'I am delighted to review the second edition of this book, *Contemporary Research in Social Media Marketing*. Social media marketing is evolving rapidly, with influencers driving content and shaping consumer journeys. The book's first edition greatly contributed to social media literature. This second edition covers various exciting topics, such as TikTok changing norms and B2B companies leveraging social media for customer engagement, and it contains many case studies, making it ideal as a textbook.'

Ranjan Kini, *Professor of Management Information Systems, Indiana University Northwest*

'*Contemporary Issues in Social Media Marketing* discusses digital marketing across different online approaches and tools. The book uncovers important digital marketing strategies and presents new avenues for research in modern marketing. The book contains many cases, making it ideal for students and business executives.'

Yllka Azemi, *Associate Professor of Marketing, Indiana University Northwest*

Contemporary Issues in Social Media Marketing

Contemporary Issues in Social Media Marketing provides the most cutting-edge findings in social media marketing, through original chapters from a range of the world's leading specialists in the area. This second edition has been fully updated with new features such as discussion questions, global case studies and examples, and material reflecting the key trends in the field, including:

- The growth in user-generated content.
- The growing influence of AI in content creation, including virtual influencers.
- The development and utilization of social media analytics.
- The use of social media as the primary search engine.
- The relationship between social media and the customer experience of the brand.

Highly regarded for its breadth of topics, range of perspectives and research-based approach, this text is perfect recommended reading for advanced undergraduate and postgraduate students studying Digital and Social Media Marketing, Contemporary Issues in Marketing and Strategic Marketing. It will also be valuable reading for academics in the field and reflective practitioners.

Subir Bandyopadhyay is a Marketing Professor at Indiana University Northwest, USA. He is a Senior Fulbright Fellow.

Bikramjit Rishi is a Professor in Marketing at the School of Management and Entrepreneurship (SME), Shiv Nadar Institution of Eminence (SNIoE), Delhi National Capital Region (NCR), India.

Contemporary Issues in Social Media Marketing

Second Edition

EDITED BY SUBIR BANDYOPADHYAY AND BIKRAMJIT RISHI

Routledge
Taylor & Francis Group
LONDON AND NEW YORK

Designed cover image: ilyaliren / Getty Images

Second edition published 2025
by Routledge
4 Park Square, Milton Park, Abingdon, Oxon, OX14 4RN

and by Routledge
605 Third Avenue, New York, NY 10158

Routledge is an imprint of the Taylor & Francis Group, an informa business

First edition published by Routledge 2018

British Library Cataloguing-in-Publication Data
A catalogue record for this book is available from the British Library

ISBN: 978-1-032-53570-8 (hbk)
ISBN: 978-1-032-53569-2 (pbk)
ISBN: 978-1-003-41265-6 (ebk)

DOI: 10.4324/9781003412656

Typeset in Dante and Avenir
by SPi Technologies India Pvt Ltd (Straive)

Contents

Contributors

Mohd Arif is an assistant professor in the Department of Mechanical Engineering and Head of Strategic Alliances and Collaborations at Sharda University, Agra, India.

Bingqian Bai researches fashion management and marketing at Manchester Metropolitan University, UK.

Subir Bandyopadhyay is a marketing professor at Indiana University Northwest, USA. He is a Senior Fulbright Fellow. He is a consultant with expertise in branding, marketing research, health-related communication, and social media marketing.

Ardion D. Beldad is an associate professor at University College Twente, the Netherlands. He studies online trust formation and maintenance.

Kruti Sanjaykumar Bhatt specializes in marketing, focusing on advertising and brand management in India.

Christy Cook is Senior Special Faculty, Digital Marketing Program in the Department of Marketing and Supply Chain Management at the Walker College of Business, Appalachian State University, USA.

Ashim Kumar Ghosh is a healthcare marketing strategist and consultant. He is pursuing PhD in digital transformation in healthcare from Symbiosis International University, India.

Hagai Gringarten teaches marketing at St. Thomas University, USA, and is the publisher and editor-in-chief of the *Journal of Multidisciplinary Research*.

Shaphali Gupta is the Mani Ayer Chair Professor of Marketing and co-chair of the Center for Research Excellence in Marketing at MICA, India. She serves as associate editor with the *Journal of Business Research* and *Journal of Strategic Marketing*.

Hannah Hameed is an assistant professor and area chair of marketing at Sharda University, Greater Noida, India. Dr Hameed combines industry experience in advertising and human resources with multiple publications.

Annmarie Hanlon teaches digital marketing and is course director of the MSc senior leadership apprenticeship at Cranfield University, UK.

Jenny Zhengye Hou is an associate professor in strategic communication at the School of Communication, Queensland University of Technology, Australia.

Ruchi Jain is a professor at Amity School of Business, Amity University Uttar Pradesh, India. Her research area is sustainable usage of technology in marketing.

Faniza Joshi is an assistant professor in Chitkara University, India, with over five years of experience in teaching.

Ilias Kapareliotis is an associate professor of marketing, specializing in luxury brand management at the American College of Greece, Athens.

Deepa Kapoor is a professor of marketing at Amity University Uttar Pradesh, India, with training, teaching and research experience in digital marketing and consumer behavior.

Manohar Kapse has more than twenty years of teaching, research, and consulting experience in statistics, machine learning, and data science in India.

Pinja Karjala holds an MSc in marketing from the Jyväskylä School of Business and Economics, University of Jyväskylä, Finland.

Heikki Karjaluoto is a professor in the Faculty of Information Technology, University of Jyväskylä, Finland.

Amandeep Kaur is an assistant professor at Mehr Chand Mahajan DAV College for Women, Chandigarh, India, and has over twelve years of teaching experience.

Sujata Khandai is a professor of marketing and the Dy. Dean (Academics) at Amity University Uttar Pradesh, India. She has rich experience in corporate, teaching, research, training, and administration.

Ruchi Khandelwal is an associate professor at Amity University Uttar Pradesh, India. She is a seasoned professional with over twenty years of experience in teaching, administration, research, and development.

George Kyparissiadis is an assistant professor and coordinator of the MA in advertising communications at the American College of Greece, Athens.

Xuan Li is a PhD candidate at the Digital Media Research Centre, Queensland University of Technology, Australia.

Nidhi Malhotra has been associated with Chitkara University, India since April 2017. She has won the University Roll of Honour and Scholarship in academics. She has more than ten years of teaching experience.

Manjushree G S is a faculty member in the MBA department at the Community Institute of Management Studies (CIMS), Bengaluru, India.

Nicholas Mathew is associated with St. Thomas University, USA, teaching international business and marketing. He also serves as a course director and faculty advisor.

Mohit Maurya is an associate professor of marketing at Sharda University, Greater Noida, India. He has nearly two decades of academic, research, and consulting experience, with several publications in esteemed journals.

Lubna Nafees is an associate professor and director of digital marketing in the Department of Marketing and Supply Chain Management at the Walker College of Business, Appalachian State University, USA.

Atanas Nik Nikolov is an associate professor of marketing and professional sales in the Department of Marketing and Sales at Coles College of Business, Kennesaw State University, USA.

Padmaja D S has more than eighteen years' experience in teaching and research areas in India.

Krishna Teja Perannagari is an assistant professor in marketing at the Indian Institute of Management (IIM) Tiruchirappalli, India. His teaching and research interests lie in customer centricity, customer experience management, and marketing analytics.

Gerald Petz is professor of e-business and head of marketing and electronic business at the University of Applied Sciences Upper Austria.

Lakshmi Raj is a PhD researcher in the management department of Christ University, Bengaluru, India, focusing on digital content marketing, influencer marketing, and social media marketing.

Bikramjit Rishi is a professor of marketing at the School of Management and Entrepreneurship (SME), Shiv Nadar Institution of Eminence Deemed to be University, Delhi, India. He has made significant contributions to the success and growth of the marketing discipline over two decades.

Daniella Ryding is a professor of fashion marketing in the Manchester Fashion Institute at Manchester Metropolitan University, UK.

Mallika Sankar M. is an assistant professor and researcher with over twenty years of experience, specializing in teaching undergraduate and postgraduate courses, supervising doctoral dissertations and theses, and editing and co-authoring research methodology books. She is a frequent speaker at public events and academic institutions.

Bhavna Sharma has been associated with the BPS Women University, India, for more than fifteen years. She has published extensively and completed a University Grants Committee-funded project.

James Stoddard is department chair and professor of marketing in the Department of Marketing and Supply Chain Management at the Walker College of Business, Appalachian State University, USA.

Nupur Taneja is a graduate and postgraduate of BPS Women University, India, and has presented papers at national and international conferences.

Uday Thareja is an accomplished industry leader with rich experience in India; and, as a corporate stalwart, leverages digital transformation through innovation.

Olli Tyrväinen is a postdoctoral researcher at the Jyväskylä School of Business and Economics, University of Jyväskylä, Finland.

Delia Vazquez is a senior lecturer in retail marketing in the School of Materials at the University of Manchester, UK.

Gianpaolo Vignali is a professor of sustainable fashion business in the Manchester Fashion Institute at Manchester Metropolitan University, UK.

Róisín Vize is a lecturer in digital marketing in the School of Marketing, Technological University Dublin, Ireland. She has research interests in B2B relationship marketing in a digital context, e-retail, and principles in sustainable digital design.

Wolfgang J. Weitzl is a professor of digital marketing at the University of Applied Sciences Upper Austria and a private lecturer at the University of Vienna, Austria.

Preface

We are excited to publish the second edition of *Contemporary Issues in Social Media Marketing* for several reasons. The first edition, published in 2018, was very popular across the world, and we received positive feedback from many readers, including academicians, practitioners, and policymakers. Also, social media marketing has advanced by leaps and bounds since 2018, with new tools such as reels and new platforms such as TikTok capturing the imagination of many users. Terms such as TikTokers, influencers, and YouTubers have become universal, transcending all language barriers.

Despite the plethora of new applications of social media marketing, its common objectives have remained unchanged since 2018: it facilitates communication between individuals, between individuals and organizations, and between organizations. Hence, it has empowered both individuals and organizations to create social and business networks.

This book contains nineteen chapters that cover a wide array of topics related to social media marketing. These chapters encompass research studies undertaken in eight countries, giving the reader a diverse perspective of how social media marketing is practiced globally. Also, like the first edition, these chapters cover applications of social media marketing in various fields, including business, branding, technology, customer engagement, customer trust, performance monitoring, and customer engagement. A key feature of this volume is that most chapters include a case study based on the topic discussed, which, hopefully, will make this volume suitable for social media marketing courses.

We begin with the chapter 'Social Media Marketing: Trends and Challenges,' which, as the title suggests, presents emerging trends in social media marketing and outlines the potential challenges social media marketers will face in the future. We have thoroughly researched the academic and managerial literature to prepare the lists of trends and challenges.

In Chapter 2, titled 'Aspects of Social Media Engagement for Luxury Brands: A Case Study Approach,' Ilias Kapareliotis and George Kyparissiadis introduce readers to some of the strategies luxury brands employ on social media. They address the brands' reasons for social media engagement, discuss relevant engagement models and practices, and provide a case study on this topic.

In Chapter 3, 'Unleashing the Potential: How Influencers Drive Digital Content Marketing,' Lakshmi Raj and Mallika Shankar M. explore the impact of influencers on facilitating digital content marketing. They employ the exploratory research synthesis method to gain insights into the current research concerning influencers and digital content marketing. They also provide a case study to shed light on how influencers drive digital content marketing.

In Chapter 4, titled 'Social Media Usage in the B2B Context,' Nicholas Matthew and Hagai Gringarten describe the opportunities, challenges and impact of social media in the business-to-business context, and provide practical suggestions on social media strategy and use for B2B firms.

In Chapter 5, titled 'Promoting Social Marketing on Social Media: Using TikTok as an Engaging Platform to Reduce Food Waste,' Jenny Zhengye Hou and Xuan Li illustrate how a popular platform such as TikTok can be leveraged to promote an important social cause such as reducing food waste. This chapter provides insights into harnessing the power of social media, ranging from compelling content creation, building long-term relationships with followers, to dynamic peer and social learning, to advance the social marketing objectives of a firm effectively.

In the next chapter, 'Optimizing User Engagement: The Synergy of Social Media Marketing and UI/UX Design,' Hannah Hameed, Mohit Maurya, and Mohd Arif explore the symbiotic relationships between social media, user interface and user experience design, and successful brand strategies. They examine how businesses leverage well-designed interfaces and engaging content to enhance user engagement and conversion rates. Using examples from leading brands such as Apple, Samsung, and Nike, they illustrate how effective UI/UX design influences consumer perceptions and fosters brand loyalty.

In Chapter 7, 'The Consumer Journey in a Social Media World,' Kruti Sanjaykumar Bhatt traces the path a consumer takes in forging a relationship with a social media platform. Specifically, she highlights how a firm's followers can become brand ambassadors. She illustrates this journey in the context of various social media platforms, including Facebook, Instagram, YouTube, TikTok, Pinterest, LinkedIn, and Twitter (X).

Chapter 8, titled 'Connecting Brands and Influencers: The Case of The Irish Blogger Agency,' contributed by Róisín Vize, explores the role of influencer marketing from a social media context, and describes how influencers are categorized according to their follower count and level of influence. The chapter highlights the benefits and drawbacks of engaging in influencer marketing, and explores the agency's role in bridging the gap between influencer and brand from the perspective of the Irish Blogger Agency.

Like Chapter 4, Chapter 9 addresses the application of social media marketing in the B2B context. Titled 'Mapping the B2B Customer Journey through Social Media Marketing,' it draws attention to a few companies that have successfully used social media in order to comprehend and aid the customer journey in the B2B domain at various stages. Authors Sujata Khandai, Ruchi Khandelwal, and Deepa Kapoor illustrate nicely how many industry leaders harness digital tools to obtain more relevant information about the customer journey that helps them in more targeted efforts leading to successful outcomes.

Chapter 10, titled 'Exploring the Impact of Para-Social Interaction: The Consumer Journey in a Social Media World with a Focus on Virtual Influencers,' investigates the impact of virtual influencers on social media platforms. Bingqian Bai, Gianpaolo Vignali, Daniella Ryding, and Delia Vazquez leverage insights from established theories, such as the Source Attractiveness Model and the Theory of Persuasion, to dissect the relationships followers maintain with virtual influencers, who are digital representations in the online space. Through an in-depth analysis of interactions with the popular virtual influencer Yexi Liu, the authors demonstrate the nuances of how digital personas reshape followers' brand perceptions and purchasing habits.

In Chapter 11, titled 'Transitioning from CRM to Social CRM in the Healthcare Industry,' Ashim Kumar Ghosh and Manohar Kapse explore the significance of customer relationship management (CRM) in this sector, emphasizing its role in building trust between providers and patients regarding healthcare products. They also examine social media strategies used by various healthcare organizations and the rise of Social CRM as a progressive approach. The chapter assesses the feasibility of integrating social media data into traditional CRM practices to enhance customer relationship management in healthcare. They emphasize the strategic importance of embracing Social CRM in healthcare, and provide insights into how healthcare organizations can use digital technologies to improve customer engagement and satisfaction.

Chapter 12, 'Consumer Persuasion by Chatbots: An Integrative Model of Social Influence,' discusses the utility of chatbots, digital tools for persuading consumers. Wolfgang J. Weitzl, Ardion D. Beldad, Gerald Petz, and Annmarie Hanlon outline the current state of scientific knowledge of chatbot communication research. Based on a comprehensive literature review, they developed an integrated model of the impact of chatbot communication on key consumer outcomes, including consumers' willingness to use and be influenced by chatbots during purchases.

In the next chapter, 'The Impact of Generational Differences on Target Audience Identification in Social Media Marketing,' Manjushree G S and Padmaja D S explore the influence of generational differences on target audience identification in social media marketing. With each generation exhibiting distinct behaviors, preferences, and communication styles, understanding these nuances becomes vital for effective audience targeting. Through behavioral analysis, managerial strategies, and case studies, this chapter provides marketers with practical guidance to optimize their marketing efforts in the dynamic landscape of generational diversity.

In Chapter 14, titled 'Social Media's Role in Customer Experience Creation: User-Generated Content Quality vs. Firm-Generated Content Quality,' Olli Tyrväinen, Heikki Karjaluoto, and Pinja Karjala evaluate the effects of user-generated and firm-generated social media content quality and social media attachment on the retail customer experience and loyalty. Based on data from surveys, experiments, and consumer interviews, they demonstrate how a retailer's participation in consumers' social media discussions affects consumer responses and loyalty outcomes. Results indicate that: user-generated content quality positively affects customers' cognitive responses; firm-generated content reduces the harmful effects of negative user-generated content on loyalty intentions; and social media attachment strengthens the impact of emotional responses on loyalty intentions. They also demonstrate that consumers' content preferences are linked to the type of product.

Chapter 15, titled 'Augmenting the Analyst: Artificial Intelligence in the Age of Social Media Big Data,' examines the use of AI tools to analyze social media data and outlines how they can provide meaningful insights into large-scale social media data. Authors Faniza Joshi, Amandeep Kaur, and Nidhi Malhotra suggest that integrating AI with social media marketing strategies can enable organizations to better understand user sentiment and optimize marketing campaigns. The chapter covers various AI-based techniques and demonstrates how AI algorithms can help us cope with the complexities of social media data.

In Chapter 16, titled 'Leveraging the Role of Social Media Platform Data in Enhancing the Effect of Cause-Related Marketing,' Krishna Teja Perannagari and Shaphali Gupta propose an approach that employs a construct-specific dictionary and Euclidean distance to empirically measure the degree of alignment between the various attributes of brand campaigns. The proposed approach offers a robust framework for evaluating the viability of CRM partnerships. The authors discuss the utility of the proposed approach using real-time case studies, underscoring the practicality of data-driven strategies.

Ruchi Jain and Uday Thareja demonstrate in Chapter 17, titled 'Social Media Renaissance with Audio Content: Bolstering a Personalized Approach,' how audio content may help companies build brands. Using a case study of Earshot Digimedia Private Limited, based in India, the authors assess how the company used audio content in sync with other digital marketing strategies for the personalization of content. The chapter demonstrates how audio content can be gainfully utilized for customer engagement in the B2B market.

In Chapter 18, titled 'Influencer Marketing and Customer Engagement through Social Media: A Promising Avenue in a New Normal,' Bhavna Sharma and Nupur Taneja examine how marketing strategies are used by social media influencers on platforms like YouTube and Instagram. The chapter evaluates the effectiveness of various tactics such as humor, polls, storytelling, question/answer sessions used by influencers in their posts, and videos to engage audiences. It also examines how influencers promote products and services, considering factors such as brand endorsements, product demonstrations, and discount offers.

The final chapter, titled 'Perceived Source Credibility of Social Media Influencers and Consumer Attitudes toward Brands: An Exploration of Differences between India and the United States,' explores the relationship between perceived source credibility of social media influencers (SMIs) and consumer attitudes toward brands. Lubna Nafees, Christy Cook, Atanas Nick Nikolov, and James Stoddard use survey data from both countries to explore the dimensions of source credibility of SMIs and compare the mechanisms at play in influencing brand attitudes. Empirical analysis suggests that SMIs' goodwill is positively related to followers' brand attitudes in India, while expertise and trustworthiness are more important in the United States.

Acknowledgements

We would like to thank everyone who helped us produce this book. First and foremost, we thank all the researchers who contributed chapters, and acknowledge the assistance from the personnel at Routledge in preparing the manuscript. We are also grateful to the reviewers for their valuable suggestions.

Many people encouraged us to write the book. The first author thanks Dean Cynthia Roberts of Indiana University Northwest School of Business and Economics for her support and encouragement. He also thanks his wife Soumita, his children Aishariya and Anusuya, his son-in-law Andrew, and his brother Sudip for their encouragement throughout the writing process.

The second author would like to express his deepest gratitude to those who contributed their time, effort, and expertise to the completion of this book. He is also grateful to Prof. Ananya Mukherjee, Vice-Chancellor of Shiv Nadar Institution of Eminence, and Prof. Sundaravaradhan Venkatesh, Dean of its School of Management and Entrepreneurship, for their support and guidance, and for providing the environment conducive to research. Thanks to my family and friends for your unwavering support and encouragement. Your patience and understanding have been a source of strength for me during this journey. Special thanks to my wife and children (Sharanya and Misha).

Thank you to all the contributors for believing in this project.

Subir Bandyopadhyay
Bikramjit Rishi

1 Social Media Marketing

Trends and Challenges

Bikramjit Rishi
Shiv Nadar Institution of Eminence Deemed to be University, Delhi - NCR

Subir Bandyopadhyay
Indiana Northwest University

Introduction

Social media is a generic term used to describe websites that connect individuals based on one or more similarities or interests. Social networks have existed since the 1990s but took off in the mid-2000s. Since then, social media has revolutionized the communication process between individuals and between individuals and organizations. As people increasingly used technology and social media grew in popularity, marketers started to take advantage of these sites to get to know their customers better, talk to them, and provide them with goods and services that met their needs (Moedeen et al., 2024; Doshi et al., 2023a). Nowadays, many businesses, especially small and medium-sized enterprises (SMEs), only talk to their customers through social media, making social media marketing a big deal. Companies began to use social media marketing because that's where the customers are, and it lets them connect with those customers directly (Bandyopadhyay, 2016; He et al., 2016).

Before venturing into social media marketing, businesses must decide what they want from it (Felix et al., 2017). Next, they need to figure out who

DOI: 10.4324/9781003412656-1

their target audience is, what social media site(s) they use most, and what messages they want to send to that audience (Rishi & Bandyopadhyay, 2018; Dwivedi et al., 2020). When you use social media correctly to share information, you can attract more people to your website, make more people aware of your brand, build brand identity and help people develop their own brand identities, and connect with audiences better. Businesses should promote a consistent brand image and give their target audience helpful content to which they can relate. Companies can also use third-party stories about their brand and include links to e-commerce sites to directly turn people who want to buy into people who actually buy (Chen & Lin, 2019). Companies can also use social media sites to offer fun material and make people feel and think about things in new ways. In return, customers can write reviews and useful tips, and spread the word about the business online (Zhang & Luo, 2016).

Usually, marketers divide their customers into segments by using different factors. This is also true for social media marketing. Different platforms use various factors to divide a market into segments and advise users on how to run campaigns. So, to run a successful social media campaign, marketers need to know the critical aspects of social media marketing. Rishi and Mohammed (2022) and Doshi et al. (2023b) suggest the following actions in selecting a good social media marketing plan:

1 Choose a Market to Focus on and Create Client Personas

The most important aspect of social media marketing is figuring out the target market and creating buyer personas, where a persona is a profile of a typical customer in a specific category based on important factors (Rishi & Kuthuru, 2021). Your social media strategy is more likely to work if you know as much about the people you want to reach as possible. A marketer should therefore gather information about a person's demographics, pain points, hobbies, and interests. You should learn where they spend time online and how they buy things (Rishi & Mohammed, 2023) in order to create profiles of individual customers or groups. A marketer can create personas based on shared events or interests.

2 Perform a Social Media Audit

This is the process of monitoring a brand on social media sites and then choosing which sites to use to promote the brand. The following factors are taken into account by a social media audit (Kietzmann et al., 2011):

- Making and analyzing a list of the social media sites where the brand is involved
- Making sure that social media profiles are set up correctly
- Comparing the current platforms with their competitors based on the number of followers, how often they post, the average number of engagements, the type of content, customer questions, and the average time it takes to answer those questions. Marketers use this information to list the company's strengths, weaknesses, opportunities, and threats (SWOT) as it will help them determine how to improve their social media profile.

3 Set Goals, Objectives, and Measurement Metrics

Buyer personas or groups can be linked to the social media audit, and then the goals, objectives, and metrics set to help determine how well the effort is going. These are linked to a timeline, which lets you see whether the brand's social media strategy is going well (He et al., 2015), as in the following examples:

- Goal: Make more people aware of the business online.
- Objectives: Get 100 percent more people to join the Facebook group in the next 12 months.
- Measurement metrics: The number of new fans joining Facebook; increase in page views.

4 Select Which Social Media Sites to Use

Marketers can choose the best platforms for building the brand's profile by looking at social media audits and consumer cohorts or personas. With increasing numbers of social media sites, it is important to know what makes each site unique so you can pick the one that best fits your business's marketing goals (Devereux et al., 2020). Bandyopadhyay (2016) provides a useful taxonomy for small business owners to utilize specific social media platforms for specific business objectives. Below, we outline the reach and capabilities of popular social media platforms:

- Facebook: With 3 billion monthly active users globally, Facebook is the most popular and influential site in its market. People share news, stories, and other material on the platform, and marketers can connect with their customers through business pages. There are also ways to advertise through Facebook Ads, Premium Ads, and paid stories (Statista, 2024a).

- X: Formerly known as Twitter, this platform has more than 368 million active users globally sharing news, information, and stories, making it popular for marketing purposes. Marketers can create personal or enhanced profile pages, and can advertise on the site through promoted tweets, trends, and accounts with higher profile (Statista, 2024b).
- LinkedIn: This is a business-to-business (B2B) social media site with more than 1 billion users worldwide. It is mainly used by employees and jobseekers for discussing and sharing news about businesses and industries. Users can create a business or product page or a networking group to interact with subscribers, and brands can also reach customers through LinkedIn Ads (Shepherd, 2024).
- YouTube: Businesses look to this video sharing platform as a way to connect with customers because of its user base of more than 265 million. The site lets users share educational and fun videos through brand or custom brand channels. To reach even more people, the site also has video ads, reach ads, and display ads (Degenhard, 2024).
- Pinterest: This platform has 498 million monthly active users, thus making it attractive to businesses. Its main goal is to share and promote trending products and websites through "boards" created by users (Macready, 2024).
- Instagram: With 2 billion active users globally, people use this site to share photos, videos (including live streams), comments, hashtags, and stories. After its purchase by Facebook, this platform can now be used for combined social media campaigns (Dixon, 2024).
- Snapchat: This has about 414 million active users globally, who can use artistic tools such as filters and lenses to share photos and videos (Statista 2024a).

5 *Ensure Meaningful Customer Experience*

A brand must choose a suitable tone of voice for social media sites to provide users with a good and friendly experience (Popli & Rishi, 2021). When designing a social media experience, marketers should consider the following questions:

- Does the chosen tone of voice (warm, friendly, playful, professional, casual, inspiring, sarcastic, authoritative, etc.) match the brand image (Effing & Spil, 2016)?
- Why are you using social media? To teach, entertain, inform, connect, sell, please, or spread the word?
- Is the brand's language easy, funny, serious, smart, or hard to understand?

Based on these, a marketer can formulate a content strategy and distribution plan to get that information to people. The content strategy and distribution plan determine the network, frequency and types of posts and content shared on each social media site (Dwivedi et al., 2020).

6 Track Performance, Analyze, and Fine-Tune

The key to success on social media is to keep track of metrics, look at the results, and make changes to your marketing plan. One needs to answer the questions below to determine whether using social media was successful (Rishi & Bandyopadhyay, 2018):

- Was it possible for the brand to reach its goals? Why or why not?
- If not, what needs to be changed so the goals can be met?
- What themes helped accomplish the goals, and which did not?
- What exactly are the topics of posts that do well?
- Which social media sites should be used, and how many times should the post be made on each one?
- How should the text look?
- What plans should the focus be on?

Emerging Trends

Social media is constantly changing over time due to many factors – including, technological innovation, data availability, data analysis methods, etc. – that enable consumers as well as businesses to harness the power of social media more than ever. Based on the ongoing changes in factors mentioned above, this section outlines some key emerging trends in social media marketing.

1 User-Generated Content (UGC)

UGC has been around for a while as advertisements in traditional media outlets were also based on ideas that marketers got from customers. However, these are now being made, shared, and sourced differently (Dwivedi et al., 2020; Mukhopadhyay et al., 2023), with changes traced back to social media sites. The rise of remixing apps such as TikTok, Instagram Reels, and Koji has given marketers new ways to connect with customers more effectively with attractive content. UGC is a new trend that helps brands create content for their customers. It lets people say what they think about brands, which will make it easier for brands and customers to connect naturally. With more people shopping online, it will become normal for users to generate more content (Halliday, 2016). To keep up with the trend, brands should give people the right tools, such as logos and labeled templates, to make good remixes. However, watching how brand images are used on social media sites is essential as it will help the business create and keep track of remixed content (Daugherty et al., 2008). Brands should also monitor their social media footprint to determine which virtual channels work best for them. It is important to keep an eye on the copied content to avoid any potential problems.

2 Memes

Memes have opened up a new way for people to interact with each other on the internet. A meme is an amusing or interesting item (such as a captioned picture or video) that is spread widely especially through social media. It is something that marketers should learn from, and they should try to use memes to build and run brand groups (Razzaq et al., 2023). Memes will convince people of new business and economic trends and problems. These problems affect the health of brands on social media and are connected to brands in some way. Memes are a huge trend that allows marketers to connect with their audiences. Brands should make material that people want to share and talk about, and they should also monitor their business logo (Malodia et al., 2022). Brands can interact with the meme communities to make their words go viral faster. However, as a marketer, you should ensure that a meme does not also cause bad feelings among people. You should also take into consideration that numerous rules may emerge around memes because of their increasing popularity (Murray et al., 2014).

3 Feelings of Nostalgia

You will remember how great life was before 2019, when people didn't need to wear face masks, use hand sanitizer, or stay away from people they didn't know. Marketers can connect current feelings with retro marketing by invoking memories of the "good old days" as nostalgia links strong, positive feelings to a brand and makes people feel better emotionally (Koetz & Tankersley, 2016). On the other hand, the word "nostalgia" became popular on social media after lockdowns because people wanted to remember those days. Research shows that people want to remember good times and forget about any current problems they are having. Nostalgia allows marketers to connect good memories with their brand as these will help people connect emotionally with the brand. Because the brand makes people feel good, it will help build a good brand image (Davalos et al., 2015; Bandyopadhyay & Serjak, 2015). The brand can use nostalgia marketing if it knows its customers well. Data from the past can help change trends and make something old look brand new, thus invoking nostalgic feelings. Going over current or old contacts can also help identify feelings people liked in the past. By using nostalgia marketing to connect with them, you can showcase your business (Andangsari et al., 2022).

4 Marketing through Conversation

Today's marketers must encourage customers to communicate with them regularly. Conversational marketing changes the message based on how the customer communicates. Consumer needs have changed since digital and social media marketing became popular. Talking to consumers is therefore essential to understand their preferences (Parida & Prasanna, 2021). People can connect on a human level through chatbots, social messaging, phone calls, and other methods. Conversational marketing can also give social media a human voice by enabling the brand and the customer to have real-time discussions. If a brand wants to use social marketing well, it must look at the customer journey and determine what harms them at each stage. The brand should therefore talk to customers to discover their problems and help brands have better conversations. They should also combine information from different sources such as emails, calls, and chats (Curran & Lennon, 2011). Marketing teams should understand what is being said in customer services to have better customer interactions. Dialogue should also be personal, so brands should "lower their voices" to achieve this. When building relationships and conversations, the focus should be on using a more approachable and authentic tone of voice (Liu & Lopez, 2016).

5 Gamification on Social Media

The global online gaming market generated revenues of around US$26.14 billion in 2023, representing an increase of 9.8 percent compared to the previous year (Clement 2024). The global COVID-19 outbreak in 2019/2020 led to a substantial increase in online gaming profits as it compelled individuals to remain at home and seek digital entertainment and means to interact with others. Although the growth trend has stabilized, online gaming remains a popular activity. Currently, there are over 1.1 billion online gamers globally, led by populations in China, South Korea, and Japan (Clement, 2024; Aydin, 2015). This gives brands a chance to market themselves through gaming groups. Even before the pandemic, Nepal et al. (2015) suggested that the best way to use and get the most out of these groups is via a three-way strategy. First, find the right communities, especially those with similar demographics, to connect the business with the customer. Second, learn about those communities, especially how the material is made and how people interact. Third, if there are no paid advertising options, join groups and ask people to share games and content related to the brand.

Emerging Challenges

1 Selecting the Right Social Media Platform

One of the main challenges faced by social media users is choosing the right platform, and it is hard for marketers to determine which sites are best for connecting with buyers. It is important for a company to match its specific objectives with specific social media platforms. Many marketers study which sites their target audiences use as there are differences between the platforms consumers and marketers use (Stieglitz et al., 2018), meaning that marketers often connect with their customers through the wrong channels. If you use paid social media, picking the wrong platforms will waste money, so marketers must be careful when choosing platforms (Rishi & Kuthuru, 2021).

To solve this problem, marketers need to know which social media sites their customers visit the most and what they do on social media. Figuring out customer demographics and social media habits is vital for creating customer profiles and providing content that fits those personas. It will help you connect with your customers better. The selection of social media sites also depends on the type of business. For example, business-to-consumer (B2C) companies tend to focus more on Facebook and X/Twitter, while B2B companies, on the other hand, tend to rely on platforms such as Google My Business and LinkedIn (Dash et al., 2023). Another thing that marketers should keep in mind is that, if they are not on the same channels as their rivals, they will miss out on conversations and sales.

2 Selecting the Right Marketing Goal on Social Media

Many brands do well in their physical shops but not necessarily on social media as brands sometimes create content and share it on social media without fully knowing what their customers' likes and dislikes (Khanom, 2023). Knowing and understanding customer behavior is therefore essential when posting information. Marketers need to know what their target customers like and don't like, and using social listening tools can help them learn more about how their customers act (Rishi & Bandyopadhyay, 2018). The brand will do better on social media if it knows its customers' demographics and behavior. For a social media effort to be successful, marketers should make an "ideal buyer persona" to reach the right people (Doshi et al., 2023b).

3 Decreasing Organic Exposure and Engagement

Organic reach has dropped significantly because of the new algorithms social media sites use. For example, only 0.31 percent of people who see organic branded material interact with it. This means that, even if you have 1000 friends, only 3.1 will see your posts, which is why ads cost more for retailers. Many marketers have trouble balancing their spending and marketing goals (Lipsman et al., 2012). Marketers need to know how the algorithms work on each social media site to get the most direct reach. You can also get more organic reach and engagement by sharing right content at the right time. Working with influencers and using UGC can help your organic reach and engagement. People now watch more videos, so marketers can use videos to answer customer's questions and resolve complaints. This will also help spread the word to more people (Chang & Chiang, 2020).

4 Sending Clear Messages and Building Trust

People are increasing losing faith in social media sites because their data has been misused, for example in cases such as Facebook sharing data with consulting firm Cambridge Analytica and the spread of disinformation or "fake news" (Habibi et al., 2014). People still trust traditional media more than social media as news sources. To overcome this problem, social media marketers can get users' permission to store and use their data. They can also win customers' trust through programs that encourage them to discuss brands, which will lead to more brand involvement in the long run

(Warren et al., 2014). The quality of the material is very important for social media marketers to attract followers and prospective followers and regularly interact with them.

5 Rising Advertising Costs

Brands with considerable funds are willing to pay for social media ads to get people to interact with them, but the cost of ads is increasing rapidly. As the number of ads grows, it becomes harder for brands to stand out and reach the people they want to reach. Among this plethora of ads, brands must spend more money to reach their target audience (Rinallo & Basuroy, 2009). Advertisements filtered or blocked by users forces brands to spend more to on ads to attract users because people's attention spans are getting shorter. As a result, social media campaigns do not give brands a good return on investment (ROI). To deal with this problem, brands can improve the quality of the material in their campaigns so that they reach more people naturally. Brands can lower the cost of their social media ads by managing their time well, being creative, and ensuring they reach the right people (Rishi et al., 2023). It is possible to reduce expenses by correctly using ad targeting and version testing tools. Interactive content, live videos, augmented reality, and story forms are some of the newest tools to help marketers reach their goals on a budget.

Despite the challenges outlined above, social media marketing will continue to flourish. Marketers will do well to harness the elements discussed in this chapter. Following the steps of social media marketing plans properly and guarding against potential challenges will help social media marketing continue to yield rich dividends.

References

Andangsari, E. W., Fitri, R. A., Hurriyati, E. A., Herlie, W. J., Prima, F. C., & Dhamayanti, M. (2022). Social media for society 5.0: Nostalgia function and social connectedness. *Proceedings of the 3rd Asia Pacific International Conference on Industrial Engineering and Operations Management* (pp. 3902–3909).

Aydin, G. (2015). Adoption of gamified systems: A study on a social media gamification website. *International Journal of Online Marketing (IJOM)*, *5*(3), 18–37.

Bandyopadhyay, S. 2016. How a cost-effective social media plan can make a difference for small business. *Journal of the Indiana Academy of Social Sciences*, *19*(1), Art. 4, 1–12.

Bandyopadhyay, S., & Serjak, R. (2005). Key success requirements for online brand management. In S. Krishnamurthy (Ed.), *Contemporary research in marketing*, Vol. 2 (pp. 146–166). IGI Global.

Chang, W. L., & Chiang, Y. S. (2020). The organic reach of online videos: Linking viewers' traits to post-viewing behaviour. *Cybernetics and Systems*, *52*(3), 191–212.

Chen, S., & Lin, C. (2019). Understanding the effect of social media marketing activities: The mediation of social identification, perceived value, and satisfaction. *Technological Forecasting and Social Change*, *140*(2), 22–32.

Clement, J. (2024). Online gaming: Statistics and facts. Accessed from https://www.statista.com/topics/1551/online-gaming/

Curran, J. M., & Lennon, R. (2011). Participating in the conversation: Exploring usage of social media networking sites. *Academy of Marketing Studies Journal*, *15*(1), 21–38.

Dash, G., Rishi, B., Akmal, S., Paul, J., & Chakraborty, D. (2023). Digitization, marketing 4.0, and repurchase intention in e-tail: A cross-national study. *Journal of Global Information Management*, *31*(1), 1–24.

Daugherty, T., Eastin, M. S., & Bright, L. (2008). Exploring consumer motivations for creating user-generated content. *Journal of Interactive Advertising*, *8*(2), 16–25.

Davalos, S., Merchant, A., Rose, G. M., Lessley, B. J., & Teredesai, A. M. (2015). "The good old days": An examination of nostalgia in Facebook posts. *International Journal of Human-Computer Studies*, *83*, 83–93.

Degenhard, J. (2024). YouTube users worldwide 2020–2029. Accessed from https://www.statista.com/forecasts/1144088/youtube-users-in-the-world

Devereux, E., Grimmer, L., & Grimmer, M. (2020). Consumer engagement on social media: Evidence from small retailers. *Journal of Consumer Behaviour*, *19*(2), 151–159. https://doi.org/10.1002/cb.1800

Dixon, S. (2024). Instagram statistics and facts. Accessed from https://www.statista.com/topics/1882/instagram/#topicOverview

Doshi, P., Nigam, P., & Rishi, B. (2023a). System quality features and continuous usage intention of social network users: A multi-group analysis with gender. *Journal of Systems and Information Technology*, *25*(4), 480–501. https://doi.org/10.1108/JSIT-07-2022-0164

Doshi, P., Nigam, P. and Rishi, B. (2023b). Customer values and patronage intention in social media networks: Mediating role of perceived usefulness. *VINE Journal of Information and Knowledge Management Systems*, Vol. ahead-of-print No. ahead-of-print. https://doi.org/10.1108/VJIKMS-07-2022-0217

Dwivedi, Y. K., Ismagilova, E., Hughes, D. L., Carlson, J., Filieri, R., Jacobson, J., Jain, V., Karjaluoto, H., Kefi, H., Krishen, A. S., Kumar, V., Rahman, M. M., Raman, R., Rauschnabel, P. A., Rowley, J., Salo, J., Tran, G. A., & Wang, Y. (2020). Setting the future of digital and social media marketing research: Perspectives and research propositions. *International Journal of Information Management*, *59*, 102168. https://doi.org/10.1016/j.ijinfomgt.2020.102168

Effing, R., & Spil, T. A. M. (2016). The social strategy cone: Towards a framework for evaluating social media strategies. *International Journal of Information Management, 36*(1), 1–8. https://doi.org/10.1016/j.ijinfomgt.2015.07.009

Felix, R., Rauschnabel, P. A., & Hinsch, C. (2017). Elements of strategic social media marketing: A holistic framework. *Journal of Business Research, 70*, 118–126. https://doi.org/10.1016/j.jbusres.2016.05.001

Habibi, M. R., Laroche, M., & Richard, M. O. (2014). The roles of brand community and community engagement in building brand trust on social media. *Computers in Human Behavior, 37*, 152–161.

Halliday, S. V. (2016). User-generated content about brands: Understanding its creators and consumers. *Journal of Business Research, 69*(1), 137–144.

He, W., Tian, X., Chen, Y., & Chong, D. (2016). Actionable social media competitive analytics for understanding customer experiences. *Journal of Computer Information Systems, 56*(2), 145–155.

He, W., Wu, H., Yan, G., Akula, V., & Shen, J. (2015). A novel social media competitive analytics framework with sentiment benchmarks. *Information & Management, 52*(7), 801–812.

Khanom, M. T. (2023). Using social media marketing in the digital era: A necessity or a choice. *International Journal of Research in Business and Social Science, 12*(3), 88–98.

Kietzmann, J. H., Hermkens, K., McCarthy, I. P., & Silvestre, B. S. (2011). Social media? Get serious! Understanding the functional building blocks of social media. *Business Horizons, 54*(3), 241–251. https://doi.org/10.1016/j.bushor.2011.01.005

Koetz, C., & Tankersley, J. D. (2016). Nostalgia in online brand communities. *Journal of Business Strategy, 37*(3), 22–29.

Lipsman, A., Mudd, G., Rich, M., & Bruich, S. (2012). The power of "like": How brands reach (and influence) fans through social-media marketing. *Journal of Advertising Research, 52*(1), 40–52.

Liu, Y., & Lopez, R. A. (2016). The impact of social media conversations on consumer brand choices. *Marketing Letters*, 27, 1–13.

Macready, H. (2024). 42 Pinterest stats that matter to marketers in 2024. Accessed from https://blog.hootsuite.com/pinterest-statistics-for-business/

Malodia, S., Dhir, A., Bilgihan, A., Sinha, P., & Tikoo, T. (2022). Meme marketing: How can marketers drive better engagement using viral memes? *Psychology & Marketing, 39*(9), 1775–1801.

Moedeen, S., Aw, E. C. X., Alryalat, M., Wei-Han Tan, G., Cham, T. H., Ooi, K. B., & Dwivedi, Y. K. (2024). Social media marketing in the digital age: Empower consumers to win big? *Asia Pacific Journal of Marketing and Logistics, 36*(1), 66–84.

Mukhopadhyay, S., Pandey, R., & Rishi, B. (2023). Electronic word of mouth (eWOM) research: A comparative bibliometric analysis and future research insight. *Journal of Hospitality and Tourism Insights*, 6(2), 404–424. https://doi.org/10.1108/JHTI-07-2021-0174

Murray, N., Manrai, A., & Manrai, L. (2014). Memes, memetics and marketing: A state-of-the-art review and a lifecycle model of meme management in advertising. In L. Moutinho, E. Bigné, & A. K. Manrai (Eds.), *The Routledge companion to the future of marketing* (pp. 331–347). Routledge.

Nepal, S., Paris, C., & Bista, S. (2015). Gamification on the social web. In S. Nepal, C. Paris, & D. Georgakopoulos (Eds.), *Social media for government services* (pp. 197–220). Springer.

Parida, D. K., & Prasanna, D. (2021). An empirical study on social media conversation to increase brand awareness: Startup organization context. *Academy of Marketing Studies Journal, 25*(4), 1–8.

Popli, S., & Rishi, B. (2021). Customer experience management: The road ahead. In S. Popli & B. Rishi (Eds.), *Crafting customer experience strategy* (pp. 199–218). Emerald.

Razzaq, A., Shao, W., & Quach, S. (2023). Towards an understanding of meme marketing: Conceptualisation and empirical evidence. *Journal of Marketing Management, 39*(7–8), 670–701.

Rinallo, D., & Basuroy, S. (2009). Does advertising spending influence media coverage of the advertiser? *Journal of Marketing, 73*(6), 33–46.

Rishi, B., & Bandyopadhyay, S. (Eds.) (2018). *Contemporary issues in social media marketing*. Routledge.

Rishi, B., & Kuthuru, N. R. (2021). A review for managerial guidelines for social media integration of IMC in digital era. In S. Das & S. Gochhait (Eds.), *Digital entertainment: The next evolution in service sector* (pp. 187–212). Palgrave Macmillan.

Rishi, B., & Mohammed, J. (2022). Design, execute, and manage promotions: Study on social media platforms. In S. Rana, A. K. Shrivastava, & S. K. Raut (Eds.), *Promotional practices and perspectives from emerging markets* (pp. 226–245). Routledge India.

Rishi, B., & Mohammed, J. (2023). Social media marketing applications and fashion brands: A South Asian perspective. In T. Tarnanidis, E. Papachristou, M. Karypidis, & V. Ismyrlis (Eds.), *Social media and online consumer decision making in the fashion industry* (pp. 267–299). IGI Global.

Rishi, B., Anand, A., & Sharma, T. (2023). An unexpected journey: Designing a social media marketing framework for small and medium enterprises (SMEs). In D. Ostic, R. Bansal, & S. A. Qalati (Eds.), *Strengthening SME performance through social media adoption and usage* (pp. 1–20). IGI Global.

Shepherd, J. (2024). 41 essential LinkedIn statistics you need to know in 2024. Accessed from https://thesocialshepherd.com/blog/linkedin-statistics

Statista (2024a). Number of monthly active Facebook users worldwide as of 4th quarter 2023. https://www.statista.com/statistics/264810/number-of-monthly-active-facebook-users-worldwide/

Statista (2024b). Number of X (formerly Twitter) users worldwide from 2019 to 2024. https://www.statista.com/statistics/303681/twitter-users-worldwide/

Stieglitz, S., Mirbabaie, M., Ross, B., & Neuberger, C. (2018). Social media analytics: Challenges in topic discovery, data collection, and data preparation. *International Journal of Information Management, 39*, 156–168.

Warren, A. M., Sulaiman, A., & Jaafar, N. I. (2014). Social media effects on fostering online civic engagement and building citizen trust and trust in institutions. *Government Information Quarterly, 31*(2), 291–301.

Zhang, M., & Luo, N. (2016). Understanding relationship benefits from harmonious brand community on social media. *Internet Research, 26*(4), 809–826.

Aspects of Social Media Engagement for Luxury Brands

2

A Case Study Approach

Ilias Kapareliotis and George Kyparissiadis
Deere – The American College of Greece

Introduction

New lifestyles and economic developments in western society have changed the beliefs and attitudes of contemporary consumers. These changes, along with others at the micro and macro level, have created demand for different types of products and services. Economic development leads to the 'need' for the latest luxury. By 'new luxury' can be understood society's demand for more advanced and sophisticated brands rather than for products. Long (2023) maintains that 'luxury brands' communicates a new world of luxury that fulfils the desire of people with the following profile characteristics:

- High income
- High spending power
- Unique psychological needs and traits
- Satisfaction of social status and taste
- Recognition of self-worth through the consumption of luxury goods.

DOI: 10.4324/9781003412656-2

Information for consumers in contemporary society is transmitted and disseminated via different media routes, both online and off. This entails the development of multiple channels and platforms. Psychological factors affect the way consumers receive, interpret and inform themselves about the world of luxury or what happens in different worlds. Furthermore, the world of luxury brands relates much more to the consumer of the twenty-first century, and establishes a new world of luxury. An interactive relationship starts from this as new relationships emanate between business and consumer.

Despite the fact that luxury brands have existed for centuries, technological developments, particularly those of social media, have increased the power of twenty-first century brands. The literature examines various forms of the luxury phenomenon fragmented by current, primarily online, trends (Aldhamiri et al., 2024; Firouznia et al., 2024; Thanasi-Boçe et al., 2024, Cruz-Ros et al., 2024). The fragmentation stems from the various social media strategies the luxury brands adopt. Attitudes, perceptions, and luxury consumers inform the engagement strategy that luxury brands deploy on social media. Here we study the various methodological lenses, and review approaches to engagement as luxury brands pursue online strategies. Marketing managers or brand managers should pay attention to the following key concepts or approaches in looking at how they can engage with luxury brand customers online:

- Brand strategies
- Social media platforms
- Communication approaches
- Consumer attitudes and perceptions
- Engagement
- Brand performance.

Study of the above variables demonstrates that luxury brand engagement online is a strong outcome not only of brand performance but also of communication used across various social media platforms, whether today or in the future. When a luxury brand requires online engagement to boost its various branding and/or marketing strategies, it should set the requirement for successful online presence in the more precise context of experience. The customer/consumer experience is strongly related to consumer behaviour.

Looking at the various media contexts in which luxury brands exist, we can conclude that they are present almost everywhere, both off- and online.

The question brand managers should ask themselves is: How can the brand continue engaging its current and potential customers, regardless of the medium the customer chooses? Engagement, the desired outcome, is the pivotal element for customer loyalty to a luxury brand. Non-luxury brands arrive at the loyalty stage without necessarily embedding the engagement stage in their strategies. Studying the various academic sources, we can conclude that engagement of the luxury customer occurs particularly within new forms of media; in other words, social media. Liadeli et al. (2023) presents a model of luxury brands' engagement on social media based on a literature review identifying key engagement characteristics and engagement sources. Table 2.1 summarizes the key characteristics of this model. It demonstrates that engagement is a multifaceted phenomenon dependent on several key factors such as macro- and micro-environments and the point of reference in specific contexts.

The following key engagement characteristics stem from a literature study:

1. Content is pivotal for the engagement and accommodation of luxury brand practices on social media.
2. Branding is at the heart of what the social media manager does, especially when it comes to luxury brands. The brand identity belongs to the past, and current practices denote the path to engagement alongside the strategies to be used.
3. Platforms play a key role in how engagement occurs, in conjunction with context and the tradition itself. The specific national context is also clear, and guides the engagement practices as well as the strategies of luxury brands.
4. The vantage point of the study of the phenomenon is vital in drawing relevant conclusions.

Table 2.1 Engagement characteristics for social media based on their sources

Source	Characteristic
Owned social media	Types of owned social media content
Sales	Brand characteristics
Social media platforms vs microblogs	Brand community size
Platform-related advertising content	Industry products vs services
Country specifics	Product lifecycle vs maturity
	Cultural characteristics
	Other characteristics

Adapted from Liadeli et al (2023).

The definition of engagement, as presented by Bazi et al. (2023, demonstrates that the concept looks more complex than it is, and has the following key characteristics:

- aesthetic quality
- celebrity endorsement
- brand loyalty
- brand love.

The concept of engagement has gained significant attention, both in the business-to-business (B2B) and the business-to-consumer (B2C) sectors, from researchers and practitioners alike, rendering the practice a prominent marketing objective. The surge in engagement started when social media accounts became increasingly attractive to business. Digital marketing content has proved crucial in the stimulation of consumer engagement.

Interestingly, engagement online is enhanced by love of the brand – a facet that encapsulates all the emotions a customer might feel in relation to the brand or due to the effects of brand engagement. We may conclude that social media allow brands to engage with their customers on a deep personal level, which is an important factor for luxury brands. The concept of engagement is multidimensional and multiscale, and includes attitudes and behaviours that in the past might have accrued to products and/or brand awareness or loyalty; however this is no longer the case.

Typologies of Engagement

Typologies of engagement that investigate the different forms engagement may take on social media are helpful for both managers and academics as they support the evaluation of engagement strategies and help design future steps and pathways. The final stage is evaluation of the various target audiences and groups reached or of the overall strategy of the luxury brands across social media.

The digital evolution, or revolution, still requires responsiveness on the part of social media users, and consumers and customers react to the luxury brand stimuli sent to them primarily online. The aim is for them to feel closer to the brand and to the media used, to instil feelings of differentiation, superiority, and heightened self-esteem. This particular strategy looks at fostering closer relationships between the particular social media platform, the consumer, and the customer profile, supporting all marketing and branding strategies both off- and online and elements of superiority of the brand. In addition, this enables users of various social media platforms to feel the brand essence – to enjoy the brand journey, touch or feel the brand (or not), and have the option to buy. The luxury brand then provides those not necessarily looking to buy but instead wishing to feel the brand the opportunity to engage at a very early stage. After considering the most up-to-date literature at the time of writing (2023), the present study identified five forms of engagement on social media:

1. **Pre-engagement**: Social media users explore the ifs and maybes of the luxury brand online experience, the medium or media used, and their willingness to.
2. **Engagement**: Users engage with their chosen brand over a long period of time. Concepts of brand loyalty and brand awareness are at play in user/customer engagement, and vice versa (Fetais et al., 2023).
3. **Lovers' engagement**: Users love the brand; they engage with it, knowing the characteristics that generate the love (Pangarkar et al., 2023).
4. **Full engagement**: In this case users buy the brand, support the brand, and act as informal brand ambassadors, a role which they then take to much higher levels (Zha et al., 2023).
5. **Passionate engagement**: Users are passionate about the brand, the experiences, opportunities, and anything else it offers as part of the overall experience, both off- and online (Bazi et al., 2023).

Levels of engagement are never considered an indication of brand equity as this does not fit with what brands have to offer overall, and could instead consist of short-term strategies.

Luxury Brands and Social Media

Luxury brands joined social media platforms hesitantly (Üçok Hughes et al., 2016), first exploring the ground to ensure they wouldn't jeopardise their distinct brand image, exclusivity, and distance from the traditional marketplace in democratising platforms where everyone could be found (Brandão et al., 2019; Weaver, 2015). In fact, style guru, brand consultant, and influential blogger Anish Bhatt said that a decade ago 'no one believed social media was a platform to talk about luxury goods. It was a place to share pictures of your lunch' (Gomelsky, 2021). In addition, it was considered that the exposure to large audiences that the mainstream social platforms afford could threaten the 'paucity' of luxury brands, one of the eight 'Ps' of luxury brand marketing (Arora, 2013). The term refers to the negative impact that 'over-revelation' and availability can have on the brand image of luxury products, and which leads luxury brands to create and maintain the perception that their goods are scarce. Arora writes that paucity can be natural (i.e. the result of scarcity of materials such as precious stones and metals), technology-driven (when infrastructure and time limit the availability of goods), or tactical-driven (when brands create the sense of rarity and uniqueness through limited editions or personalisation). Among such efforts, it is understandable that luxury brands enter the public sphere of social media prudently (Jin, 2012; Mohr, 2013).

As Hennigs et al. (2012) point out, with a carefully crafted and applied strategy, luxury brands can enhance the desire for their offerings among a large number of existing and potential customers while maintaining the exclusivity of their products through limited distribution channels and points of sale. One such brand is Chanel, which communicates its elegance and product range with clearly branded content that consists primarily of short videos. This content strategy has earned the brand over 59 and 13 million followers on Instagram and X (formerly Twitter), respectively. In return, in October 2023 Chanel only followed back three and two accounts on those platforms. However, those carefully selected accounts are also related to the brand: besides other official Chanel accounts, the brand also follows le19M, its massive creativity hub in an industrial area of Paris, and Librairie 7L, an exclusive bookshop and publishing house established in 1999 by the German fashion designer Karl Lagerfeld, the company's creative director from 1983 until his death in 2019.

This is an effective use of the 'followers' feature that brands may employ in various ways to achieve different objectives. In the case of Chanel, users are intrigued by the small number of accounts that the brand follows, and may click on the links to check out different brand offerings that help build Chanel's creative credentials and exclusive image. Other brands may employ the 'follow for follow' tactic in order to increase their number of followers by following various accounts in expectation that they will be followed back (Haydn, 2016). The ugly face of this tactic, which is in fact considered as 'spam', is the 'follow/unfollow' practice whereby the brand unfollows the accounts that have returned the favour so it appears to have more followers than follows, thus increasing its influencer credentials (Goodman, 2021).

Regarding followers of luxury brands on social media, these vary according to the two parameters of engagement and propensity to purchase, with Ramadan et al. (2018) identifying six distinct types: pragmatists, bystanders, trend hunters, image seekers, passionate owners, and prime consumers.

- 'Pragmatists' are consumers who can afford to purchase luxury brands but choose not to unless they are convinced of their utility value (He et al., 2010). They recognise the superior quality and durability of luxury goods and follow luxury brands because they want to keep an eye on the latest trends (Eastman & Eastman, 2011; Ramadan et al., 2018).

- 'Bystanders', on the other hand, cannot afford the luxury goods, and view the market with detached passivity. They are usually the greater part of a brand's online followers, but rarely engage with the content, preferring to view from a distance as the consumption of luxury goods leads them to experience cognitive dissonance and even guilt (Wu et al., 2015).
- 'Trend hunters' appreciate the fashion statements proposed by the brands, but see no reason to pay the premium prices required. Instead, they adopt the trends and display them through counterfeits or imitations (Suessmuth-Dyckerhoff et al., 2008).
- 'Image seekers' love luxury brands and buy them because they seek the status they convey. Even though luxury products are hardly within their means, these followers view the expense as an investment in quality and functionality, and, most importantly, as imparting the sophistication and status that the branded goods communicate (He et al., 2010).
- The next type consists of 'passionate owners', who display high levels of engagement with specific brands as they create strong mental associations with luxury goods in relation to special events and other milestones in their life. They are likely to purchase when they can afford to because luxury products satisfy their hedonic nature (Vigneron & Johnson, 2004).
- Lastly, 'prime consumers' recognise the functionality and quality of luxury brands, and are able to afford them. Their means allow them to not consider such goods as 'luxurious' as they loyally purchase brands that keep delivering high quality and performance that they are accustomed to (Park et al., 2008).

Each of these groups requires a different strategy to engage them online and increase their propensity to buy. Some of these approaches are discussed in the next section.

Engagement Tactics for Luxury Brands

A recent Havas Media Network report indicates that the majority of luxury goods consumers are women, who primarily buy for themselves out of self-indulgence. These high-end female consumers tend to seek inspiration for their purchases primarily through social media (see WARC, 2023). As luxury brands realise this, they employ a variety of tools and tactics to ensure that their offering and presence satisfy the need for information, inspiration, and sense of community. The desired outcome is consumer–brand engagement, which is defined as 'a consumer's positively valenced cognitive, emotional and behavioral brand-related activity during, or related to, specific consumer/brand interactions' (Hollebeek et al., 2014, p. 151).

Research has shown that consumer engagement enhances the consumer's perception of brand image (Oliveira & Fernandes, 2020; Febrian & Ahluwalia, 2021) and increases brand loyalty (Aljuhmani et al., 2023). However, careful marketing efforts are required as luxury brands must not lose touch with the traits that distinguish them from other goods, such as exclusivity, heritage, uniqueness, and association with high society (Vigneron & Johnson, 2004). In fact, it has been proven that a large number of interactions can jeopardise brand image and sense of 'premiumness'. For example, large numbers of reviews negatively impact higher-end hotels (Blal & Sturman, 2014), and high levels of engagement on behalf of the brand may result in lower-value perceptions (Park et al., 2020).

Pentina et al. (2018) identified 11 distinct behaviours that followers of luxury brands exhibit on social media, defined by the two parameters of 'effort' and 'intended counterpart', whether other users or the brand itself. These behaviours range from simply liking a page to 'proposing new use, image or interpretation for brand's products' (p. 61). All can be 'activated' by the intentional use of social media affordances, some of which are discussed below.

Content Marketing

The term 'content' refers to brand-related material that users actively choose to consume (Smulders, 2016); therefore 'content marketing' is defined as 'the creation and distribution of … compelling content in multiple formats to attract and retain customers' (Pulizzi & Barrett, 2008, p. 8). Users are attracted to such content – which can be informational, entertaining, or relational – for the perceived value it adds to their experience on social media platforms (Lou et al., 2019). One such example that stands out for its longevity and success is the 'Spirit of Travel' campaign developed by Louis Vuitton to celebrate the brand's purpose and associate its product lines with their source of inspiration. The campaign – which includes a book by Patrick Mauriès (with publisher Rizzoli), several films with brand muses such as actresses Emma Stone and Michelle Williams, and a photographic exhibition by Jean Larivière – comes to life on Instagram through compelling copy that accompanies the visuals.

Storytelling

Storytelling is considered a fundamental component of branding (Herskovitz & Crystal, 2010; Wachtman & Johnson, 2009). As luxury brands occupy a unique position in business and culture based on their 'specific aura that is strongly associated with a rich heritage, dreams, myths and legends' (König et al., 2018, p. 284), storytelling can help them connect with their users through narratives around the brand and its legacy. An example of such practice is the Gucci 'Aria' campaign that celebrated the fashion house's centennial by showcasing the collection in a beautifully shot and erotically charged narrative for adult audiences. Starring the band Måneskin and model Kristen McMenamy, and featuring music by Madonna and Massive Attack, the film attracted 2.5 million views on YouTube (over double the brand's 1 million followers) and 32K likes (Gucci, 2021). The film also reveals the legacy of the brand as it was shot at the Savoy Hotel in London, where its founder, Guccio Gucci, worked as a liftboy in his youth (Wonderland, 2021).

Storytelling tactics that communicate a brand's values and image work well with the 'image seeker' category of followers to increase their purchase intentions (Ramadan et al., 2018).

Community

Communities make consumers feel safe in interacting (Hollebeek et al., 2017) and give them the opportunity to create social ties and share information (Febrian & Ahluwalia, 2021). Among them, brand communities bring together the loyal and active customers who 'come together to achieve a collective goal and share a common enthusiasm for a specific brand' (Ozbölük, 2015, p. 412). Such a community is hosted on Instagram, and brought together 38K followers in 15 months. The Cartier Watch Community features content that showcases the horologer's creations, as well as proud collectors and their stories. The page's followers are highly involved, with an engagement rate that often reaches 5 per cent, much higher than the platform's benchmark of 0.2 per cent for the luxury and fashion sector (Landry, 2023).

Communities are also often established to participate in the Corporate Social Responsibility (CSR) activities of luxury brands. In this spirit, the creative directors of fashion house Kenzo brought to life their fascination with tigers, which features on their clothing and accessories, by partnering with WWF (the World Wide Fund for Nature) and Tiger Beer to double the number of tigers in the wild. The collaboration led to the creation of the 'Rare Stripes' capsule collection that helped communicate the brand's cause on platforms such as YouTube. To create the exclusive collection, the brand collaborated with four artists who created unique drawings inspired by real stories of captivity and suffering of tigers. When these drawings were scanned, viewers were taken to page to read the story of each tiger (WWF, 2018). The campaign won numerous awards, including the Webby for CSR in 2019 (Hawes, 2021).

Influencers

A promotional tool often employed by luxury brands to bring their offering closer to the marketplace is influencer marketing. Influencers are defined as 'people who built a large network of followers, and are regarded as trusted tastemakers in one or several niches' (De Veirman et al., 2017, p. 798). Influencer marketing relies on the assumption that a large number of followers leads to an accelerated diffusion of information (Yoganarasimhan, 2012), and on the premise that social media users trust influencers more than the brand they collaborate with (Deyo, 2023). As expected, research indicates that followers' positive attitude towards influencers is also transferred to the brand (Jin, 2018), and that the trustworthiness and perceived authenticity of influencers increases when their displayed lifestyle matches the symbolic value of the luxury brands (Lee & Watkins, 2016). As a consequence, luxury brands often collaborate with hand-picked Instagram celebrities, labelled as the 'Instafamous' by Jin et al. (2019), to launch new collections or further enhance their brand image.

Among these influencers, Chiara Ferragni stands out as one of the world's most prominent fashion bloggers and one of the 500 most influential on The Business of Fashion ratings (n.d.). She has collaborated with brands such as Hublot, Pantene, and Bulgari (Lo, 2022), but most famously holds an ongoing partnership with the fashion house of Dior. Among the many occasions that Ferragni has worked with the luxury brand is for her much-publicised wedding, for which Maria Grazia Chiuri, creative director of Christian Dior, designed the wedding and party gowns. The coverage of the event on Ferragni's Instagram account earned the brand $5.2 million in audience-driven Media Impact Value (MIV) and engagement of 5.6 million globally (Vingan Klein, 2018). In fact, the wedding's 'official hashtag', #TheFerragnez, earned approximately 67 million engagements.

However, not all of Dior's influencer campaigns have been successful. Relaunching its iconic 'saddle' bag, the company gifted it to 100 influencers and celebrities around the world, such as the models Miranda Kerr and Lena Perminova, the fashion bloggers Bryanboy, Susie Bubble, and Chiara

Ferragni, and local influencers such as Jing Tian and Leaf Greener in China. The recipients of the classic bag immediately featured it in their posts, without, however, indicating that this was a promotion for the brand, as required by national advertising regulations and the United States Federal Trade Commission's endorsement guidelines. This was quickly picked up by the fashion watchdog group Diet Prada, which drew attention to the 'sketchiness' of the campaign (Gush, 2018; Singh-Kurtz, 2022).

Aside from this, the massive coverage that the bag received within a few days through so many celebrities actually backfired for the brand as it jeopardised the 'exclusive' character of the brand and alienated its core consumers (Holloway, 2018). In addition to the above, this move by the fashion house meant that it had little control over the output of the influencers and celebrities that featured the bag. Among them, former fashion model and influencer Elle Lee in Hong Kong posted a video showing her visiting the brand's store and trying on the bag. The video was immediately criticised by users and followers for its 'kitsch' cinematography that 'makes the bag look so cheap' (Pan, 2018, para. 6).

The above indicates the importance of planning and monitoring strategic promotional collaborations with influencers on social platforms. The earned media value is often high, but must never jeopardise the brand image or consumers' perception of the exclusivity and lifestyle offered by the brand.

Exclusivity

Regarding exclusivity, another recommended tactic for luxury brands is the launch of limited-edition goods and their promotion on social media (Sotheby's Institute of Art, n.d.). To help build anticipation for these launches among followers, Instagram added the 'Drops' feature to the platform, which allows brands to announce forthcoming product releases and sales, usually for a limited amount of time (Waters, 2022). Burberry's chief creative officer, Riccardo Tisci, made several modifications to the company's release strategy following his appointment in March 2018. These included using Drops to launch the 'B Series' by releasing one new product on the 17th of each month that would be sold exclusively through the brand's Instagram and WeChat accounts, and only for 24 hours (Newbold, 2018). These releases continued for months, and included the sale of non-fungible token (NFTs) and metaverse avatars and accessories for the *Blankos Block Party* mobile game.

The sense of exclusivity and scarcity that such tactics afford can be particularly attractive to the 'trend hunter' segment of followers, who love luxury brands and follow news of them closely, but satisfy their desire for the actual goods by buying and displaying replicas (Ramadan et al., 2018). Limited series and availability of Drops may instead motivate them to purchase authentic products from brands as their desirability has an expiry date.

User-Generated Content

Long before the exclusive Drops feature, Burberry had generated high levels of engagement among followers through User-Generated Content (UGC). In October 2009 the fashion house, renowned for the iconic trench coats it has manufactured for over a century, launched its own social networking site, called 'The Art of the Trench'. The site, which is now hosted on the brand's Tumblr account, invited users to share photos and stories of themselves and their coats, creating a library of images that displayed personal style statements from around the world (Phan et al., 2011). The numerous pictures that featured on the site could be filtered by tags such as gender, colour, weather, style, and popularity (Bunz, 2009).

Followers of luxury brands become involved and engage with them through UGC, primarily in order to express themselves or to earn rewards (Connors, 2019), including the satisfaction of sharing knowledge or experiences with other people (Hasbullah et al., 2020). Their contribution is often invaluable for the brand, but obviously only as long as it is carefully curated to reflect the brand's luxury character (Gardiner, 2019). Considering that the vast majority of social media users find the content created and posted by fewer than half the brands 'authentic', UGC helps fill the gap, increasing brand value and affinity (Beveridge, 2023). In this spirit, Gucci launched the #TFWGucci hashtag to gather memes created by users featuring its watches. With TFW standing for 'That Feeling When', the memes were based on popular social media trends, showcasing humour and advanced levels of creative artistry (Anyanwu, 2017).

'Passionate owners', followers who purchase luxury goods for their emotional benefits, will particularly engage with such activities. Such tactics help establish strong emotional ties and increase communication opportunities, making these consumers feel valuable to the brand and increasing their propensity to buy (Ramadan et al., 2018).

Case Study: Lito Fine Jewelry

Following the above review of tactics and practices used by large luxury brands worldwide, it is worth considering how a relatively small brand can operate in the same environment.

Lito Fine Jewelry was founded in 1999 and quickly embraced by the market, featuring in *The New Jewelers* collection, published by Thames & Hudson (Dupon, 2012). The brand's designs are sold exclusively through the eshop, selected retailers around the world, and its flagship store, Cabinet of Curiosities, in the centre of Athens, Greece. The brand has been active on Instagram for over a decade, and has amassed more than 43K engaged followers. For the purposes of this chapter, the authors interviewed the founder and designer, Lito Karakostanoglou, and the brand's Communications Director, Theodore Lalangas, to look beyond metrics and delve into the objectives and strategy that the brand employs online.

The company sees its products as an expression of self. Through the different collections, the aim is to communicate narratives derived from myths, cultures, and stories – both new and old and universal and personal. Primarily addressing women, the brand promotes contemporary heirlooms that capture the spirit of each woman and help express her own story (Lito Fine Jewelry, 2023).

In regard to communication, Lito Fine Jewelry employs Instagram, primarily as a branding tool that allows the brand to tell its story. The main objective is consistency and coherence in the message conveyed about the brand's aesthetic and communication standards. Engagement is the second objective, and is monitored through the analytics tools provided by the platform. The brand relies on word-of-mouth, as evidenced by the constant increase in followers on the Instagram account, despite the fact it rarely runs advertisements and only appears selectively in fashion editorial content on other media.

For the purposes of this overview, the data were collected in July to October 2023, during which followers grew by 2 per cent. They consist primarily of Millennial and GenX women, who are also the brand's target groups, although several designs are also popular among younger women. Engagement among these followers is reported to be 0.36 per cent by the engagement calculator of marketing platform Phlanx, higher than the industry benchmark of 0.33 per cent (Cucu, 2024). Indicatively, the same metric for the main Instagram accounts of Dior and Chanel is 0.04 and 0.05 per cent, respectively.

For the brand, meaningful engagement demonstrated by comments and shares, as well as visits to the profile and the eshop, is more important than simple interactions such as likes. It is also notable that almost 15 per cent of the interactions are saves, particularly for posts showcasing products, highlighting potential leads for future purchases. As the communication team have noticed, engagement is higher for content that is characterised by emotion and storytelling. Product posts that feature a short narrative around the character, the occasion, or the setting attract more interactions. In the study period, the top performing post (1.2 per cent engagement) commemorated fashion designer Vivienne Westwood, who died near the end of 2022, demonstrating that users appreciate content that is not overtly promotional or product focused (Sullivan, 2020).

Other content that seems to perform well for the brand also references culture (such as art, music, and literature), which enables the brand to share with its audience sources of inspiration, as well as glimpses into brand interests. Another noteworthy finding concerns the human element in the content: it seems that users are attracted more strongly to posts featuring models (full body or close-ups) wearing the jewellery than to photos or videos of standalone products.

Regarding format, the brand primarily uploads posts and stories (single image or carousels) rather than Reels. The posts tend to focus mainly on the brand and its products, with the majority remaining permanently on profile. Most of the stories are posted directly by the designer and are used to showcase slices of life or special moments relating to the brand and herself. The fleeting character of the stories fits well with this type of content, which is viewed by users but is not entangled in the main brand narrative of the profile. Keeping an eye on the various interactions triggered by the various content themes, formats, and post types is key for the brand team to help set specific goals for diverse objectives regarding Key Performance Indicators (KPIs) such as engagement, sales, or leads.

As shown through this short case, a luxury brand aims primarily to build and sustain the brand character when utilising social media platforms such as Instagram. Brand storytelling is key to both showcasing products and as offering glimpses into the life of the brand itself – its heritage, inspiration, and input to the consumer's life. With a clear view of the customer/follower, the luxury brand adds value through narratives that reach and stir emotions, rather than rational, hard-sell promotional messages that go against what differentiates this sector of the industry from the mass market.

Discussion Questions

- What are the objectives a luxury brand aims to achieve through social media?
- What type of content or theme delivers the highest level of engagement?

Industry Recommendations

The list of engagement tactics presented in this chapter is by no means exhaustive. Although some engagement practices, such as the use of polls and giveaway contests, are not considered suitable for a luxury brand, it is worth keeping an eye on successful tactics and activation ideas that may be adapted and employed by the more exclusive brands in the market. Particularly for the younger generation – which enjoys participating in TikTok challenges, uses Snapchat filters, and applies zany stickers to their Instagram stories – the detachment of luxury brands becomes less and less relevant. However, having a strong brand personality, with clearly defined limits as to what is on par with the brand identity, is key to safeguarding brand character in the luxury goods market.

References

Aldhamiri A., Carlson, J., Vilches-Montero, S., Rahman, S. M., & Gudergan, S. P. (2024). What drives higher active customer engagement in luxury brands' social media? Measurement and contingencies. *Journal of Retailing and Consumer Services, 79*, 103804. https://doi.org/10.1016/j.jretconser.2024.103804

Aljuhmani, H. Y., Elrehail, H., Bayram, P., & Samarah, T. (2023). Linking social media marketing efforts with customer brand engagement in driving brand loyalty. *Asia Pacific Journal of Marketing and Logistics, 35*(7), 1719–1738. https://doi.org/10.1108/apjml-08-2021-0627

Anyanwu, O. (2017, March 20). *Gucci calls on digital artists for #TFWGucci collaborative project*. Fashion Network. Retrieved October 28, 2023, from https://ww.fashionnetwork.com/news/gucci-calls-on-digital-artists-for-tfwgucci-collaborative-project,806992.html

Arora, R. (2013, May 8). *8 P's of luxury brand marketing*. American Marketer. https://www.americanmarketer.com/wp-content/uploads/pdf_cache/6/4/5/1/5/64515.pdf

Bazi, S., Filieri, R., & Gorton, M. (2023, May). Social media content aesthetic quality and customer engagement: The mediating role of entertainment and impacts on brand love and loyalty. *Journal of Business Research, 160*, 113778. https://doi.org/10.1016/j.jbusres.2023.113778

Beveridge, C. (2023, July 17). *User-generated content (UGC): What it is + why it matters*. Hootsuite. https://blog.hootsuite.com/user-generated-content-ugc/#Why_is_user-generated_content_important

Blal, I., & Sturman, M. C. (2014, May 6). The differential effects of the quality and quantity of online reviews on hotel room sales. *Cornell Hospitality Quarterly, 55*(4), 365–375. https://doi.org/10.1177/1938965514533419

Brandão, A., Pinho, E., & Rodrigues, P. (2019, September 9). Antecedents and consequences of luxury brand engagement in social media. *Spanish Journal of Marketing – ESIC, 23*(2), 163–183. https://doi.org/10.1108/sjme-11-2018-0052

Bunz, M. (2009, November 9). Burberry checks out crowdsourcing with The Art of the Trench. *The Guardian*. Retrieved October 28, 2023, from https://www.theguardian.com/media/pda/2009/nov/09/burberry-art-of-the-trench

Business of Fashion (n.d.). *Chiara Ferragni*. Retrieved October 27, 2023, from https://www.businessoffashion.com/community/people/chiara-ferragni.

Connors, J. (2019, August 6). *Check out the benefits of user-generated content*. The Raven. https://raventools.com/blog/benefits-user-generated-content/

Cruz-Ros, S., Miquel-Romero, M. J., & Yee, R. W. (2024). Individuals' materialism and brand rituals and traditions as drivers of luxury brand love on social media. *Journal of Consumer Behaviour, 23*(4), 1820–1831. https://doi.org/10.1002/cb.2305

Cucu, E. (2024, February 7). *2024 social media industry benchmarks: Performance data across 22 industries*. Socialinsider. https://www.socialinsider.io/blog/social-media-benchmarks/#14

De Veirman, M., Cauberghe, V., & Hudders, L. (2017). Marketing through Instagram influencers: The impact of number of followers and product divergence on brand attitude. *International Journal of Advertising, 36*(5), 798–828. https://doi.org/10.1080/02650487.2017.1348035

Deyo, J. (2023, February 23). *81% of consumers embraced influencer marketing in the past year, study finds*. Marketing Dive. https://www.marketingdive.com/news/influencer-marketing-success-matter-study-2023/643310/

Dupon, O. (2012, November 13). *The new jewelers*. Thames & Hudson. https://thamesandhudson.com/new-jewelers-desirable-collectable-contemporary-9780500516294

Eastman, J. K., & Eastman, K. L. (2011, June 23). Perceptions of status consumption and the economy. *Journal of Business & Economics Research*, 9(7), 9–20. https://doi.org/10.19030/jber.v9i7.4677

Febrian, A., & Ahluwalia, L. (2021, September 28). Investigating the antecedents of consumer brand engagement to luxury brands on social media. *Indonesian Journal of Business and Entrepreneurship*, 7(3), 245. https://doi.org/10.17358/ijbe.7.3.245

Fetais, A. H., Algharabat, R. S., Aljafari, A., & Rana, N. P. (2023). Do social media marketing activities improve brand loyalty? An empirical study on luxury fashion brands. *Information Systems Frontiers*, *25*(2), 795–817.

Firouznia, M., Brochado, A., & Wood, C. (2024). The influence of social media communications on consumer–brand relationships in the luxury brand context: A bibliometric review. In B. Barbosa (Ed.), *Marketing innovation strategies and consumer behavior* (pp. 243–265). IGI Global.

Gardiner, S. P. (2019). Do luxury car brands market premium status in a world of likes, followers, and user-generated content. *Journal of Marketing Management*, 7(2), 18–27. https://doi.org/10.15640/jmm.v7n2a3

Gomelsky, V. (2021, October 22). Instagram: A watch brand's best friend. *New York Times*. https://www.nytimes.com/2021/10/22/fashion/watches-instagram.html

Goodman. (2021, June 24). *How to bounce back from black hat tactics that are strangling your success*. Sked Social. Retrieved October 22, 2023, from https://skedsocial.com/blog/how-to-bounce-back-from-black-hat-tactics

Gucci, (2021, September 10). *The Gucci Aria advertising campaign*. YouTube. https://www.youtube.com/watch?v=Ob570Cescv4

Gush, C. (2018, July 25). *Dior's Saddle Bag is back – along with a controversial influencer campaign*. Refinery29. Retrieved October 28, 2023, from https://www.refinery29.com/en-gb/dior-saddle-bag-influencer-disclosure.

Hasbullah, N. N., Sulaiman, Z., & Mas'od, A. (2020). User-generated content sources: The use of social media in motivating sustainable luxury fashion consumptions. *International Journal of Scientific and Technology Research*, *9*(3), 5208–5214.

Hawes, W. (2021). *Tiger Beer 'Rare Stripes'*. http://www.wezhawes.com/tiger-beer-rare-stripes#awards

Haydn. (2016, December 15). *Follow for follow: The 411 on the controversial IG growth tactic*. Kimberly Haydn Consulting. Retrieved October 22, 2023, from https://kimberlyhaydn.com/follow-for-follow/

He, Y., Zou, D., & Jin, L. (2010, November 2). Exploiting the goldmine: A lifestyle analysis of affluent Chinese consumers. *Journal of Consumer Marketing*, *27*(7), 615–628. https://doi.org/10.1108/07363761011086362

Hennigs, N., Wiedmann, K., & Klarmann, C. (2012). Luxury brands in the digital age: Exclusivity versus ubiquity. *Marketing Review St. Gallen*, 29, 30–35.

Herskovitz, S., & Crystal, M. (2010). The essential brand persona: Storytelling and branding. *Journal of Business Strategy*, *31*(3), 21–28. https://doi.org/10.1108/02756661011036673

Hollebeek, L. D., Glynn, M. S., & Brodie, R. J. (2014, May). Consumer brand engagement in social media: Conceptualization, scale development and validation. *Journal of Interactive Marketing*, 28(2), 149–165. https://doi.org/10.1016/j.intmar.2013.12.002

Hollebeek, L. D., Juric, B., & Tang, W. (2017). Virtual brand community engagement practices: A refined typology and model. *Journal of Services Marketing*, *31*(3), 204–217. https://doi.org/10.1108/JSM-01-2016-0006

Holloway. (2018, July 24). *When mass influencer marketing goes awry*. Beauty Directory. Retrieved October 28, 2023, from https://www.beautydirectory.com.au/news/business/when-mass-influencer-marketing-goes-awry

Jin, S. V. (2018, February). 'Celebrity 2.0 and beyond!' Effects of Facebook profile sources on social networking advertising. *Computers in Human Behavior*, *79*, 154–168. https://doi.org/10.1016/j.chb.2017.10.033

Jin, S. V., Muqaddam, A., & Ryu, E. (2019, March 21). Instafamous and social media influencer marketing. *Marketing Intelligence & Planning*, *37*(5), 567–579. https://doi.org/10.1108/mip-09-2018-0375

Jin, S.-A. A. (2012). The potential of social media for luxury brand management. *Marketing Intelligence & Planning*, *30*(7), 687–699.

König, J. C. L., Haase, J., Hennigs, N., & Wiedmann, K. P. (2018). … and they lived luxury ever after: Storytelling as a driver for luxury brand perception and consumer behaviour. *Luxury Research Journal*, *1*(4), 283–302. doi:10.1504/lrj.2018.090973

Landry, J. (2023, May 29). *Instagram reels stats and benchmarks*. Dash Hudson. https://www.dashhudson.com/blog/instagram-reels-performance-benchmarks

Lee, J. E., & Watkins, B. (2016, December). YouTube vloggers' influence on consumer luxury brand perceptions and intentions. *Journal of Business Research*, *69*(12), 5753–5760. https://doi.org/10.1016/j.jbusres.2016.04.171

Liadeli, G., Sotgiu, F., & Verlegh, P. W. (2023). A meta-analysis of the effects of brands' owned social media on social media engagement and sales. *Journal of Marketing*, *87*(3), 406–427. https://doi.org/10.1177/00222429221123250

Lito Fine Jewelry (2023). *Brand DNA*. Internal Document.

Lo, J. (2022, March 18). Meet the Italian Kardashians – Chiara, Valentina and Francesca Ferragni from Amazon reality show The Ferragnez, the stylish sisters and influencers who luxury brands love. *Style Magazine.* Retrieved October 28, 2023, from https://www.scmp.com/magazines/s.tyle/celebrity/article/3170988/meet-italian-kardashians-chiara-valentina-and-francesca

Long, Y. (2023, May 14). How luxury advertising captures the psychology of audience. *Frontiers in Business, Economics and Management*, *9*(1), 66–69. https://doi.org/10.54097/fbem.v9i1.8292

Lou, C., Xie, Q., Feng, Y., & Kim, W. (2019). Does non-hard-sell content really work? Leveraging the value of branded content marketing in brand building. *Journal of Product & Brand Management*, *28*(7), 773–786. https://doi.org/10.1108/JPBM-07-2018-1948

Mohr, I. (2013). The impact of social media on the fashion industry. *Journal of Applied Business and Economics*, *15*(2), 17–22.

Newbold, A. (2018, October 16). *Why you need to know about Burberry's B Series*. British Vogue. https://www.vogue.co.uk/article/burberry-monthly-drop-model-b-series

Oliveira, M., & Fernandes, T. (2020, June 10). Luxury brands and social media: Drivers and outcomes of consumer engagement on Instagram. *Journal of Strategic Marketing*, *30*(4), 389–407. https://doi.org/10.1080/0965254x.2020.1777459

Ozbölük, T. (2015). Consumption communities through a marketing lens. *International Journal of Business & Management Studies*, *4*(2), 411–417.

Pan, Y. (2018, July 23). Dior's pushy relaunch of iconic bag backfires in China. *Jing Daily.* Retrieved October 28, 2023, from https://jingdaily.com/dior-saddle-bag-china/

Pangarkar, A., Patel, J., & Kumar, S. K. (2023). Drivers of eWOM engagement on social media for luxury consumers: Analysis, implications, and future research directions. *Journal of Retailing and Consumer Services*, *74*, 103410.

Park, H., Rabolt, N. J., & Sook Jeon, K. (2008). Purchasing global luxury brands among young Korean consumers. *Journal of Fashion Marketing and Management, 12*(2), 244–259. doi:10.1108/13612020810874917

Park, M., Im, H., & Kim, H. Y. (2020, September). 'You are too friendly!' The negative effects of social media marketing on value perceptions of luxury fashion brands. *Journal of Business Research, 117*, 529–542. https://doi.org/10.1016/j.jbusres.2018.07.026

Pentina, I., Guilloux, V., & Micu, A. C. (2018, January 2). Exploring social media engagement behaviors in the context of luxury brands. *Journal of Advertising, 47*(1), 55–69. https://doi.org/10.1080/00913367.2017.1405756

Phan, M., Thomas, R., & Heine, K. (2011, November). Social media and luxury brand management: The case of Burberry. *Journal of Global Fashion Marketing, 2*(4), 213–222. https://doi.org/10.1080/20932685.2011.10593099

Pulizzi, J. & Barrett, N. (2008). *Get content, get customers: Turn prospects into buyers with content*. Bonita Springs, FL: Voyager Media.

Ramadan, Z., Farah, M. F., & Dukenjian, A. (2018, May 8). Typology of social media followers: The case of luxury brands. *Marketing Intelligence & Planning, 36*(5), 558–571. https://doi.org/10.1108/mip-01-2018-0039

Singh-Kurtz, S. (2022, July 20). *The Dior saddle bag is back – in a thinly veiled influencer ad campaign*. Quartz. https://qz.com/quartzy/1333000/users-are-rightly-suspicious-after-dior-saddle-bag-photos-flood-instagram

Smulders, T. (2016). *Why and how content marketing works for luxury. Luxury Daily.* https://www.luxurydaily.com/why-and-how-content-marketing-works-for-luxury/

Sotheby's Institute of Art (n.d.). *Luxury marketing: A deep dive into high-end branding.* Retrieved October 28, 2023, from https://www.sothebysinstitute.com/how-to-series/luxury-marketing

Suessmuth-Dyckerhoff, C., Hexter, J., & St-Maurice, I. (2008). Marketing to China's new traditionalists. *Far East Economic Review, 171*(1), 28–33.

Sullivan, M. (2020, May 28). *The 80/20 rule, explained. BrandMuscle.* Retrieved February 14, 2024, from https://www.brandmuscle.com/blog/the-80-20-rule-explained/

Thanasi-Boçe, M., Zaidi, S. F. H., Kurtishi-Kastrati, S., & Momin, M. (2024). Decoding the luxury brand attachment: The power of social media in driving consumer action in Kuwait. *Human Behavior and Emerging Technologies, 2024*(1), 9687915.

Üçok Hughes, M., Bendoni, W. K., & Pehlivan, E. (2016). Storygiving as a co-creation tool for luxury brands in the age of the internet: A love story by Tiffany and thousands of lovers. *Journal of Product & Brand Management, 25*(4), 357–364. https://doi.org/10.1108/JPBM-09-2015-0970

Vigneron, F., & Johnson, L. W. (2004, July). Measuring perceptions of brand luxury. *Journal of Brand Management, 11*(6), 484–506. https://doi.org/10.1057/palgrave.bm.2540194

Vingan Klein, A. (2018, September 4). *Chiara Ferragni earned her wedding dress designer more media value than Meghan Markle did. Fashionista.* Retrieved October 28, 2023, from https://fashionista.com/2018/09/chiara-ferragni-dior-wedding-dress-media-press-value

Wachtman, E., & Johnson, S. L. (2009). The persuasive power of story. *Marketing Management, 18*(1), 28–34.

WARC. (2023, October 23). *Feed: Luxury category needs to engage with 'Joy Rejuvenators'*. Retrieved October 25, 2023, from https://www.warc.com/content/feed/luxury-category-needs-to-engage-with-joy-rejuvenators/en-GB/8797

Waters, M. (2022, May 5). *Generate hype for your launch like 'Supreme' with the new Instagram Drops feature.* Chatdesk. https://www.chatdesk.com/blog/generate-hype-for-your-launch-with-the-new-instagram-drops-feature

Weaver, R. (2015). *Top 10: Luxury brands on social media.* Social Media Delivered. Retrieved October 27, 2023, from https://www.socialmediadelivered.com/blog/luxury-brands-on-social-media

Wonderland. (2021, September 13). *Gucci Aria.* https://www.wonderlandmagazine.com/2021/09/11/gucci-aria-campaign

Wu, M. S. S., Chaney, I., Chen, C. H. S., Nguyen, B., & Melewar, T. C. (2015). Luxury fashion brands: Factors influencing young female consumers' luxury fashion purchasing in Taiwan. *Qualitative Market Research, 18*(3), 298–319. https://doi.org/10.1108/QMR-02-2014-0016

WWF. (2018, July 21). *World's first 'Rare Stripes' collection unveiled in the name of wild tiger conservation.* https://wwf.panda.org/wwf_news/?333092/launch-of-rare-stripes-collection

Yoganarasimhan, H. (2012). Impact of social network structure on content propagation: A study using YouTube data. *Quantitative Marketing and Economics, 10*(1), 111–150.

Zha, T., Aw, E. C. X., Dastane, O., & Fernando, A. G. (2023). Social media marketing for luxury brands: Parasocial interactions and empowerment for enhanced loyalty and willingness to pay a premium. *Marketing Intelligence & Planning, 41*(8), 1138–1161.

Unleashing the Potential 3

How Influencers Drive Digital Content Marketing

Lakshmi Raj and Mallika Sankar M.
Christ University, Bengaluru

Introduction

Social media is "a group of Internet-based applications that build on the ideological and technical foundations of Web 2.0, and that allow the creation and exchange of user-generated content" (Kaplan & Haenlein, 2010, p. 61). It offers a platform for collaborative exploration, content-sharing, relationship-building, and various other purposes such as social and educational engagement (Jiao et al., 2015; Rishi & Bandyopadhyay, 2018). Social media marketing (SMM) employs social media as a promotional tool to enhance brand visibility, customer engagement, and sales (Saravanakumar & SuganthaLakshmi, 2012; Constantinides, 2014; Pourkhani et al., 2019).

Recently, the integration of influencers in social media has emerged as a prominent marketing strategy across various industries. Influencers wield individual power to sway a broad audience, and, when they endorse products or services on social media in exchange for compensation, this is termed "influencer marketing" (Glucksman, 2017; Campbell & Grimm, 2019; Campbell & Farrell, 2020). Simultaneously, digital content marketing (DCM) is a dynamic field defined as distributing valuable brand-related content on digital platforms to foster brand engagement, trust, and relationships (Hollebeek & Macky, 2019). DCM has made significant contributions

DOI: 10.4324/9781003412656-3

to consumer behavior, brand equity, online word-of-mouth (e-WOM), and purchase intention (Rowley, 2008; Pulizzi & Barrett, 2009; Baltes, 2015; Kee & Yazdanifard, 2015; Pazeraite & Repoviene, 2016; Weerasinghe, 2018; Hollebeek & Macky, 2019; Sudarsono et al., 2020; Izogo & Mpinganjira, 2022; Balio & Casais, 2021; Febrian et al., 2021; Lopes & Casais, 2022; Terho et al., 2022; du Plessis, 2022; Li et al., 2022; Trivedi, 2022).

These marketing trends signify the evolving landscape of brand promotion and consumer engagement. In 2022, the global content marketing industry generated approximately US$63 billion in revenue, with projections estimating a rise to $72 billion in 2023 and $107 billion by 2026; and the global influencer marketing market has more than doubled since 2019, reaching an estimated $21.1 billion in 2023 (Dencheva, 2023). According to Veissi (2017), influencers play a crucial role in content marketing. Therefore, this study aims to comprehensively investigate the effectiveness of influencers in driving digital content marketing, employing a detailed case study approach to elucidate how influencers harness the power of content from a marketing perspective. In this context, we examine the case of Ranveer Allahbadia to gain insights into how he, as an influencer, contributes to digital content marketing.

Significance of the Study

This study carries substantial significance, spanning the influencer marketing and digital content marketing landscape, with far-reaching implications for industry, businesses, influencers, and digital content marketers. For industry, it offers the potential to revolutionize influencer marketing practices by enhancing transparency and ethical standards, fostering stronger consumer trust and more authentic brand collaborations. Businesses can benefit from invaluable insights into optimizing influencer partnerships, gaining a deeper understanding of how influencers can boost brand visibility and engagement. Meanwhile, influencers can harness the study's insights to refine their strategies, forging stronger connections with both their audience and collaborating brands. Lastly, digital content marketers can draw practical guidance on influencer selection and content strategy, emphasizing the importance of authenticity and value creation in content marketing. In essence, this research transcends academic boundaries, reshaping the influencer marketing landscape to be more ethical, effective, and value-driven, thus influencing the future of influencer marketing and digital content marketing.

Research Methodology

This study utilizes an exploratory research synthesis approach to comprehensively examine the existing literature on influencer, influencer marketing, and digital content marketing, specifically focusing on understanding how influencers drive DCM. The influencer for the case example was chosen based on convenience sampling and his number of followers. Additionally, the study incorporates a real-life case, providing concrete evidence of how influencers actively contribute to the success of DCM strategies. By amalgamating both theoretical foundations and practical instances, this research methodology seeks to offer a holistic perspective on the role of influencers in shaping the digital marketing landscape.

The Role of Influencers in Driving Digital Content Marketing

Influencers' Impact on Marketing

Marketers are increasingly shifting some control from advertising agencies to influencers who, in exchange for compensation, share product information on social media platforms (Campbell & Grimm, 2019). This practice harnesses the influencers' unique skill sets and their intimate connections with target audiences, commonly referred to as "influencer marketing"—a strategy where individuals are remunerated for featuring a product or service on their social media accounts (Campbell & Farrell, 2020). An influencer, as defined by Freberg et al. (2010), serves as a third-party endorser who shapes audience perceptions through the use of blogs, tweets, and videos on various social media channels.

While influencers historically encompassed celebrities used in advertising endorsements (Gretzel, 2018), the landscape has evolved. Today, influencers have become leaders of opinion, professionals in their respective niches, consistently present on social media, and closely associated with specific brands, allowing them to wield considerable sway over a vast audience of potential consumers (Gretzel, 2018; Mokhare et al., 2021). There are five types of influencer classified based on their number of followers: Nano-influencers, "newcomers" with 0–10k followers; Micro-influencer "rising stars" (10k–100k); Macro-influencers occupying "the sweet spot" (100k–1 million followers); Mega-influencers, "everyday celebrities (1m+); and Celebrity influencers encompassing "the rich and famous" (1m+) (Campbell & Farrell, 2020).

According to Glucksman (2017, p. 77):

> Influencer marketing, the process of identifying, engaging, and supporting individuals who create conversations with a brand's customers, is a growing trend used in public relations initiatives. In recent years, this strategy has become predominantly centred around social media, creating an opportunity for brands to market through social media influencers.

As reported in *The State of Influencer Marketing 2020: Benchmark Report*, the influencer marketing industry experienced substantial growth, with an increase from $6.6 billion in 2019 to $9.7 billion in 2020. This growth continued, reaching a record $16.4 billion in 2022 (Influencer Marketing Hub, 2024). Influencers play a vital role in enhancing the reputation of a business or brand by increasing customer awareness and soliciting valuable feedback, thereby strengthening customer relationships (Booth & Matic, 2011; Campbell & Farrell, 2020). They are instrumental in promoting brand recognition and fostering direct connections with consumers, ultimately encouraging brand loyalty. This engagement also facilitates direct communication, trust-building, and the integration of an influencer's identity with the brand through digital media interactions (Farquhar, 1989; Booth & Matic, 2011). In addition, influencers are viewed as brand endorsers, possessing specific qualities such as confidence, authenticity, interactivity, participation level, frequency of engagement, and prominence within the market or community (Booth & Matic, 2011; Glucksman, 2017; Gretzel, 2018; Mokhare et al., 2021). Key elements of influencer marketing include appearance, content creation, credibility, genuine self-sharing/expression, and expertise (Glucksman, 2017; Tsen & Cheng, 2021; Isyanto et al., 2020):

- Appearance: The way influencers present themselves significantly affects their ability to capture the attention of their audience (Tsen & Cheng, 2021).
- Content production pertains to the influencer's ability to create captivating videos, exhibit strong writing skills, and demonstrate adeptness in photography and proficiency in photo editing (Tsen & Cheng, 2021).
- Credibility addresses the question of an individual's believability (Wiedmann & Mettenheim, 2021). A credible influencer's followers can place trust in them because they furnish reliable information and offer expert advice to address inquiries (Tsen & Cheng, 2021). For influencers to effectively convey advertising messages as part of brand marketing, they must possess credibility to be regarded as trustworthy by

consumers and social media followers, thereby instilling confidence in potential customers (Isyanto et al., 2020).

- Genuine self-sharing: Influencers engage in the authentic sharing of their personal life experiences with their followers through vlogs, blogs, and a willingness to divulge private aspects of their lives, such as relationship status, educational qualifications, family life, and more (Tsen & Cheng, 2021). This openness fosters trust among their followers, who come to believe in their opinions, and companies leverage this trust in influencers to promote their brands.
- Expertise: An influencer will be an expert in a particular area (Tsen & Cheng, 2021), and expertise denotes their level of knowledge. An expert excels in a domain to a degree that few others can achieve, often surpassing the knowledge, experience, and problem-solving skills of the general population (Wiedmann & Mettenheim, 2021). This is characterized by a high level of knowledge and proficiency within a particular domain.

The Role of Digital Content Marketing

The fundamental underpinning for a successful digital marketing strategy hinges on the presence of high-quality digital content marketing (Baltes, 2015). "Content" serves as the core of marketing material, encompassing both meaning and information through which businesses employ digital content to identify, scrutinize, and fulfill customer demands. Thus, comprehending how to effectively utilize content in marketing endeavors is central to the concept of content marketing (Rowley, 2008; Puro, 2013; Holliman & Rowley, 2014). Content marketing revolves around providing consumers with valuable marketing information, crafted, distributed, and managed within virtual spaces—all with the overarching goal of engaging both current and potential consumer bases (Pulizzi & Barrett, 2009; Pazeraite & Repoviene, 2016).

Digital content marketing specifically involves the development and distribution of pertinent, valuable, brand-associated content to current or prospective customers via digital platforms with the aim of nurturing positive brand engagement, trust, and relationships (Hollebeek & Mackyc, 2019). Notably, DCM is not confined to large corporations; it is embraced by small and medium-sized enterprises (SMEs) as well (Baltes, 2015). Marketers curate personalized, engaging, and creative content that caters to the needs of each consumer, granting them the freedom to select, explore, and read, thereby aligning with the principles of pull marketing (Kee & Yazdanifard, 2015). DCM has the power to sustain readers' interest by producing valuable content, subsequently enhancing brand loyalty among readers and establishing enduring relationships with them (Baltes, 2015; Kee & Yazdanifard, 2015).

The fundamental objectives of DCM encompass: the promotion of brand awareness; audience education, credibility and trust-building; the generation of demand and leads; nurturing subscribers; and fostering loyalty among existing clients and customers. It also aims to drive attendance at in-person events, boost sales and revenue, cultivate subscriber audiences, and support the launch of new products (Moutsos, 2022). An understanding of the optimal channels, platform-specific content, and the creation of content communities serves as compelling evidence for companies to establish connections between their brands and their target audience (du Plessis, 2017). DCM primarily focuses on content design, presentation, and dissemination. Various forms of educational and compelling content are used to attract and retain customers in exchange for customer-owned resources. This practice generates positive word-of-mouth and contributes to the establishment of sustainable and trusted brand status (Li et al., 2021).

It is therefore of utmost importance for entrepreneurs to possess effective DCM techniques to attract more visitors to their pages, keep them updated with news, and encourage repeat purchases (Ahmad et al., 2016). Digital brand content encompasses a variety of elements, including blog posts, website content, white papers, e-books and newsletters, testimonials, infographics, and multimedia content (owned media). Consumers themselves also contribute to brand content (user-generated) through their comments, feedback, and social media posts (earned media).

Finally, brand content can also be utilized as paid content promotion and social network advertising (paid media) (du Plessis, 2022). The fundamental elements of content marketing encompass relevance, informativeness, reliability, value, uniqueness, emotions, and intelligence (Pazeraite & Repoviene, 2016), as outlined below.

Relevance

As highlighted by Pazeraite and Repoviene, customers discern a brand as suitable when its content is rich in value and conveys pertinent information. This emphasis on relevant content serves as a guide through advertising, facilitating a connection with the company. For example: Patagonia is a sustainable outdoor clothing brand that uses recycled and ethically sourced raw materials to reduce its carbon footprint in manufacturing. Through its website, social media platforms, and marketing campaigns, the company shares content that highlights its commitment to environmental sustainability, ethical sourcing, and social responsibility (Patagonia, n.d.).

Informativity

Pazeraite and Repoviene further emphasize that customers benefit from being informed about the company, brand, and the processes employed to create products and services in a rational and accessible manner. This approach presents an opportunity to effectively persuade and engage consumers (Gagnon, 2014). For example: GoPro promotes informational content by providing users guidance and tips on how to maximize the use of its cameras. Through its website, blog posts, and social media channels, it shares how-to videos, photography techniques, editing tutorials, and product reviews to educate users on how to capture the best footage and create compelling content (GoPro, 2022).

Reliability

In producing reliable and adequate content, content marketing plays a crucial role (Pazeraite & Repoviene, 2016). This reliability serves as a critical element for high-quality content, fostering trust-building among prospective customers toward the brand. For example: Byju's, an e-learning platform, offers engaging and interactive lessons in various subjects, including mathematics, science, and languages. The content is developed by expert educators and is aligned with curriculum standards, ensuring accuracy and reliability (Byjus, n.d.).

Value

Gagnon (2014) points out that content used in brand marketing should exhibit a level of quality that defines its value, addressing the needs of potential customers and offering solutions to their problems. The content should encompass both functional and emotional value to establish a meaningful connection between the brand and the customer, as also highlighted by Pazeraite and Repoviene. For example: Indian online fashion store Myntra's "Style Tips for Every Occasion" series exemplifies value content by offering practical fashion advice and styling tips tailored to different occasions. Through engaging videos, informative blog posts, and interactive social media content, the company addresses the needs of its audience by providing solutions to their styling dilemmas (Myntra, n.d).

Uniqueness

To capture consumers' attention, companies must employ unique and distinctive content in the online space compared to their competitors, a concept emphasized by Pazeraite and Repoviene and by Gagnon. This unique content is instrumental in positioning the brand against competitors, creating a favorable and enduring impression in the minds of potential customers and facilitating WOM discussions about the company's unique qualities. For example: Austrian multinational Red Bull's 2012 Stratos mission, including Felix Baumgartner's unprecedented skydive, showcased unique content, solidifying the company's brand identity (Red Bull, n.d.).

Emotions

Emotions, as elucidated by Bagozzi et al. (1999), are context-dependent and emerge from evaluations of events and personal thoughts. Brand marketing content must possess a dynamic character, evoking positive or negative emotions, and incorporating entertaining elements to excite customers rather than presenting neutral content (Pazeraite & Repoviene, 2016). Emotions hold the power to predict consumer behavior and significantly influence their purchasing decision-making (Drozdova, 2014). For example: laundry detergent company Ariel India's "Dads #ShareTheLoad" campaign resonates emotionally as it portrays fathers reflecting on gender biases in household chores, sparking empathy and inspiring viewers to challenge traditional norms. Through heartfelt storytelling, the content fosters a deep connection with its audience, igniting conversations about the importance of equal participation in domestic responsibilities and promoting positive change in societal attitudes towards gender equality (Ariel India, 2016).

Intelligence

Content should demonstrate the attributes of "intelligent content", which should be both human-friendly in its comprehensibility and machine-friendly in its processability. Furthermore, it should have a persuasive impact, with content quality assessed through its ability to drive conversions; and it should have a persuasive impact, with content quality assessed through its ability to drive conversions. For example: Netflix utilizes intelligent content in its marketing strategy by analyzing user data to personalize recommendations and create original series tailored to audience preferences. Through data-driven insights, it optimizes content distribution across multiple platforms, ensuring a seamless viewing experience and driving engagement and subscription growth (Netflix, n.d).

How Influencers Drive Digital Content Marketing

Case Study: Ranveer Allahbadia

Ranveer Allahbadia is an influencer, entrepreneur, YouTuber, podcaster, and content creator. His remarkable journey encompasses a transformation from creating videos on fitness and cooking to a thriving entrepreneur in the realm of influencer marketing and podcasting. His foray into content creation on YouTube initially revolved around fitness and culinary arts, but his channel's growing popularity soon spurred diversification into self-development and style-related content, significantly expanding his influence and reach.

After a year or two dedicated to content production, Ranveer reconnected with Viraj, a former college junior. This reunion led to a pivotal realization—a noticeable gap between emerging influencers and opportunities for brand collaborations. To bridge this gap, they co-founded Monk Entertainment (Monk-E) in 2018, when Ranveer was just 24. This digital entertainment start-up, based in Mumbai, India, was established to support up-and-coming creators in the digital sphere. The company excels in various facets—including content creation, talent management, social media, brand marketing, and video production—and has a strong emphasis on cultivating personal relationships and fostering a vibrant work environment.

Despite its humble beginnings, Monk Entertainment experienced rapid growth, with a remarkable 350-percent increase within a year. It transitioned from a small team operating out of a garage to a fully fledged office with 35 employees. Along the way, it successfully managed renowned talent and executed brand launches and digital marketing campaigns for clients such as Nykaa, Sony Music, Tinder, and many others. This journey began in the basement of Ranveer's building but quickly gained momentum as the company took on various brands and creators.

The next phase steered the company toward podcasting, in around 2019. This involved collaborations with fellow YouTubers and notable figures from Bollywood, with the pinnacle being an episode featuring the Indian actress and producer Priyanka Chopra. Ranveer's podcast series witnessed a surge in popularity as he welcomed esteemed guests, including Ayushmann Khurrana, Siddharth Roy Kapur, Saif Ali Khan, and even the global icon Arnold Schwarzenegger.

Despite encountering challenges such as the disruptive impact of COVID-19 lockdowns, Ranveer adapted by shifting production to virtual Zoom calls, showcasing his resilience and unwavering commitment to engaging the audience. The podcast series showcased a rich tapestry of guests from diverse backgrounds, spanning defence experts, historians, spiritual leaders, and luminaries from the Bollywood sphere. Renowned national names such as Jay Shetty, Gaur Gopal Das, Sourav Ganguly, Rohit Shetty, G.D. Bakshi, and Amish Tripathi have graced the episodes.

Ranveer's entrepreneurial journey doesn't end there, however. In addition to Monk Entertainment and podcasting, he branched into two more ventures: Big Brainco. and Level Supermind, exemplifying his enduring dedication to personal and professional growth. The following are the awards and recognition he has received:

- Best Fashion Influencer 2019—*Cosmopolitan*
- Influencer Marketing and Best Use of Video for CSR for Monk 2020 at Foxglove Afaqs (twice)
- Youth Influencer of the Year 2019 MTV—IWM Digital Awards
- Young Entrepreneur Award 2020—*Business World*
- Digital Content Entrepreneur and Digital Content Startup of the Year 2020—Talenttrack Awards
- Impact 30 under 30 (2020)—Exchange4Media Group
- PYF International Youth Inspiration of the Year Award 2020.

Demonstrating an unswerving commitment to progress and knowledge dissemination, Ranveer launched the BeerBiceps website, which serves as a comprehensive repository of his multifaceted work, encompassing blogs, vlogs, YouTube content, podcasts, and more. It provides audiences with a centralized hub to explore the world of BeerBiceps, meticulously curated and created by Ranveer Allahbadia himself. His resounding message echoes through this platform—a call for people to relentlessly pursue personal and professional advancement regardless current location or vocation. The website stands as a heartfelt offering to Ranveer's audience, delivering invaluable insights and content for those eager to delve deeper into its journey, also known as *The Ranveer Show*.

The Ranveer Show is India's foremost long-format podcast, hosting insightful interviews with prominent individuals in various domains, such as politicians, historians, cricketers, Bollywood actors, and more. Ranveer's content is characterized by its diverse range, both in terms of his guests and the topics he explores. With a journey spanning over eight years, he has produced an impressive portfolio of over 3,000 videos and conducted 450+ podcasts, amassing an extensive and engaged audience. As of October 31, 2023, his BeerBiceps YouTube channel boasted a subscriber base of 6.37 million, and his Instagram account 2.9 million followers.

Ranveer Allahbadia's journey is an example of an influencer actively engaged in content marketing. The renowned fashion brand Ajio has entered into a pioneering partnership with *The Ranveer Show*, and will be responsible for dressing the host in distinctive themed outfits for each episode (BeerBiceps, 2023; Fashion Network, 2023).

Discussion Questions

- What are the key factors that make influencers effective in digital content marketing?
- How can brands select the right influencers for their marketing campaigns?
- How do influencers create engaging content that resonates with their followers, and how can brands leverage it?

Discussion

Influencer marketing and digital content marketing are two dynamic pillars of modern advertising, each playing a vital role in the ever-evolving landscape of brand promotion and audience engagement. On the one hand, influencer marketing relies on authentic, relatable figures with dedicated followers to communicate brand messages effectively. These influencers leverage their credibility to foster trust among their audience, making it a compelling strategy for businesses seeking to enhance brand visibility and credibility. On the other hand, digital content marketing is the canvas on which influencer marketing operates. It encompasses the creation and dissemination of valuable, engaging content. High-quality content is crucial in capturing and sustaining audience attention, a fundamental requirement for successful influencer marketing campaigns.

The interplay between influencer marketing and digital content marketing is a symbiotic one, where brands rely on influencers to deliver content that resonates with their target audience. The case study of an influencer engaged in digital content marketing serves as a real-world illustration of this synergy. It demonstrates how influencers leverage content to build connections with their audience, emphasizing the importance of authenticity and relevance in content creation. This practical instance underscores that influencer marketing is not merely about endorsements; it is also a strategic process of crafting content that adds genuine value and resonates with followers. The implications are profound, offering insights to brands, influencers, and digital content marketers.

Implications

This study has far-reaching implications in the influencer marketing and digital content marketing domains. Its offer the potential for the industry to overhaul existing practices, emphasizing transparency and ethical standards that can lead to more credible and authentic brand collaborations. This transformation can enhance consumer trust, contributing to a stronger and more sustainable industry. Businesses can reap the benefits of this study by gaining valuable insights into optimizing influencer partnerships, ultimately boosting brand visibility and engagement. This enhanced understanding can lead to more efficient resource allocation and improved return on investment.

Influencers, on the other hand, can harness the insights to refine their strategies, cultivating stronger connections with both their audience and collaborating brands. This, in turn, can pave the way for more meaningful and fruitful collaborations, contributing to long-term career success. Digital content marketers can draw practical guidance from this study, particularly in influencer selection and content strategy, as it underscores the importance of authenticity and value creation in content marketing, enabling marketers to create content that genuinely resonates with their audience.

Overall, this research transcends academic boundaries, reshaping the influencer marketing landscape to be more ethical, effective, and value-driven. It has the potential to revolutionize the industry by fostering transparency and credibility while offering practical guidance to businesses, influencers, and digital content marketers.

Future Scope and Conclusion

The study of influencer marketing and digital content marketing opens up several promising avenues for future research and industry development. Firstly, there is a growing need to explore the long-term impact and sustainability of influencer marketing campaigns. Researchers can conduct longitudinal studies to assess how influencer partnerships affect brand loyalty and consumer behavior over extended periods. Secondly, future research could delve deeper into developing and implementing ethical guidelines and best practices that not only benefit the industry but also protect the interests of consumers. Thirdly, the emerging fields of artificial intelligence (AI) and machine learning present intriguing prospects for research. The integration of AI tools to analyze influencer performance, optimize content strategies, and predict consumer behavior can be a transformative area of exploration. Additionally, the measurement of ROI and the development of standardized metrics for influencer marketing effectiveness remain ongoing challenges. Future studies could focus on refining measurement methodologies and creating industry benchmarks to better evaluate the value generated by influencer collaborations. Lastly, the global nature of digital content and influencer marketing necessitates cross-cultural research. Investigating how cultural nuances impact influencer marketing effectiveness and consumer engagement will be crucial for businesses aiming to expand their reach.

The future of research in influencer marketing and digital content marketing is vibrant and diverse, encompassing ethical considerations, long-term impact assessment, AI integration, standardized metrics, and cross-cultural studies. This evolving landscape presents exciting opportunities for scholars, practitioners, and industry stakeholders to further enrich and refine the field. In conclusion, this study underscores the pivotal role of influencers in reshaping the landscape of digital content marketing. It highlights the critical importance of transparency, authenticity, and ethical standards in fostering trust and credibility within the industry.

References

Ahmad, N. S., Musa, R., & Harun, M. H. M. (2016). The impact of social media content marketing (SMCM) towards brand health. *Procedia Economics and Finance, 37*, 331–336. https://doi.org/10.1016/S2212-5671(16)30133-2

Ariel India. (2016). *#Share the load [Video]*. YouTube. https://www.youtube.com/watch?v=wJukf4ifuKs

Bagozzi, R. P., Gopinath, M., & Nyer, P. U. (1999). The role of emotions in marketing. *Journal of the Academy of Marketing Science, 27*(2), 184–206.

Balio, S., & Casais, B. (2021). A content marketing framework to analyze customer engagement on social media. In Information Resources Management Association (Ed.), *Research anthology on strategies for using social media as a service and tool in business* (pp. 320–336). IGI Global. doi:10.4018/978-1-7998-9020-1.ch016.

Baltes, L. P. (2015). Content marketing: The fundamental tool of digital marketing. *Bulletin of the Transilvania University of Brasov: Economic Sciences, Series V*, *8*(2), 111–118.

BeerBiceps. (2023). *The Ranveer Show is stopping and ... [Video]*. YouTube. https://www.youtube.com/watch?v=hFaprk_abl0

Booth, N., & Matic, J. A. (2011). Mapping and leveraging influencers in social media to shape corporate brand perceptions. *Corporate Communications: An International Journal*, *16*(3), 184–191. doi:10.1108/13563281111156853.

Byjus. (n.d.) *Comprehensive learning programs and classes for all students*. https://byjus.com/

Campbell, C., & Farrell, J. R. (2020). More than meets the eye: The functional components underlying influencer marketing. *Business Horizons*, *63*(4), 469–479.

Campbell, C., & Grimm, P. E. (2019). The challenges native advertising poses: Exploring potential federal trade commission responses and identifying research needs. *Journal of Public Policy & Marketing*, *38*(1), 110–123. https://doi.org/10.1177%2F0743915618818576

Constantinides, E. (2014). Foundations of social media marketing. *Procedia: Social and Behavioral Sciences*, *148*(1), 40–57. https://doi.org/10.1016/j.sbspro.2014.07.016.

Dencheva, V. (2023). *Global influencer market size*. Statista. https://www.statista.com/statistics/1092819/global-influencer-market-size/

Drozdova, N. (2014). *Measuring emotions in marketing and consumer behavior: Is Face Reader an applicable tool?* [Master's thesis]. Norwegian School of Economics.

du Plessis, C. (2017). The role of content marketing in social media content communities. *South African Journal of Information Management*, *19*(1), 1–7. https://doi.org/10.4102/sajim.v19i1.866

du Plessis, C. (2022). A scoping review of the effect of content marketing on online consumer behavior. *SAGE Open*, 1–17. https://doi.org/10.1177/21582440221093042

Farquhar, P. H. (1989). Managing brand equity. *Marketing Research*, *1*(3), 24–33.

Fashion Network. (2023). *Ajio joins "The Ranveer Show" as first brand partner*. https://in.fashionnetwork.com/news/Ajio-joins-the-ranveer-show-as-first-brand-partner,1510143.html

Febrian, A., Bangsawan, S., MS, M., & Ahadiat, A. (2021). Digital content marketing strategy in increasing customer engagement in Covid-19 situation. *International Journal of Pharmaceutical Research*, *13*(1), 4797–4805.

Gagnon, E. (2014). Goodbye, B2B brand marketing: Developing content-based marketing programs for the post-marketing era. *International Management Review*, *10*(2), 68–71.

Glucksman, M. (2017). The rise of social media influencer marketing on lifestyle branding: A case study of Lucie Fink. *Elon Journal of Undergraduate Research in Communications*, *8*(2), 77–87.

GoPro (2022). *How to use GoPro HERO11 Black (instructions + tips) [Video]*. Youtube. https://www.youtube.com/watch?v=l-CaYFcBi94

Gretzel, U. (2018). Influencer marketing in travel and tourism. In M. Sigala & U. Gretzel (Eds.), *Advances in social media for travel, tourism and hospitality: New perspectives, practice and cases* (pp. 147–156). Routledge.

Hollebeek, L. D., & Macky, K. (2019). Digital content marketing's role in fostering consumer engagement, trust, and value: Framework, fundamental propositions, and implications. *Journal of Interactive Marketing, 45*, 27–41. https://doi.org/10.1016/j.intmar.2018.07.003

Holliman, G., & Rowley, J. (2014). Business to business digital content marketing: Marketers' perceptions of best practice. *Journal of Research in Interactive Marketing. 8*(4), 269–293. https://doi.org/10.1108/JRIM-02-2014-0013

Influencer Marketing Hub. (2024, June 24). *The state of influencer marketing 2020: Benchmark report*. https://influencermarketinghub.com/influencer-marketing-benchmark-report-2020/

Isyanto, P., Sapitri, R. G., & Sinaga, O. (2020). Micro influencers marketing and brand image to purchase intention of cosmetic products Focallure. *Systematic Review Pharmacy, 11*(1), 601–605.

Izogo, E. E., & Mpinganjira, M. (2022). Somewhat pushy but effective: The role of value-laden social media digital content marketing (VSM-DCM) for search and experience products. *Journal of Research in Interactive Marketing, 16*(3), 365–383. https://doi.org/10.1108/JRIM-05-2021-0146

Jiao, Y., Gao, J., & Yang, J. (2015). Social value and content value in social media: Two ways to flow. *Journal of Advanced Management Science, 3*(4), 299–306. doi:10.12720/joams.3.4.299-306

Kaplan, A. M., & Haenlein, M. (2010). Users of the world, unite! The challenges and opportunities of social media. *Business Horizons, 53*(1), 59–68. https://doi.org/10.1016/j.bushor.2009.09.003

Kee, A. W. A., & Yazdanifard, R. (2015). The review of content marketing as a new trend in marketing practices. *International Journal of Management, Accounting and Economics, 2*(9), 1055–1064.

Li, C. H., et al. (2022). Evaluating the effectiveness of digital content marketing under mixed reality training platform on the online purchase intention. *Frontiers in Psychology, 13*, 1–16. https://doi.org/10.3389/fpsyg.2022.881019

Li, F., Larimo, J., & Leonidou, L. C. (2021). Social media marketing strategy: Definition, conceptualization, taxonomy, validation, and future agenda. *Journal of the Academy of Marketing Science, 49*(1), 51–70. https://doi.org/10.1007/s11747-020-00733-3

Lopes, A. R., & Casais, B. (2022). Digital content marketing: Conceptual review and recommendations for practitioners. *Academy of Strategic Management Journal*, 21(2), 1–17.

Mokhare, K., Satpute, A., Pal, V., & Badwaik, P. (2021). Impact of influencer marketing on travel and tourism. *International Journal of Advance Research and Innovative Ideas in Education*, *7*(1), 1098–1105.

Moutsos, K. (2022, May 16). *4 content marketing goals that really matter to the business. Content Marketing Institute.* https://contentmarketinginstitute.com/articles/content-marketing-goals-matter-business

Myntra. (n.d.) *How to style*. https://www.myntra.com/studio/feed/hashtag/howto style/Studio

Netflix (n.d.) *Personalization and search*. https://research.netflix.com/business-area/personalization-and-search

Patagonia. (n.d.) *Our footprint*. https://www.patagonia.com/our-footprint/.

Pazeraite, A., & Repoviene, G. (2016). Content marketing elements and their influence on search advertisement effectiveness: Theoretical background and practical insights. *Organizacijų vadyba: sisteminiai tyrimai. Kaunas: Vytauto Didžiojo universitetas.* http://dx.doi.org/10.7220/MOSR.2335.8750.2016.75.7

Pourkhani, A., Abdipour, K., Baher, B., & Moslehpour, M. (2019). The impact of social media in business growth and performance: A scientometrics analysis. *International Journal of Data and Network Science*, *3*(3), 223–244. https://doi.org/10.5267/j.ijdns.2019.2.003

Pulizzi, J., & Barrett, N. (2009). Get content get customers: Turn prospects into buyers with content marketing. *Saxena NSB Management Review*, *2*(2), 98–100.

Puro, P. (2013). *Content marketing and the significance of corporate branding*. [Master's thesis]. Lappeenranta University of Technology, Finland.

Redbull. (n.d.) *I jumped from space* [Video]. https://www.redbull.com/us-en/videos/i-jumped-from-space

Rishi, B., & Bandyopadhyay, S. (Eds.). (2018). *Contemporary issues in social media marketing*. Routledge.

Rowley, J. (2008). Understanding digital content marketing. *Journal of Marketing Management*, *24*(5–6), 517–540. doi:10.1362/026725708X325977.

Saravanakumar, M., & SuganthaLakshmi, T. (2012). Social media marketing. *Life Science Journal*, *9*(4), 4444–4451. http://www.lifesciencesite.com/lsj/life0904/670_13061life0904_4444_4451.pdf

Sudarsono, S. S., Kamase, J., Ella, H., Rachman, A., & Dunggio, T. (2020). Big data and content marketing on purchase decisions online in Indonesia. *American Journal of Economics and Business Management*, *3*(1), 168–177. doi:10.31150/ajebm.Vol3.Iss1.123.

Terho, H., Mero, J., Siutla, L., & Jaakkola, E. (2022). Digital content marketing in business markets: Activities, consequences, and contingencies along the customer journey. *Industrial Marketing Management*, *105*, 294–310. https://doi.org/10.1016/j.indmarman.2022.06.006

Trivedi, T. (2022). Impact of digital content marketing on purchase intentions for online shopping post Covid-19 pandemic. *International Journal of Management, Public Policy and Research, 1*(2), 24–33.

Tsen, W. S., & Cheng, B. K. L. (2021). Who to find to endorse? Evaluation of online influencers among young consumers and its implications for effective influencer marketing. *Young Consumers, 22*(2), 237–253. https://doi.org/10.1108/YC-10-2020-1226

Veissi, I. (2017). *Influencer marketing on Instagram*. [Bachelor's thesis]. Haaga-Helia University of Applied Sciences, Finland. https://www.theseus.fi/handle/10024/135448

Weerasinghe, K. P. W. D. R. (2018). Impact of content marketing towards the customer online engagement. *International Journal of Business, Economics and Management, 2*(3), 217–2024.

Wiedmann, K. P., & von Mettenheim, W. (2021). Attractiveness, trustworthiness and expertise: Social influencers' winning formula? *Journal of Product & Brand Management, 30*(5), 707–725.

Social Media Usage in the B2B Context 4

Nicholas Mathew and Hagai Gringarten
St Thomas University, Florida, USA

Chapter Learning Objectives

1. Examine the opportunities and challenges in social media usage for B2B firms.
2. Describe the development of a social media strategy for B2B firms.
3. Analyze how value is created through social media by B2B firms.
4. Evaluate the measurement of social media effectiveness.

Introduction

Over the years, social media platforms have been used widely for marketing purposes both in the business-to-business (B2B) and business-to-consumer (B2C) sectors. Social media platforms have allowed companies to engage their customers, build relationships, and have ongoing conversations with them. Social media's reach can be far and wide: with more than half of the world's population using various forms of social media (Dixon, 2023), the B2B sector has a great opportunity in the social media space. Research has suggested that social media platforms are being widely used by B2B companies as part of their marketing strategy (Dwivedi et al., 2023). These B2B companies use at least one of the major platforms, such as LinkedIn, X (formerly Twitter), Facebook, and YouTube. Due to social media use, half of these companies

DOI: 10.4324/9781003412656-4

improved their marketing optimization and customer experience, and a quarter increased their revenue (Dwivedi et al., 2023; Kumar & Sharma, 2022).

Social media can help with knowledge creation for B2B companies. Knowledge creation can involve social interactions both inside and outside the company. Social media platforms provide a level of personalization in these interactions and can help the company connect with existing and potential clients at a more nuanced level; these interactions can facilitate the exchange and creation of knowledge between the company and its clients (Rishi & Bandyopadhyay, 2018). This knowledge exchange and creation, in turn, can help the company better understand and cater to client needs and wants. Thus, social media can provide an important platform for companies in the B2B sector to better serve their clients.

With B2B firms increasingly using social media channels to reach and engage with clients, it becomes imperative for us to examine B2B social media usage. Over the years, many well-known B2B firms have found success by leveraging their social media assets. For example, software firm Adobe, shipping and logistics firm Maersk, and technology firm Dell have all created value for their clients by successfully leveraging social media. While social media usage in the B2C sector has been studied widely, a greater understanding of its usage in the B2B sector is warranted (Balaji et al., 2023; Cao & Weerawardena, 2023).

With the range of external and internal stakeholders involved in the various stages of the B2B buying process – such as employees, customers, suppliers, intermediaries, and competitors – the usage of social media in the B2B sector is more complex than in the B2C sector (Balaji et al., 2023). Given the differences between B2B and B2C social media and the limited understanding of social media usage in the B2B sector, there is a need to examine social media issues in the B2B context. Thus, this chapter provides the following:

1. A framework for B2B social media strategy development.
2. A review of the opportunities and challenges in B2B social media use.
3. An examination of B2B value creation through social media.
4. Practical recommendations for measuring the effectiveness of B2B social media.

Opportunities and Challenges of Social Media in the B2B Context

Opportunities

Social media platforms provide many opportunities for B2B companies. For example, social media can help them increase customer loyalty and trust, strengthen corporate reputation and branding, improve market sensing, facilitate client co-creation, enhance client and employee engagement and empowerment, hire new employees, drive clearer communications, prospect new customers, handle objections, and improve after-sales follow-up. Social media can also facilitate the creation of relevant 'targeted customer connections' for key account managers (Tiwary et al., 2021). Further, social media platforms could provide user-generated content (UGC) – a constant flow of new information from diverse user groups from which new perspectives and themes can emerge (Agnihotri et al., 2016).

Social media platforms will help B2B firms better understand customers' needs, resolve product or service issues (jointly with clients or other social groups), acquire knowledge to adapt quickly to market changes, engage with clients, and build network ties (Chuang, 2020). For example, technology firms such as Dell, Oracle, and Intel have used X to deal with a variety of customer service issues. Firms use YouTube as a platform for incorporating video into their webpages, thereby attracting traffic to company websites and giving companies the opportunity to engage with clients. Firms use LinkedIn to connect with clients and establish professional networking ties (Iankova et al., 2019). Research has shown that X, LinkedIn, and Facebook positively impact clients' perceptions of the four elements of brand relationship strength – namely, commitment, intimacy, satisfaction, and partner quality (Pardo et al., 2022). Hence, social media can provide opportunities ranging from resolving customer service issues to strengthening the firm's brand.

Challenges

Compared to B2C, B2B firms often deal with factors such as more complex products and services, long-term business relationships, fewer but larger customers, multiple decision makers, and high-value transactions (Cao & Weerawardena, 2023; Setkute & Dibb, 2022). B2B firms may already have strong relationships with their existing clients and understand their requirements well; hence, they may see social media use as lacking benefits. Research has suggested that decision makers in B2B firms may be somewhat skeptical about the benefits of social media marketing, and feel it is incompatible with the nature of B2B markets. B2B firms also may find it difficult to identify and integrate relevant social media platforms into their digital marketing mix (see Iankova et al., 2019; Tiwary et al., 2021; Kumar & Sharma, 2022).

While B2B firms can use social media to better understand their clients' needs and wants, they need to be prepared to encounter negative feedback from different social media users. Social media platforms can be where clients and others air their concerns about a firm's products or services. There will be potential for miscommunication between the firm and clients on these platforms. Discussions on product or service malfunctions could take place; these factors could negatively impact the firm's image. Hence, the firm should be prepared and should develop a strategy to deal with potential negative encounters on social media. However, the firm can convert the challenge of these encounters into an opportunity. During social media encounters, B2B firms can increase their understanding of existing clients or potential clients, show resolve and agility in addressing their concerns, and thereby gain the confidence of the market. Engaging in continued communication with social media users will allow the firm to accumulate sufficient knowledge of market needs; this knowledge will help the firm to be better prepared to handle negative encounters or a crisis on social media.

However, continued communication on social media platforms may elicit requests from clients to resolve multiple issues with the firm's products or services. The firm may not have the human resources to respond promptly to these requests and resolve them. With the firm being unable to respond promptly, misinformation among social network actors could spread, and the firm's reputation could be damaged (Agnihotri et al., 2016).

Developing Social Media Strategy in the B2B Context

Research shows that B2B firms use social media as supportive tools in their marketing strategy to better connect with clients. For example, B2B firms use social media to support search engine optimization (SEO); drive customer traffic to the firms' homepage and/or landing page; monitor and listen to clients or potential clients; create relevant and compelling content; and generate electronic word of mouth (e-WOM) (Cawsey & Rowley, 2016; Iankova et al., 2019; Setkute & Dibb, 2022).

However, researchers and practitioners have looked at social media largely from a tactical perspective as opposed to a strategic one (Pardo et al., 2022). For example, they have studied the impact of social media tools on specific business activities or functions such as sales. However, in recent years, researchers and practitioners have begun to view social media as part of the firm's overall strategy. Social media can be used strategically to facilitate knowledge exchange and innovation throughout the firm. Social media could contribute to altering or shaping the B2B firm's position in the ecosystem in which it operates by affecting the entire marketing process rather than only certain parts of it (Pardo et al., 2022).

From a strategic perspective, researchers have argued that social media can impact business networks by enabling firms to establish their credibility through engaging in more targeted one-to-one communications with clients or potential clients (as opposed to traditional mass broadcasts). Such communications are important in the B2B context, where it is useful for firms to co-create with clients; and this co-creation can eventually lead to solid, long-lasting business relationships (Pardo et al., 2022).

A B2B company can use social media channels to communicate about the position it wants to occupy in the market. The same channels can be used by others (i.e., clients, potential clients, or other network users) to communicate what they think about the position occupied by the company. Hence, social media provides a platform for a firm to learn about itself and others. To develop a social media strategy, research has suggested that a firm needs to possess a strategic market orientation (Cao & Weerawardena, 2023). Market-oriented firms engage in effectively gathering market information, processing and then disseminating that information across the firm. Market-oriented firms successfully sense changes impacting their clients and competitors, and spot market threats and opportunities correctly. Market orientation drives the B2B firm to use social media, which, in turn, facilitates a greater understanding of the market and effective engagement with clients. Hence, the B2B firm should first develop a market orientation so as to better position it to develop a social media strategy (Cao & Weerawardena, 2023). Research has shown that social media adoption by B2B firms is also determined by organizational innovativeness, perceived usefulness of social media use for the company, the company's strategic vision and level of commitment, and the company's internal resources and capabilities.

A successful social media strategy will also enable the firm to develop brand management capabilities – that is, the firm's ability to create and maintain high levels of brand equity and to use this equity to position the firm for success in the market environment (Morgan et al., 2009). For example, firms with strong brand management capabilities can establish and maintain brand awareness among prospective and current customers and effectively differentiate their products and services. This differentiation will allow potential customers to reduce their search costs and perceived risk from the firm's products or services. In effect, a sound social media strategy can allow the firm to attract new clients, build confidence among existing and prospective clients, gain a better brand reputation, and provide assurance of product or service quality.

A B2B firm should also consider the source of social media messages. For example, if the firm creates a message and shares it on its official social media account, the message is *firm-generated content* (FGC). In contrast, if the firm's employees create messages and posts on social media, this is considered *employee-generated content* (EGC) – an example of user-generated content (Agnihotri, 2020). The B2B firm can use both FGC and EGC to ensure customer engagement and interaction with social media users. In a B2B context, message source is an important element, and plays a key role in shaping customer engagement and perception. Interestingly, research has found that UGC which includes EGC leads to more social media engagement from social media users than FGC (Balaji et al., 2023).

Developing creative social media messages is important when attempting to gain customers' attention. Prior research has indicated that different message elements, such as the content and selling cues, influence client engagement with B2B firms. For example, it was found that: features such as post length, visual complexity, and language play a role in persuading clients; interactive and creative content, emotional cues, and information richness enhance client engagement; visual aspects of the message (including colors and images) positively impact WOM behaviors; and characteristics of the source (i.e., the competence and warmth of the B2B firm's digital influencers) positively affect the client's intention to engage with the firm (see Deng et al., 2021; Balaji et al., 2023).

Table 4.1 provides a framework for B2B firms to develop a social media strategy. The framework shows a focus on certain task areas that can be

Table 4.1 Social media management matrix

Task area	Short- and long-term) goals in each area	Goals' connection to firm mission and vision	Social media activity type to achieve each goal	Platforms to be used for each activity type
Media/public relations	1, 2, 3			
Client relationship management				
Brand management				
Crisis management				
Product/service innovation management				
Sales promotions				
Internal firm use (e.g., for employees)				

Source: Adapted from Dwivedi et al. (2023) and Kasper et al. (2015).

critical for B2B firms. Firms will need to develop goals for each of these areas and ensure they align with their organizational strategic mission and vision. Then, the firm must decide on specific social media activities to achieve these goals. The social media activity types can involve publishing posts, images, audio and video content, engaging in social listening, replying to posts made by social media users, and reaching out to and networking with users (for example, inviting them to join an interest group on LinkedIn). Simultaneously, the firm must choose the platform (LinkedIn, X, Facebook, etc.) to engage in those activities.

As part of their social media strategy, firms should consider several factors when creating posts on a social media platform. For example, the firm should:

- clearly understand the goals it wants to achieve through its social media use;
- analyze the target group it is trying to reach;
- assess the content of its posts (i.e., the depth, style, and appeal);
- analyze other competing social media platform types;
- analyze the nature and structure of social media channels, including the type and diversity of users;
- review the role of moderators (for example, subject matter experts from the company connecting with social media users);
- understand the nature of public and private content, and what can be shared on social media;
- understand the ability of other actors on the platform to share and repost the firm's content;
- analyze the role of online communities in blogs and other digital spaces; and
- develop integration strategies whereby the firm's social media activity is integrated, on an ongoing basis, into other marketing communication channels, such as the firm's website or trade shows and other physical or virtual promotional events (Lashgari et al., 2018).

B2B Social Media Examples

There are B2B firms successfully using social media in several ways – for example, to leverage their corporate social responsibility (CSR) and ethics strategies, to strengthen their internal and external marketing strategies, and to highlight their values and goals. The following mini-case studies highlight organizations that have successfully used social media to build strong relationships with their stakeholders and strengthen their profiles.

Mini-Case 1: Social Responsibility Focus

Learning Objectives

This case examines the application of social media in the realms of ethics and CSR. After reading the case and working through the questions, readers should be able to do the following:

1. Identify the opportunities in using social media for corporate social responsibility initiatives.
2. Describe value creation for company stakeholders through the successful leveraging of social media.
3. Evaluate the impact of social media on a B2B firm's brand value.

WTDC, a small and medium-sized enterprise (SME), is a global logistics firm offering door-to-door transportation and foreign-trade zone (FTZ) warehousing services. The companies it serves supply B2B inventory or cargo. Since its founding in 1977, WTDC has been owned and operated by the Gazitua family with current President and CEO Sean Gazitua being the third generation from the family to lead the company.

WTDC uses social media to showcase its employees and company culture. The company's new business is primarily built on referrals, not outward solicitation. By sharing its story as a company that takes care of its employees, community, and environment, WTDC connects with the types of company with whom it wants to conduct business.

WTDC has a social media presence on Facebook, Google Business Profile, Instagram, X, LinkedIn, and Threads. It also has a company newsletter that is emailed twice a month and then posted to the company's website. Company values – as described in its four pillars (God and Family, Health and Education, Community, and WTDC) – as well as sustainability measures organized by environmental, social, and governance (ESG) initiatives are the basis for most posts to the company's social media. WTDC has several community initiatives through which it provides goods and services for those less fortunate. For example, it engages in water and school supply drives for nonprofit organizations providing residential, foster care, and other support services to vulnerable segments of society. WTDC highlights these and other community initiatives on social media.

Based on feedback from customers who have seen WTDC's social media posts, the company expanded its charitable scope to include customers and friends in the donations, thereby making a greater impact for its community partners. Thus, through social media, WTDC builds awareness of community issues and encourages its customers and others to contribute to its CSR efforts. The values and initiatives reflected in its social media posts are a principal topic of conversation during WTDC business meetings. Hence, it has successfully leveraged social media to strengthen its brand and standing within the community.

Case Theme and Implications

This case provides an overview of how a firm can develop a social media strategy to successfully connect with its primary stakeholders (e.g., customers) and secondary stakeholders (e.g., the community) by enabling the firm to involve stakeholders in its social responsibility programs. Acting ethically, which includes CSR initiatives, should form an important part of the firm's overall strategy as this will have an impact on its value proposition, with more clients willing to engage with firms that possess the correct ethical approach. One issue for firms to consider is to properly measure social media's impact in helping them achieve their CSR goals, and firms should choose appropriate metrics to measure this impact.

Discussion Questions

- Corporate social responsibility is a key part of WTDC's social media strategy. What social media metrics could it use to measure the success of its social media strategy?
- How does social media create value for WTDC?
- What concepts from this chapter can be related to WTDC's social media strategy?

Mini-Case 2: Building Value Focus

Learning Objectives

The next case examines the use of social media to build brand awareness and value. After reading the case and working through the questions, readers should be able to do the following:

1. Describe how social media is used to build relationships with customers.
2. Identify the metrics used to measure social media effectiveness.
3. Explain the ways in which brand awareness can be built through a social media strategy.

Tortuga is a globally renowned brand that leads the gourmet and 'spirit cake' category through a strong focus on innovation. It is known for its rum cakes, and has launched several new distinctive flavors. The brand strives to ensure that consumers are presented with fresh, innovative, and new options, solidifying its position in the industry. With more than 35 years of experience and annual revenues of US$10 million–15 million, Tortuga has established successful B2B partnerships with cruise channels, major North American retailers, department and grocery stores, and the gifting sector.

The Tortuga brand's social media strategy focuses on three main components: content creation, engagement, and analytics. The brand creates high-quality and engaging content that showcases and positions it in a premium way. It currently leverages content across four channels – X, Meta, Instagram, and TikTok – in the form of informative blog posts, visually appealing images, or entertaining videos. The company actively engages its existing and potential customers through UGC that helps 'humanize' the brand, which fosters a sense of community and builds trust with customers. Lastly, Tortuga uses data and analytics to deliver a superior experience and product to customers. Social media has helped the brand grow and evolve over time with its customers.

Tortuga has a strong online presence, and social media is one of the channels it uses to drive revenue and awareness. Because the channel is used as a revenue driver, key metrics include return on ad spend, cost per click, conversion, and reach. Since 2019, Tortuga has adopted an omnichannel approach, which involves positioning its brand on all online platforms and networks where its existing and potential customers are found. As a result, social media has been a major contributor to driving online revenue for the business.

With the ability to engage the desired target audience using interest and affiliate targeting, Tortuga connects and recruits new customers using tailored messages. Interest targeting refers to using engaging content to target potential clients based on their interests, while affiliate targeting involves collaborating with affiliates (i.e., organizations or individuals) to promote the brand on their platforms.

In summary, Tortuga's sophisticated social media strategy has enabled it to successfully engage with new audiences around the world and reinforce ties with existing customers.

Case Theme and Implications

This case highlights social media's ability to help the firm provide value to customers and build its brand awareness and equity. In the B2B sector, personal relationships and co-creation can play important roles in helping firms create value. In this case, we see that the firm encourages its customers to be involved in the design and delivery of social media content, thereby allowing customers to co-create an element of the firm's marketing program. This co-creation can lead to customer advocacy when they actively recommend the firm's products to others. The firm's strategy of encouraging user-generated content can be an effective tool for social media engagement and building brand value.

Discussion Questions

- Briefly describe the main components of Tortuga's brand strategy.
- Social media has provided the Tortuga brand with many benefits. Discuss how the brand could further enhance its social media strategy.
- What concepts from this chapter can be related to Tortuga's social media strategy?

Creating Value with Social Media in the B2B Context

B2B firms can create value for themselves and their clients through social media platforms in multiple ways. For example, they can use social media tools for sharing information, building trust, relationship management, and post-sale service communication among others (Tiwary et al., 2021). Value creation can be considered from both firm and client viewpoints.

Client and Firm Value Creation

Firms should understand how to use social media effectively to create value for clients. An important value-creation activity is building long-term relationships with clients. Relationship building involves client satisfaction and retention, connecting and reminding clients of the company's products and services, and client advocacy through which clients are encouraged to actively recommend the firm to others (Iankova et al., 2019; Kumar & Sharma, 2022). Social media facilitates relationship building with clients.

The use of agility is another way to create value effectively on social media: that is, the firm should use social media to respond quickly to customer needs and promptly identify market changes. Social media agility involves quick responses, appropriate efforts and actions, and the ability to build effective customer–firm relationships at low cost. Agility has become a priority for B2B relationships; hence, social media's ability to facilitate agility is important (Chuang, 2020).

Social media becomes more meaningful and effective when the firm uses it to collaborate with clients to develop new products or services as this collaboration or co-creation helps create value for both firm and clients. Clients become part of the creation and delivery of products and services, and therefore become more invested in the firm and its performance outcomes. Social media can effectively assist in client co-creation by enabling clients to build better connections with firms because they can communicate their thoughts, ideas, hopes, needs, and desires to firms more easily (Koivisto & Mattila, 2018). They can interact with other users of the firm's products or services and share ideas with them; they can experience a sense of community with these other users, identify with them, and eventually develop closer relationships with the firm and its products and services. Social media thus creates value both for clients and firms by facilitating co-creation and enabling engagement.

Social media can also help improve user trust and facilitate knowledge creation within the firm. Research has shown that firms operating in a social media environment adapt and adjust better to the information they process than firms operating in other more traditional environments (Chuang, 2020). From the firm's viewpoint, social media can support value creation activities for employees, partners, and suppliers. Social media also can be used to strengthen brand and corporate credibility (Iankova et al., 2019; Dwivedi et al., 2023).

A social media marketing strategy can be particularly helpful for B2B firms that are also SMEs. B2B firms can come in various sizes and some can be classified as SMEs, which face challenges when competing in the market due to limited financial, human capital, and organizational resources and capabilities (Cao & Weerawardena, 2023). However, SMEs can be agile and act quickly to respond to customer requests. Agility, as mentioned earlier, is important for B2B relationships; and social media can help further facilitate this agility and allow the SME to connect with clients in a quick and cost-effective way.

Performance, Effectiveness, and Reach

It is important for firms to properly measure the effectiveness of social media to allow them to understand which channels to focus on to better reach customers. B2B firms commonly use both qualitative and quantitative metrics to measure and understand social media effectiveness (Dwivedi et al., 2023; Balaji et al., 2023; Deng et al., 2021), as summarized in Table 4.2.

B2B firms can use marketing analytics tools such as Sprout Social, Hootsuite Insights, IBM analytics, HubSpot, and Brandwatch to track and measure their social media KPIs (Elevation Marketing, 2023). There are also natural language processing and machine learning technologies that identify relationships in unstructured data. Since a large amount of social media

Table 4.2 Commonly used qualitative and quantitative metrics

Quantitative Metrics	Qualitative Metrics
The number of: 1. site visits 2. comments on social media posts 3. social network connections 4. profile views 5. retweets 6. impressions 7. reactions 8. click-through rates 9. shares and comments 10. sales revenue (derived from social media campaigns) 11. return on investment (on a customer)	1. growth and value of relationships over time with target audience 2. moving from monologue to dialogue with clients 3. quality of 'leads' (i.e., prospective customers)

content is unstructured, these technologies can be helpful in providing meaningful insights (IBM, 2023).

Table 4.3 provides a sample list of social media key performance indicators that measure firms' progress in meeting their operational and strategic goals. Firms can use these indicators to measure the effectiveness of their social media strategy.

Table 4.3 Sample social media key performance indicators

KPI	Description
Website traffic source and medium	Source refers to where visitors come from, such as other sites or platforms Medium describes whether the traffic comes from organic, paid, or referral marketing sources, indicating which channels and tactics attract the most visitors
Website conversions by source	A formula that refers to the sources (e.g., social media platforms) sending prospective customers to the firm's website: Conversion rate by source = (number of conversions by source/total number of visitors by source) × 100 For example, if a YouTube article about the firm results in 5000 visitors and 500 of them submit a contact form, YouTube's conversion rate is 10% (500/5000) × 100
Engagement	Potential customers' interactions with a social media marketing campaign (e.g., in the form of likes, shares, clicks, and comments); these can result in increased brand visibility and mentions on social channels, which, in turn, creates a large pool of potential leads
Return on ad spend (ROAS)	Indicates which advertising channels are most effective in terms of revenue earned for the investment made in the channel
Share of voice	Indicates the prevalence and intensity of conversations on social media regarding brand, products, services, reputation, etc., which firms can classify as positive, negative, neutral, or ambivalent
Average order value (AOV)	Measures the average amount of money customers spend on each order made through social media channels
Cost per engagement (CPE)	The cost associated with each engagement. For example, CPE for a Facebook advertisement campaign is calculated by dividing the firm's campaign spend by the number of engagements generated: if the firm spends $100 and the campaign generates 125 engagements, CPE is $0.80 (100/125)
Cost per click (CPC)	How much the firm pays every time a user clicks on an advertisement (cost of ad divided by number of clicks)
Call to action rate (CTAR)	Number of clicks elicited from a 'call to action' (content a firm posts to drive customer engagement) divided by the number of 'views' (i.e., each time the content was viewed for at least 30 seconds)

Source: IBM (2023); Revealbot (2023); Caldwell (2023); Pirraglia et al. (2022).

One must keep in mind that there are challenges when measuring the effectiveness of social media marketing that increase skepticism among B2B firms with regard to investing in such marketing (Cawsey & Rowley, 2016; Balaji et al., 2023). For example, it is often hard to accurately measure and keep track of client engagement across earned media (such as posts others create about the firm, reviews of the firm's products or services, mentions, and tags). In addition, although B2B firms may develop certain goals for their social media marketing, determining the correct measures to assess those goals can be difficult (Balaji et al., 2023).

Social Media Policy Development

Ensuring oversight and quality control in social media marketing may also be challenging as it could be difficult to manage or control posts that are created on behalf of the company by employees, clients, potential clients, or members of the wider social media network. To better manage social media marketing, the B2B firm should therefore develop a corporate social media policy to help minimize exposure to risks arising out of suboptimal oversight or minimal quality control. Through this internal policy, the firm's employees will understand what guidelines and procedures must be followed when representing the company on social media. These guidelines and procedures can relate to the language, tone, and visual aspect of the content shared or posted on social media. The policy can specify what information can and cannot be shared, and provide guidelines for confidential information. Through a clear corporate social media policy, the firm can work to ensure that employees represent themselves and the company in a professional manner (Balaji et al., 2023).

Social Media Reach

B2B buyers are increasingly younger, more digitally oriented, and more active online. They can therefore be very demanding and engaged in the buying process. The number of such decision makers in the B2B space is growing, increasing the importance of social media as they look to its content for professional development, solutions, and inspiration (Voss, 2023).

According to a recent industry survey in the U.S. (Voss, 2023), social media was the most effective B2B channel for driving revenues among B2B marketers in 2023, with 60 percent citing it as their top choice (Figure 4.1).

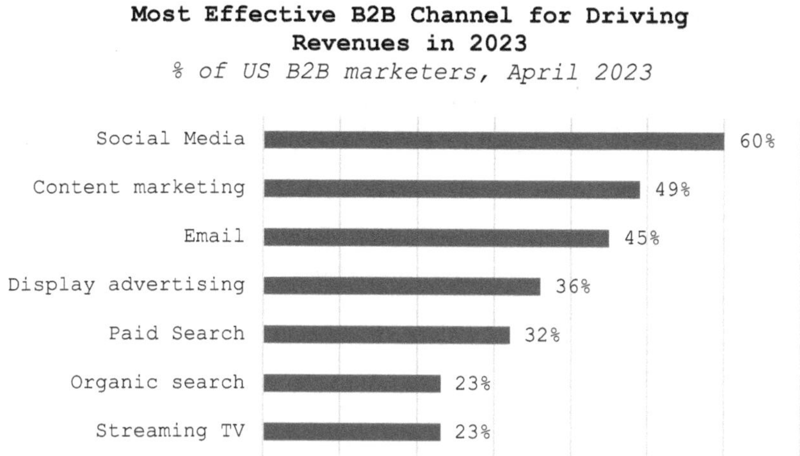

Figure 4.1 Most effective B2B channels for driving revenues in 2023
(*Source:* Wpromote & Ascend2, 2023)

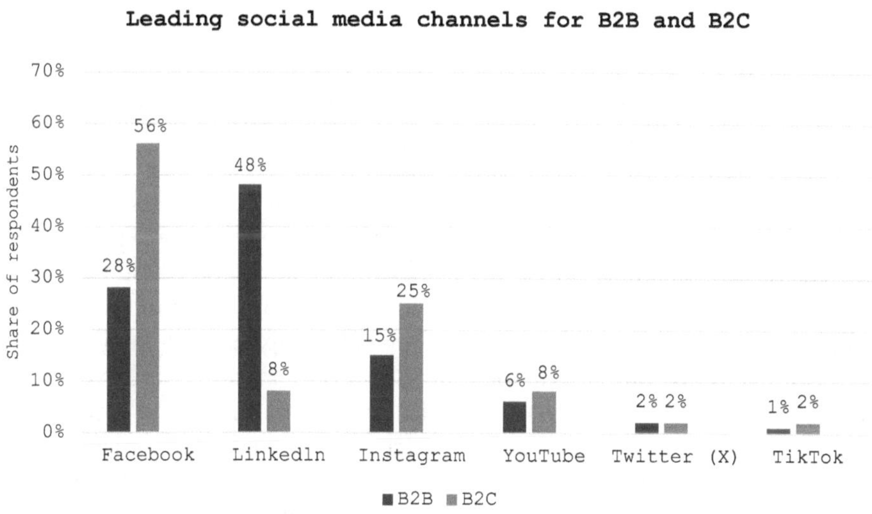

Figure 4.2 Leading social media channels for B2B and B2C
(*Source:* Dencheva, 2024)

Although Figure 4.2 shows that LinkedIn is the leading social media channel used by B2B marketers, a survey in 2023 indicated that they considered Facebook as offering the highest ROI, followed by Instagram and then TikTok and YouTube tied (Dencheva, 2024). Figure 4.2 also shows clear differences between B2B and B2C social media channels, with Facebook more popular among the latter.

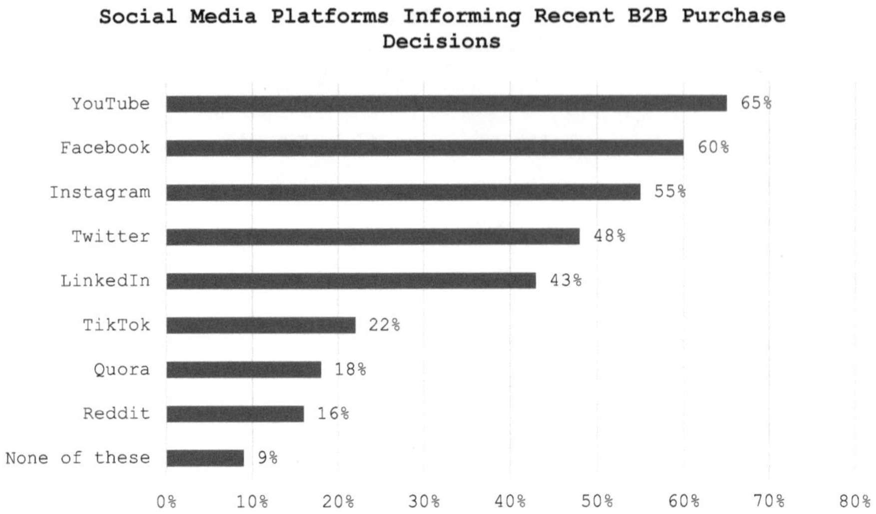

Figure 4.3 Social media platforms informing recent B2B purchase decisions
(*Source:* Gartner, 2023)

From the B2B buyer perspective, Gartner (2023) has shown that YouTube is the top social media channel influencing a B2B purchase decision, followed by Facebook, Instagram, X, LinkedIn, and TikTok (Figure 4.3).

Earlier research by Gartner (2022) also shows that B2B buyers seek third-party interactions to make sure they are making the correct purchases, such as reading customer reviews or references online and consulting with third-party experts. B2B firms can provide a space for these interactions on their social media channels wherein they can bring in third-party experts or loyal clients to talk about their products or services. B2B buyers also research the B2B firm's website, social media channels, and interactive tools (e.g., price calculators and product recommenders) to ensure they are making the correct purchase decisions. Thus, B2B firms can use their social media channels to introduce potential clients to their websites and interactive tools.

Conclusion

This chapter provided an overview of the use of social media in the B2B sector. It described the development of social media strategy and the many challenges and opportunities in B2B social media use. In addition, value creation with social media was highlighted, and issues related to performance, effectiveness, and reach outlined. In conclusion, some key issues to consider as we move forward are as follows:

1. Social media's value creation potential for both B2B clients and firms should be emphasized.
2. Social media strategy should be well integrated with the firm's wider marketing strategy.
3. Guidelines and best practices for social media use should be studied thoroughly and adopted by firms.
4. Social media's impact should be understood from both quantitative and qualitative measurement perspectives.

References

Agnihotri, R. (2020). Social media, customer engagement, and sales organizations: A research agenda. *Industrial Marketing Management, 90*, 291–299. https://doi.org/10.1016/j.indmarman.2020.07.017

Agnihotri, R., Dingus, R., Hu, M. Y., & Krush, M. T. (2016). Social media: Influencing customer satisfaction in B2B sales. *Industrial Marketing Management, 53*, 172–180.

Balaji, M. S., Behl, A., Jain, K., Baabdullah, A. M., Giannakis, M., Shankar, A., & Dwivedi, Y. K. (2023). Effectiveness of B2B social media marketing: The effect of message source and message content on social media engagement. *Industrial Marketing Management, 113*, 243–257.

Caldwell, A. (2023, March 12). *B2B marketing KPIs: 23 metrics to track*. Oracle Netsuite. https://www.netsuite.com/portal/resource/articles/business-strategy/b2b-marketing-kpis.shtml

Cao, G., & Weerawardena, J. (2023). Strategic use of social media in marketing and financial performance: The B2B SME context. *Industrial Marketing Management, 111*, 41–54.

Cawsey, T., & Rowley, J. (2016). Social media brand building strategies in B2B companies. *Marketing Intelligence & Planning, 34*(6), 754–776.

Chuang, S. H. (2020). Co-creating social media agility to build strong customer–firm relationships. *Industrial Marketing Management, 84*, 202–211.

Dencheva, V. (2024, April 30). *Most important social media platforms for B2B and B2C marketers worldwide*. Statista. https://www.statista.com/statistics/259404/most-important-social-media-platforms-for-b2b-and-b2c-marketers-worldwide/

Deng, Q., Wang, Y., Rod, M., & Ji, S. (2021). Speak to head and heart: The effects of linguistic features on B2B brand engagement on social media. *Industrial Marketing Management, 99*, 1–15.

Dixon, S. J. (2023, August 29). *Number of social media users worldwide from 2017 to 2027*. Statista. https://www.statista.com/statistics/278414/number-of-worldwide-social-network-users/

Dwivedi, Y. K., Ismagilova, E., Rana, N. P., & Raman, R. (2023). Social media adoption, usage, and impact in business-to-business (B2B) context: A state-of-the-art literature review. *Information Systems Frontiers*, *25*, 971–993.

Elevationmarketing. (2023, April 21). *6 social media KPIs for B2Bs to track*. https://elevationb2b.com/blog/6-social-media-kpis-b2bs-to-track/

Gartner. (2022, April 27). *Gartner predicts by 2025, 60% of customers will seek service information from third-party sources*. https://www.gartner.com/en/newsroom/press-releases/gartner-predicts-by-2025--60--of-customers-will-seek-service-inf

Gartner. (2023, June 8). *Gartner marketing survey finds B2B buyers value third-party interactions more than digital supplier interactions*. https://www.gartner.com/en/newsroom/press-releases/2023-06-08-gartner-marketing-survey-finds-b2b-buyers-value-third-party-interactions-more-than-digital-supplier-interactions

Iankova, S., Davies, I., Archer-Brown, C., Marder, B., & Yau, A. (2019). A comparison of social media marketing between B2B, B2C, and mixed business models. *Industrial Marketing Management*, *81*, 169–179.

IBM. (2023). *Social media analytics*. https://www.ibm.com/topics/social-media-analytics

Kasper, H., Koleva, I., & Kett, H. (2015). Social media matrix matching corporate goals with external social media activities. In E. Simperl et al. (Eds.), *The semantic web: ESWC 2012 Satellite Events, Heraklion, Crete, Greece, May 27–31, 2012. Revised Selected Papers 9* (pp. 233–244). Lecture Notes in Computer Science, Vol. 7540. Springer.

Koivisto, E., & Mattila, P. (2018). International fashion trade shows as platforms for experiential branding. *Journal of Global Fashion Marketing*, *9*(2), 161–178.

Kumar, B., & Sharma, A. (2022). Examining the research on social media in business-to-business marketing with a focus on sales and the selling process. *Industrial Marketing Management*, *102*, 122–140.

Lashgari, M., Sutton-Brady, C., Søilen, K. S., & Ulfvengren, P. (2018). Adoption strategies of social media in B2B firms: A multiple case study approach. *Journal of Business & Industrial Marketing*, *33*(5), 730–743.

Morgan, N. A., Slotegraaf, R. J., & Vorhies, D. W. (2009). Linking marketing capabilities with profit growth. *International Journal of Research in Marketing*, *26*(4), 284–293.

Pardo, C., Pagani, M., & Savinien, J. (2022). The strategic role of social media in business-to-business contexts. *Industrial Marketing Management*, *101*, 82–97.

Pirraglia, E., Giuliani, F., De Cicco, R., Di Berardino, C., & Palumbo, R. (2022). The role of emotions in B2B product advertising on social media: A family business case study. *Journal of Family Business Management*, *13*(1), 146–165.

Revealbot. (2023). *Average cost per engagement for Facebook ads*. https://revealbot.com/facebook-advertising-costs/cpe-cost-per-engagement

Rishi, B., & Bandyopadhyay, S. (Eds.). (2018). *Contemporary issues in social media marketing*. London: Routledge.

Setkute, J., & Dibb, S. (2022). 'Old boys' club': Barriers to digital marketing in small B2B firms. *Industrial Marketing Management, 102*, 266–279.

Tiwary, N. K., Kumar, R. K., Sarraf, S., Kumar, P., & Rana, N. P. (2021). Impact assessment of social media usage in B2B marketing: A review of the literature and a way forward. *Journal of Business Research, 131*, 121–139.

Voss, K. (2023, June 27). *B2B social media marketing: 3 ways marketers can connect with young buyers now*. Insider Intelligence. https://www.insiderintelligence.com/content/b2b-social-media-marketing

Wpromote & Ascend2. (2023). *2023 state of B2B digital marketing*. https://www.wpromote.com/report/2023-state-of-b2b-digital-marketing

Promoting Social Marketing on Social Media 5

Using TikTok as an Engaging Platform to Reduce Food Waste

Jenny Zhengye Hou and Xuan Li
Queensland University of Technology (QUT), Australia

This chapter aims to guide readers in achieving the following objectives:

1. Develop a comprehensive understanding of the current landscape of using social media for social marketing, exploring both its potential and limitations;
2. Gain insights into the distinctive features of TikTok, an emerging and captivating social media platform, with a focus on its dynamic functions and creative participatory mechanisms;
3. Analyse a case study illustrating how a TikTok influencer effectively utilises the platform to promote audience engagement and reduce food waste as a social marketing initiative; and
4. Provide strategic guidance for marketing practitioners, particularly in the public and not-for-profit sectors, on leveraging the affordances of social media to build broad awareness and drive positive action towards common social goals.

DOI: 10.4324/9781003412656-5

Social Marketing in the Digital Era

As a discipline born in the 1970s, social marketing involves using marketing strategies to design and implement programmes that educate the public on an important social cause (e.g., climate action, gender equity) to raise awareness or promote socially beneficial behaviours (Zhou et al., 2021). The core focus of social marketing theory and practice lies in improving the provision of public services and resources to promote the welfare and wellbeing of society. One potential approach to mitigating socioeconomic inequality is through the enhancement of public and social services. This will enhance the impact of social marketing on fulfilling its primary function as well as fostering societal progress as a whole (Feeney & Porumbescu, 2021; Rishi & Bandyopadhyay, 2018). Similar to marketing in the commercial sector, the primary emphasis of social marketing lies on the consumers, with a focus on comprehending their needs and desires, rather than employing one-way, persuasive tactics to encourage purchase behaviour (Mensah & Amenuvor, 2022). The concept of social marketing emphasises the utilisation of marketing strategies with the intention of modifying behaviour, rather than only promoting ideas or disseminating information (Li et al., 2021a). Lee and Kotler (2011) propose that social marketing should be defined as the application of business marketing principles to influence behaviour for the benefit of public or wider communities. The social marketing field should prioritise reducing the adverse ramifications of commercial actions, but exerting positive influence on policies aimed at reducing inequalities and increasing the opportunities available to marginalised populations (Brauer et al., 2021).

To put it simply, social marketing is primarily concerned with promoting social justice, equity, and inclusion by incorporating marketing thinking into practice (Brauer et al., 2021). Business marketing involves making decisions about (1) product concept, (2) price, (3) place (location), and (4) promotion. These are often referred to as the 'four Ps' of marketing (Weinreich, 2006). Weinreich has added a few more dimensions to social marketing: *publics, partnership, policy, and purse strings*. Social marketing endeavours to impact social behaviours, aiming to benefit both the target audience and society as a whole by effectively promoting ideas, attitudes, and behaviours (Wasan & Tripathi, 2014). The public participates in the project. The comprehensive scope of the 'external public' includes the target audience, secondary audiences, policymakers, and gatekeepers. Conversely, the 'internal public' refers to individuals who are involved in the process of approving or implementing the plan in some way (Finchum, 2017). 'Partnership' refers to collaborations between organisations that share similar objectives, although not necessarily identical ones (Secundo et al., 2021). Frequently, policies need to change, and media campaigns can be effective complements to social marketing (Galan-Ladero & Rivera, 2021). Lastly, the majority of organisations that develop social marketing programmes rely on financial support ('purse strings') from various sources, such as foundations, government grants, or donations (Mutum & Ghazali, 2023).

The advent and proliferation of social media provides interactive opportunities that enable marketers to promote consumer engagement and build ongoing relationships (Ashley & Tuten, 2015). Over the past decade, the benefits of social media have become increasingly evident and are used for wide-ranging purposes. For example, after the 2010 earthquake in Haiti, social media was employed to connect healthcare providers with victims, some of whom were trapped under rubble but managed to use Facebook to seek assistance (Merchant et al., 2011).

Compared to traditional advertising methods, social media platforms enable marketers to precisely target specific user segments, thus presenting cost-effective advantages (Velentza & Metaxas, 2023). Therefore, it can be argued that social media platforms provide a better opportunity to change people's behaviour with fewer resource requirements (Vedel et al., 2020). Social media provides these opportunities, changing the way consumers interact with each other and with organisations. Extensive research has shown that social media is more powerful than traditional media in building intimate relationships with consumers because it is more popular among audiences (Bannor et al., 2017).

Social marketing has been applied to many different fields for various social purposes. One area that has frequently involved social marketing is healthy lifestyle. For instance, in the context of alcohol reduction, Thompson et al. (2013) find that online and interactive promotional materials such as Facebook pages and event videos significantly increased the probability of students visiting the designated website, and that students exposed to the website reported they were more confident about reducing their alcohol consumption. This study demonstrates that social marketing and social media interaction produce positive outcomes. Similarly, Frerichs et al. (2015) conducted a study on social marketing to reduce obesity and cultivate healthy eating habits by producing a series of short videos and distributing them through social media platforms such as Facebook and YouTube. The videos highlighted the social benefits of a healthy lifestyle, with some featuring dietitians demonstrating simple recipes and advice on snacks, and explaining that healthy food would be more nutritious. According to the authors' three-year follow-up project, the target audience increased their consumption of healthy food and showed a growing inclination to confront health issues associated with obesity.

Social marketing has also been applied to promote behavioural change on other issues related to sustainable development, energy efficiency, and water conservation (Sheth & Parvatiyar, 2021). In the United States, social marketing is increasingly promoted as a core strategy to influence behaviours such as smoking, drinking, drug use, and dietary choices (Mason et al., 2021). According to the Food and Agriculture Organization of the United Nations (FAO), food waste is a worldwide issue, with an estimated 30–50 per cent of produce never consumed (Martínez-Blanco et al., 2010). Meanwhile, the COVID-19 pandemic has exacerbated famine and food shortages in the third world, thus exacerbating already severe social inequalities (Kassa & Grace, 2020). To promote less food waste, some marketing scholars have explored integrating social marketing with social media platforms with the aim of fostering meaningful connections with intended audiences (Jenkins et al., 2022).

Young et al. (2017) contended that Facebook had the potential to serve as an effective social media intervention. They were particularly interested in Facebook, arguing for its dominant position in social media; and, if the platform proved to be effective, it could offer a broader range of intervention strategies to help speed changes in consumer behaviour towards food waste. The authors assessed various types of intervention based on qualitative feasibility designed to target consumer communication channels such as magazines, social media platforms, in-store radio, posters, and local communities. They posted topics on Facebook about leftovers, asked users to discuss their favourite recipes for leftovers, directed users to a website on reducing food waste, called 'Love Food Hate Waste' and encouraged households to use up surplus food and promoted discussion among consumers.

Some researchers have found that food has become a popular way of displaying consumers' lifestyles among the vast amount of content shared on social media (Lahath et al., 2021). In the context of Instagram, with hundreds of millions of food-related posts shared on the app, people believe these posts help show others how good their lives are and help them feel good about themselves when posting pictures of their food. Evans-Lacko et al. (2013) maintain that regularly updating and using a variety of content (including informational content, images, and links) can be effective in maintaining communication with existing social media followers as well as reaching new audiences.

Since the interactive nature of social media provides a variety of communication opportunities, scholars and experts are actively trying to combine social media with social marketing (Li et al., 2021a). However, the role of social media in marketing is still under-researched. According to Dooley et al. (2014), there is a major deficiency in the understanding of social marketing practitioners, who often lack adequate knowledge of social media utilisation and communication management. In their study of social marketing participants, in-depth interviews highlight that some practitioners lack a comprehensive understanding of social media platforms that require a significant amount of time to acquire proficiency in navigating them. Particularly in the public and non-profit sectors, limited budgets and time prevent marketing managers from fully harnessing the potential of social media. Published content online may not resonate with audiences due to ineffective communication, thus minimising the effectiveness of social media to disseminate marketing messages.

Nevertheless, it is believed that social media has the potential to play a major role in addressing consumer-level food waste. The increasing number of platforms has generated significant amounts of information and impact from marketers, social media influencers, and lay people. Researchers have begun to recognise the potential of social media for information dissemination but still lack precise understanding of how social media engagement, including on TikTok, can translate content into shifting behaviours to reduce food waste. The present strategies employed to address such behaviour – such as adverts/billboards on various platforms (e.g., buildings, buses, TV) and face-to-face encounters – are characterised by high costs, significant time requirements, and limited effectiveness. New communication methods such as trending social media platforms should therefore be employed. Suitable models need to be developed to evaluate different factors that contribute to the production, distribution, and consumption of effective messaging. In what follows we discuss one of the most engaging social media platforms—TikTok—in relation to promoting food waste reduction.

TikTok: An Engaging Social Media Platform

TikTok, a short video app, is an international development derivative of Douyin, and launched in 2016 by ByteDance in Beijing for the domestic market in China. TikTok is accessible across 155 countries in 75 languages (Mohsin, 2020), and globally was the most downloaded iPhone application during January 2021. TikTok has since achieved significant popularity, especially among young audiences (Zhang et al., 2024). With the fast-growing number of users, it is prevalent in spreading information globally (Mohsin, 2020). Users browse the app eight times a day for a total average of 45 minutes, which drives substantial traffic. As an entertainment app, all the trending topics and popular news stories are discussed on TikTok, which easily creates hot topics to guide users to discuss and follow them. The advantage of simple communication makes it easier for topics related to social causes to be seen, shared, and discussed by users. In recent years, TikTok has increasingly also been used for both commercial promotion (Yuan et al., 2022) and the dissemination of public information (Comp et al., 2021), indicating great potential for growth.

The main feature of TikTok, the 'For You Page' (FYP), displays popular video content that users can scroll through endlessly on their phones. According to Valdovinos Kaye et al. (2020), individuals can easily imitate videos they watch, creating new versions in a few simple steps using the same sound effects and templates—a viral spreading effect that has made the platform even more popular. Every video is tagged by a hashtag, which makes it easier for people to find the content they are interested in. In September 2021, the BBC reported that TikTok had surpassed YouTube in terms of average viewing time in both the United States and the United Kingdom. TikTok's rapid development shows that the way it interacts with users is so engaging that it can easily attract large audiences (Mohsin, 2020).

Medina Serrano et al. (2020) identified four levels of communication on TikTok:

1. This level corresponds to when users watch the videos but do not actively engage with the content.
2. This includes basic responses, mainly referring to sharing or liking the video.
3. The user posts a comment in response to a video.
4. The final level allows users to respond with a 'duet', a distinctive feature of TikTok whereby users react to the original post with the 'reply video' function. The duet is more like a real-time, face-to-face conversation than a passive response, which makes the interaction between host and user more personal.

TikTok provides a highly user-friendly method of creating and duetting videos in just a few steps using templates with the same sound/vision/caption effects. This kind of viral spreading effect has made TikTok even more popular (Li et al., 2021b). It seems to be an effective way of interacting, and is a feature that no other social media sites afford (Omar & Dequan, 2020). It also allows users to create a duet to show off their creativity in expressing their opinions. The duet function makes TikTok more powerful and interactive than other social media platforms, a useful aspect when studying the impact of TikTok in relation to social causes.

To investigate the relationship between TikTok and social marketing, it is important to assess current research findings, especially to examine the potential impact and effect of TikTok. This platform garners significant attention because of its diverse content offerings and its participatory culture of active user engagement. Some studies have indicated that the marketing and commercial value of TikTok will influence young customers' decision-making and encourage them to purchase products (Xiao et al., 2023). A number of corporations are currently utilising it as a strategic marketing platform, with well-known companies such as Sony Pictures, Samsung, Nike, and Adidas already having loyal fans or followers on TikTok.

Some researchers also suggest that TikTok can be an invaluable and influential platform for disseminating important global messages. Indeed, it was praised for facilitating the dissemination of important public health information during the pandemic (Barker, 2020), including the promotion of wearing masks and washing hands to reduce community transmission of the coronavirus. Crucially, since the pandemic, TikTok has no longer been a social media platform just for entertainment. Scientists around the world continued to post video updates on TikTok concerning the virus, self-quarantine measures, and vaccine progress. TikTok appears to have played a significant role in the dissemination of information about public health and community wellbeing (Basch et al., 2021). Nevertheless, its role and potential in changing the norms and behaviours around broad social issues (e.g., food waste) have been under-analysed.

An Illustrative Example: Promoting Food Waste Reduction on TikTok

The features unique to TikTok—the 'For You Page' and the 'duet' functionalities—maximise content publicity and user engagement in trending topics or even facilitate promoting a particular (desired) social behaviour (e.g., reducing food waste). These two novel features can enable a social cause to be widely promoted and easily accepted, as exemplified by many videos on TikTok that teach viewers how to reduce waste by making full use of leftovers (Bölükbaş et al., 2021; Phillipov, 2016). The following example illustrates the impact of TikTok on marketing/promoting this social cause through bespoke videos created by an influencer to encourage sustainability and engage, educate, and persuade the audience to actively save food.

The influencer with the username @thegreenhub1 has had a significant impact on the virtual community on TikTok. She introduces herself in videos on her homepage about sustainable living. Her videos feature promoting sustainable living practices, including several aspects related to the natural environment, thus gaining popular support from followers. It is worth noting that the videos are divided into three playlists, each containing practical content about reducing food waste and promoting sustainability, as outlined below.

Food Waste Recipes

These videos explore innovative approaches to addressing food waste, offering practical tips for daily routines to effectively use and cook with leftover food. Followers can learn about innovative ways to reduce food waste by exploring how to make the most of food. For example, one video shows how to make soup from fruit and vegetable skins/peels that would otherwise be thrown away: more than a dozen kinds can be frozen, and then boiled into a delicious and nutritious soup. It is essential for people across all sectors of society to get involved in efforts to reduce food waste. Indeed, one follower of @thegreenhub1 expressed appreciation for the quality of the soup and commended the source of inspiration.

Food Storage Tips

This set of videos provide comprehensive and practical food storage guidelines. They guide TikTok users with fundamental principles and strategies to effectively keep food and enhance its longevity and flavour while optimising the preservation process for a diverse range of produce. For example, one teaches people how to soak the roots of fresh, green, leafy vegetables in a container of water, refrigerate for 10 minutes, and then put them in a cloth bag or food storage box, which can extend their best-before eating time by 1–2 weeks. Some followers left messages such as "Thank you for this tip, very practical for me."

Ways I Reduce Food Waste

This group of well-designed videos provide a variety of delicious recipes to reduce food waste, particularly addressing meals that are frequently thrown away by individuals who lack cooking skills. The influencer introduces innovative recipes that smartly rescue and transform discarded fruit and vegetables into tasty dishes. Followers were greatly impressed by her educational demonstration of how to prepare a rich soup and dip using overripe avocados with darkened skin, with the visual presentation of the dish looking quite appealing.

In terms of influence, @thegreenhub1 has attracted 194,000 loyal followers and her videos have amassed a staggering 350.1 million likes, indicating her undeniable impact on the world of sustainable living. At the heart of her content is a constant flow of information. The videos produced for different purposes not only have appealing visual elements that are characterised by vivid and authentic tones, but also possess a highly educational intent in an effectively engaging manner. Specifically, instead of preaching about the importance of reducing food waste, this influencer offers practical tips on how to do so in everyday life. Through her videos, she shares various methods of reducing food waste in all aspects of life (e.g., through reuse) that followers can learn about. By following her strategies, TikTok users can not only reduce daily costs but also achieve tangible results in reducing food waste.

Followers of @thegreenhub1 actively engage with her by commenting and sharing their own experiences while also expressing their gratitude for her valuable insights. For example, one follower commented, "That's good advice! Lots of people throw away hard bread!! Can save!" The significance of her guidance and the positive influence of her tips on people who are interested in minimising food waste are heightened by the motivation of saving money. Another TikTok user expressed gratitude, saying: "This recipe is perfect when I've grown too many zucchini, tomatoes and basil and don't know what to do with them, thank you!" Reviews of her page continue to show the viability of her recipes, with another user commenting: "Nice reminder. How do you know I bought too much red cabbage?" This not only praised the influencer's content but also highlighted how her advice resonated with fans' daily lives, fostering a sense of understanding and connection.

In general, the comment list provides a space where followers can: express gratitude; exchange knowledge, experience, and tips; and seek further advice through fostering a dynamic and engaging online community that focuses on the principles of sustainable living and mitigation of food waste. Videos such as these have shown a great potential to educate followers (especially younger followers) about the importance of sustainability and avoiding food waste. Influencers can also offer economical recipe suggestions to younger viewers, as well as tips on using leftovers for cooking.

In summary, TikTok can indeed be an important educational tool to raise public awareness and develop social norms around reducing food waste. The interactive element of the platform's comment area plays a significant role in fostering a community that is dedicated to sustainability and reducing food waste. This is evident through the high level of participation observed on @thegreenhub1's videos.

Discussion Questions

- How do the 'For You Page' and 'duet' features of TikTok help in the promotion and acceptance of social concerns in a distinctive manner, particularly in the context of reducing food waste?
- How does @thegreenhub1 skilfully use the capabilities of TikTok to captivate, enlighten, and convince her audience about sustainable living and the reduction of food waste?

Concluding Remarks

The example of a TikTok influencer's social marketing practice in promoting food waste reduction has shed light on the fact that popular social media platforms such as TikTok can make important contributions to serving social causes and the public interest. Traditional social marketing relies heavily on adverts, campaigns, and petitions – mainly delivered through traditional and mass media as one-way publicity, persuasion, and mobilisation. In comparison, social media offers new potential not only to effectively reach a large cohort of audience members and draw their attention to appealing audio-visual content. More importantly, it can also engage them in active conversations and possible behavioural changes to implement a particular social marketing initiative (e.g., reducing food waste). This is mainly because of the strong participatory mechanism and interactive culture embedded in social media platforms so that individuals are empowered to freely express ideas, opinions, and creativity while, at the collective level, learning from and influencing each other with regard to achieving a common goal. In other words, the great potential of social media as a social learning and collective action platform warrants further exploration.

As shown in this chapter, social media platforms such as TikTok offer an enormous 'marketplace' for spreading ideas and information regarding the reduction of food waste to achieve the United Nation's Sustainable Development Goals 2030. TikTok provides a quality platform for presenting social marketing initiatives in a more engaging way than traditional media and other social networking sites. TikTok content creators or influencers utilise a variety of multimedia tools (such as videos, pictures, and compelling stories) to encourage public understanding and spread information to viewers regarding how to reduce food waste on a societal level. These short videos effectively communicate social marketing topics with accuracy, detail, and audio-visual appeal. Influencers can leverage the advantages of these videos to disseminate messages about reducing food waste, effectively reach a vast number of followers, and increase awareness and proactive engagement with the issue of food waste.

TikTok also provides both influencers (content creators) and users with the ability to establish mutually supportive communities online by co-creating shareable content via the functionality of duet. In this process, the community can naturally develop a shared understanding and a set of common values toward the social issue, laying important ground for developing the shared social norm that encourages and guides practical action. The area for comments on TikTok also creates an environment conducive to fostering the exchange of knowledge, experience, or even problems and challenges among viewers-as-content-producers. Establishing a community sense, in turn, encourages increased engagement and motivation among individuals (Hou, 2018), hence facilitating their adherence to collective behaviours aimed at (in this case) reducing food waste.

Overall, social media platforms like TikTok possess significant yet under-explored potential to contribute to the advancement of social marketing, especially to facilitate sustainable development. Their various interactive and participatory functions can be better utilised to enable incremental changes in the behaviour chain—from raising awareness, changing perceptions and attitudes, and developing social norms to effecting real behaviours at different time points. Their peer-to-peer influence and social learning dynamics can be better navigated to foster fandom—groups of loyal followers, advocates, and activists—to enact particular social marketing initiatives in the pursuit of human wellbeing, prosperity, and sustainability. This chapter serves as a departure point sparking a call for more empirical studies and professional practice to fully employ the affordances of social media such as TikTok for social marketing purposes.

References

Ashley, C., & Tuten, T. (2015). Creative strategies in social media marketing: An exploratory study of branded social content and consumer engagement. *Psychology & Marketing*, *32*(1), 15–27.

Bannor, R., Asare, A. K., & Bawole, J. N. (2017). Effectiveness of social media for communicating health messages in Ghana. *Health Education*, *117*(4), 342–371.

Barker, M. (2020). TikTok continues to grow, but new challenges await. *Marketing Week*. Retrieved from https://www.marketingweek.com/tiktok-challenges-await/

Basch, C. H., Fera, J., Pierce, I., & Basch, C. E. (2021). Promoting mask use on TikTok: Descriptive, cross-sectional study. *JMIR Public Health and Surveillance*, *7*(2), e26392.

BBC. (2021). *TikTok overtakes YouTube for average watch time in US and UK*. Retrieved from https://www.bbc.com/news/technology-58464745

Bölükbaş, R., Sarıkaya, G. S., & Yazıcıoğlu, İ. (2021). Analysis of food waste and sustainability behavior in Turkish television cooking shows. *International Journal of Gastronomy and Food Science*, *24*, 100336.

Brauer, M., Dumesnil, A., & Campbell, M. R. (2021). Using a social marketing approach to develop a pro-diversity intervention. *Journal of Social Marketing*, *11*(4), 469–488. doi:10.1108/JSOCM-09-2020-0174.

Comp, G., Dyer, S., & Gottlieb, M. (2021). Is TikTok the next social media frontier for medicine? *AEM Education and Training*, *5*(3), 1–4.

Dooley, J. A., Jones, S. C., & Iverson, D. (2014). Using Web 2.0 for health promotion and social marketing efforts: Lessons learned from Web 2.0 experts. *Health Marketing Quarterly*, *31*(2), 178–196.

Evans-Lacko, S., Malcolm, E., West, K., Rose, D., London, J., Rüsch, N., … Thornicroft, G. (2013). Influence of Time to Change's social marketing interventions on stigma in England 2009–2011. *British Journal of Psychiatry*, *202*(s55), s77–s88.

Feeney, M. K., & Porumbescu, G. (2021). The limits of social media for public administration research and practice. *Public Administration Review*, *81*(4), 787–792. doi:10.1111/puar.13276.

Finchum, A. (2017). Marketing missions: A case study for the social marketing mix. *Global Journal of Business Pedagogy*, *1*(1), 11–18. doi:10.47177/GJBP.01.01.2017.011.

Frerichs, L., Brittin, J., Robbins, R., Steenson, S., Stewart, C., Fisher, C., & Huang, T. T. K. (2015). SaludABLEOmaha: Improving readiness to address obesity through healthy lifestyle in a Midwestern Latino community, 2011–2013. *Preventing Chronic Disease*, *12*(2), E20. doi:10.5888/pcd12.140328.

Galan-Ladero, M. M., & Rivera, R. G. (2021). *Applied social marketing and quality of life: Case studies from an international perspective*. Cham: Springer.

Hou, J.Z. (2018). Integrating community and relationship building into universities' social media marketing: Implications from a case study. In B. Rishi, & S. Bandyopadhyay (Eds.). *Contemporary issues in social media marketing* (pp. 31–45). London: Routledge. https://doi.org/10.4324/9781315563312-3

Jenkins, E. L., Brennan, L., Molenaar, A., & McCaffrey, T. A. (2022). Exploring the application of social media in food waste campaigns and interventions: A systematic scoping review of the academic and grey literature. *Journal of Cleaner Production*, *360*, 132068. doi:10.1016/j.jclepro.2022.132068

Kassa, M. D., & Grace, J. M. (2020). Race against death or starvation? COVID-19 and its impact on African populations. *Public Health Reviews*, *41*(1), 1–17.

Lahath, A., Omar, N. A., Ali, M. H., Tseng, M.-L., & Yazid, Z. (2021). Exploring food waste during the COVID-19 pandemic among Malaysian consumers: The effect of social media, neuroticism, and impulse buying on food waste. *Sustainable Production and Consumption*, *28*, 519–531.

Lee, N. R., & Kotler, P. (2011). *Social marketing: Influencing behaviors for good*. Thousand Oaks, CA: SAGE Publications.

Li, F., Larimo, J., & Leonidou, L. C. (2021a). Social media marketing strategy: Definition, conceptualization, taxonomy, validation, and future agenda. *Journal of the Academy of Marketing Science*, *49*(1), 51–70. doi:10.1007/s11747-020-00733-3.

Li, Y., Guan, M., Hammond, P., & Berrey, L. E. (2021b). Communicating COVID-19 information on TikTok: A content analysis of TikTok videos from official accounts featured in the COVID-19 information hub. *Health Education Research*, *36*(3), 261–271. https://doi.org/10.1093/her/cyab010

Martínez-Blanco, J., Colón, J., Gabarrell, X., Font, X., Sánchez, A., Artola, A., & Rieradevall, J. (2010). The use of life cycle assessment for the comparison of biowaste composting at home and full scale. *Waste Management*, *30*(6), 983–994.

Mason, A., Narcum, J., & Mason, K. (2021). Social media marketing gains importance after Covid-19. *Cogent Business & Management*, *8*(1), 1–17. doi:10.1080/23311975.2020.1870797.

Medina Serrano, J. C., Papakyriakopoulos, O., & Hegelich, S. (2020). Dancing to the partisan beat: A first analysis of political communication on TikTok. Paper presented at the 12th Association for Computing Machinery (ACM) Conference on Web Science.

Mensah, K., & Amenuvor, F. E. (2022). The influence of marketing communications strategy on consumer purchasing behaviour in the financial services industry in an emerging economy. *Journal of Financial Services Marketing*, *27*(3), 190–205. doi:10.1057/s41264-021-00121-0.

Merchant, R. M., Elmer, S., & Lurie, N. (2011). Integrating social media into emergency-preparedness efforts. *New England Journal of Medicine*, *365*(4), 289–291.

Mohsin, M. (2020). TikTok statistics that you need to know in 2020. Retrieved from https://www.oberlo.com/blog/tiktok-statistics

Mutum, D. S., & Ghazali, E. M. (2023). *Consumers, society and marketing: A sustainability perspective*. Cham: Springer.

Omar, B., & Dequan, W. (2020). Watch, share or create: The influence of personality traits and user motivation on TikTok mobile video usage. *Journal of Interactive Mobile Technologies*, *14*(4), 121–137. https://doi.org/10.3991/ijim.v14i04.12429

Phillipov, M. (2016). 'Helping Australia Grow': Supermarkets, television cooking shows, and the strategic manufacture of consumer trust. *Agriculture and Human Values*, *33*(3), 587–596.

Rishi, B., & Bandyopadhyay, S. (Eds.) (2018). *Contemporary issues in social media marketing*. London: Routledge.

Secundo, G., Del Vecchio, P., & Mele, G. (2021). Social media for entrepreneurship: Myth or reality? A structured literature review and a future research agenda. *International Journal of Entrepreneurial Behaviour & Research, 27*(1), 149–177. doi:10.1108/IJEBR-07-2020-0453.

Sheth, J. N., & Parvatiyar, A. (2021). Sustainable marketing: Market-driving, not market-driven. *Journal of Macromarketing, 41*(1), 150–165. doi:10.1177/0276146720961836.

Thompson, E. B., Heley, F., Oster-Aaland, L., Stastny, S. N., & Crawford, E. C. (2013). The impact of a student-driven social marketing campaign on college student alcohol-related beliefs and behaviors. *Social Marketing Quarterly, 19*(1), 52–64.

Valdovinos Kaye, D. B., Rodriguez, A., Langton, K., & Wikstrom, P. (2020). You made this? I made this: Practices of authorship and (mis)attribution on TikTok. *International Journal of Communication, 15*, 3195–3215.

Vedel, I., Ramaprasad, J., & Lapointe, L. (2020). Social media strategies for health promotion by nonprofit organizations: Multiple case study design. *Journal of Medical Internet Research, 22*(4), e15586.

Velentza, A., & Metaxas, T. (2023). The role of digital marketing in tourism businesses: An empirical investigation in Greece. *Businesses, 3*(2), 272–292. doi:10.3390/businesses3020018.

Wasan, P. G., & Tripathi, G. (2014). Revisiting social marketing mix: A sociocultural perspective. *Journal of Services Research, 14*(2), 127.

Weinreich, N. K. (2006). What is social marketing? Weinreich *Communications*, 10.

Xiao, L., Li, X., & Zhang, Y. (2023). Exploring the factors influencing consumer engagement behavior regarding short-form video advertising: A big data perspective. *Journal of Retailing and Consumer Services, 70*, 103170. doi:10.1016/j.jretconser.2022.103170.

Young, W., Russell, S. V., Robinson, C. A., & Barkemeyer, R. (2017). Can social media be a tool for reducing consumers' food waste? A behaviour change experiment by a UK retailer. *Resources, Conservation and Recycling, 117*, 195–203.

Yuan, L., Xia, H., & Ye, Q. (2022). The effect of advertising strategies on a short video platform: Evidence from TikTok. *Industrial Management + Data Systems, 122*(8), 1956–1974. doi:10.1108/IMDS-12-2021-0754.

Zhang, Y., Liu, C., & Lang, C. (2024). How luxury fashion brands leverage TikTok to captivate young consumers: An exploratory investigation using video analytics. *Journal of Marketing Analytics*. doi:10.1057/s41270-023-00276-w.

Zhou, S., Blazquez, M., McCormick, H., & Barnes, L. (2021). How social media influencers' narrative strategies benefit cultivating influencer marketing: Tackling issues of cultural barriers, commercialised content, and sponsorship disclosure. *Journal of Business Research, 134*, 122–142. doi:10.1016/j.jbusres.2021.05.011.

Optimizing User Engagement

6

The Synergy of Social Media Marketing and UI/UX Design

Hannah Hameed, Mohit Maurya
Sharda School of Business Studies, Sharda University, India

Mohd Arif
Anand School of Engineering and Technology, Sharda University, Agra

Out of all the changes the global business landscape has witnessed in the past few decades, the most profound and promising has been the confluence of technology and design into generating immersive user experiences across all brand-user touchpoints. Among the most significant drivers of this have been social media platforms and digital media channels (Rishi & Bandyopadhyay, 2018).

According to the *Digital 2023 Global Overview Report* (We Are Social, 2023), worldwide digital advertising expenditure in 2021 was estimated at 522.5 billion U.S. dollars, and projections indicate that this is expected to surge to 836 billion by 2026. Moreover, a whopping 68 percent of the total global population are active mobile phone users, and another 65 percent are now online. These statistics not only emphasize the pivotal role of the digital consumer but also highlight the vast potential of social and digital media in shaping the experiences of both customers and brands. An exceptional, lasting, and captivating customer experience empowers businesses to fortify their brand identities and secure a competitive advantage (Watulingas & Permana, 2020). Despite the extensive attention devoted by scholars and industry

DOI: 10.4324/9781003412656-6

experts to comprehending user experiences and the realm of social media marketing, the *Global Digital Report* revealed some unexpected insights.

While social media has been growing fast, it is slowing slightly. In 2024, the number of new social media users only rose by 3 percent, or 137 million new users. The question is why is this happening? There could be a few reasons. First, in some places, almost everyone who wants to be on social media already is, so there are fewer new users available to join. Second, people might be getting a little tired of spending so much time online. It's like eating too much of your favorite food; after a while you might not want as much. This slowdown in social media growth reminds us how important it is to continually improve the user experience. When there are fewer new users, it's even more crucial to keep the existing users happy. This means social media platforms must work to make their websites and apps more fun, useful, and easy to use. They should also focus on showing users the content they really like. This trend compels brand managers and the academic community to delve into the underlying factors contributing to this slowdown. It underscores the escalating significance of enhancing the overall user experience, considering not only functional utility but also embracing the more pleasurable and emotionally gratifying aspects of engagement. Thus, interfaces between technology and users must be high on functionality, aesthetics, personalization, and overall experience.

The worth of an enhanced user experience, popularly known as user interface/user experience (UI/UX) design, is an aspect acclaimed globally by digital marketers and brand strategists. It is the experience that customers have with a brand across the digital landscape—basically, the crux of what the brand *means* to the customer in the long run. With new perspectives of Marketing 5.0, which focuses on human-centric design and creating immersive, intimate, and long-lasting emotional experiences, it is imperative to fully understand the significance of delivering the best UI/UX to a digitally savvy, empowered, and futuristic audience base.

This chapter seeks to delve into the various dimensionalities of what UI/UX stands for in the context of social media marketing and the digital consumer landscape. It will also deepen this understanding through a relevant case study.

The Confluence of Technology and Design

Relevant research and practitioner viewpoints have established the important link between user experience/interface and marketing outcomes, as both are key elements of creating an overall enhanced and effective experience for all stakeholders during the process of building and experiencing brand (Goel et al., 2022; Algharabat et al., 2020; Watulingas & Permana, 2020). The combination of technology and design is a major force in today's business world, especially in social media and digital marketing. From strategic planning to marketing campaigns and the delivery of solutions through technology based on artificial intelligence (AI), this fusion has changed the way we engage with these platforms. Social media is all about connecting people and technology through designs to make it more enjoyable, engaging, and accessible. Sites and applications use advanced tech such as AI and augmented reality (AR) to offer users personalized experiences, with sleek and user-friendly designs that make it easy to navigate through content. Consider Apple's user interface, which leverages cutting-edge technology to craft a user experience that streamlines navigation and, in turn, greatly enhances the overall experience. Additionally, social media platforms use clever algorithms to show us content we will like. This mix of technology and design keeps us hooked and helps companies target their audiences effectively. The use of multimedia, interactive interfaces, and eye-catching visuals enhances our experience.

In digital and social media marketing, technology and design are equally vital. Businesses analyze data to understand what customers like, leading to personalized ads. Their websites, apps, and ads are designed to look good and be easy to use. They may even use augmented reality to create captivating experiences. This combination of tech and design is not just a trend; it's the future. It shapes how businesses connect with us and how we interact with the digital world.

The massive shift to mobile and online life has had a huge impact on how people and brands interact. Digital and social media have transformed user experiences: for customers, it means ads and content that are more personalized and relevant to their interests; for brands, it's a powerful way to reach and engage with their target audience. The digital advertising revolution is not just a passing trend; it's here to stay. It's changing the way businesses and people connect and communicate. As more of our lives become digital, the role of digital interfaces in shaping our experiences becomes increasingly important.

The Essence of UI/UX Design

UI/UX design is like the engine behind our digital experiences. It's all about making things work well and making users feel good when using websites and applications. UI stands for 'user interface', which means how online interfaces *look* and how users interact with them. UX is 'user experience', which is all about how a user *feels* when browsing a website or using an app. Think of it this way: if you visit a website that looks nice and it's easy to find what you need , that's because of UI/UX design. This design is not just about making things pretty; it's about making you happy when you use them.

Functionality leads to a more hedonic aspect of how we interact with brands and products online. Digital marketers and brand experts focus strongly on UI/UX design because it is how they make you see and feel about a brand online. If a brand's website or app is user-friendly and enjoyable, people are more likely to form a positive impression of that brand. It is like walking into a clean and well-organized store; you're more likely to shop there again. Thus, UI/UX design is vital in the digital world because it's about creating a great, enjoyable experience for users, which also helps brands make a good impression on their customers.

The design of user interfaces and user experiences has become crucial in producing engaging digital interactions for users as brand–customer experience has taken center stage. It can be difficult to understand the subtle differences and interactions between UI and UX. Though closely related, UX focuses on the more comprehensive elements of user behavior and satisfaction, whereas UI emphasizes visual design and front-end development.

User experience (UX) is the term used in marketing to describe the process of creating products and services that provide consumers with relevant and meaningful experiences. To produce designs that are aesthetically beautiful, intuitive, and easy to use, research must be done to understand customer needs and preferences. UX designers therefore prioritize features such as a product's look, feel, and usability to provide a positive user experience. They also take into account information architecture, visual design principles, and user research while making products that cater to the individual demands of customers. To guarantee a smooth user experience across disciplines, UX designers frequently collaborate with engineers, marketers, and other designers in multidisciplinary teams. The creation of goods that users find helpful, simple to use, and intuitive is the aim of UX design.

Another crucial element of user experience is interactive design, which focuses on developing interactive features and elements that promote user participation and engagement—such as clickable buttons, animations, and micro-interactions. In addition to improving the overall user experience, these interactive components are essential for drawing in visitors and achieving intended marketing goals. UX design goes one step further by placing more emphasis on the user's overall experience and happiness. In the realm of digital marketing and social media, a satisfying user experience is essential. It entails developing user-friendly interfaces, guaranteeing quick page loads, and putting in place obvious calls to action. Increased customer loyalty, conversion rates, and user retention are all correlated with flawless UX.

The user interface would be the first thing users encounter, and so can be defined as their first impression (Mishra et al., 2015). The goal of UI design is to make a digital platform that is both aesthetically pleasing and intuitive to use. This is especially crucial in the social media arena, where users expect positive and easy connections. Effective digital marketing initiatives can benefit from a well-designed UI, which strengthens brand identity and promotes user engagement. Usability, or the ease with which people can navigate and engage with a website or application, is one important factor.

Showcasing Successful Brand Strategies

Social media is an essential component of our lives, transforming the way we communicate, reshaping our worldview, and changing how we consume information. It is also crucial in helping to create user-centric, visually appealing, and engaging digital experiences that propel the success of online marketing efforts. Interestingly, it has a significant impact on user experience design in the digital sphere outside of personal life. Businesses can produce and distribute information that connects with their audiences through well-designed interfaces. Additionally, according to a study by Ferreira et al. (2023), integrating social media strategies with UI/UX design enhances user satisfaction and retention. Canziba (2018) provides practical insights and techniques for developers to effectively integrate UX design principles into their workflow, bridging the gap between design and development for enhanced user experiences. Studies have reinforced and shown how marketing initiatives can be made more effective by using visually appealing and straightforward elements, which improve engagement and conversion rates (Sasisuriyaphoom, 2021; Yablonski, 2020).

In order to create online shopping experiences that imitate the simplicity and satisfaction of real purchasing, e-commerce platforms must use UI and UX design. Businesses may increase sales and cultivate consumer loyalty by optimizing product presentation and expediting the buying process. For example, consider the user-friendly design of the iPhone. The sleek and intuitive interface (the UI) and the overall experience of using it (the UX) have helped establish Apple as a brand known for quality and user satisfaction. People enjoy using iPhones because of the experiential design process, which positively influences their perception of the Apple brand.

Many brands have become masters at using social media and UI/UX design to attract customers. Take Samsung for instance, whose user-friendly interfaces make using products like the Galaxy S series of phones a delight. Further, the company has triumphed with social media integration. But how does this impact their customer base? And what about Nike? That company's mobile app goes further: it mixes social sharing with personalized product recommendations. How does that make users more engaged? Let us dig a bit deeper. The fact that Apple's gadgets are so easy to use makes us happy. That is good UI/UX design at work. And when we see how well they do on social media, it reinforces our trust in the brand. The Nike app is like a personal shopping assistant. It suggests stuff users might like, making their shopping experience fun, and you can share finds with friends on social media, which makes it all the more exciting.

But this is not just about the big players, as even brands like JK Tyres, Motorsports, and Royal Enfield are using Instagram filters to create unique and fun experiences on social media. It helps them connect with both existing and potential consumers and builds brand image. So it's not just about selling stuff; it's about creating immersive, ultramodern, and user-friendly experiences that keep us coming back for more.

How Do Brands Use Technology?

Let us elaborate on how this confluence is utilized by brands.

Personalized User Experience

Brands use technology-driven user interfaces to give their audiences a more personalized and engaging social media experience. According to Kumar et al. (2019), brands that leverage AI and machine learning (ML) technologies can analyze user behavior to tailor content and recommendations, thereby enhancing user satisfaction and loyalty. Additionally, Krishnan et al. (2022) discuss how chatbots and immersive graphic designs play a critical role in creating interactive and engaging user experiences, leading to higher levels of customer engagement. Brands may gain greater awareness of their target audience, deliver personalized content, and sustain positive and engaging user interactions by utilizing chatbots (AI) to create 'try me on' features and immersive graphics. This can result in greater online presence, improved conversion rates, and a rise in brand loyalty. Amazon is one e-commerce site that makes use of customized user experiences. To give specialized product recommendations, individualized search results, and specialized marketing messages, the company makes use of user data, browsing history, purchase history, and other behavioral information. Users find that this customization improves their overall shopping experience and motivates them to find and buy products that better suit their interests and preferences.

E-commerce websites that have well-designed UI/UX are guaranteed to be user-friendly, intuitive, and visually appealing. UI/UX elements that enhance the user experience include straightforward product classification, easy checkout processes, and efficient navigation (Danesh, 2023). These design principles not only improve the overall usability of the site but also contribute to greater customer satisfaction and increased sales.

Enhanced Visual Content

Consider a well-known e-commerce website that employs AI-driven image optimization, for instance. When a user visits the website, AI algorithms analyze the user's device, internet connection speed, and browsing preferences. This allows the AI to offer product photos that are adequately optimized, resulting in a fast download time for users without sacrificing quality. When users have a smooth and visually appealing experience, they are more inclined to stay on the website and browse products, which not only reduces bounce rates (the number of people landing on and then leaving a page), but also increases the possibility of conversions. The 'wishlist' feature, 'similar product recommendations', and 'try me on' tools on popular fashion, interior, and lifestyle websites are visual delights for customers. They help them build strong positive attitudes towards brands, and ensure more intentions to return to the websites. Gunawan et al. (2021) emphasized the critical role of intuitive design in fostering positive user interactions on e-commerce platforms. To efficiently grab users' attention and deliver messages, high-quality images and animations are employed. UI/UX design therefore helps optimize pictures, videos, and other media to enhance the user experience and improve loading times.

Real-Time Engagement

Instant answers to queries are provided by chatbots and AI-driven customer support representatives, thus increasing user engagement. These chatbots can also help with transactions, such as making purchases, scheduling services, or resolving problems directly via the social media network.

This seamless interaction not only boosts user engagement but also enhances the customer's overall experience by providing instant and efficient solutions to their needs. Bag et al. (2022) explore how artificial intelligence technologies enhance user engagement and conversion rates in digital marketing, emphasizing the pivotal role of AI in personalizing customer experiences and driving effective marketing strategies. For example, leading Indian fashion e-commerce company Myntra recently introduced an AI-driven chatbot named Maya, making use of the capabilities of OpenAI's ChatGPT to improve its customers' shopping experience. Maya aims to assist users explore Myntra's vast selection of products by answering queries, thus making the shopping process seamless and more enjoyable.

User Behavior Analysis

As AI-driven insights enable companies to precisely customize their communications, personalization and relevance have become the cornerstones of brand communication. In addition to improving audience engagement, this dynamic response to user reactions also strengthens client bonds, ensuring a more robust and successful brand–consumer relationship. Suadamara (2024) explores the opportunities and challenges in UX design for e-commerce websites, emphasizing that optimizing UX can lead to increased customer satisfaction and conversion rates. The study also discusses the complexities involved in balancing aesthetic appeal with functional usability. Consider Amazon's 'Recommended for you' and 'Customers who bought' widgets, which are estimated to account for approximately 35 percent of its sales, with 56 percent of consumers likely to make additional purchases through them. The 'Customers who bought this item also bought' algorithm is used to harness crowd wisdom, which can drastically improve cross-sales and overall revenue and impact long-term customer loyalty. This is enabled by UI/UX designs and interfaces.

Automated Content Creation and AI-Powered Ads

Graphic design tools that are driven by technology are adept at creating eye-catching images that can be used in posts and ads, which increases the visual appeal and impact of brand messages. By streamlining content development and ensuring the delivery of attractive graphics, this integration of UI/UX technology helps create a marketing plan that is more effective overall and uses fewer resources. Attractive video advertising and strategically placed digital advertisements within e-commerce websites capture and engage online clients. These commercials make use of the potency of skillfully composed visual material and flawless user interfaces to entice viewers, improve their whole buying experience, and eventually increase conversions. Together, these components guarantee that consumers notice the advertisements and find them engaging and interactive, making the online purchasing experience more enjoyable.

Asante et al. (2023) examine how AI elements enhance consumer engagement on e-commerce platforms, highlighting their effectiveness in personalizing shopping experiences and optimizing consumer interactions to boost engagement and sales. By analyzing user behavior and preferences, they deliver relevant content and personalized recommendations, making the interface more intuitive and user-friendly. This attracts consumers' attention while also improving convenience and levels of satisfaction, strengthening the bond between the company and its patrons in the process.

Social Listening

Social listening is a useful technique that involves monitoring and evaluating online forums and social media conversations in real time to learn what people are saying about a product, company, or subject. Gupta and Bansal (2023) present a novel approach to consumer engagement through AI-driven emotional recognition in digital ads. Their research illustrates how AI can analyze and interpret consumers' emotional responses to advertisements in real-time.

AI-driven solutions have revolutionized social listening by automating processes and providing more precise and thorough data analysis. This transformation enhances the accuracy and depth of insights obtained from monitoring and evaluating online forums and social media conversations in real time. User UI/UX design and 'sentiment analysis' are crucial for determining the success and branding of e-commerce platforms and online purchasing experiences. Sentiment analysis helps brands understand public opinion, enabling them to adapt their strategies accordingly. Sentiment analysis tools examine reviews, comments, and other feedback from customers in order to determine how the general public feels about a company or its offerings. This provides insightful information on what consumers find appealing or unappealing about the online store or its features.

Behera et al. (2024) further highlight the transformative power of AI in customer engagement from an e-retailer's perspective in the era of Retail 4.0. They emphasize how AI-driven e-marketing strategies can significantly enhance consumer engagement and satisfaction. Integrating these AI technologies into e-commerce platforms allows retailers to deliver more personalized and impactful experiences, thereby strengthening customer relationships.

Friction Reduction

Well-designed UI/UX helps reduce friction during the online purchasing process. For instance, consumers may find desired products quicker and with less frustration thanks to search feature that are easier to use and readily available.

Gamification

Gamification features can significantly enhance user experiences in e-commerce and online shopping platforms when combined with effective UI/UX design. Elements such as badges, points, and rewards can motivate users to interact more with the platform. For instance, an e-commerce site may offer loyalty points for every purchase, thus encouraging repeat business. Effective UI/UX design ensures that gamification features are easily included in the platform's user interface and that there are obvious ways for users to interact with them. User-friendly menus, buttons, and icons are essential (Mominzada et al., 2022; Meder et al., 2018; García-Jurado et al., 2021). Well-designed UI/UX also includes feedback systems to let users know about their achievements and rewards in the gamification system, such as through notifications and animations. As a result, the encounter is more fulfilling and captivating.

Accessibility should be given top priority in UI/UX design so that all users, including those with disabilities, can utilize the gamification features, as this inclusive strategy improves the overall user experience. When gamification is skillfully incorporated into UI/UX design, routine actions like browsing products or checking out can become entertaining and enjoyable endeavors. User input gathered via gamification features might also offer ideas for additional UI/UX design enhancements, creating a never-ending cycle of innovation.

Dimensional Mapping of UI/UX Elements

The five elements of user experience design, from abstract to concrete, are strategy, scope, structure, skeleton, and surface—a model created by

Table 6.1 Dimensions of UI/UX

User Interface (UI)	User Experience (UX)
Visual design	Interactive design
Graphics and colors	Emotionally engaging
Layout and typography	Aesthetics
User navigation and widgets	Content design, storytelling
Ease of use	Contextual elements
Branding	Information architecture
Input controls	User research
Informational components	Wireframes and prototypes

designer Jesse James Garrett in *The Elements of User Experience* (2022 [2002]. As shown in Table 6.1, UX design encompasses the entire process, while UI design primarily focuses on the surface.

Case Study

The microblogging platform X (formerly Twitter), has over 217 million active daily users, making it a crucial part of your marketing strategy. It's not just about the large user base; X ranks as the world's seventh most popular network, with predictions of over 340 million active users in 2024. However, with 350,000 tweets sent every minute and a whopping 500 million daily, achieving your marketing goals on the platform requires a strategic and savvy approach to capture and retain your audience's attention.

A well-designed UI/UX ensures a seamless and intuitive conversion of online retail and social interaction platforms. This has turned thoughtless scrolling into something meaningful. Brands now focus on social media platforms that may turn an experience into a transaction moment while driving commercially successful outcomes. Businesses undoubtedly face cadences, and therefore need better connections to their consumers. Therefore, whatever is required—whether AI, metaverse, Clubhouse, or Threads—is used to create efficiencies for business. Adoption of AI in increasingly specialized, tailor-made applications across sectors can mark the onset of significant disruptions within their respective categories. The increasing momentum of AI technology as a fundamental tool in the realms of business, government, healthcare, and academia may leave slow adopters at a distinct disadvantage.

Marketers prefer owned channels as they help with prioritizing budgets. With smaller innovation budgets the focus has shifted to direct-to-consumer (DTC/D2C) and performance marketing. UX is all about crafting user-friendly designs to make websites, apps, technology, and even physical products as easy and enjoyable to use as possible. As UX is design-oriented, it doesn't require expertise in visual design to work in this field; it focuses on delivering a great customer experience through design and empathy. Social media marketing promotes your brand on company platforms, often managed by a social media marketing manager. The key to in-app monetization is improving UX and adding value to continued usage or gameplay while simultaneously increasing engagement. Many users sign up for free downloads but soon have to subscribe to in-app purchases to increase functionality or user experience, or simply to remove ads, etc. For instance, popular gaming apps improve user UX by offering durable in-app purchases such as ad removal or bonus game levels.

UI/UX design enhances marketing strategies in several ways, such as boosting search engine optimization (SEO) potential, collecting user feedback, understanding customer needs, identifying user issues, and improving conversion rates. It also enhances the customer service experience, creates intuitive interfaces, refines website navigation, maintains visual appeal, and ensures brand consistency. UI and UX design plays a crucial role in how your audience engages with your product, fostering trust and credibility, improving user engagement metrics for SEO, optimizing calls to action, personalization, targeted messaging, and ultimately increasing brand awareness.

For example, X offers an '@anywhere' platform that will allow websites to easily integrate its features, the idea being to offer the X experience anywhere on the web seamlessly. This would enable users to navigate third-party sites such as *The Times of India*, giving them X content without the need to leave the page they're currently viewing. This brings a range of functionality to your website with practically no prerequisite technical capabilities. Keeping tabs/pages open means you can browse regularly visited sites with tweets from friends, celebrities, companies, media outlets, fictional characters, and more. This would enable you to recreate these open, engaging interactions, providing a new level of value for visitors without sending them to the parent site (X/Twitter.com). In other words, you could follow any account and be followed by any account.

As a result of this, companies have started interacting with customers, celebrities have connected with fans, governments have become more transparent, and people have started discovering and sharing information in a new, participatory manner. Options include the ability to:

- use twitter usernames on your website into links automatically
- show hovercards revealing users' details on rollover
- tweet directly from your website
- embed tweets in your website as well in YouTube videos

- sign in to third-party sites with a Twitter/X ID
- enable a journalist's byline to show her Twitter/X profile and allow people to follow her through the article on any other website
- tweet about a video from its YouTube page
- discover new Twitter/X users/accounts from, say, Yahoo's home page.

Recently, the platform has adopted a content strategy to support both longer-format and video-first posts. It offers a diverse range of Application Programming Interfaces (APIs) that empower developers to construct applications interacting with the platform. APIs serve as the conduits through which various software systems communicate, facilitating the integration of technologies to improve the overall user experience.

As one of the leading social media networks, Twitter/X is an ideal platform for businesses aiming to promote their products and services as they can use its Ads API to create and oversee their advertising campaigns seamlessly within the platform's ecosystem. Leveraging this API, companies can craft and personalize their advertisements, pinpoint specific target audiences, and monitor campaign performance in real time. For instance, tools for managing social media marketing, such as Buffer, enable users to schedule their marketing activities, relying on Twitter APIs to obtain analytical insights from the platform. Buffer can showcase crucial metrics such as tweets/retweets, replies, clicks, and more.

Twitter/X has numerous bots that utilize its API to perform automated tasks. Twitter bots are automated accounts that carry out actions such as tweeting, retweeting, following, and sending direct messages in response to software commands. For example: *TinyCareBot* sends reminders for self-care activities; *Grammar Police* identifies grammatical errors; and *Netflix Bot* announces new Netflix content. These bots operate using the Twitter API, which not only supports basic functions but also enables event-based notifications.

Another well-known API enhancing user experience is the 'Log in with Facebook/Twitter/Google' capability seen on many websites. This is quite useful because, rather than entering users' social media accounts (a probable security risk), applications with this capability use these platforms' APIs to authenticate the user with each login.

Understanding Twitter Trends

Twitter/X quickly spreads the word on various topics. When a word, phrase, or hashtag becomes popular, it's a 'trending topic' or 'trend'. Marketers use trends to stay informed about ongoing conversations and understand their audience. Twitter is all about staying current. Watching declining trends helps marketers avoid outdated topics.

Twitter Circle is a way for you to form a private audience, allowing you to send exclusive tweets to a group of your choice, with a maximum of 150 participants. Only people in your Twitter Circle can view the content and engage with those particular tweets. As a marketer, your circle could consist of important brands and influencers. This feature can be used to establish your brand as a trusted source of information or to share industry insights tailored to your audience.

Twitter Communities are a great marketing tool as they allow you to create or join groups of similar accounts and share content related to common interests, thus helping you build your brand, audience, and community.

Twitter Spaces is like a live audio chat room, and is a great tool for brands and businesses. You can use Spaces for live questions and answer (Q&A) or ask me anything (AMA) forums, or industry-specific discussions with active audiences. It's a way to establish your brand as a thought leader. Although social audio on Twitter is new, live audio is powerful and can help you engage your audience in real time.

Twitter Lists are curated feeds from selected accounts that let you tune into important discussions and influential people because Twitter feeds are often full of countless conversations with a lack of focus on what matters to businesses. You can create as many lists as you need (up to 1000); and, unlike the main feed, which uses the platform's algorithm, list tweets appear in chronological order, making it easier to track current events. You can build lists for competitors, industry leaders, and your team. Remember, however, that they are public, so name them carefully. This takes some time, but it's worth it for efficient and strategic Twitter use.

Discussion Questions

- Analyze the benefits and challenges of using Twitter bots for automated marketing tasks. How do these bots enhance user experience and engagement according to the case study?
- Discuss the role of UI/UX design in improving social media marketing outcomes on platforms like Twitter. How do elements like AI, in-app purchases, and tailored user experiences contribute to achieving marketing goals? Use details from the case study to illustrate your points.

Conclusion

Social media and digital marketing have fundamentally transformed the way businesses connect with their audiences. Effective UI/UX design is the bridge that connects these platforms to users, enabling brands to convey their messages and build relationships. This is a dynamic, ever-changing field that plays a crucial role in shaping the success of marketing strategies in the digital age. While UX captures the entire interaction—including the user's thoughts and emotions about the interaction—UI focuses on efficiency, effectiveness, and satisfaction (i.e., the user's ability to use an interface). The goal of user-centered design is to facilitate seamless and productive user experiences. Meeting both pragmatic and hedonistic user needs is essential for a smooth and satisfying online customer journey, which hinges on a good user experience.

The rise of online shopping, voice search, and personalized recommendations has made intuitive and responsive design a critical component for retaining customers. Additionally, the integration of AI and machine learning technologies allows for more tailored and predictive user experiences, further enhancing engagement and conversion rates. As businesses continue to innovate and adapt to these changes, a focus on user-centric design will remain pivotal in driving sustainable growth and customer loyalty.

References

Algharabat, R., Rana, N. P., Alalwan, A. A., Baabdullah, A., & Gupta, A. (2020). Investigating the antecedents of customer brand engagement and consumer-based brand equity in social media. *Journal of Retailing and Consumer Services, 53*, 101767.

Asante, I. O., Jiang, Y., Hossin, A. M., & Luo, X. (2023). Optimization of consumer engagement with artificial intelligence elements on electronic commerce platforms. *Journal of Electronic Commerce Research, 24*(1), 7–28.

Bag, S., Srivastava, G., Bashir, M. M. A., Kumari, S., Giannakis, M., & Chowdhury, A. H. (2022). Journey of customers in this digital era: Understanding the role of artificial intelligence technologies in user engagement and conversion. *Benchmarking: An International Journal, 29*(7), 2074–2098.

Behera, R. K., Bala, P. K., Rana, N. P., Algharabat, R. S., & Kumar, K. (2024). Transforming customer engagement with artificial intelligence e-marketing: An e-retailer perspective in the era of retail 4.0. *Marketing Intelligence & Planning, 42*(7), 1141–1168.

Canziba, E. (2018). *Hands-on UX design for developers: Design, prototype, and implement compelling user experiences from scratch*. Packt Publishing.

Danesh, B. A. (2023). *E-commerce UI/UX* (Doctoral dissertation, University of Applied Sciences Technikum, Vienna).

Ferreira, M. S., Antão, J., Pereira, R., Bianchi, I. S., Tovma, N., & Shurenov, N. (2023). Improving real estate CRM user experience and satisfaction: A user-centered design approach. *Journal of Open Innovation: Technology, Market, and Complexity*, *9*(2), 100076.

García-Jurado, A., Torres-Jiménez, M., Leal-Rodríguez, A. L., & Castro-González, P. (2021). Does gamification engage users in online shopping? *Electronic Commerce Research and Applications*, *48*, 101076.

Garrett, J. J. (2022 [2002]). *The elements of user experience: User-centered design for the web and beyond* (2nd ed.). New Riders.

Goel, G., Tanwar, P., & Sharma, S. (2022, January). UI-UX design using user-centred design (UCD) method. *In 2022 International Conference on Computer Communication and Informatics (ICCCI)* (pp. 1–8). IEEE.

Gunawan, R., Anthony, G., & Anggreainy, M. S. (2021, October). The effect of design user interface (UI) e-commerce on user experience (UX). *In 2021 6th International Conference on New Media Studies (CONMEDIA)* (pp. 95–98). IEEE.

Gupta, T., & Bansal, S. (2023). AI-driven emotional recognition in digital ads: A novel approach to consumer engagement. *Journal of Marketing & Supply Chain Management*, *2*(3), 1–7. https://doi.org/10.47363/JMSCM/2023(2)131.

Krishnan, C., Gupta, A., Gupta, A., & Singh, G. (2022). Impact of artificial intelligence-based chatbots on customer engagement and business growth. In T. Hong, L. Serrano-Estrada, A. Saxena, & A. Biswas (Eds.), *Deep learning for social media data analytics* (pp. 195–210). Cham: Springer.

Kumar, V., Rajan, B., Gupta, S., & Pozza, I. D. (2019). Customer engagement in service. *Journal of the Academy of Marketing Science*, *47*, 138–160.

Meder, M., Plumbaum, T., Raczkowski, A., Jain, B., & Albayrak, S. (2018, October). Gamification in e-commerce: Tangible vs. intangible rewards. In *Proceedings of the 22nd International Academic Mindtrek Conference* (pp. 11–19). New York: Association for Computing Machinery.

Mishra, A., Dash, S., & Malhotra, N. K., 2015. An integrated framework for design perception and brand equity. *AMS Review*, *5*, 28–44.

Mominzada, T., Abd Rozan, M. Z. B., & Aziz, N. A. (2022). Consequences of user experience in a gamified e-commerce platform. *International Journal of Electronic Commerce Studies*, *13*(1), 113–136.

Rishi, B., & Bandyopadhyay, S. (Eds.). (2018). *Contemporary issues in social media marketing*. London: Routledge.

Sasisuriyaphoom, P. (2021). *Marketing 5.0: How to improve user experience with digital solutions* (BA dissertation, Thammasat University, Thailand).

Suadamara, R. (2024). Opportunity and challenges in UX design for e-commerce website. *Engineering, MAthematics and Computer Science Journal (EMACS)*, *6*(2), 157–162.

Watulingas, E. B., & Permana, D. (2020). The influence of user interface, user experience and digital marketing toward purchase intention. *International Humanities and Applied Science Journal*, *3*(2), 35–39.

We Are Social. (2023). *Digital 2023: Global overview report*. https://wearesocial.com/wp-content/uploads/2023/03/Digital-2023-Global-Overview-Report.pdf

Yablonski, J. (2020). *Laws of UX: Using psychology to design better products and services*. O'Reilly Media.

The Consumer Journey in a Social Media World

7

Kruti Sanjaykumar Bhatt
B. V. Patel Institute of Management, Uka Tarsadia University, India

Introduction

Social media has become an integral aspect of consumer behavior, and enables marketers to reach billions of users worldwide. Marketers focus on benefits such as convenience, product search, and brand relationships for developing social media strategies. As usage continues to advance, brands must adapt their strategies to recent trends and consumer preferences on social media platforms. Approximately 4.9 billion users spend around two hours on social media platforms, with around 2 billion active users worldwide. Considering revenue generation, video platforms are expected to contribute the highest return by using pop-up advertisements between content to attract new customers and encourage repeat purchases from the existing customer base. The contribution of influencers and social commerce has increased dramatically, as identified on Instagram and YouTube. Consumers access social media platforms using mobile devices. In the digital age, consumers not only expect honesty from brands with an online presence, but also follow recommendations from influencers or on social media platforms, as seen in the case of the Itzy Ritzy brand discussed later.

Youngsters are the key consumers of these platforms. Consumers stay updated with information on new trends, find them convenient, and also discover content in their respective interest areas, termed "personalization

DOI: 10.4324/9781003412656-7

benefit". Consumers have a larger set of choices regarding purchases, including international brands.

Demographics of Social Media Users

Businesses need to focus on the kind of consumers they will be serving on social media platforms, and can better understand the demographic profile and other associated details of target customers by asking the following questions:

- Who are the target customers worldwide?
- Which age groups would the business like to serve?
- Which residential or service area is the business targeting?
- What income group should the business target?
- What household structure is the target – nuclear, joint, or extended?
- Which occupations/professions should it target?
- Are there any specific hobbies, tastes, or preferences of target customers that need to be considered?
- Does the business need to target customers interested in trendy products?

In sum, to enter the social media world, marketers need to understand the demographics of their target market. Not only are the younger generations increasing their social media usage, but older generations are also adopting it gradually. Based on geography, education, income, and gender distributions, marketers need to target customers using a multichannel approach on various social media platforms.

In general, the social media user base is young, urban, and increasingly diverse. For example, the Asia-Pacific region has the major share of social media users worldwide, accounting for 59.9% of total users, compared to North America with 6.7%. Women aged 18–29 are most likely to make purchases based on influencer content. The use of Facebook is declining among younger customers due to the emergence of other social media platforms. Instagram and Snapchat are becoming more popular among users aged 18–29, while LinkedIn caters to college graduates and professionals. TikTok has seen enormous growth among Gen Z (born between about 1997 and 2012), with 1 billion monthly active users worldwide (Pew Research Center, 2024). Consumers start using social media platforms at around the age of 12, and usage declines comparatively declines with age. Gen Z comprises the major users of Instagram (71%) and Snapchat (65%). Millennials (1981–1996) primarily use Facebook (29.9%). Women are more inclined towards Instagram (48.2% of users), Pinterest (76.2%), and Snapchat (51%); and men mostly use LinkedIn (57%) and Twitter (61.29%). According to Auxier (2021), 50% of women aged 18–29 have made purchases based on influencer content, compared to 36% of men in the same age group, indicating that it is easier to attract and influence female customers for impulsive purchases than male customers.

Regarding countries, the Philippines has the most social media saturation, with 98.6% of internet users, along with Indonesia, Malaysia, and Thailand. The U.S. has the most Facebook, Instagram, LinkedIn, and Snapchat users: 55% of LinkedIn users there are in high-income households; TikTok, YouTube, Snapchat, and Facebook are used by the low-income population; and Pinterest is used by 45% of users with a household income above $100k. India has the most YouTube and TikTok users. The majority of college graduates use different social media networks. Digital India has therefore upgraded access to increase the usage of social media platforms across education levels for academic betterment (Newberry, 2024).

The Consumer Journey

Social media users can be novices or experts, depending on people's skills and interests when choosing a social media platform and spending time on it for different tasks. Some may just like to follow a page, while others would like to be part of a specific community. Others still may consider advertisements for different products and services, make purchases, or alert others to the page or social media platform. By considering the consumer journey and improving touchpoints on platforms, brands can easily engage audiences, drive sales, and build resonance across the customer lifecycle (Rishi & Bandyopadhyay, 2018). Regularly observing performance metrics and adapting to new consumer behaviors will be key factors if brands are to remain successful in the social media world.

Social media has a substantial influence on consumers' behavioral decisions. Generating engaging content and developing relationships are key contributors to converting followers into purchasers. Strategies such as competitions, offers, and other incentives can encourage followers to purchase. Turning buyers into advocates requires delivering excellent service and positive experiences. Advocates are shaped through loyalty programs, tailored communication, and making customers feel valued. They have a considerable impact through word-of-mouth (WOM) marketing and recommendations, help attract potential customers, and can lead to repeat business.

Stages of Consumers' Social Media Journey

According to Dixon (2024), a consumer goes through five main stages in the social media journey with a brand:

1. **Awareness**: Consumers gain knowledge about a brand, its products, and services through social media advertisements, influencer content, and organic content. This information creates a base about the brand in the minds of consumers.
2. **Consideration**: Reviews, discussion forums, and interaction with respective brands empower consumers to compare options available online and consider some of them as meeting their requirements for a product or service.
3. **Decision**: Using shopping-related posts, consumers make purchase decisions for a product/brand. This can also be termed behavioral intention to purchase and use the product/brand.
4. **Retention**: Brands provide after-sales services and exclusive deals to retain customers for longer periods, which can lead to repeat purchases.
5. **Advocacy**: Satisfied customers recommend the brand to others through reviews, shares, and tags, which helps build a positive attitude towards a brand.

Key Metrics for Measuring the Consumer Social Media Journey

The report by Newberry (2024) includes the following key metrics:

- *Reach* – the number of people who see the content
- *Engagement rate* – likes, shares, and comments as a percentage of reach
- *Conversions* – behavioral intention, such as purchase and other goals
- *Click-through rate* – clicks on the links as a percentage of impressions
- *Audience growth rate* – increase in the number of followers over a period of time
- *Net promoter score* – customer satisfaction and loyalty.

Various social media platforms (such as Facebook, Instagram, TikTok, LinkedIn, and Twitter) influence the consumer journey in exceptional ways based on their features and target market demographics. Strategies for enhancing the consumers' social media journey include forming shareable content, leveraging the credibility and fame of influencers, responding to feedback, providing exclusive deals, and incentivizing recommendations.

The consumers' social media journey has grown significantly over the past decade due to smartphones and the provision of audiovisual content. Emerging trends include live chat and video, transient content, interactive commerce, and cybernetic influencers. For example: the Facebook experience ranges from awareness of the brand to advocacy of the brand; Instagram impacts visual content-based product identification and shopping; Twitter enables real-time chats with brands; and TikTok initiates awareness among younger audiences.

An effective social media strategy needs consumers to progress through the journey from follower to buyer to advocate. A strong understanding of user psychology and tactics to move them through each stage is crucial for brands looking to maximize the value of their social media presence. Nowadays, businesses also need to monitor trends to attract customers, such as using a trendsetter song in making reels on Instagram or Facebook. As a result of using the trendy song, people will enjoy your reel and recommend it. Another example is the use of Artificial Intelligence (AI) in making interesting advertisements to attract customers on social media platforms. These platforms can be the best way not only to influence people, communicate thoughts to communities, and sell products; they can also be used for consultations and discussions about particular problems and much more. Once hooked, a customer can also become a seller, partner, or influencer for a brand.

Strategies for Converting Followers into Buyers

- Creating shareable and more engaging content, such as videos and contests.
- Partnering with relevant influencers to build brand awareness and inclusion in the consideration set for purchase.
- Responding promptly to consumer feedback and queries on social media platforms.
- Offering special deals and discounts to consumers.
- Encouraging satisfied customers to leave positive reviews and recommendations.
- Sharing real-time lifestyle content and videos to build long-lasting relationships with social media consumers (Qualtrics, 2023a, 2023b).

Turning Buyers into Advocates

Retaining buyers is a key challenge nowadays as customers have a broad spectrum of market players selling highly similar products, which can lead them to switch brands. The following are recommendations to help retain customers (RingCentral, 2023).

- rs need to run loyalty programs on a continuous basis with rewards to encourage frequent repeat purchases and referrals from existing customers.
- Personalized communication showcasing their areas of interest through recommendations makes loyal customers feel valued and helps strengthen emotive connections.
- Providing exceptional services at the time of purchase and after sale validates the brand's commitment to customer satisfaction.
- Posting user-generated content (UGC) and testimonials helps develop credibility and trust between brands and consumers.
- Asking for feedback regularly or after each transaction, along with implementing changes where necessary, makes customers feel heard.

Brand advocates give two or three times more referrals than usual marketing campaigns, which accelerates growth. Advocates improve brand reputation by endorsing a positive brand image and protecting it from criticism. Advocates' word-of-mouth marketing helps attract new customers at a comparatively lower cost than usual marketing tactics. Advocates have a higher lifetime value with reference to the brand through increased loyalty, the number of referrals, and frequent purchases (Thorne, 2023; All Business, 2022).

Understanding Social Media Platforms

Understanding different social media platforms helps brands develop strategies to better cater to consumers for various reasons, such as to:

- create networks or communities
- generate leads or business
- promote products from social media platforms
- hire people
- spread awareness or educate consumers
- entertain and engage users to gain a sustainable customer base
- provide the existing customer base with customer relationship management (CRM).

However, simply choosing the right platform is not enough; businesses also need to keep an eye on the competition. Competitor analysis is significant in retaining advocates for respective brands. Businesses need to understand the SWOT (Strength, Weakness, Opportunity, Threat) aspects of their brands and products as well as those of the competition. The following outlines some of the most popular social media platforms.

Facebook

The customer journey on Facebook usually starts when consumers become aware of a brand. Main Facebook touchpoints at this awareness stage include ads, organic posts from the brand, and posts from influencers and friends. At the evaluation stage, consumers decide whether or not a brand meets their requirements. It starts with observing the page and profile of the brand, watching posted videos, and reading reviews, which prompts the Facebook algorithm to show them more content from the brand. At the purchase stage, consumers decide to buy the brand. Consumers interact with brands in various ways such as:

- **Ads**: Brands pay to promote new products or attract new customers for existing products through sponsored posts, reels, and stories.
- **Organic content**: This consists of posts, reels, live videos, and stories posted directly to audiences.
- **Friends' post**: Discussions by a user's friends about brand content are shown in the consumer's feed.
- **Influencer posts**: Influencers become partners with the brand and promote the brand's content to their followers.

Tracking Consumer Engagement on Facebook

Brands can track consumer engagement through Facebook Analytics and Page Insights, considering page views, actions, reach, and follower demographics. When followers are online, engagement can be observed through their top posts. Through likes, shares, and comments, consumers' reactions and responses to posted content can be evaluated. Analytics can also be obtained through ad performance and conversations with consumers, and the data should be used to continually improve brand content and strategy in the long term.

Key Parameters

- **Page content**: Brand pages consist of audiovisual content, photographs, tabs to provide key information, and shopping features, along with information about recent trends and exclusive offers for customers.
- **Reviews**: These play an important role in evaluating brands as consumers rely heavily on them when choosing a product or service. Having a brand in the consideration set is therefore an important parameter.
- **Events**: Brands create Facebook events that users can follow and register for in their calendars.
- **Live shopping**: Tagging products in their live videos ensures brand products are instantly visible.
- **Messaging**: Consumers contact brands with questions about new arrivals or to ask for any clarity they need on the performance of brands (Synup, n.d.; Campos, 2020).

Twitter/X

Twitter (rebranded as X in 2023) is an important channel for appealing to consumers throughout the shopping journey. Designing campaigns to align with consumers' motivations and behaviors for different retail categories leads to success. Originality, quick responses, and understanding core consumer communities are crucial parameters for the platform. Consumers use it to research products, receive recommendations, and find deals. Positive brand conversations can shift consumer perceptions toward purchase intent, while negative conversations provide opportunities for improvement. Businesses should avoid over-branding and inauthentic messages. This is a significant channel for customer service as consumers want quick responses to their feedback and complaints. The platform also provides facilities for social networking and blogging, and helps users be good content creators or writers as they need to be concise in posts.

Instagram

Consumers use Instagram to identify new products, conduct research, and make purchase decisions. Brands can augment the consumer experience at every stage through strategic content along with features such as Highlights, giving a seamless path to purchase. Tracking brand performance through Instagram metrics provides dynamic data to improve the journey. Most Instagram users use the platform for 6–10 years, having initially joined it due to peer pressure, an interest in photography, and wanting to feel inclusive.

Instagram has evolved from being a platform simply for posting photographs into a robust e-commerce marketplace, with features such as Instagram shop, shoppable post, product tags, and droppable links in stories to empower consumers in product discovery and purchases through the app. Messaging helps consumers resolve queries and they can also post feedback. Metrics such as reach, engagement rate, and website clicks have become significant for understanding the consumers' journey and optimizing marketing strategies (Suarez, 2020).

LinkedIn

This platform is specifically used by business people, professionals, and graduates to establish professional connection and networks in relevant fields. A major use of LinkedIn is job searches by college / university graduates, and it is a reliable source of up-to-date information on respective business fields.

Key Features of LinkedIn

- **Feed**: Users consume content here, a key place where brands gain visibility through moments of truth.
- **Profile**: Users create professional profiles for personal branding and establishing credibility.
- **Content creation**: Users create images, text posts, and videos to share industry insights and thought leadership.
- **Groups**: Niche content is shared among members of the same industry fields.
- **Messaging**: Direct messages are used for networking and for maintaining connections.
- **Job search**: New career opportunities can be identified through networking, the platform's internal job search engine.

Pinterest

For consumers looking for something on social media about their interests and passions, Pinterest is a must as its greater visibility of content makes it highly conducive to browsing and finding new things. The platform initially attracts consumers through interest, who then end up purchasing a product. Brands can easily and effectively engage customers on this platform, which has more than 200 million active users worldwide because of its visibility and inspiration to engage shoppers. Features such as Lens, Buyable Pins, and Taste Graph make it easy for consumers to purchase products based on their interests. The majority of "Pinners" use the platform for purchases, and it drives ten times more branded product searches than other social media platforms, as reflected in the brands' return on ad spend (ROAS). Survey results show that investment in this platform gives double the amount of revenue. There is also opportunity for growth as the average saturation of ads for the platform is only around 25%.

Pinterest provides a positive environment for those users who dream, plan, and find relevant ideas as brands share visually appealing lifestyle content. Users actively follow brand accounts that provide information and inspiration, and brands engage users through promising content and participation in group boards (Bordelon, 2020; Kudhail, 2023).

Key Ways Consumers Use Pinterest

Consumers use Pinterest for advice/information/inspiration on topics such as home décor, fashion, recipes, do-it-yourself (DIY) projects, travel destinations, etc. by searching keywords or browsing suggested and interesting profiles and themes. The platform has billions of "pins" (bookmarks for desirable content) that users can share with their friends directly through messages, and thus increase the number of followers of a brand. By creating inspiration boards, users can plan events such parties, weddings, and holidays.

Key Features of Pinterest

- **Lens**: Users can point a virtual camera to look for ideas and snap anything of interest.
- **Taste graph**: This uses AI to realize Pinners' tastes and offers recommendations relevant to their ideas and accounts.
- **Buyable pins**: Enables direct purchases.
- **Pincodes**: These scan the codes in stores or print to surface-related pins and drive site traffic.

YouTube

YouTube has billions of active users, and is an essential platform for brands to engage consumers through their social media journey, mainly by leveraging user data, community building, and customized video ad campaigns. Its algorithms observe users' online behavior and accordingly make relevant recommendations that lead to purchases. Entertainment, music, education, and "how-to" content are popular genres on the platform to attract a diversified demographic profile, but like other platforms, children and young people are key users. If brands do not want to lose users, they should avoid repetitive and irritating ad campaigns; short, story-based, entertaining ads can engage users more easily.

The Consumer Journey on YouTube

1. Discovery and Exploration

YouTube's algorithms analyze data from users' browsing history to recommend relevant content, providing users with new topics, brands, products, etc. It is a useful platform for early discovery of products because of its wide reach and engagement, with "unboxing" and product review videos enabling consumers to see products before purchase. YouTube is the second largest search engine worldwide, with the top searches being for musical content for entertainment.

2. Consideration and Intent

The majority of users use this platform to search for information about a brand or product before an actual purchase decision. Brands can provide important informative ads about product or services before and within videos. Ads need to connect viewers emotionally to encourage them to buy, so creative storytelling concepts can be useful here. Users prefer short ads (6–15 seconds) to longer ads of around 30 seconds.

3. Advocacy and Loyalty

YouTube attracts passionate brand advocates and loyal communities through vloggers, influencers, and content creators because they provide credibility to users – they believe influencers and content creators more than ads by brands. YouTube communities revolve around collective interests such as fashion, music, gaming, food, etc., which ultimately provides brands with loyal consumers. Brands should therefore use YouTube analytics to optimize video strategy and understand return on investment (Antoniadis et al., 2019; Ceci, 2024).

TikTok

TikTok has revitalized consumers' social media journey through its algorithm-driven identification, engaging video format, and long-lasting relationships between brands, content creators, and users. Key discriminators in TikTok are its infinite loop engagement model to disrupt the traditional marketing funnel and information concentration. By using these aspects, brands can successfully reach and influence customers. The "For You Page" (FYP) and short-form video format create an extremely engaging user experience that leads to product discovery and purchase intent. The FYP is used to analyze users' likes and browsing habits to offer personalized and relevant content. Users of this platform can also find and learn new things to inspire them, making it important not only for entertainment but also for educational content.

Collaborations with content creators can increase reach for potential users of the platform. Users believe that "lifting spirits" impacts purchase decisions by emphasizing the need for inspirational (success stories) and problem-solving content. TikTok's algorithm enables better ad discovery through better memory encoding than other digital video platforms. Its strategy of one video at a time allows for grainy user feedback for the algorithm, and features such as duets and stitches allow content remixing. TikTok users are also more likely to share purchases made via the app, and more likely to tag a brand after a purchase than users of other platforms (TikTok for Business, n.d.; Agius, 2023; Adsmurai, n.d.).

Table 7.1 summarizes the operational mechanisms behind the social media platforms discussed here.

Navigating the Social Media Landscape: The Itzy Ritzy Journey

Babycare and parenting lifestyle brand Itzy Ritzy was founded in 2007, with the aim of helping new parents on their parenting journey – a kind of social strategy for community building. Its products are available through multiple retail and online sales channels, as well as through its own website, and are made of 100% food-grade silicone, risking no harm to babies. Most are for the pre-toddler age group (6–18 months). Abundant positive reviews of products can be observed on its e-commerce website, and the brand has a presence on Facebook, Instagram, Twitter, Pinterest, and YouTube.

Shopping tabs are available for parents, baby products, and gifting, and include diaper bags, how to organize bags, what to take on the go, and accessories, with collection options available. Baby products cover categories such as teething, pacifiers, toys, and feeding. For gifting, products are organized by price range based on features, and include items such as travel bags and hospital bags. A "chat with us" option provides a list of frequently asked questions (FAQs). A customer can select directly from the questions

Table 7.1 Summary of key operational aspects of social media platforms

	Facebook	Instagram	Twitter	LinkedIn	TikTok	YouTube	Pinterest
Purpose	Social connection	Sharing content	Stay updated	Professional network	Share short-term content	Create, watch, and share videos	Identify and save ideas
Content	Posts, photographs, articles, videos	Photo, stories, videos	Tweets, short messages	Professional articles and updates	Short videos, creative content	Tutorials, videos, vlogs, unboxing content	Images and ideas
Engagement	Like, share, comment	Like, comment, message	Like, reply, retweet	Like, comment, share	Like, comment, share	Like, comment, share, subscribe	Comment, pins, share
Feed	Posts from friends	Content based on interest	Tweets can be seen in timeline	Professional content	Professional and trending videos	Recommended videos	Recommended content
Privacy	Select who can see posts	Control who can see stories	Decide on account visibility	Can control professional visibility	Limited privacy control	Control video visibility	Control visibility of pins
Promotion	Sponsored posts, targeted ads	Sponsored content and shopping	Trends, promoted tweets	Job posts, sponsored content	In-feed ads	Sponsored content, ads before videos	Shopping ads, promoted pins
Communication	Privacy in chat with friends	Direct message	Tweet, direct message	Professional message	Comment, direct message	Videos, community tabs, comment	Comment, direct message
User Demographics	Wide, no specific age group or occupation	Youngsters	Fans of recent news	Professional and business people	Youngsters and creative people	Diverse	DIY users

by clicking on the link or leave a message on the tab. Other tabs are available for new arrivals, bestsellers, and sale products in the outlet. Customers can join the mailing list by email and subscribe to the brand for relevant notifications.

Itzy Ritzy is a prime example of the importance and power of online community building worldwide. It has used Instagram to build a strong network of followers, and has tapped into people's mindset regarding games, live streaming, videos, competitions, puzzles, and giveaways, where customers show interest in and inclination towards content from their favorite influencers. Influencers present Itzy Ritzy products in Instagram posts and TikTok videos; giveaways and competitions are used to increase engagement; and posts highlight new arrivals / launches and feature lifestyle-based photography. The company interacts with followers by reposting user photos / videos and answering product-related questions to manage customer relationships. Followers often tag friends and share personal anecdotes. Giveaways receive hundreds of comments, and competitions drive high engagement as followers are eager to participate.

Since joining Twitter in 2009, Itzy Ritzy has gained over 15k followers. It later expanded to other social media platforms such as Instagram (with strong engagement) and Facebook, and uses blogs effectively to stay in touch with customers. The company's strategy revolves around presenting their products in real-life parent / baby situations, thus providing a helpful guide to new parents. It also leverages content generated by users and influencer partnerships, with UGC often featuring in social media posts, prompting positive responses to its community-focused approach (Itzy Ritzy, n.d.).

Discussion Questions

1. How does Itzy Ritzy enhance its presence and influence on social media?
2. Elaborate on Itzy Ritzy's strategies to stay engaged with customers to understand and fulfill their requirements.

Conclusion

Nowadays, it is imperative for businesses to be present on social media platforms and to use them effectively. The most important factor in selecting the best platform to reach a target audience is understanding the consumer. Brands need to examine platforms carefully to see whether they are the ideal fit for achieving their objectives. Influencer partnerships can be a key strategy for drawing in and retaining younger customers for long-term gains. Brands also need to post relevant updates on social media channels in order to create strong customer networks. The path of consumers on social media platforms progresses from awareness, brand visibility, and engagement, to creating a good impression, and finally to interactive dialogue.

References

Adsmurai. (n.d.). *Your all-in-one tech marketing partner.* https://adsmurai.com/en/articles/tiktok-metrics-to-analyze

Agius, N. (2023, September 21). *TikTok launches new tool for improved insight into customer journey.* Search Engine Land. https://searchengineland.com/tiktok-attribution-analytics-measurement-customer-journey-432298

All Business. (2022). *6 effective ways to convert customers into brand advocates*. Available at: https://www.allbusiness.com/6-effective-ways-convert-customers-brand-advocates-8990-1.html (Accessed: 04 June 2024).

Antoniadis, I. I., Saprikis, V. S., & Karteraki, E. (2019). Consumers' attitudes towards advertisement in YouTube. In A. Kavoura, E. Kefallonitis, & A. Giovanis (Eds.), *Springer proceedings in business and economics* (pp. 253–261). Cham: Springer. https://doi.org/10.1007/978-3-030-12453-3_29

Auxier, B. (2021). *Social media use in 2021*. Pew Research Center. Available at: https://pewresearch.org/internet/2021/04/07/social-media-use-in-2021 (Accessed: 04 June 2024).

Bordelon, L. (2020). *How can brands use Pinterest?* The Social Element. Available at: https://thesocialelement.agency/how-can-brands-use-pinterest (Accessed: 04 June 2024).

Campos, J. (2020, February 5). *How to create a Facebook marketing plan that models your customer journey.* Social Media Examiner. Available at: https://socialmediaexaminer.com/how-to-create-facebook-marketing-plan-models-customer-journey (Accessed: 04 June 2024).

Ceci, L. (2024, September 2). *YouTube: Distribution of global audiences 2024, by age and gender.* Statista. https://statista.com/statistics/1287137/youtube-global-users-age-gender-distribution

Dixon, S. J. (2024). *U.S. social network users 2023, by income.* Statista. Available at: https://statista.com/statistics/1337616/us-distribution-leading-social-media-platforms-by-income (Accessed: 04 June 2024).

Itzy Ritzy (n.d.). *Ritzy rewards loyalty program.* https://itzyritzy.com/pages/ritzy-rewards

Kudhail, V. (2023, September 20). *Don't sacrifice your brand values for performance.* Pinterest. https://business.pinterest.com/nl/blog/why-inspiration-matters

Newberry, C. (2024). *109 social media demographics marketers need to know in 2024*. Social Media Marketing & Management Dashboard. Available at: https://blog.hootsuite.com/social-media-demographics/ (Accessed: 04 June 2024).

Pew Research Center. (2024). *Social media fact sheet*. Available at: https://pewresearch.org/internet/fact-sheet/social-media (Accessed: 04 June 2024).

Qualtrics. (2023a). *Customer journey stages: Your ultimate guide*. Available at: https://qualtrics.com/experience-management/customer/customer-journey-stages (Accessed: 04 June 2024).

Qualtrics. (2023b). *What is social media customer service?* Available at: https://qualtrics.com/experience-management/customer/social-media-customer-service (Accessed: 04 June 2024).

RingCentral. (2023). *A complete guide to customer journey management via social media*. Available at: https://ringcentral.com/gb/en/blog/a-complete-guide-to-customer-journey-management-via-social-media (Accessed: 04 June 2024).

Rishi, B., & Bandyopadhyay, S. (Eds.). (2018). *Contemporary issues in social media marketing*. London: Routledge.

Suarez, M. (2020). *Instagram marketing funnels: The 5 stage customer journey. Medium*. Available at: https://medium.com/@manuels81/instagram-marketing-funnels-the-5-stage-customer-journey-7eab7649cf9d (Accessed: 04 June 2024).

Synup. (n.d.). *How to track Facebook engagement*. Available at: https://synup.com/how-to/track-facebook-engagement (Accessed: 04 June 2024).

Thorne, T. (2023). *How to turn customers into brand advocates*. LinkedIn. Available at: https://linkedin.com/pulse/how-turn-customers-brand-advocates-tanya-thorne (Accessed: 04 June 2024).

TikTok for Business. (n.d.). *Advertising products and marketing solutions*. https://tiktok.com/business/en-US/blog/tiktok-drives-greater-audience-engagement

8 Connecting Brands and Influencers

The Case of the Irish Blogger Agency

Róisín Vize
Technological University Dublin, Ireland

The advent of the Internet has revolutionized the way information is shared, consumed, and marketed. Unlike the initial phase of Web 1.0, which focused on one-way information dissemination, the emergence of Web 2.0 transformed the online landscape by enabling user-generated content (UGC) and fostering connections among individuals, brands, and consumers. Early forms of digital communication sites, such as blogs, provided users with a platform for personal expression, documentation, and connecting with others. Moreover, the integration of content allowed bloggers to incorporate advertisements within their blog content, providing a stream of revenue to the blog owner and ad exposure for the brand to the bloggers' audience (Lou & Yuan, 2019; Rishi & Bandyopadhyay, 2018).

The subsequent evolution to Web 3.0 has been driven by the proliferation of mobile devices and applications, which have propelled the rise of prominent social media platforms (Appel et al., 2020). Platforms such as Instagram, Facebook, and TikTok empower individuals to cultivate substantial followings and engage with their audiences on a more personal level. These tertiary influencers can significantly shape consumer purchase decisions (Haenlein et al., 2020; Ye et al., 2021). Research suggests that

DOI: 10.4324/9781003412656-8

influencer-produced branded content has more organic, authentic, and direct contact with potential consumers than more formally constructed brand-generated ads (Conde & Casais, 2023; Borges-Tiago et al., 2023)

The Role of Influencer Marketing

In the increasingly competitive social media environment influencer marketing is quickly evolving from ad hoc promotions and endorsements to strategic partnerships between brands and influencers. Marketers are recognizing the value of incorporating their marketing messages into influencers' narratives over an extended period, resulting in greater engagement and more authentic connections from followers (Conde & Casais, 2023; de Oliveira Santini et al., 2020; Kim & Kim, 2021). Influencer marketing is a approach wherein marketers and brands strategically collaborate with chosen influencers to develop and promote branded content which is then disseminated to the influencers' dedicated follower base as well as to the target audience of the brands involved (Leung et al., 2022).

Fundamentally, influencer marketing is a type of endorsement marketing where an individual makes recommendations about a brand to ultimately drive sales. The popularity of social media influencers has grown exponentially in recent years, making this tactic an integral component of a brand's marketing communications strategy. Broadly speaking, social media influencers are content creators who have a large and engaged following on social media platforms. According to the Interactive Advertising Bureau (IAB, 2018, p. 5), influencers are those who are deemed to 'have the potential to create engagement, drive conversion, and/or sell product/services with the intended audience. These individuals can range from celebrities to more micro-targeted professional or non-professional "peers".' Influencers can be categorized according to the number of followers on their social media accounts.

Influencer Types

Social media influencers are recognized as ordinary individuals who have a substantial number of followers on social media (Conde & Casais, 2023). Their ability to influence people's attitude and behaviour is considered above average (De Veirman et al., 2017), and they are often sought out for their perceived expertise and for advice (Belanche et al., 2021). The five influencer categories are nano, micro, macro, mega, and celebrity.

Nano-Influencers

Influences in this category have fewer than 10k followers and are typically starting out on their influencer career. However they have great personal influence and are generally regarded as highly authentic by their follower base, resulting in the best engagement rates of all influencer categories (Campbell & Farrell, 2020; Ooi et al., 2023). They have niche and loyal followers providing lucrative prospects for the brands they wish to engage with as they are more open to unpaid partnerships and 'gifted' promotions to help build their influencer position. Nano-influencers may be strategically looking to enter the commercial influencer marketing space, or they may have grown their following organically through their personal social media interactions.

Micro-influencers

These influencers have a comfortable follower base of between 10k and 100k followers on social media, yet they still command significant sums of money per endorsement. They often partner with multiple and diverse brands and industries. They tend to rely on engaging video posts to connect with their audience and to increase perceptions of accessibility and authenticity. Research suggests that micro-influencers' recommendations are considered more genuine than those made by celebrities (Breves et al., 2019; Kim & Kim, 2021). Marketing managers are increasingly working with micro-influencers as they recognize the connections these influencers have to the needs and interests of their followers. They are also often perceived as more credible and trustworthy brand endorsers than mega-influencers or those with celebrity status (Boerman, 2020; Conde & Casais, 2023).

Macro-Influencers

Members of this category are extremely successful but have yet to gain celebrity status. They have a follower count of between 100k and 1 million, and tend to be highly selective in the brands they partner with as the fit between brand, product/service, and influencer must align. They tend to have a more diverse audience than micro-influencers. Macro-influencers' audiences view them as experts in their subject area and often aspire to be like them in their own lives (Conde & Casais, 2023; Campbell & Farrell, 2020). They also tend to have strong engagement rates and can leverage substantial brand exposure at a fraction of the cost of their mega and celebrity counterparts.

Mega-Influencers

These are individuals who have gained celebrity status on social media but were not considered 'celebrities' prior to their social media expertise. They have 1 million or more followers, which enables them to garner significant sums of money per sponsored post. They are highly visible and recognizable, and can influence or create global trends (Conde & Casais, 2023) as their endorsements more persuasive than those of celebrity influencers (Borges-Tiago et al., 2023).

Celebrity Influencers

Unlike mega-influencers, celebrity influencers are well known and recognized outside of social media, and typically use social media to support their careers and propagate brand partnerships. They also have over 1 million followers and cultivate major endorsement deals with global brands. They can carry high levels of perceived expertise, but tend to have low engagement rates overall as perceptions of authenticity and credibility can be compromised and viewed cynically given the vast sums of money they are paid per post (Belanche et al., 2021; Borges-Tiago et al., 2023). However, posts that are not sponsored or gifted can have high levels of engagement and purchase influence.

Influencer Marketing: Opportunities and Challenges

Navigating the complex landscape of influencer marketing in the social media landscape requires expertise and a lot of strategic planning (Mero et al., 2023). Research suggests that the greatest challenges faced by organizations regarding social media are a prevailing lack of knowledge about how to effectively identify relevant influencers to promote the brand, and how to co-ordinate and implement influencer marketing as a strategic marketing tool (Cartwright et al., 2021; Leung et al., 2022).

The worldwide market for influencer marketing platforms is expected to reach US$24.1 billion by 2025, up from an estimated $21.1 billion in 2023 (HubSpot, 2023; Markets and Markets, 2024). According to the HubSpot

State of Marketing 2023 report, 89 per cent of marketers who already use influencer marketing plan to keep on using this tactic or increase their investment in influencer marketing in 2023 (Santiago, 2023). This makes good business sense given that 72 per cent of Gen Z (born about 1997–2012) and Millennials (1981–1996) follow influencers on social media and that 50 per cent of millennials trust product recommendations from influencers they follow, compared to 38 per cent from their favourite celebrities (He et al., 2023). It is therefore reasonable to assert that brands collaborating with influencers as part of their integrated marketing communications strategy is not going to cease anytime soon. Influencers today have become opinion leaders and act as brand ambassadors on social media. Research suggests that influencers have been described as somewhere between friends and distant celebrities – like friends who share interests, values, and lifestyles (Belanche et al., 2021; Breves et al., 2019). Using a common language, they are able to share advice with their followers on topics of mutual interest with the aim of establishing close long-term relationships (Tafesse & Wien, 2018).

Industry and academic research shows that influencer marketing can provide substantial benefits, such as strong return on investment (ROI) for engagement and reach. Influencers have already established high levels of trust with their followers, and partnering with them can create a ripple effect with perceptions of trust and credibility towards the brand (Belanche et al., 2021; Conde & Casais, 2023). Brand awareness is considered the bedrock of a firm's sales strategy (Bareda et al., 2015), and brand exposure is considered a fundamental advantage to engaging with influencers (Lou & Yuan, 2019). Source credibility theory asserts that the effectiveness of a product or brand endorsement is determined by the endorser's perceived credibility (Ohanian, 1990; Ooi et al., 2023). This is appraised by the endorser's personality traits and characteristics – such as physical attractiveness, likeability, and familiarity – as well as by their perceived fit with the product or brand they endorse (Breves et al., 2019).

Recent research shows a significant link between source credibility and the attitude–intention–behaviour model of actual purchase behaviours (Ooi et al., 2023). This in turn enhances customer loyalty (Tafesse & Wien, 2018), reduces churn, and produces valuable user-generated content (Hudders et al., 2021). Influencer marketing has a positive impact on search engine optimization (SEO) rankings, particularly when influencers mention a brand in blogs or videos. This generates high-quality backlinks to the brand's website that major search engines reward. Traffic to the website is therefore highly targeted and helps brands cut through noise online and reach targeted audiences (HubSpot, n.d.), resulting in greater potential for conversions and brand advocacy through consumer word of mouth (WOM).

Nonetheless, marketers who run campaigns in-house have cited finding influencers to participate in their campaigns as the 'most significant' challenge they face, and have ranked this as their top concern when planning influencer marketing campaigns (Influencer Marketing Hub, 2023). The management of influencer marketing has multiple stages and can be a time-consuming and difficult process. It involves: detailed planning and objective setting; identifying key criteria for influencer selection; preparation and co-ordination of campaign briefs and contractual agreements; content creation and campaign implementation; and a post-campaign evaluation stage to measure performance (Mero et al., 2023). It is therefore a challenging and laborious landscape to navigate, plan, and manage that requires considerable knowledge, expertise, and investment. In the rapidly evolving landscape of influencer marketing, agencies can play a pivotal role in addressing these challenges and connecting brands with influencers.

Case Study: The Irish Blogger Agency

The Irish Blogger Agency is Ireland's first dedicated agency for influencer marketing. Its CEO, Sinéad Carroll, established the agency in 2015 following 15 years in the banking and finance sector. Sinéad, always had a passion for creativity, design, and fashion, and very quickly immersed herself in the digital world, running her successful fashion and lifestyle blog, Yummy Mummy Fashion, and founding the successful Into the West Blogger Network in 2014. Having experienced first-hand the power of influencer marketing (before the concept became a household term), and following many requests from brands asking her to connect them with 'the right people', Sinéad spotted a gap in the market, which was to be the bridge connecting brands and influencers. Drawing on her entrepreneurial mindset, she set up Mini Media, a digital marketing and web design company. Its success led to the creation of the Irish Blogger Agency, a dedicated agency providing influencer marketing solution services to companies, specializing in micro- and macro-influencers.

Sinéad formed a partnership with Swedish company Mikz Alliance, which developed an online business-to-business (B2B) marketplace for influencer marketing by linking influencers with brands through sophisticated data-driven technology. This has enabled the Irish Blogger Agency to access a revenue-generating 'influencer ecosystem' that facilitates identifying relevant influencers, strategizing, and managing and executing campaigns as well as post-campaign analysis reports. Currently the platform has 881 influencers, with a global reach of over 18 million. The Irish Blogger Agency is the only Irish member with access to this platform, and is currently Ireland's leading agency for micro-influencers. Through strategic collaboration, brands and influencers can forge authentic connections aligned with campaign objectives and drive meaningful engagement with target audiences efficiently and with measurable impact.

Connecting Brands and Influencers

The Irish Blogger Agency has a significant network of influencers from a vast number of sectors, including beauty, food, fashion, lifestyle, entertainment, business, and many more. The technology facilitates a user journey that is simple and seamlessly integrated into a streamlined and consistent experience for both brand and influencer. The flexibility of the technology enables the brand or the influencer to control who they connect with, as well as campaign brief development, pricing, implementation, and measurement. The process is relatively straightforward and does not require specialized technical skillsets.

- **Brand sign-up**: A brand signs up with Irish Blogger Agency through its influencer marketing platform, they create an account and search among thousands of influencers from around the globe. There are filters available in the screening process to help find the right influencer for a campaign – for example, gender, engagement rate, location, interests, platforms, media channels, etc. The brand can create a campaign, set a budget, select and invite influencers for the campaign, and also hire the influencer through the platform after exchanges and agreement on the brief. The terms and conditions (T&Cs) are also agreed prior to campaign launch. Post-campaign analytics are accessible and available to share.
- **Influencer sign-up**: This follows a similar process – influencers create an account on the platform, to which they link their current live social media platforms, websites, and/or blogs. After selecting an agency to work with, they will be alerted to any campaigns that go live on the platform, and T&Cs are also agreed. The price of the activity is based on analysis of a number of factors, such the influencers, the audience, total visibility, the production budget, demand, and brand value.

If the brand is experienced in influencer marketing, understands the process of campaign development, and in a position to identify influencers who align with the brand during the selection process, the potential to expand market reach, build brand awareness, and funnel traffic directly to the client company can be realized relatively quicker and with less effort than it takes to build an audience from scratch. However, for businesses that are still exploring this relatively new form of marketing, it can be a daunting task. If services/products are specialized and have high levels of credence attributes can be difficult for a firm to articulate its needs or evaluate the outcome of the service/product prior to purchase. Smaller businesses or brands that are new to the market, that have very limited or no prior experience of digital marketing, are more willing to employ the consultancy services of a third-party agency to provide an end-to-end solution (Vize et al., 2013). The Irish Blogger Agency has the digital marketing expertise and experience, the technical skillset, industry knowledge, and network connections necessary to traverse the complexities of influencer partnerships and campaign management on behalf of clients. Its main goal is to ensure the influencer promoting a brand is a strong champion of the brand even before the commercial partnership is accepted.

Managerial Recommendations

This chapter offers many important insights that will help marketing managers better understand, implement, and manage influencer marketing strategies. It is important to recognize that one size does not fit all when considering integrating influencer marketing as a persuasive communications tool. A lot of work needs to be done at all stages of the process – that is, management and assessment before, during, and after a campaign (Tafesse & Wien, 2018). The following sections describe areas of consideration and offers recommendations for brand marketers when embarking on the road to influencer marketing.

Pre-Campaign Planning

Define Marketing Goals and Target Audience

Prior to looking for a specific influencer, the brand should have a well-defined vision of its marketing goals (Effing & Spil, 2016). Common marketing goals include increase brand awareness, drive engagement, boost sales and revenue, enhance brand reputation, launch a new product, or simply increase social media followers. Sinéad Carroll of the Irish Blogger Agency suggests that knowing what you want to achieve and who you want to reach will help you narrow your search and find influencers who can help you reach your goals. Scanning and researching influencers who not only have an engaged following and create content that aligns with the brand's values, but who also work in the brand's industry or niche are important parts of the pre-selection process.

Influencer Selection: Evaluate and Connect

When evaluating influencers, it is important to analyse their engagement rate as it is a good indicator of how active and engaged their followers are (De Veirman et al., 2017; Tafesse & Wood, 2021). Evaluate their audience demographic to align fit between the brand's intended target audience and the influencer's followers. Influencers who have worked with brands of similar status and have created content that aligns with the firm's brand values are more likely to be selected as part of the consideration set in the search for the right influencer. Sinéad Carroll asserts that the key to building relationships with influencers is simple. She suggests getting them to pay attention to you before you need something from them – that is, follow, share, and comment. Follow them on social media pages or wherever there is most activity; increase engagement by sharing posts and social media updates; add comments and start discussions – become visible and noticeable. This can be done by adding insights, asking questions, or expanding on the influencer's advice. Do this regularly and consistently, but not to overdo it.

Once the influencer knows who you are, it is time to connect. Once connections have been established, specify what you can offer. Share marketing goals and discuss opportunities. It is important not to focus solely on what the influencer can give you, but also to think about what you can offer in return. Building a relationship with the influencer can help ensure a successful collaboration and long-term partnership (Breves et al., 2019; Mero et al., 2023).

Set a Budget and Price a Campaign

Pricing an influencer campaign can be complex and dependent on several factors, such as size, engagement rate of the influencer's following, the type of content they will create, and the duration of the campaign. Generally, influencers with larger numbers of followers and high engagement rates will charge more for their services (IAB, 2018). A simple Instagram post will be less expensive than a full video production, photo shoot, live stream, or omni-channel campaign. Longer campaigns are less expensive on a per-post basis but may require greater total investment, and usage rights need to be agreed early on. The usage rights the brand requires for the influencer's content, such as the ability to reuse it in further campaign, may also impact costs (Appel et al., 2020).

Contractual Agreements: Terms and Conditions

A legal document that outlines the T&Cs agreed between the brand and the influencer is essential prior to hiring (Tafesse & Wien, 2018). The agreement may include:

- **Deliverables**: a list of specific content that the influencer is responsible for, such as posts, stories, reels, or videos. It should also include deadlines for each.
- **Compensation**: what the influencer will receive for their services, whether a flat fee, a fee per post, or a gift.
- **Usage rights**: what rights the brand has to the influencer's content, including the ability to reuse the content in future campaigns.
- **Disclosure requirements**: content must comply with advertising regulations – for example, #ad #sp #gift #collab #paidpartnership.
- **Confidentiality clause**: provisions for protecting confidential information shared between the parties.
- **Governing law and jurisdiction**: this will apply in the event of a legal dispute.
- **Signatures**: both parties must sign the agreement to indicate their acceptance of the terms and conditions.

Campaign Implementation Stage: Manage and Monitor

Prepare and Co-ordinate Content and Platform

Here it is necessary to specify the parameters of the campaign, be clear about expectations, and be willing to compromise. It is important to set out clear guidelines prior to launch so that the influencer can create content that aligns with the campaign goals – for example, core message, tone of the creatives, hashtags, URLs, content type (reel, story, post, video. etc.). However, there should be enough room for the influencer's creativity to be visible during the campaign to maintain their personality and authenticity with followers (Tafesse & Wien, 2018). Content is typically tailored to fit the culture of specific social media platforms, but sometimes it may need to be co-created and distributed via the brand's channels, in which case the firm's target audience and the campaign idea should guide platform choice (Breves et al., 2019).

Post-Campaign Evaluation Stage

To assess the performance of the influencer marketing campaign a number of metrics should be utilized (Influencer Marketing Hub, 2023; Primasiwi et al., 2021). These could include:

- **Impressions**: the number of times the content was viewed
- **Engagement**: the content generated comments, shares, likes, video views, podcast listeners
- **Conversions**: the number of people taking a desired action, such as purchases, sign-ups, and subscriptions
- **Brand sentiment**: the overall perception of the brand among the target audience aligned with hashtags and mentions.

Post-campaign evaluation is important on many levels. For example, it assists with evaluating return on investment for brand awareness, engagement, and sales. Interrogation of performance data helps identify the best-performing influencers as well as providing deeper insights into audience behaviour. This information also helps marketing managers identify areas for improvement, therefore putting them in a better position to optimize future influencer marketing campaign strategies (Kostyk & Huhmann, 2021; Borges-Tiago et al., 2023).

Conclusion

The commercialization of influencer marketing has led to a proliferation of ordinary individuals with a keen interest in a specific topic, hobby, or product/service category looking to become 'influencers'. Additionally, professionalization of the sector has led to an increase in marketing agencies and brands focusing on influencer marketing as a communications tactic (Ooi et al., 2023). The key difference between influencers and A-list celebrities is the close connections they share with their audiences and followers (Borges-Tiago et al., 2023). Influencer marketing will continue to gain momentum in the coming years. There is a recognition that the advertising industry must adapt to this new reality of interactive content, emerging technologies, and social media platforms as well as to the production, consumption, and co-creative methods of marketing. The effectiveness of the influencer market cannot be ignored by marketing managers. They need to recognize this and prepare to embrace influencer marketing within their marketing and communications campaigns, and to consider how this emerging marketing method may improve their overall brand strategies and performance goals (Influencer Marketing Hub, 2023; Ooi et al., 2023). Utilizing the services of a third-party agency that specializes in influencer marketing might just be the connection needed to build successful influencer marketing partnerships going forward.

Discussion Questions

1. Describe the opportunities and challenges a firm may experience when adopting influencer marketing.
2. You are hired as a digital marketing campaign manager for a fast-moving consumer goods (FMCG) brand. Develop a step-by-step guide for the communications team to help execute successful influencer marketing campaigns for the brand.

References

Appel, G., Grewal, L., Hadi, R., & Stephen, A. T. (2020). The future of social media in marketing. *Journal of the Academy of Marketing Science*, *48*(1), 79–95. https://doi.org/10.1007/s11747-019-00695-1

Belanche, D., Casaló, L. V., Flavián, M., & Ibáñez-Sánchez, S. (2021). Building influencers' credibility on Instagram: Effects on followers' attitudes and behavioral responses toward the influencer. *Journal of Retailing and Consumer Services*, *61*. https://doi.org/10.1016/j.jretconser.2021.102585

Boerman, S. C. (2020). The effects of the standardized Instagram disclosure for micro- and meso-influencers. *Computers in Human Behavior*, *103*, 199–207. https://doi.org/10.1016/j.chb.2019.09.015

Borges-Tiago, M. T., Santiago, J., & Tiago, F. (2023). Mega or macro social media influencers: Who endorses brands better? *Journal of Business Research*, *157*, 113606. https://doi.org/10.1016/j.jbusres.2022.113606

Breves, L. P., Liebers, N., Abt, M., & Kunze, A. (2019). The perceived fit between Instagram influencers and the endorsed brand: How influencer-brand fit affects source credibility and persuasive effectiveness. *Journal of Advertising Research, 59*(4), 440–454. https://doi.org/10.2501/JAR-2019-030

Campbell, C., & Farrell, J. R. (2020). More than meets the eye: The functional components underlying influencer marketing. *Business Horizons, 63*(4), 469–479. https://doi.org/10.1016/j.bushor.2020.03.003

Cartwright, S., Liu, H., & Raddats, C. (2021). Strategic use of social media within business-to-business (B2B) marketing: A systematic literature review. *Industrial Marketing Management, 97*, 35–58. https://doi.org/10.1016/j.indmarman.2021.06.005

Conde, R., & Casais, B. (2023). Micro, macro and mega-influencers on Instagram: The power of persuasion via the parasocial relationship. *Journal of Business Research, 158*. https://doi.org/10.1016/j.jbusres.2023.113708

de Oliveira Santini, F., Ladeira, W. J., Pinto, D. C., Herter, M. M., Sampaio, C. H., & Babin, B. J. (2020). Customer engagement in social media: A framework and meta-analysis. *Journal of the Academy of Marketing Science, 48*(6), 1211–1228. https://doi.org/10.1007/s11747-020-00731-5

De Veirman, M., Cauberghe, V., & Hudders, L. (2017). Marketing through Instagram influencers: The impact of number of followers and product divergence on brand attitude. *International Journal of Advertising, 36*(5), 798–828. https://doi.org/10.1080/02650487.2017.1348035

Effing, R., & Spil, T. A. M. (2016). The social strategy cone: Towards a framework for evaluating social media strategies. *International Journal of Information Management, 36*(1), 1–8. https://doi.org/10.1016/j.ijinfomgt.2015.07.009

Haenlein, M., Anadol, E., Farnsworth, T., Hugo, H., Hunichen, J., & Welte, D. (2020). Navigating the new era of influencer marketing: How to be successful on Instagram, TikTok, & Co. *California Management Review, 63*(1), 5–25. https://doi.org/10.1177/0008125620958166

He, A., Zink, N., Roeschke, L., Tassin, C., Tran, K., & Moquin, E. (2024). *Report: How brands can succeed at influencer marketing*. Morning Consult. https://pro.morningconsult.com/analyst-reports/influencer-marketing-trends-report

HubSpot. (n.d.). *What is inbound marketing?* https://www.hubspot.com/inbound-marketing

Hudders, L., De Jans, S., & De Veirman, M. (2021). The commercialization of social media stars: A literature review and conceptual framework on the strategic use of social media influencers. *International Journal of Advertising, 40*(3), 327–375. https://doi.org/10.1080/02650487.2020.1836925

IAB. (2018). *Inside influence: Why publishers are increasingly turning to influencer marketing and what that means for marketers. Interactive Advertising Bureau.* https://www.iab.com/wp-content/uploads/2018/01/IAB_Influencer_Marketing_for_Publishers_2018-01-25.pdf

Influencer Marketing Hub. (2023). *The state of influencer marketing 2023: Influencer marketing benchmarking report.* https://influencermarketinghub.com/ebooks/Influencer_Marketing_Benchmark_Report_2023.pdf

Kim, D. Y., & Kim, H. Y. (2021). Trust me, trust me not: A nuanced view of influencer marketing on social media. *Journal of Business Research, 134*, 223–232. https://doi.org/10.1016/j.jbusres.2021.05.024

Kostyk, A., & Huhmann, B. A. (2021). Perfect social media image posts: Symmetry and contrast influence consumer response. *European Journal of Marketing, 55*(6), 1747–1779. https://doi.org/10.1108/EJM-09-2018-0629

Leung, F. F., Gu, F. F., & Palmatier, R. W. (2022). Online influencer marketing. *Journal of the Academy of Marketing Science, 50*(2), 226–251. https://doi.org/10.1007/s11747-021-00829-4

Lou, C., & Yuan, S. (2019). Influencer marketing: How message value and credibility affect consumer trust of branded content on social media. *Journal of Interactive Advertising, 19*(1), 58–73. https://doi.org/10.1080/15252019.2018.1533501

Markets and Markets (2024). *Influencer marketing platform market report.* https://www.marketsandmarkets.com/Market-Reports/influencer-marketing-platform-market-294138.html

Mero, J., Vanninen, H., & Keränen, J. (2023). B2B influencer marketing: Conceptualization and four managerial strategies. *Industrial Marketing Management, 108*, 79–93. https://doi.org/10.1016/j.indmarman.2022.10.017

Ohanian, R. (1990). Construction and validation of a scale to measure celebrity endorsers' perceived expertise, trustworthiness, and attractiveness. *Journal of Advertising, 19*(3), 39–52. https://doi.org/10.1080/00913367.1990.10673191

Ooi, K. B., Lee, V. H., Hew, J. J., Leong, L. Y., Tan, G. W. H., & Lim, A. F. (2023). Social media influencers: An effective marketing approach? *Journal of Business Research, 160*, 113773. https://doi.org/10.1016/j.jbusres.2023.113773

Primasiwi, C., Irawan, M. I., & Ambarwati, R. (2021). Key performance indicators for influencer marketing on Instagram. In *Proceedings of the 2nd International Conference on Business and Management of Technology (ICONBMT 2020)* (pp. 154–163). Dordrecht: Atlantis Press.

Rishi, B., & Bandyopadhyay, S. (Eds.). (2018). *Contemporary issues in social media marketing*. London: Routledge.

Santiago, E. (2023, March 20). *The state of content marketing in 2023 [Stats & trends to watch]*. HubSpot. https://blog.hubspot.com/marketing/state-of-content-marketing-infographic

Tafesse, W., & Wien, A. (2018). Implementing social media marketing strategically: An empirical assessment. *Journal of Marketing Management, 34*(9–10), 732–749. https://doi.org/10.1Figure080/0267257X.2018.1482365

Tafesse, W., & Wood, B. P. (2021). Followers' engagement with Instagram influencers: The role of influencers' content and engagement strategy. *Journal of Retailing and Consumer Services*, *58*, 102303. https://doi.org/10.1016/j.jretconser.2020.102303

Vize, R., Coughlan, J., Kennedy, A., & Ellis-Chadwick, F. (2013). Technology readiness in a B2B online retail context: An examination of antecedents and outcomes. *Industrial Marketing Management*, *42*(6), 909–918. https://doi.org/10.1016/j.indmarman.2013.05.020

Ye, G., Hudders, L., De Jans, S., & De Veirman, M. (2021). The value of influencer marketing for business: A bibliometric analysis and managerial implications. *Journal of Advertising*, *50*(2), 160–178. https://doi.org/10.1080/00913367.2020.1857888

Mapping the B2B Customer Journey through Social Media Marketing 9

Deepa Kapoor, Ruchi Khandelwal and Sujata Khandai
Amity School of Business, Amity University, Uttar Pradesh, India

Introduction

The art of selling may sound familiar, but it has been the most elusive and evolving topic in marketing since its inception. Markets change, customers change, paradigms change, and so do the process and techniques of selling. Business-to-consumer (B2C) selling is a widely researched and discussed topic in academia as the process involved is clearly visible, However, since business-to-business (B2B) selling has traditionally taken place within the confines of retail or purchasing organisations, it is invisible to the public at large. However, in the digital world, as B2B marketing has become more open and transparent, the interest of researchers in exploring these strategies has increased enormously.

Digital media has provided an array of tools that companies have begun to use to connect and engage with customers (Rishi & Bandyopadhyay, 2018). Customers, on the other hand, have also been impacted through this new method of buying and selling, and their customer journey has taken a new turn. Companies began to engage customers through blogs, video content, social forums, online communities, 24/7 online support, product

DOI: 10.4324/9781003412656-9

demos, influencers, employee advocacy, etc. This chapter gives an overview of the B2B customer journey and how it has been impacted by the evolution of social media. It further discusses case studies of a few industry giants that have used social media marketing successfully in engaging customers at each stage of their journey, offering relevant communication and aiding their decision-making.

B2B and B2C Selling

Businesses are realizing the opportunities to capture the market both in the B2B and the B2C domains. Although the potential is immense in both worlds and marketing principles are similar, doing business in these two domains varies and each has its own challenges. Both domains are highly competitive. For example, in the B2C arena, companies might invest in creating distinct brand images, whereas in B2B the focus might be more on offering memorable experiences and building relationships that can engage customers for long periods and result in sustained business.

Customers make decisions differently in the B2B and B2C domains, and this is the essence of the marketing approach used by companies toward them. As the customer's buying journey shapes up differently, companies a variety of tools and processes in dealing with them. B2B sales typically take longer and involve more effort than B2C sales, but the rewards they generate in the form of volume and potential profit are comparatively greater.

Further, what differentiates these two domains is their approach to buying. While B2C customers normally make their own decisions, they may be influenced by peers and others. In contrast, B2B decision-making involves a number of people, each of whom has to be influenced through a focused approach to marketing communication and selling. It has also been proposed in the literature that B2C decisions may sometimes be emotional but that B2B decisions are largely rational (Saha et al., 2014). Another striking difference between these two approaches is the predominance of the marketing message (Rėklaitis & Pilelienė, 2019): communication content is primarily selling-focused in B2C and information-rich in B2B. One common factor, however, is the emergence and increasing prevalence of online and digital tools for communication, both in B2B and B2C. The applicability and use of these tools may again differ in these two domains.

The B2B Customer Journey

Significance of Customer Journey

According to Towers and Towers (2022), the customer journey refers to the engagement of customers with several types of touchpoint in the decision-making process. The concept is relevant from the perspective of understanding consumer behaviour and designing effective marketing strategies as it can enrich and broaden traditional research on organisational buying (Sheth, 1973). The journey reflects a detailed map of how customer awareness is generated – the number of encounters that customers experience from purchase to post-purchase. Businesses need to study the customer journey to improve these experiences.

Research shows that, rather than focusing on the entire customer journey, companies generally focus on individual customer touchpoints. The majority of the existing literature covers the customer journey in parts rather than presenting all the touchpoints (Baxendale et al. 2015). It is therefore imperative for businesses to study and analyse various phases of the customer journey as it is complex and impacted by a range of factors. A deeper understanding of the customer journey can help organisations improve their customers' experiences: "Identifying the journeys that matter most can be beneficial even when companies don't have a nagging customer service problem – the effort can help them find a competitive differentiator" (Rawson et al., 2013).

In numerous studies, attempts have been made to generalise B2B buying patterns (Lemon & Verhoef, 2016; Steward et al., 2019, Witell et al., 2020). B2B buying is divided into multiple linear stages showing information-seeking or decision-making behaviour of buyers, and includes both pre- and post-purchase stages (Johnston & Lewin, 1996). The customer journey concept is customer-centric and studying it can help B2B marketers develop a comprehensive understanding of an organisation's individual members' purchasing paths and a broader view of buyers' purchasing process comprising various touchpoints (Edelman & Singer, 2015; Jaakkola & Terho, 2021). Building on the knowledge of these touchpoints, B2B firms can create and deliver more customised customer experiences (Figure 9.1). The B2B customer journey is long and complex, with customers going through a variety of experiences to reach their goals (Becker & Jaakkola, 2020). With buyers having access to information from numerous digital sources, the customer journey concept has gained considerable importance for understanding buyers' decision-making process.

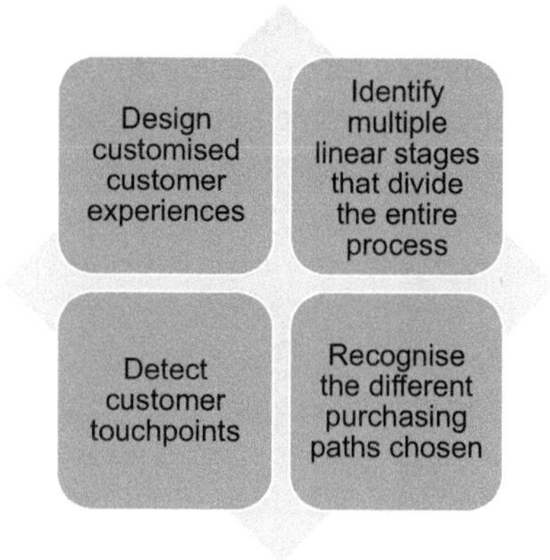

Figure 9.1 Significance of studying the B2B customer journey

Stages of the Customer Journey

Research shows that an organisation's purchasing process is increasingly complex and mostly non-linear, with B2B buyers going through numerous digital and social touchpoints in their journey – from awareness to purchase to post-purchase (Herhausen et al., 2019; Lundin & Kindström, 2023; Mele & Russo-Spena, 2022). Each touchpoint in the journey serves a distinct purpose, depending on the specific stage at which the customer is interacting; therefore, touchpoints should be treated differently as they solve problems through supporting activities such as gathering information, facilitating payment, and so on (Rusthollkarhu et al., 2022). In the service sector, the customer journey is part of a provision process, and includes customer engagement in value generation and value consumption. This involves both consumer and service provider, and includes the delivery and consumption of services.

The relevant literature not only emphasises the customer's perspective but also highlights the supplier's processes such as designing, analysing the journey, guiding, and engaging customers during the journey. From the customer's perspective, the journey emphasises the role of decision-making in the value-creation process of identifying and finding solutions. From the provider's perspective, the customer journey conceptualises sales and marketing processes that are important for the provider's value capture logic. The literature shows that it is easier to understand the structure of customer journeys when they are divided into stages – for example, pre-core, core, and post-core service encounters (Voorhees et al., 2017) or pre-purchase,

purchase, and post-purchase interactions. Progression through the customer journey is usually divided into phases and can be studied as relational processes designed to meet customer needs (Witell et al., 2020; Hamilton et al., 2021). Current literature suggests that customer journeys are changing, with recurring cycles and loyalty loops and a shift in focus from a purchase decision to a long-term iterative process (De Keyser et al., 2020; Siebert et al. 2020).

It is important to map customer journeys using timelines. The stages depend on the type of product or service, are recurrent, and can be defined as discovery, research, purchase, delivery, and after-sales – that is, from pre-purchase to post-purchase. Studies indicate that product usage may act as a base for initialising a new journey. Two kinds of B2B buying situations are observed: one that starts as a new journey; and the continuation of that journey. The customer journey has been described through three stages of the buying process – pre-purchase, purchase, and post-purchase – that can also be considered as comprising five stages: consider, evaluate, buy, loyalty loop, and new journey (Edelman & Singer, 2015). Consider and evaluate represent the pre-purchase stage; buy is the purchase stage; and the loyalty loop phase is associated with both the purchase and the post-purchase stage. The key stages of the journey generally involve awareness, consideration, purchase, and retention and advocacy (Figure 9.2), although the specifics may vary depending on the industry, market, and individual customer preferences.

The characteristics of the buying process have changed from just focusing on individual transactions to maintaining customer relationships and networks throughout the journey. The best part is that maintaining relationships

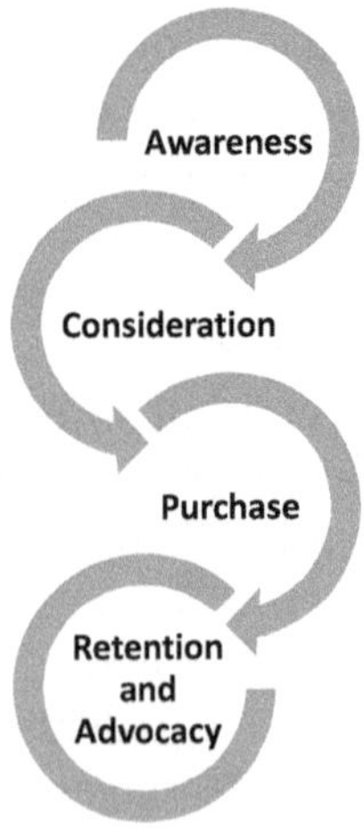

Figure 9.2 Stages of the B2B customer journey

is no longer the responsibility of the supplier alone but of the customer too, so it is crucial to manage buyer–seller relationships for both parties. Business customer journeys can vary as per relationships: transactional relationships tend to be short term, whereas relational ones are long term. This in turn can have an impact on profitability (Lindgreen et al., 2006).

The Impact of Digitalisation on the B2B Customer Journey

There has been a drastic change in B2B sales as interactions between buyers and sellers due to the rise of digital channels. Advances in information technology (IT) have brought about changes in customer behaviour and made customers' paths non-linear and complex. B2B buyers rely heavily on information to support their buying decisions, and increasingly make use of digital sources to collect this information at different stages. They use various keywords and browse multiple web pages seeking information about sellers before executing a deal.

Since buyers are increasingly engaged in information searches, B2B marketers have a massive amount of behavioural data about customers at their disposal for effective decision-making. Data enables a better understanding of the customer buying journey. The availability of big data is of great help to buyers and sellers in analysing complex customer behaviour and understanding the customer journey through technological interactions. Competition among B2B suppliers has been triggered by digitalisation as buyers have more options and are no longer dependent on specific geographical location.

The B2B environment today provides new opportunities for conducting businesses using digital platforms that generate massive amounts of information that can be analysed by B2B marketers to create more customer-centric marketing strategies (Marvasti et al., 2021). With millennials and Gen Z entering decision-making positions in their businesses, the role of selling through digital platforms has increased over time.

The Adoption of Social Media by B2B Organisations

Recently there has been a surge in research in both academia and industry on the role of social media in supporting product development, sales, customer service, and building brands generally (Michaelidou et al., 2011). With more user-generated content (UGC) on social media, social media has become more trustworthy as an information source than other communication platforms, which is reflected in customers relying heavily on social media to gather information about products and services.

Social media marketing in the B2C context has shown that customers today are more connected to each other, which has greater implications for the market. The same applies as a reason to adopt social media in a B2B setting as customer expectations are evolving; they now expect better experiences using new technologies. Although social media marketing is still at a nascent stage in the B2B context, businesses are recognising its benefits as it can be used effectively for a number of marketing activities, for example, by generating electronic word-of-mouth (eWOM), which is more cost-effective than traditional methods for scaling up brand awareness in a short time.

Businesses have improved their social media presence to increase engagement and build trust among customers by creating awareness and showcasing their expertise. Further, social media can be used to identify and attract new business partners and to improve communication and interaction with customers. By using social media platforms, B2B marketers can respond to various queries and connect emotionally with customers. In addition, social media analytics can reveal the position of both the business and its competitors, which can help in understanding customer problems and needs. Social media marketing as a communication channel helps in developing better relationships with partners, leading to trust and loyalty (Agnihotri et al., 2012).

Adoption of social media can create positive attitudes toward brands and higher purchase intention among customers as compared to traditional media. Marketers are extensively using social media platforms as marketing communication tools as they generate high word-of-mouth by expanding the reach of messages and making them go viral. It is therefore crucial for B2B marketers to implement social media tools as they lead to increased interaction and help manage resource limitation through improved buyer and seller relationships. One of the main issues for B2B companies is lead generation. Social media platforms help in getting better leads by providing opportunities for marketers to target key decision-makers by reinforcing brand image. Implementing effective social media marketing strategies supports search engine optimisation (SEO) and overall content marketing efforts. Platforms such as Facebook and LinkedIn provide tools for B2B marketers to acquire qualified leads and connect with existing business partners creatively.

B2B brands encourage customers to share new and innovative ideas on their social media platforms, supporting organisational innovation. Social media results in better performance and gives companies a competitive advantage by building resources. Research shows that the adoption of the latest technologies and social media sites such as X (formerly Twitter), LinkedIn, and Facebook is higher in innovative B2B organisations, with evidence of a positive correlation between company innovation and the use of X in small and medium-sized enterprises (SMEs) (Wamba & Carter, 2013).

Online interactions provide valuable feedback to marketers, which helps them improve engagement with existing customers and reach out to new customers. Data generated through social media is used to tailor companies' offerings as per customer needs, adding to business partners' value. Figure 9.3 gives a brief overview of various digital tools that a B2B marketer can use through the four stages of the customer journey, depending on company focus and customer requirements.

The overall impact of customisation can lead to higher sales and return on investment (ROI) over time. Social media marketing supports B2B marketing in achieving the following goals:

- Boosting sales
- Increasing market share
- Retaining and improving customer loyalty
- Customer engagement
- Earning customers' trust
- Reputation building.

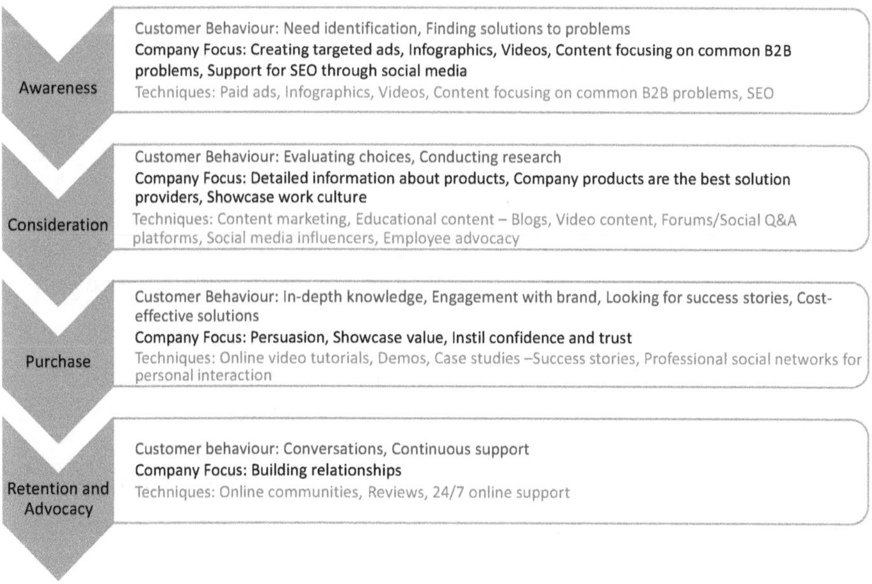

Figure 9.3 B2B marketer's online toolkit

Challenges to Adopting Social Media in B2B Marketing

The majority of CEOs of B2B companies believe that social media is not right for them. Although social media marketing offers numerous advantages in B2B selling, there are several barriers to its adoption in B2B businesses (Buehrer et al., 2005). Swani et al. (2014) suggest that one of the key challenges is implementing successful social media strategies. This can be attributed partly to lack of knowledge on how to use social media sites for achieving B2B marketing goals. Adoption of social media in the B2B sector is slow because marketers lack positive attitudes towards its usefulness. They consider social media platforms more appropriate for the B2C than the B2B sector. There is a misconception among B2B marketers that social media tools do not fit the B2B context as prospective customers rely more heavily on face-to-face interaction. It is believed that business partners require a personal approach to building relationships, which is not possible in an online environment. There is a lack of personal touch in online marketing, which is a must in converting leads to final customers and building long-term relationships (Michaelidou et al., 2011).

Another factor that hinders the adoption of social media is the fear of losing personal confidential information. Lack of control over information exchange on social media platforms is restricting its use as losing information to competitors will have a negative impact on B2B sales. One of the benefits of social media is providing opportunities for two-way communication, which is perceived as a drawback by B2B marketers leading to the non-usability of social media platforms.

Case Studies

The following case studies exemplify how various companies have made use of social media marketing to enhance engagement during the customer journey.

Cisco: Connecting through Brand Storytelling

In the words of American advertising executive Bill Bernbach, "If you don't have a good story, you are not going to have a good ad" (Dixit, 2023). Although storytelling is difficult to implement in the B2B sector, it is very effective. Research shows that almost 50 per cent of B2B customers will buy if they emotionally connect with a brand. Brand storytelling as a communication method utilises stories to establish connections with existing and prospective customers. By sharing simple human stories, businesses engage emotionally with their customers, which in turn increases brand affinity and boosts sales. Brand storytelling can be done through various mediums, such as videos, infographics, blogs, and case studies. It is important for brands to select a format that resonates deeply with the prospective target audience.

Strategy

As a pioneer in brand storytelling, American multinational digital communications technology conglomerate Cisco has used digital stories to engage audiences for years. It launched "The Network", a website featuring news stories about technology, in 2011 and produced *The Network Effect*, a documentary series about the history and future of telecoms, in 2012.

Cisco employs storytelling to make its complex services more relatable to businesses. Its content marketing campaign "Never Better" showcases interactive digital stories that illustrate how organisations from across industries leverage Cisco's technology for their benefit. Each story begins with "There's never been a better time ..." and is presented in the form of written content, images, and documentary-style videos on an infographic-style web page. This campaign highlights real cases from customers and partners. Cisco demonstrates how its technology is revolutionizing industries and countries, from providing access to clean water to making jobs safer and cities smarter. Content sections encourage readers to explore deeper and uncover strong storylines about the issues faced by various companies and how Cisco technology has enabled its clients to innovate. A two-page case study for potential customers is transformed into a storytelling journey, leaving readers to "turn the page" and acquire additional knowledge about the company.

Results

The campaign secured more than 723,000 engagements, 34,000 partnership activations, and 300 million social comments (Enderle, 2021). "Never Better" has experienced a steady stream of positive responses from media channels and users due to its unique blend of human interactivity and technological precision.

Case Questions

- How does incorporating brand storytelling into various touchpoints along the customer journey enhance the overall customer experience?
- What role does brand storytelling play in shaping customers' perceptions and emotions throughout their journey with a brand?
- How does brand storytelling contribute to building trust and credibility with customers, especially in B2B industries?

IBM Voices: Engagement through Employee Advocacy

This case illustrates how to improve brand engagement through influencer marketing. Research indicates that 77 per cent of B2B marketers believe that their potential customers seek guidance from industry professionals, and 74 per cent agree that implementing influencer marketing strategies enhances the overall experience of customers and prospects with the brand (TopRank Marketing, 2020). B2B may involve selling to businesses, but decision-makers are people. People want human interaction: they buy from people, not from brands; whether B2C or B2B, customers trust individual opinions more than formal company advertisements. It has been observed that B2B brands implementing employee advocacy have higher engagement than brands that do not. Employees sharing corporate information on their personal social media profiles helps enhance the company's presence and reputation. Employee advocacy adds the experiences of individuals to the company's marketing strategy.

Implementation

The company's advocacy programme, "IBM Voices", encourages employees to share content on social media and other platforms. It provides "IBMers" with relevant coaching and assistance to promote its brand on social media. In addition to external influencers, IBM has been focusing on its own employees to talk about the brand to connect with target audiences. Attention has shifted slightly, away from brand content to subject matter experts and other developers within the company possessing extensive knowledge about its products and services.

Through this programme, employees can share valuable content, industry knowledge, and cutting-edge innovations. By elevating their voices, in addition to promoting IBM's expertise and innovative solutions, employees strengthen their personal branding. This method is a powerful combination of personal and company branding. IBM's employees serve as genuine brand ambassadors, amplifying the company's message and values. This creates a strong emotional bond with customers, which in turn significantly improves brand perception, fostering trust and loyalty among IBM's global customers.

Results

Content posted by an employee in this scheme attracts much better engagement than through any other channel of a brand. There are 500 thought leaders in the IBM Voices programme, and leads generated through employee advocacy have a seven-fold conversion rate compared to other leads (Raman & Raman, 2024).

Case Questions

- How can organisations use social media platforms to enhance the influence of employee advocacy programmes?
- What obstacles can companies face when trying to establish employee advocacy programmes, and what strategies can be employed to overcome them?

HubSpot: Conversions through Demos and Video Tutorials

In the B2B scenario, software solutions have a profound influence, affecting multiple teams and business segments. Specifically, complex software necessitates training and changes to management, which demands substantial support from the entire organisation. The importance of software demonstrations becomes apparent in such situations, as they are often the difference between signing a contract and losing a lead. A good interactive product demo allows leads to see how a company can resolve their issues.

Strategy

HubSpot offers an all-in-one customer relationship management (CRM) solution for sales, marketing, and inbound marketing. It is designed to help align the company's sales and marketing efforts, increase sales enablement and ROI, and optimise inbound marketing strategies to generate more qualified leads. It helps companies drive traffic, convert leads, and establish customer relationships. With its cloud-based infrastructure, the platform ensures seamless synchronisation of data across teams and devices, guaranteeing instant and automatic updates.

HubSpot's inbound marketing strategy is designed to align with how today's buyers research products or services by providing useful information that informs and engages them along the way. The company aims to guide and inform customers throughout their entire journey. Inbound marketing is all about creating content and experiences that engage and excite potential customers.

HubSpot is one of the best examples in the B2B sector of targeting customers using content creation, providing a wide range of educational content – such as blog posts, videos, webinars, and e-books – to engage potential customers. For example, its YouTube channel (with 368K subscribers and 725 videos at the time of writing) focuses on product demos for target customers. Harnessing the power of interactive demos leads to an impressive 8.5 per cent increase in conversion rates, making it 1.7 times more effective than simple screenshots (Kevens & Marcotullio, 2024). HubSpot has had a lot of success using demos as one of its leading marketing tools; the impact of those demos on potential buyers is undeniable, showcasing their pivotal role in driving successful software sales.

HubSpot has established a robust community of marketers and businesses centred on its platform, emphasising education and collaboration. With a wide range of tools and training programmes, such as HubSpot Academy, it helps businesses hone their marketing skills and keep abreast of industry trends.

The company's social media statistics – whether its YouTube channel, blog, or the HubSpot Academy – show its prominence in inbound marketing, leading to higher conversion rates.

Case Questions

- What types of content perform best in demos and video tutorials for driving conversions?
- What is the role of demos and video tutorials in building customer purchase intention and post-purchase satisfaction?

SAP: Leveraging the Online Community for Customer Support and Advocacy

Online communities provide platforms for B2B customers to interact with customers, whether of the same or other products. They help reduce the burden on customer support teams, and members get several solutions to their queries from these forums. Estimates show that, in effective online communities, companies can reduce their customer support tickets by 50 per cent. In addition, these communities create brand advocates who respond positively to other members, generating huge amounts of user-generated content. Shared stories of one community member can support another member's decision-making.

Strategy

German software multinational SAP launched its online community in 2003 to offer a platform for technical discussion. Later, with an increasing number of members, the community was expanded, providing a platform to share ideas, learn, and connect. SAP's online communities have undergone changes from time to time, with forums acting as places to foster the generation of ideas through crowdsourcing. The forums also provide the benefit of engaging with millions of customers at product or service launches, with information shared utilised to create business cases for future IT investment and implementation.

To ensure quality content in the SAP community, a team of moderators and volunteers review contributions and manage submissions to meet expectations. SAP initiated a points system to motivate members to contribute to the community. In 2013, it introduced missions and badges associated with members who contribute, which, in turn, helped build individual online personas.

The SAP mentor programme is another way it which the company acknowledges its community members. Mentors are considered leaders in the community because they are best at sharing company expertise and support future improvement in its offerings. They also help customers improve their capabilities using SAP technologies by organising events for knowledge sharing.

Results

SAP believes in building solutions and providing continuous support to customers in using those solutions. According to its Community Administrator (craigcmehil, 2023), the community has 2.7 million posts, 798K members, and gets over 3 million unique visitors per month. The SAP community therefore plays a crucial role in the company's global success by providing support for its various partners.

Case Questions

- How do online communities promote a feeling of belonging among customers, resulting in higher brand advocacy?
- How does active participation in online communities play a crucial role in building trust and credibility with customers?
- How can companies use online communities to gain valuable feedback and insights that can be used for product development and other marketing strategies?

Conclusion

The customer journey has changed drastically with digitalisation. Social media platforms offer new touchpoints for engagement, empowering customers with more knowledge. A thorough understanding of the customer journey enables companies to design and deliver personalised experiences across various touchpoints. Having insights into their customers' behaviour and pain points allows companies to cultivate stronger relationships with customers at every stage of the journey. The effective use of various digital tools helps B2B organisations optimise their operations, improve customer satisfaction, and drive business growth across all stages of the customer journey. To harness the power of evolving social media platforms to achieve the best results, B2B companies need to continually adjust their strategies.

There are numerous challenges regarding the adoption of social media marketing for B2B companies; but the benefits associated with creating brand visibility, lead generation, better customer engagement, and better market insights make it worthwhile for businesses to adopt social media and succeed in today's digital era.

References

Agnihotri, R., Kothandaraman, P., Kashyap, R., & Singh, R. (2012). Bringing "social" into sales: The impact of salespeople's social media use on service behaviors and value creation. *Journal of Personal Selling & Sales Management, 32*(3), 333–348.

Baxendale, S., Macdonald, E. K., & Wilson, H. N. (2015). The impact of different touchpoints on brand consideration. *Journal of Retailing, 91*(2), 235–253. https://doi.org/10.1016/j.jretai.2014.12.008

Becker, L., & Jaakkola, E. (2020). Customer experience: Fundamental premises and implications for research. *Journal of the Academy of Marketing Science, 48*(4), 630–648. https://doi.org/10.1007/s11747-019-00718-x

Buehrer, R. E., Senecal, S., & Pullins, E. B. (2005). Sales force technology usage – reasons, barriers, and support: An exploratory investigation. *Industrial Marketing Management*, 34(4), 389–398.

craigcmehil. (2023, August 31). *A new home in the new year for the SAP community.* SAP Community. https://community.sap.com/t5/welcome-corner-blog-posts/a-new-home-in-the-new-year-for-the-sap.community/bc-p/13574448

De Keyser, A., Verleye, K., Lemon, K. N., Keiningham, T. L., & Klaus, P. (2020). Moving the customer experience field forward: Introducing the touchpoints, context, qualities (TCQ) nomenclature. *Journal of Service Research, 23*(4), 433–455. https://doi.org/10.1177/1094670520928390

Edelman, D. C., & Singer, M. (2015). Competing on customer journeys: You have to create new value at every step. *Harvard Business Review, 93*(11), 88.

Dixit, P. (2023, July 10). *Unlock the power of B2B brand storytelling!* Medium. https://medium.com/@pavasdixit/unlock-the-power-of-b2b-brand-storytelling-a4286922002c

Enderle, R. (2021, January 28). *Best practice: How Cisco revitalized its brand.* Datamation. https://www.datamation.com/trends/best-practice-how-cisco-revitalized-its-brand/

Hamilton, R., Ferraro, R., Haws, K. L., & Mukhopadhyay, A. (2021). Traveling with companions: The social customer journey. *Journal of Marketing, 85*(1), 68–92. https://doi.org/10.1177/0022242920908227

Herhausen, D., Kleinlercher, K., Verhoef, P. C., Emrich, O., & Rudolph, T. (2019). Loyalty formation for different customer journey segments. *Journal of Retailing, 95*(3), 9–29. https://doi.org/10.1016/j.jretai.2019.05.001

Jaakkola, E., & Terho, H. (2021). Service journey quality: Conceptualization, measurement and customer outcomes. *Journal of Service Management, 32*(6), 1–27. https://doi.org/10.1108/josm-06-2020-0233

Johnston, W. J., & Lewin, J. E. (1996). Organizational buying behavior: Toward an integrative framework. *Journal of Business Research, 35*(1), 1–15.

Kevens, J., & Marcotullio, N. (2024, February 12). *How interactive demos improve review site product profile pages – with Natalie Marcotullio*. B2B SaaS Reviews. https://b2bsaasreviews.com/interactive-demos-review-site-profiles/

Lemon, K. N., & Verhoef, P. C. (2016). Understanding customer experience throughout the customer journey. *Journal of Marketing, 80*(6), 69–96. https://doi.org/10.1509/jm.15.0420

Lindgreen, A., Palmer, R., Vanhamme, J., & Wouters, J. A. (2006). Relationship-management assessment tool: Questioning, identifying, and prioritizing critical aspects of customer relationships. *Industrial Marketing Management, 35*(1), 57–71.

Lundin, L., & Kindström, D. (2023). Digitalizing customer journeys in B2B markets. *Journal of Business Research, 157*, 113639. https://doi.org/10.1016/j.jbusres.2022.113639

Marvasti, N. B., Huhtala, J. P., Yousefi, Z. R., Vaniala, I., Upreti, B., Malo, P., ... & Tikkanen, H. (2021). Is this company a lead customer? Estimating stages of B2B buying journey. *Industrial Marketing Management, 97*, 126–133.

Mele, C., & Russo-Spena, T. (2022). The architecture of the phygital customer journey: A dynamic interplay between systems of insights and systems of engagement. *European Journal of Marketing, 56*(1), 72–91. https://doi.org/10.1108/ejm-04-2019-0308

Michaelidou, N., Siamagka, N. T., & Christodoulides, G. (2011). Usage, barriers and measurement of social media marketing: An exploratory investigation of small and medium B2B brands. *Industrial Marketing Management, 40*(7), 1153–1159.

Raman, V., & Raman, V. (2024, April 13). *10 stats that prove the importance of employee advocacy*. Neal Schaffer. https://nealschaffer.com/employee-advocacy-statistics/

Rawson, A., Duncan, E., & Jones, C. (2013, September). The truth about customer experience. *Harvard Business Review*. https://hbr.org/2013/09/the-truth-about-customer-experience

Rėklaitis, K., & Pilelienė, L. (2019). Principle differences between B2B and B2C marketing communication processes. *Management of Organizations: Systematic Research, 81*(1), 73–86.

Rishi, B., & Bandyopadhyay, S. (Eds.). (2018). *Contemporary issues in social media marketing*. London: Routledge.

Rusthollkarhu, S., Toukola, S., Aarikka-Stenroos, L., & Mahlamäki, T. (2022). Managing B2B customer journeys in digital era: Four management activities with artificial intelligence-empowered tools. *Industrial Marketing Management, 104*, 241–257. https://doi.org/10.1016/j.indmarman.2022.04.014

Saha, S. K., Aman, A., Hossain, M. S., Islam, A., & Rodela, R. S. (2014). A comparative study on B2B vs. B2C based on Asia Pacific region. *International Journal of Scientific & Technology Research, 3*(9), 294–298.

Sheth, J. N. (1973). A model of industrial buyer behavior. *Journal of Marketing, 37*(4), 50. https://doi.org/10.2307/1250358.

Siebert, A., Gopaldas, A., Lindridge, A., & Simões, C. (2020). Customer experience journeys: Loyalty loops versus involvement spirals. *Journal of Marketing*, 84(4), 45–66. https://doi.org/10.1177/0022242920920262

Steward, M. D., Narus, J. A., Roehm, M. L., & Ritz, W. (2019). From transactions to journeys and beyond: The evolution of B2B buying process modeling. *Industrial Marketing Management*, 83, 288–300.

Swani, K., Brown, B. P. & Milne, G. R. (2014). Should tweets differ for B2B and B2C? An analysis of Fortune 500 companies' Twitter communications. *Industrial Marketing Management*, 43, 873–881.

TopRank Marketing. (2020). *State of B2B influencer marketing report*. http://2020.influencermarketingreport.com/

Towers, A., & Towers, N. (2022). Framing the customer journey: Touch point categories and decision-making process stages. *International Journal of Retail & Distribution Management, 50*(3), 317–341.

Voorhees, C. M., Fombelle, P. W., Gregoire, Y., Bone, S., Gustafsson, A., Sousa, R., & Walkowiak, T. (2017). Service encounters, experiences and the customer journey: Defining the field and a call to expand our lens. *Journal of Business Research, 79*, 269–280.

Wamba, S. F., & Carter, L. (2013). Twitter adoption and use by SMEs: An empirical study in system sciences. In *46th Hawaii International Conference on System Sciences (HISS)* (pp. 2052–2049). https://doi.org/10.1109/HICSS.2013.577

Witell, L., Kowalkowski, C., Perks, H., Raddats, C., Schwabe, M., Benedettini, O., & Burton, J. (2020). Characterizing customer experience management in business markets. *Journal of Business Research*, 116, 420–430.

10

Exploring the Impact of Para-Social Interaction

The Consumer Journey in a Social Media World with a Focus on Virtual Influencers

Bingqian Bai
Manchester Metropolitan University, UK

Gianpaolo Vignali
Manchester Metropolitan University, UK

Daniella Ryding
Manchester Metropolitan University, UK

Delia Vazquez
University of Manchester, UK

1 Introduction

The digital revolution, characterized by the proliferation of platforms such as TikTok and Douyin, has ushered in an era where interactions transcend traditional boundaries, giving rise to the phenomenon of virtual influencers

DOI: 10.4324/9781003412656-10

(Aichner et al., 2021; Cao et al., 2021). These entities, while being digital constructs, play a pivotal role in the intricate web of social media interactions, commanding attention akin to their human counterparts. Their presence raises critical questions about the nature of celebrity, influence, and the evolving dynamics of consumer relationships in the digital age (Rishi & Bandyopadhyay, 2018). Virtual influencers, underpinned by sophisticated algorithms and design principles, engage with audiences, fostering para-social relationships that have historically been associated with traditional media figures.

These one-sided interactions, where audiences form bonds with figures they regularly engage with but do not receive direct personal interaction in return, have taken on new dimensions in the context of virtual influencers. The implications of these interactions are profound, not just from a sociological and psychological perspective but also in terms of their impact on consumer behaviour, notably influencing purchasing decisions. As these digital entities become increasingly integrated into marketing strategies and consumer engagement models, it becomes imperative to understand their rise, functioning, and influence.

The digital space's analysis, with platforms like TikTok and Douyin at its epicentre, highlights the transformative nature of technology and its impact on consumer–influencer relationships. Virtual influencers, while representing a convergence of design, technology, and marketing, have emerged as formidable forces in the digital content landscape. Their presence and the relationships they foster challenge traditional notions of influence, trust, and consumer engagement. Rooted in the dynamics of para-social interactions, these relationships exert significant influence on consumer behaviours, evidenced by shifts in purchasing patterns and brand perceptions.

This chapter offers a comprehensive exploration of the virtual influencer phenomenon. It begins by tracing the ascent of these digital protagonists, highlighting the confluence of technological advancements and evolving societal norms that have catapulted them to fame. The narrative then delves into the intricate dynamics of para-social relationships in the online space, shedding light on the underpinnings of these unique digital–human connections. Utilizing Yexi Liu as a case study, the chapter furnishes a detailed perspective on the engagement patterns between virtual influencers and their vast audiences. Anchored in robust theoretical frameworks, sections probe the direct implications of these engagements, particularly in shaping consumer behaviours and driving purchase intentions.

This chapter aims to weave a rich tapestry of insights, seamlessly integrating perspectives from digital media, psychological research, and consumer behaviour studies. Concluding the discourse, potential challenges confronting virtual influencers are addressed, with the aim of offering pragmatic recommendations for industry stakeholders.

2 The Emergence and Definition of Video-Sharing Platforms

The term "social media" was coined a long time ago. Darrell Berry is thought to have introduced the term while developing "Matisse", an online media environment in 1994 (Vugec, 2023). In academic discourse, "social media" is often interpreted as a comprehensive classification, encompassing elements ranging from social networking platforms and image-sharing applications to blogs, among other digital interfaces (Aichner et al., 2021). Since around 2000, social media platforms have evolved beyond their initial perceptions as mere digital tools or technological services. Today, they serve as pivotal spaces where individuals shape and experience their digital existence, a transformation that has attracted significant attention (Aichner et al., 2021). People with similar interests or goals find a space to gather in digital communities, which provide organized online venues for engagement, such as chat forums. Additionally, online social platforms present opportunities for users to distribute content, showcase their identities, and establish connections with others. Numerous platforms – such as TikTok, Douyin, Facebook, YouTube, and Instagram – are included in this broad category (Cao et al., 2021). Notably, these platforms are multilingual, fostering connections among users across a range of political, economic, and cultural backgrounds. Different social media platforms have different numbers of monthly active users. As of April 2024, Facebook was the foremost platform, boasting 3,065 million active users monthly (Statista, 2024).

Building on the outline above, it is evident that the spectrum of social media platforms available to the general populace is vast. The emergence of Web 2.0 heralded profound shifts in the social media terrain. Businesses can now choose from over 13 distinct social media types to advertise their products or services, encompassing blogs, business-centric networks, and general social networks, among others (Thomas and Fowler, 2021). However, this chapter will narrow its scope to examine the impact of virtual influencers on China's Douyin platform. Consequently, only video-sharing platforms, being the most pertinent to virtual influencers, will be detailed.

Video-sharing platforms facilitate the creation and exploration of videos, emphasizing the cultivation of a community centred on content production and distribution (Yuan et al., 2021). Douyin, recognized globally as TikTok, is a mobile application dedicated to brief videos. It enables users to craft, upload, and disseminate original video content (Fung Business Intelligence, 2018). Both TikTok and Douyin, under the umbrella of Chinese tech company ByteDance, have witnessed exponential growth as video-sharing platforms (Yang & Ha, 2021). By 2022, TikTok's global user base surged to 1.7 billion, a rise of 60 per cent from 2020, compared to 639.4 million users reported for Douyin in 2021. In 2022, TikTok clinched the title of the most downloaded application globally, amassing 672 million downloads (Statista, 2023b). As of April 2024, it was one of the fastest developing social media platforms, with 1,582 million active users monthly (Statista, 2024), and projections suggest its user count will escalate to around 2.25 billion by 2027 (Statista, 2023a).

TikTok and Douyin predominantly host short videos, typically under a minute, and incentivize users to craft and replicate videos, spurring trends across the platforms (Yang & Ha, 2021). Despite their shared functionalities and tech prowess, the two cater to distinct audiences: Douyin only serves the Chinese market, adhering to its censorship norms, and ensuring all content is China-centric, whereas TikTok collects global content (Yang & Ha, 2021). The former includes a unique auditory watermark, "Douyin", that concludes videos on that platform, thus bolstering brand recognition (Yang & Ha, 2021). TikTok's core lies in its algorithm-driven content recommendations and entertainment quotient.

Platforms such as YouTube and TikTok enable users to post and view both personal and commercial videos, with interactive features allowing comments. Promotional costs on such platforms often undercut those of traditional television ads (Thomas & Fowler, 2021). A 2022 survey highlighted that 15 per cent of business-to-business (B2B) marketers ranked TikTok just 2 per cent below Facebook in offering optimal returns. Moreover, over a third of those surveyed deemed TikTok the prime platform for global content outreach (Statista, 2023c).

3 The Rise of Virtual Influencers

The surge in digital technology and the growth of virtual agencies have elevated the prominence of virtual influencers across social media platforms. These digital figures not only generate content on these platforms that appeals to their followers but also foster active interactions, making them feel akin to genuine personalities (Arsenyan and Mirowska, 2021). In essence, virtual influencers are computer-generated personalities designed to mirror human behaviours on online platforms (Kim & Park, 2023). The line distinguishing these influencers from actual humans is often blurred due to their intricate design. They are crafted with precision to ensure their appearance and traits align closely with human features, thereby making them relatable to their audience (Khan & Sutcliffe, 2014). The design process is rigorous, aiming to enhance their visual appeal and charisma.

By incorporating attributes that resonate with users, virtual influencers can forge genuine bonds with their audience (Khan & Sutcliffe, 2014). Narration also plays a pivotal role in their design. By weaving human-like stories and experiences, they can emulate genuine human interactions. These narratives, rich with familiar experiences and emotions, are instrumental in creating a sense of connection. This mirroring of real-life experiences and the ability to establish relatability has enabled virtual influencers to nurture robust bonds in the digital realm, ensuring sustained engagement (Hanus & Fox, 2015).

Leveraging the prowess of advanced technologies, especially artificial intelligence (AI), virtual influencers have carved a niche for themselves. By deploying AI-driven algorithms, they have an edge in dissecting user data, ensuring their content is tailored to their audience's preferences and fostering more personalised engagements on social platforms (Moustakas et al., 2020). The digital domain has witnessed the emergence of influential virtual figures such as Lil Miquela, boasting 2.84 million followers on Instagram since 2016, and Shudu Gramm (hailed as the premier AI supermodel), who collaborates with top-tier fashion brands and renowned magazines (Sands et al., 2022). Their surging popularity over recent years is hard to miss, especially on image-centric platforms like Instagram. Here their striking visuals, coupled with traits that users find relatable, have made them forces to be reckoned with. Their unique content, seamlessly integrated into the social media milieu, has been pivotal in their soaring popularity (Moustakas et al., 2020).

The concept of virtual influencers, heralding the next phase of virtual idols and YouTubers, emerged in 2016 (Conti et al., 2022). There are two primary categories when it comes to virtual influencers: those modelled after Japanese-style anime and those resembling real humans. The anime-styled influencers typically exhibit features such as smaller mouths and oversized eyes. An example is Noonoouri, who, despite her non-human design, has seamlessly been integrated into human-centred social networks (Arsenyan & Mirowska, 2021).

As digital tech has evolved, there has been a shift towards more lifelike virtual influencers producing content that closely mirrors human output (Arsenyan & Mirowska, 2021). Studies suggest that these human-like virtual influencers, due to their more realistic appearance, hold more allure than traditional fashion idols (Conti et al., 2022). Often labelled simply as "influencers", they are not just digital spectacles but active participants in marketing drives and social initiatives. A case in point is Lil Miquela, who is at the forefront of such campaigns (Drenten & Brooks, 2020). The success stories of such influencers have paved the way for the birth of many more, all vying for a slice of the digital influence pie.

The realm of virtual influencers in the digital landscape is marked by a blend of promise and challenges. As highlighted by Conti et al. (2022), virtual influencers serve as a testament to technological advancement, opening avenues for brands to seamlessly blend reality with the digital world. Their strengths – including adaptability, exclusivity, brand safety, and innovation – equip brands with unprecedented control over their marketing narratives. The ability to meticulously craft every aspect of a virtual influencer ensures consistent brand alignment, while their innovative nature can captivate audiences and position brands as forward-thinking.

However, the challenges associated with virtual influencers, such as limited following compared to human influencers and potential societal implications, remain undeniable (Conti et al., 2022). Their inherent digital nature can inhibit genuine human connections, creating a gap in authenticity and trust (Moustakas et al., 2020). The financial implications of maintaining their presence, and the possible detachment they might foster with their audiences, further underscore the complexities involved. As such, brands exploring collaborations with virtual influencers must navigate this landscape with a clear understanding of both their potential and their limitations.

4 Para-Social Interaction in the Digital Age: The Impact on Social Media Influencers

The concept of "para-social interaction" shows the emotional connections viewers or listeners establish with characters from various media, be they real or fictional. This phenomenon spans various media forms, from movies and TV to radio (Giles, 2002). Rather than indicating a long-standing bond, this interaction is ephemeral, lasting only for the duration of the media content's exposure (Dibble et al., 2016). Interestingly, this one-sided relational dynamic is not limited to fictional characters; it extends to media figures such as social media influencers. This theory originated from viewers' reactions to human portrayals on TV, where they began to perceive these characters not as mere representations but as real people they felt close to (Horton & Wohl, 1956). The emotional tie cultivated makes these characters pivotal in viewers' lives, creating an illusion of personal familiarity and understanding akin to friendship (Chung & Cho, 2017). Such para-social interactions elevate the viewers' level of attachment. For example, fans might become deeply invested in TV celebrities or news anchors, leading them to seek more insights into these figures' lives off the screen (Hartmann & Goldhoorn, 2011). Notably, while the concept was initially associated with traditional media, it has seamlessly transitioned into the digital age, influencing interactions on the internet beyond its conventional confines of TV and radio (Labrecque, 2014).

Online social media platforms serve as fertile ground for para-social interaction (Farivar et al., 2022), where users naturally connect with like-minded individuals, paving the way for the emergence of para-social bonds (Bane et al., 2010). A myriad of elements – including an influencer's appeal, societal identity, and their effect on followers' emotional states such as sympathy or loneliness – contribute to fostering para-social ties (Hwang & Zhang, 2018). To boost engagement, social media platforms prioritize forging genuine connections between influencers and their audience. These platforms allow influencers a direct channel to their audience, giving followers intimate glimpses into their daily lives (Aw & Chuah, 2021). The ripple effects of para-social interactions extend to various online domains – from social networking sites and e-commerce platforms to blogs (Labrecque, 2014). Even if consumers never meet these influencers face to face, they often harbour profound emotional connections with them (Schnickel, 1985).

Research into para-social interaction is not new; however, its lens has transitioned from traditional celebrities to today's social media influencers (Aw & Chuah, 2021). Evidence suggests that active engagement on social media amplifies the para-social dynamic with influencers (Chung & Cho, 2017). The allure and credibility of influencers are pivotal in shaping this interaction. Influencers with compelling aesthetics and trustworthiness find it easier to establish emotional ties with their audience (Sakib et al., 2020; Sokolova & Kefi, 2020).

Interestingly, both human influencers and AI characters on interactive social media can evoke para-social feelings (Jin et al., 2021). When influencers portray nuanced and relatable personas, the depth of the para-social bond intensifies. This suggests that a well fleshed-out character magnifies this connection (Ballantine & Martin, 2004), a principle that holds true for both human–AI and consumer–influencer interactions (Rafaeli & Ariel, 2007; Banks & Bowman, 2016).

The implications of para-social interaction are not just emotional; they have commercial ramifications too. As a potent driver behind followers' purchasing decisions, the depth of their para-social bond can sway them to heed influencers' recommendations (Lee and Watkins, 2016). The bond influencers cultivate with their audience plays a significant role in their ability to sway consumer choices (Aw & Labrecque, 2020). An influencer's personality is the key to building para-social interactions, which in turn benefits both the influencer and the brands they represent (Aw & Chuah, 2021). The content influencers disseminate on social platforms is foundational for fostering ties with followers and enhancing message clarity (Martínez-López et al., 2020). Existing research suggests that the influence of endorsements by influencers on brand perception and buying decisions is channelled through para-social interactions (Hwang & Zhang, 2018). A deep emotional bond with an influencer often translates to positive sentiments toward the brands they support (Jin et al., 2021). Furthermore, when influencers showcase specific products or brands as their favourites, audiences often interpret this as genuine sharing, elevating the influencer's perceived trustworthiness (Ferchaud et al., 2018).

To sum up, para-social interactions strongly affect how consumers perceive and act towards both influencers and promoted brands, emphasizing their critical role in today's marketing landscape.

5 The Theoretical Background of Virtual Influencers' Impact on Sales

Virtual influencers, digital personas often created with advanced technologies such as AI, are emerging as a captivating trend in both the social media realm and the commercial sector. Their unique appeal resonates with a global audience. As their prominence rises, it is crucial to delve into how these figures influence consumer actions, especially their buying decisions. This section introduces the theoretical backdrops used to analyse virtual influencers' motivations and their consequent impact on purchase intention and sales.

While past studies have delved into the link between both real and virtual influencers and consumer buying intentions (Ki & Kim, 2019; Aw & Labrecque, 2020), this chapter focuses on two core theories: the Theory of Persuasion and the Source Attractiveness Model. By unpacking these theories and related hypotheses, the chapter aims to illuminate the pathways through which virtual influencers shape consumer choices. This exploration will offer insights into the dynamics between virtual influencers and consumer intentions. Table 10.1 summarizes these theoretical frameworks.

Table 10.1 Theoretical frameworks for purchase intention

Theory of Persuasion	Source Attractiveness Model
Followers create perceptions based on the personal attributes of the influencer, which can subsequently shape their behaviour	Assesses the attractiveness and value of an information or promotion source based on elements such as credibility, expertise, trustworthiness, and likability

The Theory of Persuasion

While its origins remain somewhat unclear, this theory offers profound insights into the intricacies of the influencer paradigm within the realm of social media (Masuda et al., 2022). Defined in scholarly literature, persuasion encompasses the intricate process of shaping or altering an individual's beliefs or actions, notably influencing purchasing behaviours (Dotson & Hyatt, 2000). Within the social media landscape, followers' perceptions of influencers are intricately moulded by the discernible attributes these influencers present.

Drawing on the Theory of Persuasion, Masuda et al. (2022) posited that such attributes play a pivotal role in directing the purchasing inclinations of followers. Within the digital ecosystem of social media, the inherent traits of influencers can significantly mould the perceptions and narratives followers construct about them. Such perceptions, as delineated by those authors, can instigate peripheral processing in followers, subsequently guiding their behaviour. When examining the tenets of the Theory of Persuasion in the context of social media influencers, a notable correlation emerges: the way followers interpret attributes such as an influencer's trustworthiness can steer their behaviour and purchasing decisions. Specifically, an influencer deemed trustworthy by followers is more likely to influence their purchase decisions. This metric is often a product of followers' discernment of the influencer's personal traits.

The Source Attractiveness Model

McGuire's (1985) Source Attractiveness Model provides an analytical lens to evaluate the allure and desirability of a communicator or an information source by considering an array of factors. Central to this model is the interplay between the endorser's similarity, recognizability, and appeal in determining the potency of the conveyed message. The theoretical significance of the model is underscored by its elucidation of how an appealing source can shape an individual's attitudinal disposition.

The role of influencers on social media extends beyond mere content creation; their charm and magnetism actively bolster brand perceptions (Hermanda et al., 2019). Digital influencers' appeal significantly directs consumers toward or away from purchase decisions (Torres et al., 2019). These internet icons, celebrated for their aesthetics and lifestyles, emerge as benchmarks for their followers, who often aspire to replicate their success and way of living (Okazaki et al., 2014). Consequently, a positive view of these influencers augments consumers' willingness to buy products and services they endorse (Branchik & Chowdhury, 2017).

6 The Challenge of Using Virtual Influencers

Virtual influencers, although presenting numerous opportunities, come with various challenges. This section compares virtual influencers with their human counterparts, and addresses specific intrinsic attributes of these influencers that may be problematic.

There is a notable disparity in followership between human and virtual influencers. For instance, even a comparatively less-followed human influencer such as Kylie Jenner has around 400 million followers, dwarfing the count of over 6.8 million for the top virtual influencer, Lu do Magalu. Conti et al. (2022) contend that this gap may stem from two main factors: (1) virtual influencers' sphere of influence is typically restricted to social media, whereas renowned human influencers are often famous beyond these platforms: and (2) the relatively recent emergence of virtual influencers means many people might still be unfamiliar with them. Additionally, the authors suggest that only 60 per cent of virtual influencer followers are real people, a significantly smaller ratio than their human counterparts.

Diving deeper into the attributes of virtual influencers, a multifaceted landscape of challenges emerges, with one of the most prominent issues being the representation of these influencers. The overwhelming portrayal of many as females sets skewed standards of beauty, style, and culture, potentially jeopardizing the future landscape of media and cultural representation (Moustakas et al., 2020). This issue is deeply intertwined with the inherent pitfalls of social media, where a platform's dynamics often pushes users to rely heavily on social validation and positive feedback, potentially exacerbating negative self-perceptions and concerns about body image (Sands et al., 2022).

Furthermore, as technology continues to blur the boundaries between the virtual and the real world, it causes unique discomfort among some consumers that becomes especially poignant when virtual influencers begin to mirror human likenesses with unsettling accuracy. Such hyper-realistic portrayals can be deeply unsettling for many, creating a challenge for brands. They must therefore carefully navigate the design of these influencers, striving for human resemblance without veering into the realm of the uncanny. Alongside appearance, the inherent nature of virtual influencers, with their inability to convey authentic emotions and lived experiences, can act as a deterrent for deeper consumer engagement and trust (Sands et al., 2022).

With the rise of virtual influencers, the delineation between them and their human counterparts has become increasingly hazy, causing a ripple effect in consumer expectations. Consumers now demand heightened levels of authenticity and transparency. While the authenticity of human influencers can sometimes come under scrutiny, virtual influencers face even more scepticism given their inherently digital origin and the fact that they are primarily driven by profit and brand objectives (Moustakas et al., 2020). In terms of transparency, an evolving consumer landscape seeks to understand the deeper motivations, values, and narratives behind the brands and influencers they choose to follow (Guthrie, 2020). In the long run, this amplified demand for authenticity and transparency might prompt more defined regulatory interventions, ensuring a clearer framework for the use and portrayal of virtual influencers.

Moreover, the vulnerabilities associated with the AI-driven nature of virtual influencers cannot be ignored. Their programmable nature renders these digital entities susceptible to malicious external interference, ranging from trolling to more severe forms of sabotage and cyber-attack. Such vulnerabilities, if not addressed, could also erode brand trust and value (Demsar et al., 2021; Sands et al., 2022).

As looking to the future, with the growing ubiquity of virtual entities, is is clear that regulatory and ethical considerations will become more paramount. Comprehensive measures will be essential to safeguard consumers from potential malfeasance that could arise from these technological advancements. Notably, companies such as Meta (Facebook's parent entity) are already at the forefront, crafting ethical frameworks for virtual influencers to ensure greater transparency in content creation and responsibility (Guthrie, 2020). With such proactive measures, a future where consumers can clearly discern real from virtual influencers is anticipated, potentially ushering in a new era of virtual influencer-based marketing. Nonetheless, marketers should tread carefully and be vigilant about potential intellectual property challenges when designing and popularizing unique virtual influencers.

7 Case Study: The Use of Virtual Influencers in Purchase Intention

From the discussion so far, the significant role of para-social interactions between virtual influencers and their audience, especially in influencing buying decisions, is clear. By focusing on a specific case study, this section will further explore how virtual influencers impact purchase intentions.

On October 31, 2021, a virtual influencer named Yexi Liu, adorned with Chinese-style makeup, was introduced to the public on her eponymous Douyin account through a concept video lasting less than three minutes. Since then, the account has showcased 48 videos, each featuring unique styles and themes. The combined impact of these videos has led to a follower count of 8.36 million and an impressive 43.55 million likes. The initial video itself has been a significant hit, collecting close to 3.6 million likes. Its popularity ensured Yexi Liu's appearance on Douyin's trending list for a whole week, highlighting her strong online presence.

Most video viewers are drawn to the narrative that showcases the interplay between two realms, as depicted in the film. This creates a virtual environment termed "the metaverse", which can mirror the real world but also stands apart from tangible reality, offering users a deeply immersive and experiential journey (Li & Liang, 2023).

In the narrative surrounding Yexi Liu, the creative team went beyond just crafting a singular virtual persona. They infused Yexi Liu with distinctive thoughts, emotions, and behavioural patterns that set her apart from human society. This led to the creation of an intricate virtual realm that intersects with the real world yet also stands distinct from it. Within this space, real-world individuals engage with the digital entity, Yexi Liu. Their interactions drive the storyline of short videos, culminating in the emergence of a virtual civilization that parallels the real world yet remains its own unique entity (Fang & Shen, 2021).

On March 18, 2022, Yexi Liu began a landmark collaboration with the French multinational cosmetics firm Clarins, marking her debut in commercial endorsements. A promotional video was released in which Yexi Liu, wearing a traditional white dress, promotes the brand. While men online often favour dynamic effects, women are drawn to aesthetics and emotional content. To cater to both, the marketing team blended technology and beauty, striking a balance to appeal to all. This approach gave Yexi Liu a distinct edge in her endorsements.

In a partnership with the Chinese company Xiaopeng (XPeng) Motors, manufacturers of electric vehicles, Yexi Liu used captivating visuals to highlight the cars' advanced features, seamlessly blending her virtual persona with the products' technical prowess. Yexi Liu now endorses various premium products, ranging from mobile phones to luxury cosmetics. Despite being virtual, she competes at the top in commercial endorsements thanks to her marketing team's strategy – carefully shaping Yexi Liu's image before capitalizing on her commercial potential (Feng, 2022).

While Yexi Liu is undoubtedly embarking on a promising trajectory, transitioning seamlessly from conception to tangible success, her journey is not without foreseeable challenges. Her meteoric rise and immense popularity bring with them concerns about authenticity in visual communication. Initially branded as a virtual beauty blogger, she is not the first to face scepticism. For instance, when the Chinese virtual icon Ling Ling endorsed Gucci lipstick, the very nature of virtual influencers posed a credibility challenge. Consumers found it difficult to trust virtual influencers that, inherently, cannot genuinely experience or consume a product (Li & Liang, 2023). Such a dissonance goes against long-standing consumer expectations of influencers truly using and vouching for products. Scholars have warned of the ramifications of capital-driven artificial intelligence, fearing that it could inadvertently force AI to act as a tool that assimilates and drains human creativity and spiritual labour. Furthermore, with the advent of major capital players, the future of ordinary content creators and consumers remains uncertain.

In reflecting on the tremendous success of Yexi Liu, it is clear that the realm of digital influencers has evolved considerably. Yexi Liu's success – built on a delicate fusion of rich narratives, cutting-edge technology, and strategic marketing – challenges traditional conceptions of influencer authenticity. While her virtual nature presents an obvious advantage in adaptability and commercial endorsement, it simultaneously ignites debates on trustworthiness in influencer marketing. The scepticism faced by virtual influencers like Yexi Liu brings into focus the age-old importance of authenticity in the world of endorsements. Additionally, the intertwining of massive capital operations with the genesis of virtual influencers raises questions about the future of content creation and the potential monopolization of the digital space. As technology and capital continue to shape this nascent world, the real challenge lies in preserving genuine creativity and ensuring a level playing field for all content creators.

8 Conclusion and Discussion

Exploration of the digital landscape, particularly on platforms such as TikTok and Douyin, underscores the transformative impact of technology on consumer–influencer dynamics (Yang & Ha, 2021). Virtual influencers – a blend of design, technology, and marketing strategies – have secured a prominent position in the digital content arena. These entities not only redefine traditional concepts of influence, trust, and consumer engagement but also profoundly affect consumer behaviours, as evidenced by changes in purchasing trends and brand perceptions (Statista, 2023c; Thomas & Fowler, 2021).

Incorporating Yexi Liu as a case study in this chapter provides a comprehensive demonstration of the interactions between virtual influencers and their audiences. The influence of Yexi Liu in the digital realm and the nature of interactions with consumers present a detailed picture of the intricacies of para-social relationships in the current digital context.

Drawing on theoretical frameworks such as the Theory of Persuasion and the Source Attractiveness Model, the chapter examined the multifaceted nature of interactions between consumers and virtual influencers. Such frameworks highlight the importance of trust, authenticity, and perceived relatability in determining consumer responses in the digital milieu. As advancements in artificial intelligence and graphics continue, the domain of virtual influencers is expected to witness further evolution. This ever-changing landscape offers both challenges and opportunities for businesses, content creators, and academic researchers, emphasizing the need for ongoing adaptation and a nuanced understanding of emerging digital interaction paradigms.

The prominence of virtual influencers suggests a potential future where distinctions between reality and the virtual world may further diminish. Brands and marketers face the task of operating in this mixed reality, striving to harness the influence of virtual entities while ensuring sustained authenticity and trust. Recognizing and utilizing the para-social relationships between consumers and virtual influencers will become increasingly crucial. The role of these relationships, not limited to the present context, is expected to be a central element of digital marketing and consumer research in the coming years. Staying informed about these trends is essential for stakeholders to effectively navigate and capitalize on the opportunities presented by the realm of virtual influencers.

9 Future Research Directions

A comprehensive review and synthesis of the current literature has revealed several research gaps and potential avenues for future exploration. These insights not only pave the way for the broader trajectory of virtual influencer research but also hold specific significance for the realm of para-social interactions. The authors believe that, by addressing these gaps and capitalizing on the suggested directions, the academic community can attain a more nuanced understanding of the intricate dynamics between virtual influencers and their audiences (Table 10.2).

Table 10.2 Future research directions

Research Gaps and Future Directions	Source
The rise and potential of virtual influencers in the marketing landscape are acknowledged; however, there is limited understanding of how to effectively integrate them into brand strategies and measure their impact in the evolving digital ecosystem	Sands et al. (2022)
Future investigations should focus on assessing the perceptions and viewpoints of followers and consumers who interact with virtual influencers in the digital realm	Moustakas et al. (2020)
Various avenues for studying virtual influencers have been proposed (from psychological impact to performance metrics), but a significant gap remains in understanding the comprehensive managerial implications of their reputation on conversion/sales; their potential to complement or eventually replace human roles (particularly in marketing sector) requires in-depth exploration across various academic disciplines and policy considerations	Batista da Silva Oliveira & Chimenti (2021)
Although existing frameworks and studies have touched on the categorization and perception of virtual influencers, there is scant research on nuanced cultural preferences concerning their realism, aesthetic choices, and perceived personalities; the influence of cultural context on consumer preferences for virtual influencer attributes (from appearance to perceived autonomy) warrants deeper exploration to understand global reception and engagement patterns	Zhou et al. (2024)
There is a significant need for qualitative research to delve deeper into consumer perceptions across different product categories and cultures; and understanding tangible business outcomes (e.g. the direct effects of virtual influencers on sales using actual data) remains largely unexplored and presents a valuable direction for future inquiries	Al Masri et al. (2023)

References

Aichner, T., Grünfelder, M., Maurer, O., & Jegeni, D. (2021). Twenty-five years of social media: A review of social media applications and definitions from 1994 to 2019. *Cyberpsychology, Behavior, and Social Networking, 24*(4), 215–222.

Al Masri, Y., Hamdenh, S., Al-Dmour, R., & Al-Okaily, M. (2023). Can computer virtual influencers replace human influencers in the future? An empirical investigation in the age of digital transformation. *Jordan Journal of Business Administration, 19*(4). https://doi.org/10.35516/jjba.v19i4.1430

Arsenyan, J., & Mirowska, A. (2021). Almost human? A comparative case study on the social media presence of virtual influencers. *International journal of Human–Computer Studies, 155*, 102694.

Aw, E. C. X., & Chuah, S. H. W. (2021). "Stop the unattainable ideal for an ordinary me!" Fostering parasocial relationships with social media influencers: The role of self-discrepancy. *Journal of Business Research, 132*, 146–157.

Aw, E. C. X. , & Labrecque, L. I. (2020). Celebrity endorsement in social media contexts: understanding the role of parasocial interactions and the need to belong. *Journal of Consumer Marketing, 37*(7), 895–908.

Ballantine, P. W., & Martin, B. A. S. (2004). Forming parasocial relationships in online communities. *Advances in Consumer Research*, 13(2), 197–202.

Bane, C. M., Cornish, M., Erspamer, N., & Kampman, L. (2010). Self-disclosure through weblogs and perceptions of online and "real-life" friendships among female bloggers. *Cyberpsychology, Behavior, and Social Networking, 13*(2), 131–139.

Banks, J., & Bowman, N.D. (2016). Avatars are (sometimes) people too: Linguistic indicators of parasocial and social ties in player–avatar relationships. *New Media & Society*, 18(7), 1257–1276.

Batista da Silva Oliveira, A., & Chimenti, P. (2021). "Humanized robots": A proposition of categories to understand virtual influencers. *Australasian Journal of Information Systems, 25*(1). https://doi.org/10.3127/ajis.v25i0.3223

Branchik, B. J., & Chowdhury, T. G. (2017). Men seeing stars: Celebrity endorsers, race, and the male consumer. *Journal of Marketing Theory and Practice*, 25(3), 305–322.

Cao, D., Meadows, M., Wong, D., & Xia, S. (2021). Understanding consumers' social media engagement behaviour: An examination of the moderation effect of social media context. *Journal of Business Research*, 122, 835–846.

Chung, S., & Cho, H. (2017). Fostering Parasocial relationships with celebrities on social media: Implications for celebrity endorsement. *Psychology & Marketing, 34*(4), 481–495.

Conti, M., Gathani, J., & Tricomi, P.P. (2022). Virtual Influencers In Online Social Media. *IEEE Communications Magazine, 60*(8), 86–91.

Demsar, V., Brace-Govan, J., Jack, G., & Sands, S. (2021). The social phenomenon of trolling: Understanding the discourse and social practices of online provocation. *Journal of Marketing Management, 37*(11–12), 1058–1090.

Dibble, J. L., Hartmann, T., & Rosaen, S.F. (2016). Parasocial interaction and parasocial relationship: Conceptual clarification and a critical assessment of measures. *Human Communication Research, 42*(1), 21–44.

Dotson, M. J., & Hyatt, E. M. (2000). Religious symbols as peripheral cues in advertising: A replication of the elaboration likelihood model. *Journal of Business Research*, *48*(1), 63–68.

Drenten, J., & Brooks, G. (2020). Celebrity 2.0: Lil Miquela and the rise of a virtual star system. *Feminist Media Studies*, *20*(8), 1319–1323.

Fang L., & Shen, H. (2021). Changes in technology and civilization: A conceptual study of the metaverse. *Metaverse*, *2*(2). http://dx.doi.org/10.54517/met.v2i2

Farivar, S., Wang, F., & Turel, O. (2022). Followers' problematic engagement with influencers on social media: An attachment theory perspective. *Computers in Human Behavior*, *133*, 107288.

Feng, Y. (2022). The rise of virtual image endorsement in visual culture context. In *2022 4th international conference on economic management and cultural industry, 1622–1629*.

Ferchaud, A., Grzeslo, J., Orme, S., & LaGroue, J. (2018). Parasocial attributes and YouTube personalities: Exploring content trends across the most subscribed YouTube channels. *Computers in Human Behavior*, *80*, 88–96.

Giles, D. C. (2002). Parasocial interaction: A review of the literature and a model for future research. *Media Psychology*, *4*(3), 279–305.

Guthrie, S. (2020). Virtual influencers: More human than humans. In S. Yesiloglu & J. Costello (Eds.), *Influencer marketing: Building brand communities and engagement* (pp. 271–285). London: Routledge.

Hanus, M. D., & Fox, J. (2015). Persuasive avatars: The effects of customizing a virtual salesperson's appearance on brand liking and purchase intentions. *International Journal of Human–Computer Studies*, *84*, 33–40.

Hartmann, T., & Goldhoorn, C. (2011). Horton and Wohl revisited: Exploring viewers' experience of parasocial interaction. *Journal of Communication*, *61*(6), 1104–1121.

Hermanda, A., Sumarwan, U., & Tinaprillia, N. (2019). The effect of social media influencer on brand image, self-concept, and purchase intention. *Journal of Consumer Sciences*, *4*(2), 76–89.

Horton, D., & Richard Wohl, R. (1956). Mass communication and para-social interaction: Observations on intimacy at a distance. *Psychiatry*, *19*(3), 215–229.

Hwang, K., & Zhang, Q. (2018). Influence of parasocial relationship between digital celebrities and their followers on followers' purchase and electronic word-of-mouth intentions, and persuasion knowledge. *Computers in Human Behavior*, *87*, 155–173.

Jin, S. V., Ryu, E., & Muqaddam, A. (2021). I trust what she's #endorsing on Instagram: Moderating effects of parasocial interaction and social presence in fashion influencer marketing. *Journal of Fashion Marketing and Management*, *25*(4), 665–681.

Khan, R. F., & Sutcliffe, A. (2014). Attractive agents are more persuasive. *International Journal of Human–Computer Interaction*, *30*(2), 142–150.

Ki, C., & Kim, Y. (2019). The mechanism by which social media influencers persuade consumers: The role of consumers' desire to mimic. *Psychology & Marketing, 36*(10), 905–922.

Kim, H., & Park, M. (2023). Virtual influencers' attractiveness effect on purchase intention: A moderated mediation model of the product–endorser fit with the brand. *Computers in Human Behavior, 143*, 107703.

Labrecque, L. I. (2014). Fostering consumer–brand relationships in social media environments: The role of parasocial interaction. *Journal of Interactive Marketing, 28*(2), 134–148.

Fung Business Intelligence. (2018, August 30). *Uncovering the emerging players in China's e-commerce (Issue 1): Short video platform – Douyin.* https://www.fbicgroup.com/internal-site/wp-content/uploads/documents/1CNE_Douyin.pdf

Lee, J. E., & Watkins, B. (2016). YouTube vloggers' influence on consumer luxury brand perceptions and intentions. *Journal of Business Research, 69*(12), 5753–5760.

Li, D., & Liang, T. (2023). A new path of visual communication from the perspective of the metaverse: Take Liu Yexi's internet communication spectacle as an example. *SHS Web of Conferences, 167*, 2013

Martínez-López, F. J., Anaya-Sánchez, R., Fernández Giordano, M., & Lopez-Lopez, D. (2020). Behind influencer marketing: Key marketing decisions and their effects on followers' responses. *Journal of Marketing Management, 36*(7–8), 579–607.

Masuda, H., Han, S.H., & Lee, J. (2022). Impacts of influencer attributes on purchase intentions in social media influencer marketing: Mediating roles of characterizations. *Technological Forecasting & Social Change, 174*, 121246.

McGuire, W. J. (1985). Attitudes and attitude change. In G. Lindzey & E. Aronson (Eds.), *Handbook of social psychology*, Vol. 2 (pp. 233–346). New York: Random House.

Moustakas, E., Lamba, N., Mahmoud, D., & Ranganathan, C. (2020). Blurring lines between fiction and reality: Perspectives of experts on marketing effectiveness of virtual influencers. In *2020 international conference on cyber security and protection of digital services (cyber security)*, 1–6.

Okazaki, S., Dìaz-Martìn, A. M., Rozano, M., & Menendez-Benito, H. D. (2014). How to mine brand tweets: Procedural guidelines and pretest. *International Journal Of Market Research, 56*(4), 467–488.

Rafaeli, S., & Ariel, Y. (2007). Assessing interactivity in computer-mediated research. In A. Joinson, K. McKenna, T. Postmes, & U.-D. Reips (Eds.), *Oxford handbook of internet psychology* (pp. 71–88). Oxford: Oxford Academic.

Rishi, B., & Bandyopadhyay, S. (Eds.). (2018). *Contemporary issues in social media marketing*. London: Routledge.

Sakib, M. N., Zolfagharian, M., & Yazdanparast, A. (2020). Does parasocial interaction with weight loss vloggers affect compliance? The role of vlogger characteristics, consumer readiness, and health consciousness. *Journal of Retailing and Consumer Services, 52*, 101733.

Sands, S., Ferraro, C., Demsar, V., & Chandler, G. (2022). False idols: Unpacking the opportunities and challenges of falsity in the context of virtual influencers. *Business Horizons, 65*(6), 777–788.

Schnickel, R. (1985). *Intimate strangers: The culture of celebrity.* Garden City, NY: Doubleday.

Sokolova, K., & Kefi, H. (2020). Instagram and YouTube bloggers promote it, why should I buy? How credibility and parasocial interaction influence purchase intentions. *Journal of Retailing and Consumer Services, 53*, 101742.

Statista. (2023a). *Number of TikTok users worldwide from 2018 to 2027.* Available at: https://www.statista.com/forecasts/1142687/tiktok-users-worldwide.

Statista. (2023b). *Leading mobile apps worldwide in 2022, by downloads.* Available at: https://www.statista.com/statistics/1285960/top-downloaded-mobile-apps-worldwide/

Statista. (2023c). *Social media platforms that were most effective for content distribution according to marketers worldwide in 2022.* Available at: https://www.statista.com/statistics/1297727/social-media-content-marketing/

Statista. (2024). *Most popular social networks worldwide as of April 2024, by number of monthly active users.* Available at: https://www.statista.com/statistics/272014/global-social-networks-ranked-by-number-of-users/

Thomas, V. L., & Fowler, K. (2021). Close encounters of the AI kind: Use of AI influencers as brand endorsers. *Journal of Advertising, 50*(1), 11–25.

Torres, P., Augusto, M., & Matos, M. (2019). Antecedents and outcomes of digital influencer endorsement: An exploratory study. *Psychology & Marketing, 36*(12), 1267–1276.

Vugec, D. S., Pivar, J., & Stjepić, A.-M. (2023). Preliminary study of the gender differences in the habits of social media usage across the student population. *In Proceedings of FEB Zagreb international odyssey conference on economics and business*, 444–457.

Yang, Y., & Ha, L. (2021). Why people use TikTok (Douyin) and how their purchase intentions are affected by social media influencers in China: A uses and gratifications and parasocial relationship perspective. *Journal of Interactive Advertising, 21*(3), 297–305.

Yuan, L., Xia, H., & Wang, B. (2021). An empirical study on the effectiveness of advertising strategies on a short-video sharing platform. In *Proceedings of the 2021 2nd international conference on internet and e-business*, 56–62.

Zhou, X., Yan, X., & Jiang, Y. (2024). Making sense? The sensory-specific nature of virtual influencer effectiveness. *Journal of Marketing, 88*(4), 84–106.

Transitioning from CRM to Social CRM in the Healthcare Industry

11

Ashim Kumar Ghosh
Symbiosis International (Deemed University), Pune, India

Manohar Kapse
Jaipuria Institute of Management Indore, India

Introduction

Customer Relationship Management (CRM) is a commonly used term in business. It is not new and must have existed in its original form since the beginning of business. However, its importance has grown with the advent of digital technology and the changing landscape of business practices driven by increased competition. These factors have caused CRM to evolve and develop from its original form to the one we have today, making it even more critical for businesses. In today's business world, CRM solutions are not just tools but drivers of growth, delivering a competitive advantage. Thus, companies worldwide, irrespective of industry, size, or location, understand the importance of having an intelligent CRM solution to support their operations. Lamrhari et al. (2022) defined CRM as a business strategy that integrates internal processes and functions with external networks, using technology and scientific methods to identify new customers, build long-term customer relationships, retain customers by meeting their needs, and reduce churn rates while minimizing marketing and customer service costs.

DOI: 10.4324/9781003412656-11

For healthcare service providers such as hospitals and other medical institutions, CRM is an effective communication channel with patients, building relationships and sharing information with them promptly. In the pharmaceutical and medical device manufacturing and marketing industry, CRM has a more diverse role in maintaining and supporting relationships with various stakeholders, including healthcare practitioners, medical institutions, distributors, and patients.

In modern society, social media platforms such as Facebook, Twitter, LinkedIn, YouTube, and Google have become indispensable, significantly altering the dynamics of communication, information sharing, and collaborative content creation (Rishi & Bandyopadhyay, 2018). Many businesses use social media to promote their brand and products while improving communication with their customer base (Siakas et al., 2014). Introducing social media into the healthcare industry has significantly altered the landscape of customer relationships. Today, healthcare professionals and patients actively use social media to search for information, share experiences, and engage in dialogue. This shift has changed relationship dynamics by giving customers access to extensive information and allowing them to express their opinions on various social media platforms freely. Therefore, exploring the integration of social media and CRM is essential.

Social CRM (or CRM 2.0) combines social media and social networking platforms with traditional CRM strategies and practices. Companies can use Social CRM to engage with customers, interact with them directly, and monitor their social impact in a modern and convenient way (Paliouras & Siakas, 2017). The primary goal is to use social media channels to improve customer interactions, personalize experiences, and increase overall customer satisfaction.

This chapter explores the transformation roadmap of Customer Relationship Management to Social CRM in pharmaceutical and medical device companies supplying healthcare products. In doing so, it highlights the importance of CRM in healthcare and its critical role in building trust for relevant products among healthcare providers/professionals (HCPs) and consumers. It also looks into the social media strategies of different healthcare companies. Finally, it explores the rise of Social CRM (CRM 2.0) and the scope of integrating social media data into traditional CRM practices.

The following are the objectives of this chapter:

- **Highlight the significance of CRM in healthcare**: Emphasize the crucial role of CRM in the healthcare industry, focusing on its impact on building trust among healthcare providers and consumers regarding healthcare products.

- **Explore social media strategies**: Examining the strategies implemented by different types of healthcare companies and analysing how they engage with various stakeholders in the digital landscape.
- **Learn about the emergence of Social CRM (CRM 2.0)**: Its rise as a progressive approach, examining its features and potential benefits in the context of healthcare companies.
- **Assess the scope of integration**: Evaluate the possibilities and scope for integrating social media data into traditional CRM practices, exploring how this integration can enhance Customer Relationship Management within the healthcare sector.

The chapter employs a mixed-method approach involving three diverse healthcare companies. It assesses their CRM and social media strategies, focusing on customer engagement and insights, patient relationships and education, brand promotion, social listening, and business impact. A semi-structured questionnaire aids data collection, aiming to comprehend company feedback and perceptions about various types of CRM and social media tools, their integration, benefits, and challenges. The findings will showcase the path to successful transitions from CRM to Social CRM in healthcare settings, proposing strategies, addressing challenges, and encouraging healthcare organizations to embrace Social CRM for improved customer engagement and satisfaction.

In addition, a case study of USV Private Limited demonstrates the practical implementation of these strategies. This real-world application provides valuable insights into how companies like USV navigate the complexities of transitioning to Social CRM, offering a blueprint for others in the industry to follow. By showcasing the success of USV's initiatives, the chapter underscores the importance of testing theoretical frameworks in live organizational settings to validate their efficacy and relevance.

Literature Review

The Evolution of CRM in Healthcare

Customer Relationship Management software enables businesses to gain deeper insights into their customers and improve communication with them. Understanding customer behaviour and preferences enables businesses to tailor services and increase satisfaction. CRM involves technological tools and strategic approaches to improve customer interaction management processes (Anshari et al., 2019), and relies heavily on technology for better customer communication and data management (Harrigan et al., 2011; Jayachandran et al., 2005). According to Harrigan et al. (2011), these processes enhance marketing performance by increasing market awareness, reducing costs, building customer loyalty, increasing competitiveness, and maximizing customer profitability. With the advancement of information technology (IT), electronic services have become more common in improving service standards. Electronic Customer Relationship Management (e-CRM) has therefore evolved into an essential component of providing high-quality services in various industries, demonstrating an impressive integration of IT and traditional CRM practices (Singh et al., 2023). Companies can gain insights into the behaviours of both existing and potential customers by combining CRM tools with web or app technology. This will assist them in developing specific strategies and activities that may persuade customers to conduct transactions and make decisions (Nisar & Prabhakar, 2018).

The evolution of CRM in healthcare companies has been fast with advancements in technology and evolving consumer expectations. CRM systems are adapted to meet the unique needs of healthcare product companies, enhance relationships with healthcare providers, and optimize internal processes. Integrating technologies such as electronic health records (EHRs), telemedicine solutions, and healthcare and patient portals has changed how healthcare companies manage client interactions, prioritizing personalized care and improving engagement (Smith & Johnson, 2015).

The Emergence of Social CRM in Healthcare

Recent trends in CRM include the adoption of Social CRM, integrating social media platforms to enhance customer engagement and leveraging technological advancements for efficient data management (Fernando et al., 2023). This evolution reflects the growing importance of integrating social media interactions into CRM systems (Lamrhari et al., 2022). Social CRM facilitates various interactions and applications, enabling businesses to create social communities, connect with customers, and utilize social data for predictive purposes (Awasthi & Sangle, 2012; Choudhury & Harrigan, 2014). With robust technical features, Social CRM enables users to create and share content effectively (Harrigan et al., 2015).

Also referred to as CRM 2.0, the emergence of Social CRM introduces a new dimension to healthcare companies, improving communication and providing valuable insights for product design (Garcia & Rodriguez, 2016). As healthcare product companies embrace new technologies, the evolving CRM landscape promises to improve customer relations, streamline operations, and offer a more client-centric healthcare product experience. Moreover, businesses are encouraged to utilize social monitoring tools for frequent customer engagement and timely responses to changing needs. At the same time, managers must invest in social media to enhance Customer Relationship Management, adjust business processes for digital marketing, and allocate marketing resources effectively (Luo et al., 2024).

The evolution of CRM into Social CRM was prompted by the transformative impact of social media communications, altering communication patterns between younger generations and companies (Dewnarain et al., 2019). Social CRM enables precise analysis by examining conversations on social media platforms, facilitating the delivery of programmes aligned with customer interests and preferences (Anshari et al., 2019). However, challenges in using social CRM in healthcare organizations persist, including awareness gaps, inconsistent use of social media alongside existing CRM systems, and the absence of policies and privacy measures for shared information (Rupert et al., 2020).

Limited Research on Social CRM within Healthcare

The existing literature on social CRM indicates that more research into social CRM adoption is needed. While factors influencing the adoption of CRM, electronic CRM, mobile CRM, and Social CRM have been explored in certain studies, more research is needed on social CRM adoption in the healthcare context (Jalal et al., 2021). Despite the significant advancements in scientific research on Social CRM, there needs to be more emphasis on comprehensively demonstrating the fundamental influencers, challenges, and business benefits associated with it (Anshari & Almunawar, 2012). Future research should therefore focus on empirical studies to investigate the primary challenges of adopting Social CRM in specific domains. Cross-sectional studies would be particularly advantageous in thoroughly comprehending this subject matter. Similarly, future research should empirically investigate Social CRM notable benefits and potential consequences across various businesses. There is also an opportunity for further investigation to develop and examine a comprehensive structural model that encompasses the crucial determinants and outcomes of applying social CRM (Anshari & Almunawar, 2012).

The Current State of CRM in the Healthcare Industry

Healthcare is an industry focused on creating products and services that enhance and save human lives. From disease prevention and diagnosis to treatment and care, healthcare covers the entire spectrum of human life.

In such a dynamic and innovative industry, staying competitive is vital, and this is particularly true given the informed and engaged nature of healthcare consumers. Customer retention is critical in this industry because new customers are expensive to acquire and because repeat business represents trust and quality. CRM gathers comprehensive patient data in healthcare to facilitate effective communication, establish positive rapport, and provide timely information. It also includes tracking patients' progress and making necessary adjustments to their care (Benz & Paddison, 2004).

CRM plays a vital role in today's operational framework of pharmaceutical and medical device companies. Healthcare companies have a multifaceted role in developing and enhancing relationships with various stakeholders, including healthcare providers, practitioners, distributors, patients, and others. Building robust relationships with healthcare providers and practitioners is essential as they are the direct contact for recommending and utilizing various healthcare products. However, with patients becoming more engaged and empowered in managing their health, healthcare product suppliers recognize the significance of direct patient engagement. Today's CRM tools assist in creating and sharing targeted and informative content addressing concerns that contribute to patient well-being.

CRM Tools Used by Healthcare Companies

A proficient CRM tool with intelligent features for tracking sales and marketing efforts, managing the sales pipeline, and integrating business functions is valuable to leadership teams in healthcare companies. Such a tool can help with customer acquisition and retention by providing insights into planned efforts and their implementation. The customers of healthcare companies are widespread and served by local representatives, so centralizing customer data using features such as customer database management in a sophisticated CRM tool helps streamline operations. Features like call planning and reporting, and interactive dashboards for tracking key performance indicators (KPIs) ensure effective sales team management.

Healthcare companies commonly use a range of CRM tools to manage relationships with patients, healthcare providers, and stakeholders, as outlined below:

- *Sales and marketing*: These platforms cater to healthcare product sales, marketing campaigns, and lead management, enabling companies to interact with healthcare professionals, manage marketing strategies, and track sales efforts. Examples: Salesforce, Veeva, TOTALytics.

- *Patient relationship management*: Designed to manage relationships with patients, PRM systems focus on patient engagement – managing patient records, scheduling appointments, and facilitating communication between healthcare providers and patients. Example: Solutionreach.
- *Enterprise*: These systems often encompass sales, marketing, and customer service, enabling healthcare companies to manage interactions across departments and stakeholders. Examples: SAP, Oracle, and Salesforce.
- *Customer service*: These CRMs focus on managing interactions and support services for healthcare product consumers and healthcare professionals, facilitating issue resolution and providing information about healthcare products. Example: Zendesk.
- *Product management*: These CRMs focus on managing healthcare product data, inventory, and information related to product features, specifications, and compliance. They assist in tracking product development, maintaining regulatory compliance, and managing product information databases. Examples: PTC Windchill, Veeva.
- *Partner relationship management*: PRM systems manage relationships with distributors, suppliers, and other business partners in the healthcare industry. These CRMs facilitate collaboration, communication, and support among supply chain business partners. Example: Impartner.

Each type of CRM serves a specific purpose. The choice of system therefore often depends on a company's specific needs, objectives, and primary area of focus – whether patient care, pharmaceutical sales, medical devices, or healthcare services.

The Significance of Social CRM in the Healthcare Industry

Social media serves as a space for dialogue, knowledge-sharing, and networking, profoundly influencing decision-making processes for both healthcare practitioners and patients. Leveraging social media in the context of CRM can be instrumental in aggregating valuable insights from these interactions. Social CRM, built on Web 2.0, should include features from social networks. Integrating data from social media platforms with traditional CRM systems offers an opportunity to obtain a more comprehensive understanding of healthcare practitioners' and patients' needs, preferences, and behaviours. Integrating social networks into a strategy helps healthcare organizations connect with customers by understanding what they need from the services. Through conversations on social networks, customers can freely express praise or criticism of the organization. These networks also serve as a platform for patients with the same conditions to share their experiences (Anshari & Almunawar, 2012). By amalgamating social media data with existing CRM, healthcare companies can refine their strategies, tailor their services more effectively, and better address the evolving demands and expectations of their stakeholders.

Critical Components of Social CRM in Healthcare

Based on the literature review and earlier studies, we identified the following important factors needed to determine the need/success of integrating Social CRM with traditional CRM in healthcare. We then studied them from the perspective of three diverse healthcare companies for presentation in this chapter.

Data integration and security: Ability to integrate social CRM data with existing CRM systems (sales, marketing) while maintaining data security and compliance with healthcare regulations.

Customer insights and analytics: The ability to derive actionable insights from social CRM data integrated with existing CRM, allowing for more informed sales and marketing strategy decisions.

Lead management and opportunity identification: Features supporting the identification of leads and opportunities derived from social interactions for sales and marketing efforts in the healthcare manufacturing domain.

Operational efficiency: Assessing how integration impacts operational processes and whether it streamlines workflows for improved efficiency.

Impact on sales and marketing strategies: Understanding how integration affects sales and marketing strategies and whether or not it contributes to more effective targeting and campaigns.

Research Design and Methodology

We used a mixed-method approach comprising a case study of three healthcare companies and a pilot quantitative study focused on those companies.

Case Studies

The objective here was to gain insights into the types of CRM and social media tools and strategies used and the potential benefits and significant barriers in implementing Social CRM strategies in healthcare companies.

Therefore, a qualitative research approach, specifically the case study methodology, was employed. Recognized as a systematic approach within the qualitative research paradigm, case study allows in-depth exploration of specific contexts or scenarios with well-defined boundaries, offering a means to investigate unique or recurring conditions. This methodology can serve as a model for deriving and replicating generalizable insights (Creswell & Poth, 2016). While providing rich and detailed data for a deeper understanding of specific situations, it is essential to acknowledge the limitations of case study research – such as the potential lack of generalizability due to its focus on particular cases and the potential for bias and subjectivity in data collection and analysis. Despite these limitations, the case study methodology remains valuable for comprehending complex phenomena in various fields.

Pilot Quantitative Research

The primary objective of this follow-up pilot quantitative research was to understand and investigate the scope of the transition from traditional CRM to Social CRM. We aimed to collect initial quantitative insights from three diverse healthcare companies regarding their CRM and social media practices. The insights from this chapter will serve as a foundation for more in-depth research involving many companies in the future. The benefits of this mixed approach include:

- Depth and breadth: Gaining in-depth insights and rich qualitative data from case studies while also collecting broader trends and patterns from quantitative data.
- Focused resources: A targeted approach for pilot research minimizes resource requirements and allows for exploring the context-specific factors influencing CRM and social media integration.
- Informed next steps: The findings can guide the development of larger-scale quantitative studies or interventions in the future.

Sampling

Knowing the multifaceted landscape of healthcare – comprising pharmaceuticals, diagnostics, medical devices, and medical disposables, and each catering to diverse products and customer segments – we chose three healthcare companies of distinct nature from a strategic perspective. By examining the status and strategies of their existing CRM and social media implementation, we aimed to find common ground and uniqueness in each sector. This approach provides scope to assess the potential advantages and challenges associated with adopting a Social CRM strategy within the dynamic realm of healthcare.

- *Company A*: This prominent player in the medical device industry specializes in creating innovative healthcare solutions in infusion therapy and vascular access, delivering high-quality medical products globally.
- *Company B*: This industry leader is known for its innovative and cutting-edge dental technology and equipment. It is recognized for manufacturing and supplying advanced solutions that enhance dental care globally.
- *Company C*: A prominent Indian pharmaceutical company renowned for its commitment to advancing healthcare through research, development, and production of a diverse range of products for various therapeutic areas. It is dedicated to improving global access to quality healthcare solutions.

Data Collection

The method used was a semi-structured questionnaire divided into three sections of open-ended qualitative questions and closed quantitative questions (Table 11.1). This hybrid questionnaire was designed to create a balance by offering the flexibility of open questions for respondents to express thoughts freely and the structured format of closed questions to collect quantifiable data.

We engaged with key stakeholders such as senior managers from three healthcare companies' marketing, digital, and IT departments. Interviews were conducted personally over video calls in two phases. In the first phase, we asked qualitative questions, and, based on their feedback and our learning from the literature review, we designed the follow-up quantitative questions for the pilot survey and reconnected to get the same. Each participant was given a questionnaire at the beginning of the interview, which lasted for 20–30 minutes in each phase. All the participants were highly engaged and willingly shared the information. The data collection method was adapted from Dewnarain et al. (2019).

Data Analysis

A thematic analysis was carried out using the data collected from the open-ended qualitative questions to find the common themes and patterns across

Table 11.1 Semi-structured questionnaire format

Section	Objective	Qualitative Aspects	Quantitative Aspects
1	Assess current use and perceptions of types of CRM	1. Types of CRM used and reason for using	1. Suitability of CRM type on scale of most to least importance
2	Explore the use, perceived benefits, and challenges of social media tools	1. Which platform used; frequency and purpose of using social media 2. Future investment plan	1. Preference of various social media platform 2. Factors measured for success of social media efforts
3	Study Social CRM use by integrating social media with CRM and associated insights	1. Interest and importance	1. Evaluate and prioritize social media platforms based on important criteria for social CRM features 2. Attribute ranking to determine success of integrating social media data with traditional CRM

the three companies involved in the case study. We identified similarities and differences in their responses. For instance, patterns emerged where all three companies highlight a common CRM type but differ in their perceptions of their suitability in the healthcare business.

We used the qualitative findings in the development of quantitative closed questions. The data from quantitative questions were used for basic inferential statistics looking into pilot sample size, and the same data was used to summarize and analyse the quantitative data. We also compared the quantitative results with qualitative insights, and combined the findings to draw comprehensive conclusions. We used charts, graphs, and tables to represent the patterns identified visually, and created bar charts and tables to show the frequency of specific responses. Finally, a cross-case analysis to compare and contrast the findings helped identify overlapping patterns that were consistent or divergent across the companies.

Results and Discussion

We linked the analysis and findings to various research objectives (see Table 11.1) to demonstrate how they address the critical questions posed in the research, as outlined below.

Objective 1: Assess Current Use and Perceptions of Types of CRM

Qualitative Findings

All three companies had employed diverse CRM systems for over five years, tailored to specific needs by specific departments. In some cases, different modules for different functions were made available within a single CRM application: for example, Veeva CRM has modules for sales, marketing, and product management.

As shown in Table 11.2, sales and marketing CRM and enterprise CRM are commonly utilized across all organizations, irrespective of product and business type. Company B and C use partner relationship management (PRM) CRM, and only Company A used product management CRM. Results show that they do not use CRM for patient relationships and customer service.

Quantitative Findings

Based on the qualitative findings, we examined which CRM systems were important to the sample healthcare companies. We also included types of CRM not currently used by those companies but otherwise used by many others.

As shown in Figures 11.1 and 11.2, the importance of different CRM types varies among companies. On a scale of 1 (least important) to 5 (most important), Partner Relationship emerged as crucial for all, with Company A planning its implementation; sales and marketing and enterprise CRM types held general significance; and product management was also considered highly important.

Table 11.2 Type of CRM systems used by the sample companies

	Sales and Marketing	Patient Relationship	Enterprise	Customer Service	Product Management	PRM
Company A						
Company B						
Company C						

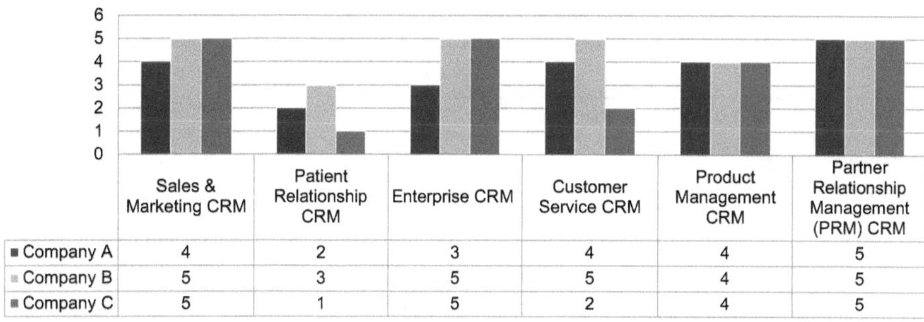

Figure 11.1 Importance of CRM types

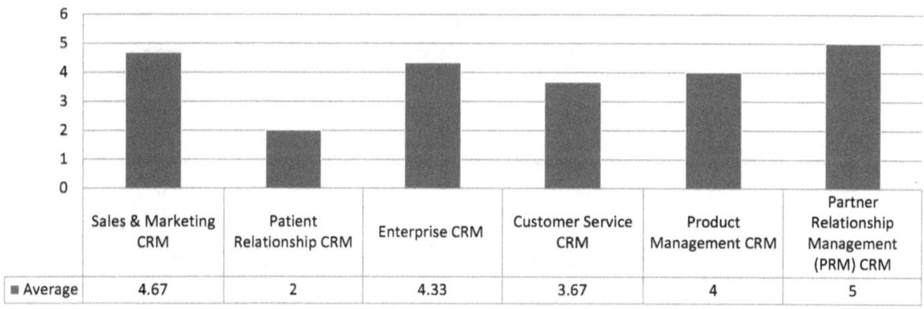

Figure 11.2 Mean ranking of CRM types

Objective 2: Explore the Use, Benefits, and Challenges of Social Media Tools

Qualitative Findings

All companies reported longstanding use of various social media platforms – mainly LinkedIn, X (Twitter), Facebook, YouTube, and Instagram – with plans to incrementally increase budgets (Table 11.3). However, as shown in Table 11.4, companies differed in the frequency of social media posts, driven

Table 11.3 Social media platforms used by the sample companies

	LinkedIn	X (Twitter)	Facebook	YouTube	Instagram
Company A					
Company B					
Company C					

Table 11.4 Frequency of posts per week

	Once	Twice	Three times
Company A			
Company B			
Company C			

Table 11.5 Purpose of using social media

	Customer (HCP) engagement and insights	Customer support and training	Brand promotion and marketing	Patient education and awareness	Employer branding and recruitment	Attract investors
Company A						
Company B						
Company C						

by distinct purposes such as patient education, brand promotion, customer support, and training.

The companies use social media for different purposes. However, patient education awareness and brand promotion are common to all three companies. For medical equipment companies, customer support and training are essential, whereas for companies listed on the Indian stock exchange, attracting investors is an important factor (Table 11.5). As informed by the respondents, challenges regarding social media strategy included measuring impact, low customer conversion, and expectations of a more significant impact.

Quantitative Findings

Based on qualitative feedback, we measured the companies' preferences for different social media platforms on a scale of 1–5 (least to most preferred). As shown in Figure 11.3, this revealed that YouTube is the most popular platform across all three companies. This aligns with its effectiveness regarding patient education and awareness, which are the primary goals of all three. LinkedIn and Facebook also scored highly, with X/Twitter the least preferred, as shown in Figure 11.4.

As shown in Figures 11.5 and 11.6, Facebook was preferred for paid promotions due to its large user base and lower advertising costs. This was followed by Instagram and YouTube, with LinkedIn the least preferred due to its high cost.

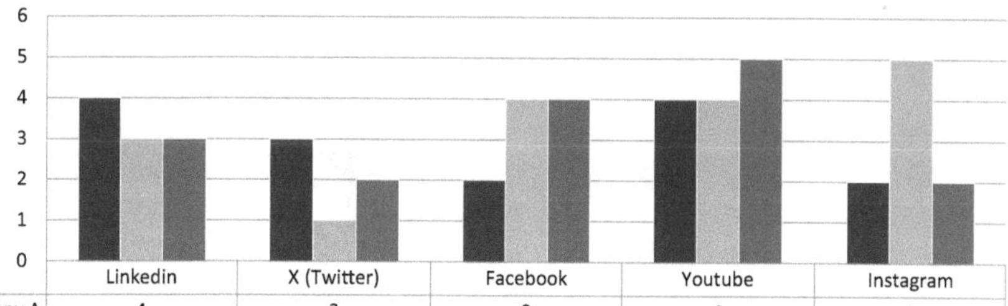

	Linkedin	X (Twitter)	Facebook	Youtube	Instagram
Company A	4	3	2	4	2
Company B	3	1	4	4	5
Company C	3	2	4	5	2

Figure 11.3 Preference for social media platforms

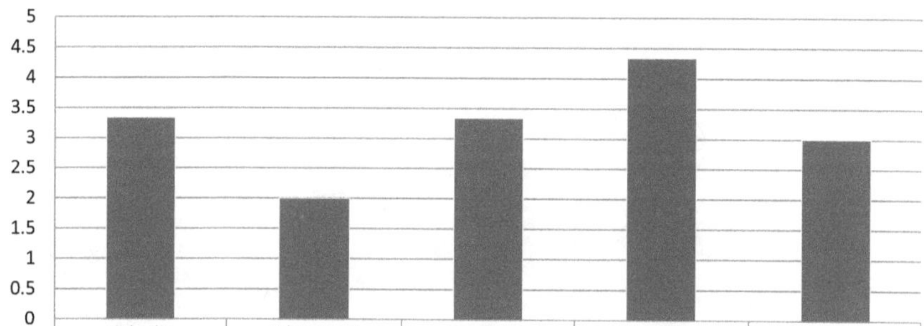

	Linkedin	X (Twitter)	Facebook	Youtube	Instagram
Average	3.33	2	3.33	4.33	3

Figure 11.4 Mean preference for social media platforms

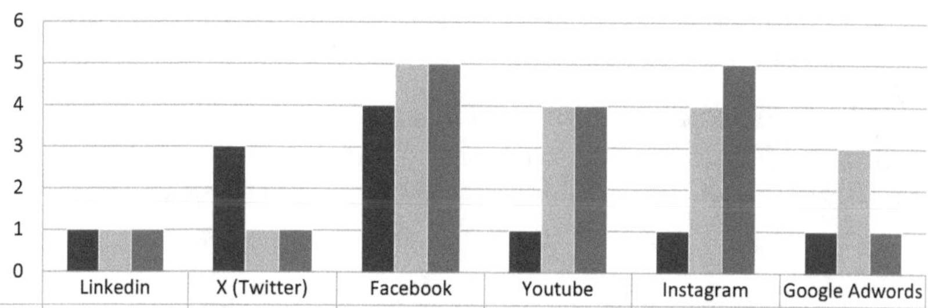

	Linkedin	X (Twitter)	Facebook	Youtube	Instagram	Google Adwords
Company A	1	3	4	1	1	1
Company B	1	1	5	4	4	3
Company C	1	1	5	4	5	1

Figure 11.5 Platform preference for paid promotions

Figure 11.7 shows the criteria considered important for evaluating the success of social media efforts: conversion metrics are top, followed by return on investment (ROI). However, no specific model or scale for a quantitative measure of ROI is available, but the general consensus is that it would be a game-changer to have a model around the same.

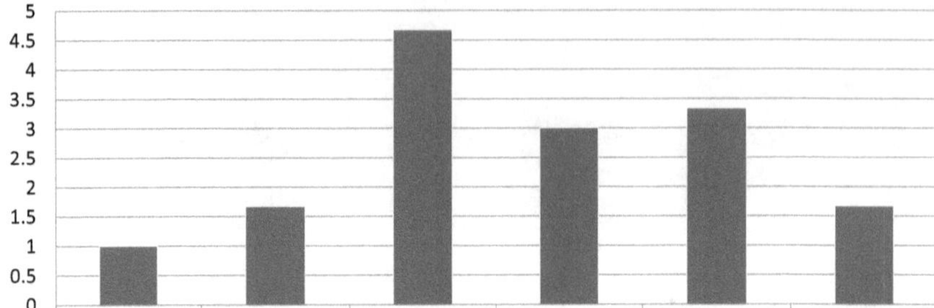

	Linkedin	X (Twitter)	Facebook	Youtube	Instagram	Google Adwords
Average	1	1.666666667	4.666666667	3	3.333333333	1.666666667

Figure 11.6 Mean platform preference for paid promotions

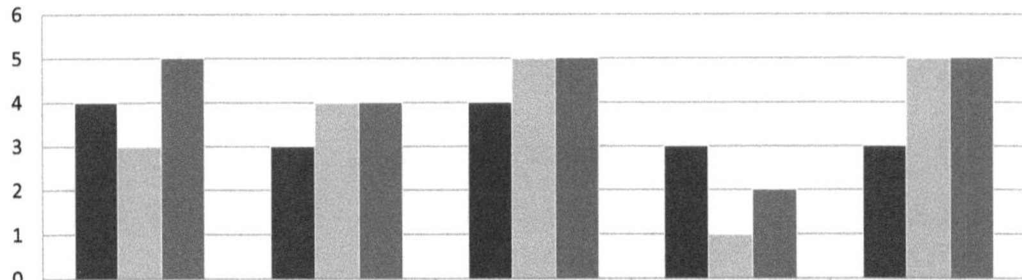

	Engagement Metrics	Reach and Impressions	Conversion Metrics	Sentiment Analysis	Return on Investment (ROI)
Company A	4	3	4	3	3
Company B	3	4	5	1	5
Company C	5	4	5	2	5

Figure 11.7 Importance of criteria for evaluating success of social media promotions

Calculation of the average rankings for these criteria based on feedback from all respondents shows conversion metrics as the most important, followed by ROI, engagement metrics, and reach and impressions (Figure 11.8).

Objective 3: Study Social CRM Use by Integrating Social Media with CRM and Associated Insights

Qualitative Findings

Awareness of Social CRM was limited, with only Company A having some knowledge of it. All respondents recognized the importance of social

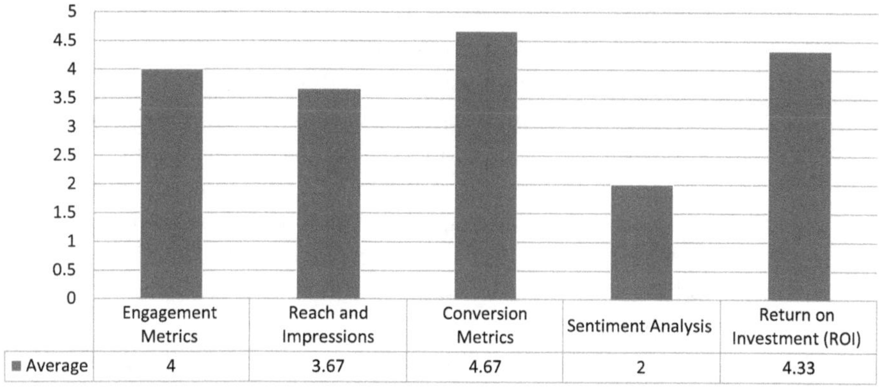

Figure 11.8 Mean importance of criteria for evaluating success of social media promotions

media data for refining customer offerings, designing communication, and improving touch points for HCPs and patients. Nevertheless, there was a shared feeling that a more structured approach – integrating social media data into traditional CRM using CRM 2.0 or Social CRM – would be highly beneficial.

Quantitative Findings

A weighted scoring method was applied to prioritize social media platforms based on crucial attributes for Social CRM, as outlined in the following step-by-step analysis:

1. Define criteria and assign weight: We identified the following criteria based on qualitative feedback from respondents regarding the purpose of using social media and on literature reviews: customer engagement and insights; customer support and training; brand marketing and promotion; patient education and awareness; employer branding; and and recruiting. We then asked respondents from each company to weight each criterion based on its importance, with weighting totalling 100 per cent.
2. Feedback: We collected feedback from each company on the performance of the social media platforms based on the criteria defined in Step 1, using a scale of 1–5 indicating worst to best performance.

3. Calculate weighted scores: We calculated the weighted scores for each social media platform by multiplying each respondent company's score for the criterion by the weight assigned to that criterion.
4. Sum weighted scores to analyse individual company preferences: We calculated the total weighted scores by summing the weighted scores given by each company for each social media option across all criteria, and then compared the total weighted scores for each option across all respondents. Based on the defined criteria, the social media platform with the highest total weighted score is the preferred choice for that particular company.
5. Analyse collective preferences: In the final step we calculated each platform's average total weighted score across all companies, which provided an overall perspective on supplier performance.

As shown in Table 11.6 for Company A, LinkedIn was the preferred platform based on the criteria defined, followed by Facebook.

Table 11.7 shows that YouTube was the most preferred platform for Company B, followed by Facebook and Instagram, while LinkedIn ranked below average.

As shown in Table 11.8 for Company C, YouTube was the preferred platform, followed by LinkedIn and Facebook.

Table 11.6 Weighted scores for Company A

Criteria	**Weighting**	**LinkedIn**	**X (Twitter)**	**Facebook**	**YouTube**	**Instagram**
Customer (HCP) engagement and insights	0.2	0.4	0.2	0.6	0.6	0.2
Customer support and training	0.1	0.1	0.1	0.2	0.4	0.1
Brand marketing and promotion	0.3	1.2	1.2	1.2	0.9	1.2
Patient education and awareness	0.2	0.4	0.6	0.8	0.4	0.6
Employer branding and recruiting	0.2	1	0.2	0.2	0.2	0.2
Total	**1**	**3.1**	**2.3**	**3**	**2.5**	**2.3**

Table 11.7 Weighted scores for Company B

Criteria	**Weighting**	**LinkedIn**	**X (Twitter)**	**Facebook**	**YouTube**	**Instagram**
Customer (HCP) engagement and insights	0.3	0.6	0.6	1.5	1.5	1.5
Customer support and training	0.2	0.4	0.4	0.8	1	0.8
Brand marketing and promotion	0.2	0.6	0.2	0.8	0.8	0.8
Patient education and awareness	0.2	0.4	0.4	1	1	1
Employer branding and recruiting	0.1	0.5	0.1	0.1	0.1	0.1
Total	**1**	**2.5**	**1.7**	**4.2**	**4.4**	**4.2**

Table 11.8 Weighted scores for Company C

Criteria	**Weighting**	**LinkedIn**	**X (Twitter)**	**Facebook**	**YouTube**	**Instagram**
Customer (HCP) engagement and insights	0.3	1.5	1.2	1.5	1.5	1.2
Customer support and training	0.1	0.2	0.1	0.5	0.5	0.2
Brand marketing and promotion	0.2	0.6	0.4	0.8	0.6	0.4
Patient education and awareness	0.3	1.2	0.9	1.2	1.5	1.2
Employer branding and recruiting	0.1	0.5	0.1	0.1	0.2	0.1
Total	**1**	**4**	**2.7**	**4.1**	**4.3**	**3.1**

Figure 11.9 shows the average total weighted scores of the various social media platforms across all companies.

Looking into the insights gained from both analyses, we found that: YouTube and Facebook are the preferred platforms for Companies A and B in terms of individual preference as well, as they scored high across all companies; X/Twitter was the least preferred platform both at the individual level and across all companies.

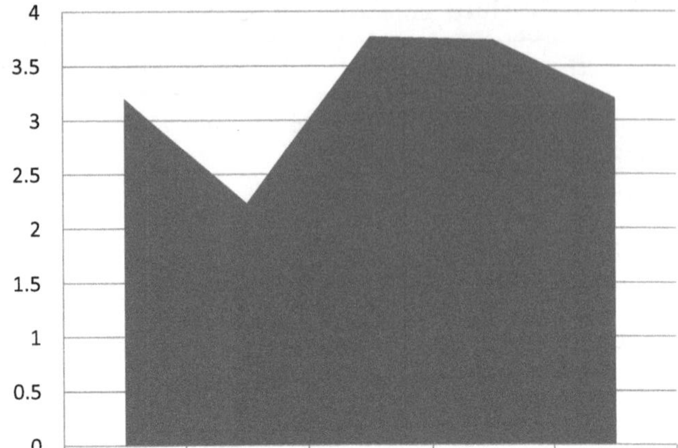

	Linkedin	Twitter	Facebook	Youtube	Instagram
■ Average Total Weighted score	3.2	2.23	3.77	3.73	3.2

Figure 11.9 Average total weighted scores for platforms across all companies

Important Attributes for the Success of Social CRM

Based on qualitative feedback and the literature review, we listed specific attributes important in determining the success of Social CRM by integrating social media data in CRM. We then asked respondents to rank those attributes on a scale of 1–5, with higher scores reflecting more importance.

As shown in Figure 11.10, customer insights and data security are considered the most essential factors in determining the success of social CRM, whereas operational efficiency will have the least impact.

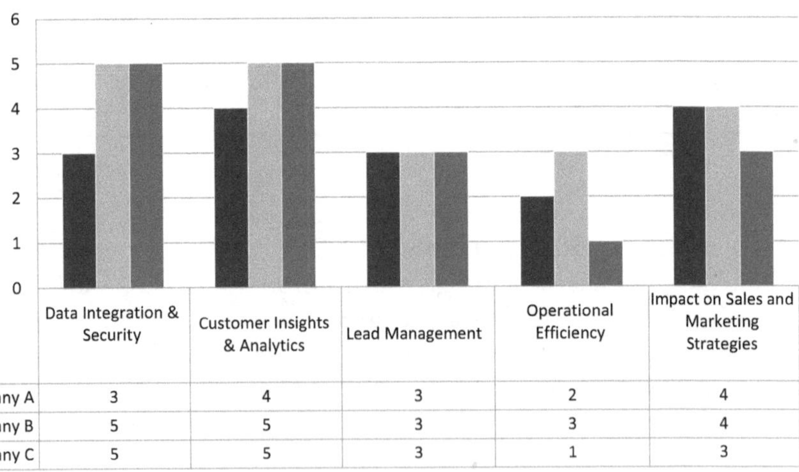

	Data Integration & Security	Customer Insights & Analytics	Lead Management	Operational Efficiency	Impact on Sales and Marketing Strategies
■ Company A	3	4	3	2	4
■ Company B	5	5	3	3	4
■ Company C	5	5	3	1	3

Figure 11.10 Attributes important for Social CRM success at company level

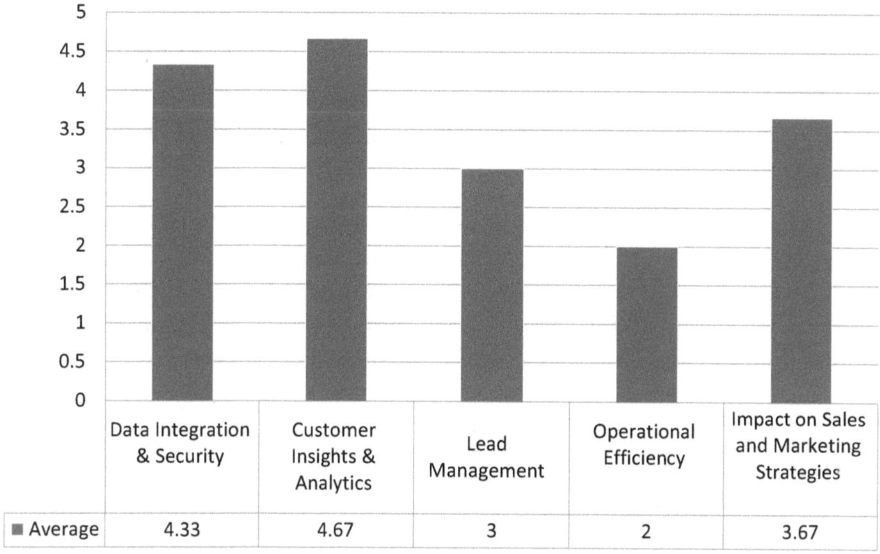

Figure 11.11 Attributes important for Social CRM success across all companies

Averages calculated across all respondents confirm the same findings (Figure 11.11), although impact on sales and marketing is also an essential factor in determining the success of Social CRM.

Case Study: USV Private Limited – Practical Transition from CRM to Social CRM

Introduction

In the ongoing exploration of the transition from CRM to Social CRM in the healthcare industry, the case of USV Private Limited – a leading Indian pharmaceutical and biotechnology company – provides a compelling narrative of practical implementation. As discussed earlier in the chapter, qualitative and quantitative data was meticulously collected and analysed to better understand the changing landscape of Customer Relationship Management in healthcare. To complement these findings, we examine USV's transformative journey.

USV Private Limited launched a strategic initiative using Social CRM strategies to improve engagement with patients and healthcare professionals. This case study investigates the methodology and outcomes of USV's initiatives using secondary sources such as social media platforms, company reports, and industry publications. By examining this company's approach, we can gain valuable insights into the practical implications of implementing Social CRM in the healthcare sector.

Background

USV Private Limited, with over six decades of experience in pharmaceutical manufacturing, research, and marketing, has emerged as India's leader in therapeutic segments such as cardiology and diabetology. USV's commitment to being a trusted health partner is demonstrated by its market leadership in the oral anti-diabetic and cardiovascular disease segments.

Campaign Initiatives and Methodology

In keeping with this commitment, in 2016 the company launched two effective campaigns – 'HALT Diabetes' and 'HALT Heart Attack' – in response to India's rising rates of diabetes and heart disease. These campaigns, integrating Social CRM strategies in marketing initiatives, aimed to educate patients about preventive measures, treatment options, and lifestyle changes using engaging content and interactive sessions led by healthcare professionals.

- *HALT Heart Attack* mainly used Facebook and YouTube, with a small presence on X/Twitter and Instagram.
- *HALT Diabetes* also focused on the Facebook and YouTube platforms.

Both campaigns aimed to increase public awareness of heart attacks and diabetes. Over 1000 healthcare professionals actively participated, sharing educational content via videos, posts, and live sessions.

Platform Engagement

- Facebook: The HALT Heart Attack FB page was created in August 2017, and has garnered significant engagement, with 201K likes and 209K followers. Posts by over 500 healthcare professionals contributed to raising awareness about heart health. The HALT Diabetes page was launched in December of that year, and amassed 167K likes and 187K followers. It primarily featured live sessions by expert medical professionals, attracting large audiences.

- YouTube: HALT Heart Attack and HALT Diabetes channels have hosted numerous educational videos and sessions, garnering thousands of subscribers and millions of views since their inception in 2016.
- Twitter (X): The @HALT_HA channel started in April 2020 with the aim of increasing awareness about heart attacks and cardiovascular disease.
- Instagram: HALT Heart Attack was created in September 2023 and has 371 followers sharing valuable health awareness messages.

Implementation and Engagement

USV directed users to informative resources such as articles, infographics, and webinars on disease awareness, lifestyle changes, and treatment options via targeted advertising campaigns and collaborations with healthcare influencers. Interactive quizzes and surveys were also used to assess audience knowledge and tailor content appropriately.

The company encouraged public participation by hosting live question and answer (Q&A) sessions with healthcare experts, organizing virtual fitness challenges, and soliciting user-generated content (UGC) via hashtag campaigns. USV aims to establish itself as a reliable resource in the disease management space by instilling a sense of community and support in its social media followers.

Outcome

The HALT Diabetes and HALT Heart Attack campaigns had extensive reach and engagement on social media platforms, with thousands of shares, likes, and comments on educational posts and videos. Live sessions frequently attracted thousands of viewers. USV Private Limited increased the impact of its campaigns and reached a larger audience by collaborating with healthcare influencers and using targeted advertising. Furthermore, the company experienced increased website traffic and enquiries about its diabetes management and heart care products, indicating individuals' growing interest in taking charge of their health.

Integration with CRM

USV seamlessly integrated Social CRM initiatives into its existing CRM system, streamlining data collection, analysis, and customer engagement. It also personalized communications by gathering valuable insights from social media interactions, addressing patient enquiries quickly and cultivating long-term relationships with patients and healthcare professionals.

Conclusion of the Case Study

The USV case demonstrates the successful transition from traditional CRM to Social CRM in the healthcare industry. This company effectively used social media platforms to raise awareness about critical health conditions and strengthen stakeholder relationships. It also improved health outcomes and brand loyalty among its users. This comprehensive case study is consistent with the findings discussed in the chapter, emphasizing the importance of transitioning to Social CRM to effectively engage patients and healthcare professionals in the changing healthcare landscape.

Summary of Key Findings

This chapter examined three healthcare companies – representing diverse sectors such as medical devices, dental technology, and pharmaceuticals – that have been actively using various CRM systems for over five years. The qualitative insights provided an understanding of the CRM applications used by these businesses, with a particular emphasis on sales and marketing functions. The pilot quantitative research investigated the importance of various types of CRM, revealing differences in preference between the companies.

Regarding social media, all three companies have consistently used platforms such as LinkedIn, X/Twitter, Facebook, YouTube, and Instagram to educate patients and promote their brands, among other purposes. The qualitative data highlighted challenges such as measuring impact and low customer conversion. At the same time, the quantitative analysis shed light on the preferred platforms for paid promotions and the criteria identified as critical for assessing social media success.

The chapter also emphasized the importance of Social CRM integration in healthcare – specifically data security, customer insights, efficient lead management, and alignment with operational processes. According to the findings, businesses should consider a strategic approach to social media and CRM integration that balances the unique needs of their industries while leveraging the strengths of the various social media platforms.

Conclusion

In this chapter, we used a mixed-methods approach to investigate the complex process of integrating Social Customer Relationship Management (CRM) with traditional CRM in the healthcare industry. The findings provide valuable insights into the current state of CRM and social media use in healthcare organizations. Despite differences in preferences and challenges, the study emphasizes the importance of tailored strategies aligned with organizational needs. Furthermore, limited awareness of Social CRM creates opportunities for further research and implementation in the healthcare domain.

The transition from CRM to Social CRM opens up numerous opportunities for healthcare companies to improve patient engagement and brand loyalty and drive positive health outcomes. Healthcare organizations can establish themselves as trusted partners on the path to better health and well-being by implementing innovative strategies and leveraging the power of social media. The case study of USV Private Limited demonstrates the successful integration of Social CRM strategies into marketing initiatives, resulting in increased engagement with patients and healthcare professionals. By embracing this evolution in Customer Relationship Management, healthcare organizations can meet the changing needs of patients and stakeholders and drive transformative change throughout the healthcare system.

Future Research Directions

Future research in Social CRM in healthcare should focus on the specific challenges that healthcare organizations face when implementing these strategies. Exploring industry-specific challenges and regulatory considerations would contribute to a more customized understanding. Furthermore, longitudinal studies that track the evolution of social CRM practices over time may provide insights into the long-term impact and viability of such strategies in the ever-changing healthcare landscape.

References

Anshari, M., & Almunawar, M. N. (2012). Framework of social customer relationship management in e-health services. *Journal of e-Health Management*, Article 766268. https://ibimapublishing.com/articles/JEHM/2012/766268/

Anshari, M., Almunawar, M. N., Lim, S. A., & Al-Mudimigh, A. (2019). Customer relationship management and big data enabled: Personalization and customization of services. *Applied Computing and Informatics*, *15*, 94–101.

Awasthi, P., & Sangle, P. S. (2012). Adoption of CRM technology in multichannel environment: A review (2006–2010). *Business Process Management Journal*, *18*(3), 445–471.

Benz, G., & Paddison, N. (2004). Developing patient-based marketing strategies. *Healthcare Executive*, *19*(5), 40–42.

Choudhury, M. M., & Harrigan, P. (2014). CRM to social CRM: The integration of new technologies into customer relationship management. *Journal of Strategic Marketing*, *22*(2), 149–176.

Creswell, J. W., & Poth, C. N. (2016). *Qualitative inquiry and research design: Choosing among five approaches* (4th ed.). Los Angeles: SAGE Publications.

Dewnarain, S., Ramkissoon, H., & Mavondo, F. (2019). Social customer relationship management in the hospitality industry. *Journal of Hospitality Research*, *1*(1), 1–14. http://htmjournals.com/jh/index.php/jh/article/view/1

Fernando, E., Sutomo, R., Prabowo, Y. D., Gatc, J., & Winanti, W. (2023). Exploring customer relationship management: Trends, challenges, and innovations. *Journal of Information Systems and Informatics*, *5*(3), 984–1001.

Garcia, C., & Rodriguez, M. (2016). Social CRM in healthcare: Opportunities and challenges. *Journal of Healthcare Information Management*, *23*(2), 78–92.

Harrigan, P., Soutar, G., Choudhury, M. M., & Lowe, M. (2011). Modelling CRM in a social media age. *Journal of Direct, Data and Digital Marketing Practice*, *12*(1), 9–23.

Harrigan, P., Soutar, G., Choudhury, M. M., & Lowe, M. (2015). Modelling CRM in a social media age. *Australasian Marketing Journal*, *23*(1), 27–37.

Jalal, A. N., Bahari, M., & Tarofder, A. K. (2021). Transforming traditional CRM into social CRM: An empirical investigation in Iraqi healthcare industry. *Heliyon*, *7*, e06913.

Jayachandran, S., Sharma, S., Kaufman, P., & Raman, P. (2005). The role of relational information processes and technology use in customer relationship management. *Journal of Marketing*, *69*(4), 177–192.

Lamrhari, S., El Ghazi, H., Oubrich, M., & El Faker, A. (2022). A social CRM analytic framework for improving customer retention, acquisition, and conversion. *Technological Forecasting & Social Change*, *174*, 121275. https://doi.org/10.1016/j.techfore.2021.121275

Luo, Z., Guo, J., Benitez, J., Scaringella, L., & Lin, J. (2024). How do organizations leverage social media to enhance marketing performance? Unveiling the power of social CRM capability and guanxi. *Decision Support Systems*, *178*, 114123.

Nisar, T., & Prabhakar, G. (2018). Trains and Twitter: Firm-generated content, customer relationship management and message framing. *Transportation Research Part A: Policy and Practice, 113*, 318–334.

Paliouras, K., & Siakas, K. (2017). Social customer relationship management: A case study. *International Journal of Entrepreneurial Knowledge, 5*(1), 20. doi:10.1515/ijek-2017-0002

Rishi, B., & Bandyopadhyay, S. (Eds.). (2018). *Contemporary issues in social media marketing*. London: Routledge.

Rupert, D. J., Moultrie, R. R., Read, J. G., Jacqueline, B., Bornkessel, A. S., Donoghue, A. C. O., & Sullivan, H. W. (2020). Perceived healthcare provider reactions to patient and caregiver use of online health communities. *Patient Education and Counseling, 96*(3), 320–326.

Siakas, K., Kermizidis, R., & Kontos, K. (2014). Using social media in business as a tool for open innovations. In *Business-related scientific research conference (ABSRC 2014)*, Milan, Italy, 10–12 December.

Singh, P., Kumar, V., & Kataria, S. (2023). A serial mediation model for investigating the impact of e-CRM services on customer loyalty in the Indian healthcare industry. *Journal of Relationship Marketing, 22*(1), 62–86.

Smith, A., & Johnson, B. (2015). The evolution of customer relationship management in the healthcare industry: A comprehensive review. *Journal of Healthcare Management, 17*(3), 45–58.

12 Consumer Persuasion by Chatbots

An Integrative Model of Social Influence

Wolfgang J. Weitzl
Digital Business Institute, University of Applied Sciences Upper Austria, Austria

Ardion D. Beldad
University College Twente, University of Twente, the Netherlands

Gerald Petz
Digital Business Institute, University of Applied Sciences Upper Austria, Austria

Annmarie Hanlon
Cranfield School of Management, Cranfield University, UK

1 Introduction

In the digital era, retailers and service companies increasingly use *chatbots* instead of human employees to assist prospective, current, and former customers during their online journey. Companies use chatbots as virtual representatives to interact with customers and to provide solutions to their problems (Mende et al., 2019). Chatbots often act as personal assistants, supporting customers in

DOI: 10.4324/9781003412656-12

various situations such as seeking information, answering queries, or building social relationships (Chung et al., 2020; Huang et al., 2007).

Chatbots have been rolled out on social media platforms including Facebook, Skype, and WeChat. For instance, the Domino's restaurant chain offers a chatbot to order pizza online via Facebook Messenger (Luo et al., 2019). Other companies such as Coca-Cola, L'Oréal, and Michael Kors provide human-to-chatbot interactions via diverse online channels and use chatbots in various forms, ranging from interactive avatars (Keeling et al., 2010) to animated pictures (Zanker et al., 2011) and human-like animated agents simulating human salespersons (Verhagen et al., 2014).

A chatbot is a computer program that emulates conversation with humans through text messages, navigation buttons, or with simulated voices to provide a particular service (Aleedy et al., 2019). Specifically, it is "a machine conversation system [that] interacts with human users via natural conversational language" (Shawar & Atwell, 2005, p. 489), or "a software that accepts natural language as input and generates natural language as output, engaging in a conversation with the user" (Griol et al., 2013, p. 760). As such, a chatbot is a special form of computer agent; it could be described as a 'social bot' as it is designed to communicate with humans and act as a substitute for other humans by mimicking human-to-human communication (Edwards et al., 2016) by employing machine learning and artificial intelligence (AI) technology (Araujo, 2018).

The ability of chatbots to engage in human-like conversations facilitates various customer services in more effective ways (Hollebeek et al., 2021), and can improve customer experiences by reducing customers' efforts and allowing them to save time (Mimoun et al., 2017). They can provide consumers with useful information. For instance, consumers can ask questions in their own words to get answers from chatbots instead of referring to a company website's frequently asked questions (FAQs).

Companies can benefit in different ways from introducing chatbots into their business operations. Dialogues between consumers and chatbots during the customer journey help companies understand their customers' preferences, expectations, and requirements so that they are in a better position to meet their needs (Rishi & Bandyopadhyay, 2018). Furthermore, chatbots can provide customized recommendations as well as automated assistance, which results in heightened customer satisfaction (Ruan & Mezei, 2022), more favorable product evaluation, and increased purchase intention (Sivaramakrishnan et al., 2007).

Chatbots can also lead to significant cost savings by eliminating the need to employ human service representatives (Hsu & Lin, 2023). Additionally, they can provide uninterrupted 24/7 services, especially when human agents are not available (Joy et al., 2022), providing prompt and real-time answers to customers' queries (Chung et al., 2020). While a human agent can typically only respond to requests from a single consumer at any given time, chatbots can handle numerous consumer queries simultaneously (Cheng et al., 2021). Such abilities enable companies to expand the scope and efficiency of their support services.

One company that has benefited from chatbots is toy manufacturer Lego, which introduced its conversational agent 'Ralph' to help customers navigate its product portfolio and select the perfect gift. This chatbot has its own personality and is valued by customers for the enjoyable interactions. As a result, Ralph helped drive 25 percent of sales from social media and reduce the costs per conversation by more than 70 percent (Davies, 2022). Hence, it is unsurprising that the trend for using chatbot in the business sector will accelerate. Furthermore, it has been projected that chatbots will provide 95 percent of all customer service interactions occurring online by 2025 (Clark, 2020). In 2022, the global chatbot market was valued at 3.02 billion USD, and is expected to reach 24.54 billion USD by 2030 (Cognitive Market Research, 2023) and sustain an annual growth rate of 24 percent (Pantano & Pizzi, 2020).

Over recent decades, research into the effectiveness of interactions between humans and chatbots has accelerated (e.g., Kasilingam, 2020; Rese et al., 2020). However, the scope of published studies into the impact of chatbot communication is large and fragmented. Various studies have attempted to identify the factors that increase consumers' acceptance of chatbots and determine their persuasive influence on consumer behavior (e.g., Beldad et al., 2016). At the same time, research has produced somewhat contradictory findings, specifically concerning the role of anthropomorphic cues (Qiu & Benbasat, 2009). Hence, it is difficult to draw meaningful conclusions. Furthermore, researchers have used diverse approaches to investigate the chatbot phenomenon, and little has been done to integrate the findings of prior studies. In this chapter, we therefore review the current status of research postulating chatbots' process of personal influence, where the interaction between a communicator (i.e., a chatbot as the sender) and a receiver (i.e., an individual consumer) can influence a consumer's purchase decisions.

2 An Integrative Framework of the Impact of Chatbot Communication

Hovland (1948, p. 371) defines social communication as "the process by which an individual (the communicator) transmits stimuli (usually verbal symbols) to modify the behavior of other individuals (communicatees)". Based on the overall framework of 'who says what to whom and with what effect', this includes four major elements: (1) the communicator (source), which refers to the person who transmits the communication; (2) the stimulus (content), which means the message being transmitted by the communicator; (3) the receiver (audience), or the individual who responds to the communication; and (4) the response (main effect), or the receiver's mental or behavioral reaction to the communicator.

In this chapter, we review selected works on the impact (responses) of chatbot communication. 'Chats' represent a new form of social communication content (stimulus) involving information-seeking consumers (receivers) and information-giving social bots (communicators). We review key academic studies and identify variables related to the four elements of social communication (responses, stimuli, receivers, and communicators). Furthermore, we develop an integrative model and discuss the relationships between the critical elements. The 'computers as social actors' (CASA) paradigm (Nass & Moon, 2000) implies that a social influence model is appropriate for identifying the main factors affecting chatbot influence. According to this paradigm, individuals tend to apply human social rules and expectations, similar to other humans, when interacting with computers. This tendency increases when more social cues are provided or a system exhibits human-like behavior – which is typically the case with chatbot communication. This behavior may be related to human-like qualities of (1) text messages like linguistic cues (Holtgraves et al., 2007) and (2) chatbot characteristics such as the name of the agent (e.g., a human- vs. a machine-like name), which might influence anthropomorphic perceptions.

Several scholars argue that the influence of anthropomorphism (the tendency to imbue the real or imagined behavior of non-human agents with human-like characteristics, motivations, intentions, or emotions) can be understood from the perspective of dual process models of persuasion – such as the elaboration likelihood model (ELM; Petty & Cacioppo, 1986) or the heuristic-systematic model (HSM; Chaiken, 1980). A fast and intuitive process leads to a quick classification of an object as human-like (mindless anthropomorphism), while a reflective process includes a conscious effort to evaluate the extent of humanness (mindful anthropomorphism) (Lu et al., 2022). Our model highlights the social cues emitted by chatbot messages (stimuli) and chatbots (communicators) affecting consumer responses in relation to either an explicit or an implicit mental process, which is likely to be moderated by receiver and contextual characteristics. Figure 12.1 summarizes our integrative framework.

2.1 Responses

Chat communication is expected to elicit a certain response from a receiver. Such a response could be attitudinal, intentional, or behavioral, which are three

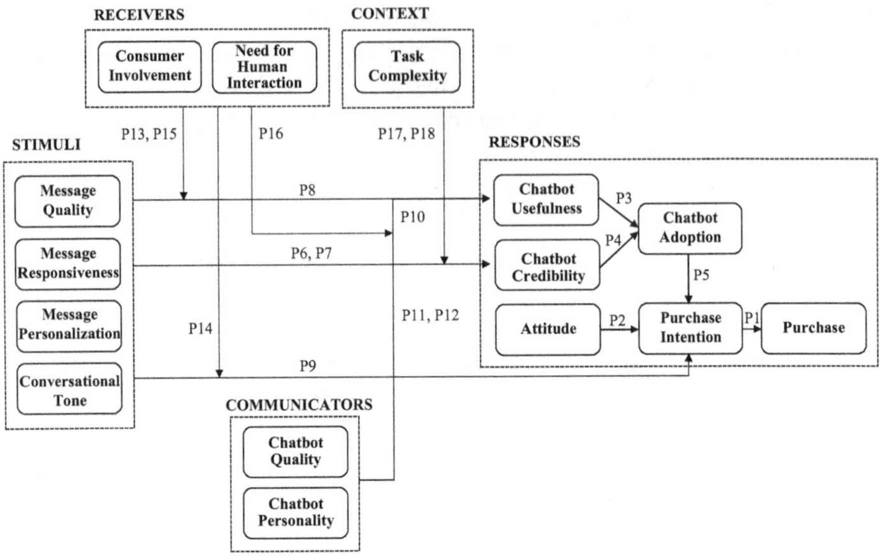

Figure 12.1 Integrative framework of the impact of chatbot communication

commonly studied outcomes of chatbot interactions (e.g., Yen & Chiang, 2021). The interrelationships of these three variables are well-established and validated in research into consumer online behavior. For instance, by reviewing earlier literature, Chang et al. (2005) conclude that attitude has a consistent impact on online purchase intention, which subsequently translates to online purchases. This sequence of impacts is supported by the theory of reasoned action (TRA; Fishbein & Ajzen, 1980) and the theory of planned behavior (TPB; Ajzen, 1991). From these points, two propositions are advanced:

P1. *Purchase intention is positively related to actual purchase.*
P2. *Attitude is positively related to purchase intention.*

Chatbot adoption, referring to the acceptance and use of conversational agents as customer assistants while making a purchase decision (Pizzi et al., 2021), has been extensively investigated in previous studies (e.g., Pillai & Sivathanu, 2020; Rese et al., 2020). Two factors are reported to impact chatbot adoption:

- perceived usefulness – i.e., the extent to which consumers believe that using chatbots and the virtual agents' given information will enhance their purchase decision (Ashfaq et al., 2020; Kasilingam, 2020); and

- chatbot credibility – consumers' perception of the reliability of the chatbot interaction process and information trustworthiness (Song et al., 2022).

The information adoption model (Sussman & Siegal, 2003) claims that perceived usefulness, chatbot credibility, and chatbot adoption are theoretically linked. This model has been used to describe the factors influencing an individual's reception of information provided in computer-mediated communication (CMC) contexts. Originating from ELM (Petty & Cacioppo, 1986), the model suggests that the influence of (a message's) information quality and perceived credibility on chatbot adoption is mediated by chatbot usefulness. By applying the information adoption model, both chatbot usefulness and chatbot credibility should have a positive relationship with chatbot adoption. Hence:

P3. *Chatbot usefulness is positively related to chatbot adoption.*
P4. *Chatbot credibility is positively related to chatbot adoption.*

Chatbot interactions can be characterized as a form of social influence that can impact consumers' purchasing decisions. Chatbots provide information as an external source, which – similar to the role of social influence in the theory of reasoned action – can improve consumers' decisions. As an example, experiments by Lo Presti et al. (2021) revealed that customers' interaction with chatbots could enhance the purchase intention process. This decision to interact is a manifestation of adoption, which we assume to have a direct impact on consumers' purchase intention. Hence, our fifth proposition is:

P5. *Chatbot adoption is positively related to purchase intention.*

2.2 Stimuli

The *stimulus* pertains to the message transmitted by the communicator (i.e., the chatbot). Researchers have identified numerous factors related to chatbot messages determining consumer responses, such as information delay (Cheng et al., 2022). In this chapter, we focus on the impact of four factors prevalent in the chatbot literature: conversational tone, message responsiveness, quality, and personalization.

Verbal cues are reported to affect consumer responses, including perceptions (e.g., Araujo, 2018; Go & Sundar, 2019). Specifically, the conversational tone of a message furnishes consumers with feelings of a human-like interaction when communicating with a chatbot (Deuter et al., 2013). For example, certain social cues in chatbot dialogues trigger consumers to regard the interaction as human-like as those cues are typically observed in human-to-human conversations (Feine et al., 2019). Examples include: (1) language style (i.e., linguistic variations used in a chatbot message) when perceived as informal, relational, empathetic, being open to dialogue, enjoyable, and invitational; and (2) the ability to express emotions, such as including emojis (Liu et al., 2023), or emotional wording (e.g., warm messages; Kull et al., 2021). The positive effects of conversational chatbot communication on consumers have been repeatedly demonstrated in previous research (e.g., Li & Wang, 2023; Lu et al., 2022). Additionally, a 'conversational human voice' (CHV) is found to positively relate to trust, a concept closely associated with credibility (e.g., Kelleher, 2009).

P6. *Conversational tone is positively related to chatbot credibility.*

The literature on chatbot effects underscores that perceived message responsiveness can enhance chatbots' credibility, perceived social presence, and other favorable consumer responses by increasing 'humanness' (Go & Sundar, 2019; Schuetzler et al., 2020; Jiang et al., 2022). Human-to-human dialogue is typically governed by conversational norms such as relation: it describes the expectation that the dialogue partner will provide a tailored response by adjusting it according to the ongoing conversation (Schuetzler et al., 2020).

Go and Sundar (2019) argue that a key characteristic of interpersonal communication is the dialogic process, or 'contingency', as responses depend on preceding messages. They describe the extent of contingency in message exchange as 'message interactivity'. A high level of interactivity enhances the anthropomorphic nature of the conversation because it mimics responsiveness. This further enhances perceived social presence, which is an important driver of trust (Lu et al., 2016). Chatbot message interactivity has been repeatedly found to increase various variables mirroring consumers' reliance on chatbots (Chung et al., 2020; Ciechanowski et al., 2019; Luo et al., 2019). Hence, the next proposition is advanced:

P7. *Message responsiveness is positively related to chatbot credibility.*

When using dual process theories of persuasion such as ELM (Petty & Cacioppo, 1986) or HSM (Chaiken, 1980) in the chatbot context, scholars typically consider the quality of the response (i.e., accuracy, format, completeness, and currency of information produced) as an important cue carefully processed via the central route, while other factors (such as source credibility) act as peripheral cues (e.g., Song et al., 2022). When consumers are motivated and able to process information cognitively, they pay attention to quality factors such as information accuracy, relevance, sufficiency, and timeliness (Gao et al., 2015). Accuracy, for instance, means that the message provides the most current and relevant information (Huang & Chueh, 2021). The information adoption model argues for a direct relationship between the argument quality of a message – resembling the information quality provided by chatbots' messages – and information usefulness (Cheung et al., 2008). Therefore, we propose that:

P8. *Message quality is positively related to chatbot usefulness.*

Personalization aims at treating consumers as unique entities and customizing messages based on their preferences (Kalyanaraman & Sundar, 2006). A personalized chatbot message containing recommendations that match consumers' tastes, needs, and preferences is therefore expected to be more persuasive than a standardized message, and could amplify positive attitudes and stronger purchase intention (Rhee & Choi, 2020).

From the perspective of ELM, this is to be expected since consumers who follow the central route are more likely to rate the chatbot message as highly persuasive when it matches their preferences. This message persuasiveness heightens consumers' willingness to buy the recommended product or brand (Norris & Wu, 2021; Bleier et al., 2019). However, this effect occurs only when a moderate personalization approach is used because extreme forms of personalization (hyperpersonalization) can trigger uncomfortable feelings – i.e., the 'uncanny valley effect' (Ciechanowski et al., 2019). These points prompt the next proposition:

P9. *(Moderate) message personalization is positively related to purchase intention.*

2.3 Communicators

The *communicator* is the chatbot that transmits the message. It is reported that people judge chatbots during their conversations based on various attributes, such as communication quality and chatbots' perceived personality. People also make inferences from additional cues, including the chatbot's name (Go & Sundar, 2019) or 'gender' (Beldad et al., 2016; McDonnell & Baxter, 2019), or disclosure timing (Huang & Dootson, 2022).

Communication quality is an important factor that creates value (i.e., improves decision-making efficiency) and affects consumer responses (Mimoun et al., 2017). Chatbot communication must meet the requirements of dimensions of communication quality such that the recipient has a favorable experience of high-quality interaction and responds positively during the process (Mohr & Sohi, 1995). Previous research indicated that chatbots' accuracy, competence, attractiveness, and openness influence consumer responses (e.g., Mou & Xu, 2017). For example, competence covers chatbots' abilities, including communication skills, capability, knowledge, intelligence, and efficiency (Kervyn et al., 2012). Competent chatbots can process customer queries and deliver useful information through high-quality interaction characterized by smoothness, accuracy, and completeness. Thus, they help consumers successfully achieve their communication goals (Cheng et al., 2022).

Research shows that consumers tend to focus on chatbots' competence when, for instance, the perceived purchase risk is high (Wang et al., 2017). This aligns with the central processing route of the ELM. When consumers feel that chatbots can improve their performance and productivity through the customer journey, perceived chatbot usefulness increases (Ashfaq et al., 2020). Accordingly, the perception that a chatbot can solve problems and provide customized answers results in heightened credibility (Chung et al., 2020). Additionally, chatbot competence is linked to credibility-based trust (Yen & Chiang, 2021). Therefore, we postulate that:

P10. *Chatbot quality is positively related to chatbot usefulness.*
P11. *Chatbot quality is positively related to chatbot credibility.*

To mimic humans, many chatbots are programmed to have individual personalities and affective qualities, such as interest (Banchs, 2017; Radziwill & Benton, 2017), as lack of personality has been found to push users away from the dialogue (Adamopoulou & Moussiades, 2020). Similarity-attraction theory claims that people prefer to interact with individuals who are similar to themselves. The same holds for interaction with non-human entities as individuals favor personality-congruent language style by the agent (Nass & Moon, 2000). Furthermore, congruency between the user and the perceived personality of the chatbot expressed through its interaction style results in a positive evaluation of the technology (Ruijten & Cuijpers, 2020).

These studies suggest that when consumers deem a chatbot's personality to be similar to theirs – through the verbal and non-verbal cues it transmits – they are more likely to identify with such an agent (Shumanov & Johnson, 2021) and perceive it as credible. Hence:

P12. *Chatbot personality is positively related to chatbot credibility.*

2.4 Receivers

The *receiver* is the person responding to a message. The effect of a message is likely to vary among different individuals. The same content can trigger very different reactions (Chaiken, 1980), depending on factors such as the recipient's traits, experiences, and perceptions (e.g., privacy risk). For instance, research on information adoption has shown that receivers' experience and knowledge moderate central influences (e.g., the argument included in a message) as well as peripheral influences (e.g., the subject matter of the message) on information acceptance in the context of computer-mediated communication (Sussman & Siegal, 2003). In the chatbot literature, consumer characteristics such as expertise and involvement play a critical moderating role and determine the influence of chatbot messages (e.g., language style) and entity perceptions (e.g., social role) on consumer reactions (Li & Wang, 2023).

Scholars have further investigated factors related to recipient characteristics, such as gender, age, values, consumer skepticism and resistance, personal innovativeness, and certainty of needs (Kasilingam, 2020; Zhu et al., 2022). One key factor appears to be receivers' involvement, or the extent of an object's personal relevance to an individual, which has a strong influence on information processing (Johnson & Eagly, 1989). Some studies have already demonstrated that involvement can be a moderator of the chatbot effect during the consumer decision-making process. For instance, it is suggested that heightened involvement increases preference for competent chatbot communication, while less involved individuals are inclined to prefer warm messages that have high relational focus and encourage social proximity between individuals (Roy & Naidoo, 2021).

This aligns with the key assertions of dual process theories claiming that highly involved individuals are motivated to engage in an effortful cognitive process through the central route by focusing on argument quality. In contrast, individuals with little involvement tend to rely heavily on peripheral cues (e.g., platform reputation). Therefore, the following propositions are advanced:

P13. *Consumer involvement moderates the relationship between message quality and chatbot usefulness.*

P14. *Consumer involvement moderates the relationship between message quality and purchase intention.*

Various studies have focused on the role of 'need for human interaction' (NHI) in consumer responses such as adoption intent (e.g., Sheehan et al., 2020; Song et al., 2022; Ashfaq et al., 2020). This concept relates to consumers' desire for human contact during a specific experience (Dabholkar & Bagozzi, 2002).

Many individuals prefer to interact with other humans (Sheehan et al., 2020), so are considered to have a high NHI, while others avoid human interaction (Meuter et al., 2000). It is suggested that individuals with high NHI favor interactions with human service agents and are less likely to accept chatbots as they are regarded as less compatible with their own desires. These individuals believe they obtain a better experience from humans because they are more capable of dealing with various problems in complex situations (Ashfaq et al., 2020).

Individuals with high NHI also perceive various issues with chatbots, which could increase their uncertainty about the chatbots' performance and contribute to feelings of discomfort (Ashfaq et al., 2020; Luo et al., 2019). They think that chatbots are not sincere enough (Shin & Jeong, 2020). Consumers with high levels of NHI have lower expectations of chatbots than individuals with low NHI (Ashfaq et al., 2020) – a difference that affects consumers' requirements for message and chatbot quality (Song et al., 2022). It is therefore proposed that:

P15. *Need for human interaction moderates the relationship between message quality and chatbot usefulness.*

P16. *Need for human interaction moderates the relationship between chatbot quality and chatbot usefulness.*

2.5 Contextual Factors

Consumers' responses are contingent on various contextual factors, such as platform type, brand, purchase type, and task complexity (Cheng et al., 2022). The task-technology fit theory (Goodhue & Thompson, 1995) postulates that technology interaction is considered satisfying when a technology meets consumers' needs and requirements for a specific task (e.g., choosing a product). Following this theory, the characteristics of the task can moderate the relationship between chatbot attributes (e.g., message content) and consumer perceptions, attitudes, and intentions. Previous studies (e.g., Dayan & Di Benedetto, 2010) note that, when a decision problem is too complex to address, consumers may doubt a chatbot's problem-solving ability when they receive standardized or warm, empathetic responses from it. Therefore, we propose that:

P17. *Task complexity moderates the relationship between conversational tone and chatbot credibility.*

P18. *Task complexity moderates the relationship between message quality and chatbot credibility.*

3 Michael Kors: A Case Study on the Effect of Chatbot Communication

Michael Kors, a US retailing brand that sells various consumer goods (clothes, accessories, jewelry, etc.), has used a chatbot solution to address the needs of their global audience since 2018. By introducing a chatbot accessible via Facebook Messenger, the company aimed to enhance the customer experience during three stages of the customer journey: (1) building brand awareness; (2) increasing brand knowledge by enhancing product discovery as well as using aspirational storytelling to cultivate consumers' brand consideration; and (3) providing personalized experiences and FAQ handling in the post-purchase phase.

Depending on consumers' origin and interests, the chatbot triggers various content journeys. Global audiences, for instance, can gain access to the latest trends from New York Fashion Week, shop for selected influencers' looks, and view backstage video content. Consumers in the US also have the opportunity to discover and shop for new products, with the 'New Arrivals' feature guiding selling experiences with shoppable looks. Users can pose questions in a free-text manner, to which the chatbot provides answers and highlights products available in the online shop. The chatbot can also answer more than 100 FAQs covering various topics. To further tailor the customer experience, messages are personalized and sent periodically to those who have interacted with the chatbot. These features led to 45,000 new users per month (Forbes, 2018). This success is attributable to several message-related factors (e.g., message quality and personalization) that our review considers pivotal for cultivating positive consumer responses in a given shopping context (i.e., low task complexity).

4 Discussion

In this chapter, we provided an overview of current scientific knowledge in the field of chatbot communication. In doing so, we consolidated the earlier findings of our literature analysis and developed an integrated model for the impact of chatbot communication on consumer outcomes. By applying the classic framework for social communication, we identified five critical components for our model: communicators, stimuli, receivers, responses, and contextual influences. Our review shows that each component includes various factors that are critical to the success of chatbots in business settings. Effectively designing chatbots that consumers are willing to use is contingent on a thorough understanding of those factors.

Businesses are well advised to refrain from the erroneous premise that designing chatbots simply to deal with customers' information needs and queries will suffice to enhance satisfaction with customer service. Our review of the literature clearly indicates that the effects of chatbot-related factors on consumer outcomes such as attitude and actual behavior are predicated on a complex interplay of considerations related not only to the sender (chatbot) but also to the receiver (customers) and the context of the interaction. The proposed integrative framework that emerged from our review captures this complexity.

Given the impact of customer characteristics and preferences on the link between chatbot message quality and customer responses, the design of the chatbot and the way it interacts with customers must recognize the fact that customers do not constitute a monolithic category. This is a challenge that merits attention since variation in customers' preference for a specific type of chatbot use is contingent on specific needs, such as the 'need for human interaction' (NHI). Must a non-humanlike chatbot still be employed when customers have high NHI? Should customers have the option to interact with a specific form or type of chatbot according to their NHI level and the context of the interaction (e.g., dealing with a complex problem or queries concerning expensive products)?

The global reach of chatbots is a trend worth exploring, especially as they are increasingly employed by multinational companies. For practitioners and researchers, the question primarily concerns the potential implications of customer values, especially those tied to customers' cultural membership, in adopting chatbots when interacting with companies. One can only ask whether individuals who value security (Schwartz & Bardi, 2001) or have high uncertainty avoidance (Hofstede, 2001) would be receptive to information from a non-human customer service agent. How should a chatbot be designed to match the culturally shaped expectations and preferences of customers from across the globe?

While the body of literature in chatbot research has grown significantly in recent years, studies into the persuasive effects of chatbot interactions are still superficial and often lack validation, with findings still often controversial. This chapter provided an overview of how the key determinants are related, and advanced several propositions on their influence on key response variables for future research. Although our review was enriched by the expanding literature on chatbot adoption, one point that resonates from this chapter is the importance of considering theories on social influence to better understand elements that make chatbots effective online sales representatives. Our review gives practitioners and scholars a first understanding of the main persuasive factors altering consumer attitudes, but more empirical insights into their role are still required.

References

Adamopoulou, E. & Moussiades, L. (2020). Chatbots: History, technology, and applications. *Machine Learning with Applications*, *2*, 100006.

Ajzen, I. (1991). The theory of planned behavior. *Organizational Behavior and Human Decision Processes*, *50*(2), 179–211.

Aleedy, M., Shaiba, H., & Bezbradica, M. (2019). Generating and analyzing chatbot responses using natural language processing. *International Journal of Advanced Computer Science and Applications*, *10*(9), 61–68.

Araujo, T. (2018). Living up to the chatbot hype: The influence of anthropomorphic design cues and communicative agency framing on conversational agent and company perceptions. *Computers in Human Behavior*, *85*, 183–189.

Ashfaq, M., Yun, J., Yu, S., & Loureiro, S. M. C. (2020). I, Chatbot: Modeling the determinants of users' satisfaction and continuance intention of AI-powered service agents. *Telematics and Informatics*, *54*, 101473.

Banchs, R. E. (2017). On the construction of more human-like chatbots: Affect and emotion analysis of movie dialogue data. In *2017 Asia-Pacific Signal and Information Processing Association Annual Summit and Conference (APSIPA ASC)*, 1364–1367.

Beldad, A., Hegner, S., & Hoppen, J. (2016). The effect of virtual sales agent (VSA) gender–product gender congruence on product advice credibility, trust in VSA and online vendor, and purchase intention. *Computers in Human Behavior*, *60*, 62–72.

Bleier, A., Harmeling, C. M., & Palmatier, R. W. (2019). Creating effective online customer experiences. *Journal of Marketing*, *83*(2), 98–119.

Chaiken, S. (1980). Heuristic versus systematic information processing and the use of source versus message cues in persuasion. *Journal of Personality and Social Psychology*, *39*(5), 752–766.

Chang, M. K., Cheung, W., & Lai, V. S. (2005). Literature derived reference models for the adoption of online shopping. *Information & Management*, *42*(4), 543–559.

Cheng, X., Bao, Y., Zarifis, A., Gong, W., & Mou, J. (2021). Exploring consumers' response to text-based chatbots in e-commerce: The moderating role of task complexity and chatbot disclosure. *Internet Research*, *32*(2), 496–517.

Cheng, X., Zhang, X., Cohen, J., & Mou, J. (2022). Human vs. AI: Understanding the impact of anthropomorphism on consumer response to chatbots from the perspective of trust and relationship norms. *Information Processing & Management*, *59*(3), 102940.

Cheung, C. M., Lee, M. K., & Rabjohn, N. (2008). The impact of electronic word-of-mouth: The adoption of online opinions in online customer communities. *Internet Research, 18*(3), 229–247.

Chung, M., Ko, E., Joung, H., & Kim, S. J. (2020). Chatbot e-service and customer satisfaction regarding luxury brands. *Journal of Business Research, 117*, 587–595.

Ciechanowski, L., Przegalinska, A., Magnuski, M., & Gloor, P. (2019). In the shades of the uncanny valley: An experimental study of human–chatbot interaction. *Future Generation Computer Systems, 92*, 539–548.

Clark, S., (2020). 5 ways chatbots improve employee experience. Available at: https://www.reworked.co/employee-experience/5-ways-chatbots-improve-employee-experience/ (Accessed: 6 November 2023).

Cognitive Market Research (2023). *Chatbot market report 2023* (Global edition). Available at https://www.cognitivemarketresearch.com/chatbot-market-report (Accessed: 7 November 2023).

Dabholkar, P. A. & Bagozzi, R. P. (2002). An attitudinal model of technology-based self-service: Moderating effects of consumer traits and situational factors. *Journal of the Academy of Marketing Science, 30*, 184–201.

Davies, N. (2022). 9 effective ecommerce chatbot examples from successful brands. Available at: https://gettalkative.com/info/ecommerce-chatbot (Accessed: 6 November 2023).

Dayan, M. & Di Benedetto, C. A. (2010). The impact of structural and contextual factors on trust formation in product development teams. *Industrial Marketing Management, 39*(4), 691–703.

Deuter, K., Procter, N., & Rogers, J. (2013). The emergency telephone conversation in the context of the older person in suicidal crisis. *Crisis, 34*, 262–272.

Edwards, A., Edwards, C., Spence, P. R., Harris, C., & Gambino, A. (2016). Robots in the classroom: Differences in students' perceptions of credibility and learning between "teacher as robot" and "robot as teacher". *Computers in Human Behavior, 65*, 627–634.

Feine, J., Morana, S., & Gnewuch, U. (2019). Measuring service encounter satisfaction with customer service chatbots using sentiment analysis. In *Proceedings of the 14th International Conference on Wirtschaftsinformatik (WI2019)*. Siegen, Germany.

Fishbein, M. & Ajzen, I. (1980). *Understanding attitudes and predicting social behavior*. Prentice-Hall.

Forbes (2018). Michael Kors revamps Android wear models and adds a chatbot to the mix. Available at: https://www.forbes.com/sites/paullamkin/2018/01/31/michael-kors-revamps-android-wear-models-and-adds-a-chatbot-to-the-mix/?sh=2fe9c4b745b8 (Accessed: 6 November 2023).

Gao, L., Waechter, K. A., & Bai, X. (2015). Understanding consumers' continuance intention towards mobile purchase: A theoretical framework and empirical study – a case of China. *Computers in Human Behavior, 53*, 249–262.

Go, E. & Sundar, S. S. (2019). Humanizing chatbots: The effects of visual, identity and conversational cues on humanness perceptions. *Computers in Human Behavior, 97*, 304–316.

Goodhue, D. L. & Thompson, R. L. (1995). Task-technology fit and individual performance. *MIS Quarterly, 19*(2), 213–236.

Griol, D., Carbó, J., & Molina, J. M. (2013). An automatic dialog simulation technique to develop and evaluate interactive conversational agents. *Applied Artificial Intelligence, 27*(9), 759–780.

Hofstede, G., (2001). *Culture's consequences: Comparing values, behaviors, institutions and organizations across nations. SAGE* Publications.

Hollebeek, L. D., Sprott, D. E., & Brady, M. K. (2021). Rise of the machines? Customer engagement in automated service interactions. *Journal of Service Research, 24*(1), 3–8.

Holtgraves, T. M., Ross, S. J., Weywadt, C. R., & Han, T. L. (2007). Perceiving artificial social agents. *Computers in Human Behavior, 23*(5), 2163–2174.

Hovland, C. I. (1948). Social communication. *Proceedings of the American Philosophical Society, 92*(5), 371–375.

Hsu, C. L. & Lin, J. C. C. (2023). Understanding the user satisfaction and loyalty of customer service chatbots. *Journal of Retailing and Consumer Services, 71*, 103211.

Huang, D. H. & Chueh, H. E. (2021). Chatbot usage intention analysis: Veterinary consultation. *Journal of Innovation & Knowledge, 6*(3), 135–144.

Huang, J., Zhou, M., & Yang, D. (2007). Extracting chatbot knowledge from online discussion forums. In *Proceedings of the 20th International Joint Conference on Artifical Intelligence (IJCAI'07)*, 423–428.

Huang, Y. S. S. & Dootson, P. (2022). Chatbots and service failure: When does it lead to customer aggression. *Journal of Retailing and Consumer Services, 68*, 103044.

Jiang, H., Cheng, Y., Yang, J., & Gao, S. (2022). AI-powered chatbot communication with customers: Dialogic interactions, satisfaction, engagement, and customer behavior. *Computers in Human Behavior, 134*, 107329.

Johnson, B. T. & Eagly, A. H. (1989). Effects of involvement on persuasion: A meta-analysis. *Psychological Bulletin, 106*(2), 290–314.

Joy, A., Zhu, Y., Peña, C., & Brouard, M. (2022). Digital future of luxury brands: Metaverse, digital fashion, and non-fungible tokens. *Strategic Change, 31*(3), 337–343.

Kalyanaraman, S. & Sundar, S. S. (2006). The psychological appeal of personalized content in web portals: Does customization affect attitudes and behavior? *Journal of Communication, 56*(1), 110–132.

Kasilingam, D. L. (2020). Understanding the attitude and intention to use smartphone chatbots for shopping. *Technology in Society, 62*, 101280.

Keeling, K., McGoldrick, P., & Beatty, S. (2010). Avatars as salespeople: Communication style, trust, and intentions. *Journal of Business Research, 63*(8), 793–800.

Kelleher, T. (2009). Conversational voice, communicated commitment, and public relations outcomes in interactive online communication. *Journal of Communication, 59*(1), 172–188.

Kervyn, N., Fiske, S. T., & Malone, C. (2012). Brands as intentional agents framework: How perceived intentions and ability can map brand perception. *Journal of Consumer Psychology, 22*(2), 166–176.

Kull, A. J., Romero, M., & Monahan, L. (2021). How may I help you? Driving brand engagement through the warmth of an initial chatbot message. *Journal of Business Research, 135*, 840–850.

Li, M. & Wang, R. (2023). Chatbots in e-commerce: The effect of chatbot language style on customers' continuance usage intention and attitude toward brand. *Journal of Retailing and Consumer Services, 71*, 103209.

Liu, D., Lv, Y., & Huang, W. (2023). How do consumers react to chatbots' humorous emojis in service failures. *Technology in Society, 73*, 102244.

Lo Presti, L., Maggiore, G., & Marino, V. (2021). The role of the chatbot on customer purchase intention: Towards digital relational sales. *Italian Journal of Marketing, 2021*(3), 165–188.

Lu, B., Fan, W., & Zhou, M. (2016). Social presence, trust, and social commerce purchase intention: An empirical research. *Computers in Human Behavior, 56*, 225–237.

Lu, L., McDonald, C., Kelleher, T., Lee, S., Chung, Y. J., Mueller, S., & Yue, C. A. (2022) Measuring consumer-perceived humanness of online organizational agents. *Computers in Human Behavior, 128*, 107092.

Luo, X., Tong, S., Fang, Z., & Qu, Z. (2019). Frontiers: Machines vs. humans: The impact of artificial intelligence chatbot disclosure on customer purchases. *Marketing Science, 38*(6), 937–947.

McDonnell, M. & Baxter, D. (2019). Chatbots and gender stereotyping. *Interacting with Computers, 31*(2), 116–121.

Mende, M., Scott, M. L., van Doorn, J., Grewal, D., & Shanks, I. (2019). Service robots rising: How humanoid robots influence service experiences and elicit compensatory consumer responses. *Journal of Marketing Research, 56*(4), 535–556.

Meuter, M. L., Ostrom, A. L., Roundtree, R. I., & Bitner, M. J. (2000). Self-service technologies: Understanding customer satisfaction with technology-based service encounters. *Journal of Marketing, 64*(3), 50–64.

Mimoun, M. S. B., Poncin, I., & Garnier, M. (2017). Animated conversational agents and e-consumer productivity: The roles of agents and individual characteristics. *Information & Management, 54*(5), 545–559.

Mohr, J. J. & Sohi, R. S. (1995). Communication flows in distribution channels: Impact on assessments of communication quality and satisfaction. *Journal of Retailing, 71*(4), 393–415.

Mou, Y. & Xu, K. (2017). The media inequality: Comparing the initial human–human and human–AI social interactions. *Computers in Human Behavior, 72*, 432–440.

Nass, C. & Moon, Y. (2000). Machines and mindlessness: Social responses to computers. *Journal of Social Issues, 56*(1), 81–103.

Norris, C. J. & Wu, E. (2021). Accentuate the positive, eliminate the negative: Reducing ambivalence through instructed emotion regulation. *Emotion, 21*(3), 499–512.

Pantano, E. & Pizzi, G. (2020). Forecasting artificial intelligence on online customer assistance: Evidence from chatbot patents analysis. *Journal of Retailing and Consumer Services, 55*, 102096.

Petty, R. E. & Cacioppo, J. T. (1986). The elaboration likelihood model of persuasion. In L. Berkowitz (Ed.), *Advances in experimental social psychology*, Vol. 19 (pp. 123–205). New York: Academic.

Pillai, R. & Sivathanu, B. (2020). Adoption of AI-based chatbots for hospitality and tourism. *International Journal of Contemporary Hospitality Management, 32*(10), 3199–3226.

Pizzi, G., Scarpi, D., & Pantano, E. (2021). Artificial intelligence and the new forms of interaction: Who has the control when interacting with a chatbot? *Journal of Business Research, 129*, 878–890.

Qiu, L. & Benbasat, I. (2009). Evaluating anthropomorphic product recommendation agents: A social relationship perspective to designing information systems. *Journal of Management Information Systems, 25*(4), 145–182.

Radziwill, N. M. & Benton, M. C. (2017). Evaluating quality of chatbots and intelligent conversational agents. *arXiv*, 1704.04579.

Rese, A., Ganster, L., & Baier, D. (2020). Chatbots in retailers' customer communication: How to measure their acceptance? *Journal of Retailing and Consumer Services, 56*, 102176.

Rhee, C. E. & Choi, J. (2020). Effects of personalization and social role in voice shopping: An experimental study on product recommendation by a conversational voice agent. *Computers in Human Behavior, 109*, 106359.

Rishi, B., & Bandyopadhyay, S. (Eds.). (2018). *Contemporary issues in social media marketing*. London: Routledge.

Roy, R. & Naidoo, V. (2021). Enhancing chatbot effectiveness: The role of anthropomorphic conversational styles and time orientation. *Journal of Business Research, 126*, 23–34.

Ruan, Y. & Mezei, J. (2022). When do AI chatbots lead to higher customer satisfaction than human frontline employees in online shopping assistance? Considering product attribute type. *Journal of Retailing and Consumer Services, 68*, 103059.

Ruijten, P. A. & Cuijpers, R. H. (2019). Does a friendly robot make you feel better? In *2019 28th IEEE International Conference on Robot and Human Interactive Communication (RO-MAN)*, 1–6.

Schuetzler, R. M., Grimes, G. M., & Giboney, J. S. (2020). The impact of chatbot conversational skill on engagement and perceived humanness. *Journal of Management Information Systems, 37*(3), 875–900.

Schwartz, S. H. & Bardi, A. (2001). Value hierarchies across cultures: Taking a similarities perspective. *Journal of Cross-Cultural Psychology, 32*(3), 268–290.

Shawar, B. A. & Atwell, E. S. (2005). Using corpora in machine-learning chatbot systems. *International Journal of Corpus Linguistics, 10*(4), 489–516.

Sheehan, B., Jin, H. S., & Gottlieb, U. (2020). Customer service chatbots: Anthropomorphism and adoption. *Journal of Business Research, 115*, 14–24.

Shin, H. H. & Jeong, M. (2020). Guests' perceptions of robot concierge and their adoption intentions. *International Journal of Contemporary Hospitality Management, 32*(8), 2613–2633.

Shumanov, M. & Johnson, L. (2021). Making conversations with chatbots more personalized. *Computers in Human Behavior, 117*, 106627.

Sivaramakrishnan, S., Wan, F., & Tang, Z. (2007). Giving an "e-human touch" to e-tailing: The moderating roles of static information quantity and consumption motive in the effectiveness of an anthropomorphic information agent. *Journal of Interactive Marketing, 21*(1), 60–75.

Song, M., Xing, X., Duan, Y., Cohen, J., & Mou, J. (2022). Will artificial intelligence replace human customer service? The impact of communication quality and privacy risks on adoption intention. *Journal of Retailing and Consumer Services, 66*, 102900.

Sussman, S. W. & Siegal, W. S. (2003). Informational influence in organizations: An integrated approach to knowledge adoption. *Information Systems Research, 14*(1), 47–65.

Verhagen, T., Van Nes, J., Feldberg, F., & Van Dolen, W. (2014). Virtual customer service agents: Using social presence and personalization to shape online service encounters. *Journal of Computer-Mediated Communication, 19*(3), 529–545.

Wang, Z., Mao, H., Li, Y. J., & Liu, F. (2017). Smile big or not? Effects of smile intensity on perceptions of warmth and competence. *Journal of Consumer Research, 43*(5), 787–805.

Yen, C. & Chiang, M. C. (2021). Trust me, if you can: A study on the factors that influence consumers' purchase intention triggered by chatbots based on brain image evidence and self-reported assessments. *Behaviour & Information Technology, 40*(11), 1177–1194.

Zanker, M., Bricman, M., & Jessenitschnig, M. (2011). Cost-effective development of virtual sales assistants. *New Directions in Intelligent Interactive Multimedia Systems and Services, 2*, 1–11.

Zhu, Y., Zhang, J., Wu, J., & Liu, Y. (2022). AI is better when I'm sure: The influence of certainty of needs on consumers' acceptance of AI chatbots. *Journal of Business Research, 150*, 642–652.

13

The Impact of Generational Differences on Target Audience Identification in Social Media Marketing

Manjushree G S
CIMS, Bengaluru, India

Padmaja D S
Surana College, Bengaluru, India

Introduction

In the digital era, pinpointing target audiences on social media is crucial for marketing success. This chapter focuses on the importance of considering generational differences when defining audiences. We explore the distinct features and behaviours of different generations to arm marketers with strategies for connecting effectively with their intended demographic groups (Smith, 2020; Johnson & Williams, 2019).

In social media marketing, it is vital for companies to understand how different generations use the various platforms in order for them to better identify their target audiences. Targeting specific generations helps marketers create campaigns that appeal to their unique preferences and behaviours,

DOI: 10.4324/9781003412656-13

making their marketing more relevant and effective, and thus leading to better results (Lee & Kim, 2021).

As businesses increase their involvement on social media, it becomes even more crucial to identify their target audience accurately. The online environment is filled with individuals from different generations who have unique traits and purchasing habits. By understanding these generational differences, businesses are able to create customized marketing strategies that resonate deeply with their desired customers. This not only boosts engagement and conversions but also strengthens the brand's overall social media presence, ensuring that marketing campaigns make a lasting impression on their intended audience (Martinez & Gomez, 2022; Thompson & Davis, 2018; Rishi & Bandyopadhyay, 2018).

Given that businesses need to focus on understanding their target audience, this chapter provides a thorough look at how to identify ideal customers using behavioural, research, and managerial techniques. It examines how social media marketing can help companies reach specific groups and improve their overall marketing effectiveness. The goal is to equip managers with the necessary tools to effectively utilize social media data for precise customer targeting, customizing marketing campaigns, and enhancing performance. The chapter is packed with real-world examples and research-based advice to help businesses master audience segmentation using social media. It is therefore a valuable resource for marketers aiming to enhance their targeting strategies and for business owners seeking to make the most of their marketing investments.

The chapter explores the significant role that generational differences play in shaping target audience identification strategies in the realm of social media marketing. In an era where each generation exhibits unique behaviours, preferences, and communication styles, understanding and effectively engaging with different generational segments has become crucial for marketers aiming to optimize their social media campaigns. This chapter aims to provide insights into the implications from both the consumer and the managerial perspective, shedding light on the behavioural analysis techniques, managerial strategies, and case studies that enable marketers to identify and engage with diverse generational audiences on social media platforms. It aims to achieve the following objectives:

1. Understand generational characteristics and social media use: This chapter seeks to delve into the distinct characteristics and social media usage patterns exhibited by the different generations – Baby Boomers, Generation X, Millennials, and Generation Z. By examining their preferences and behaviours marketers can gain a comprehensive understanding of how generational differences impact target audience identification.

2. Explore behavioural analysis techniques for generational targeting: By analysing the motivations, goals, and preferences of the generations, marketers can develop more effective strategies to engage and resonate with their target audiences on social media.
3. Provide effective managerial strategies that marketers can employ to optimize their generational targeting efforts on social media platforms. The chapter will emphasize the importance of tailoring content and messaging for each generation, leveraging platform-specific approaches, and optimizing content formats to maximize engagement and relevance.
4. Showcase relevant case studies and implications to provide practical insights and illustrate the impact of generational differences on target audience identification. By examining successful campaigns in this domain, marketers can gain inspiration and learn from real-world examples.

The chapter will also discuss the broader implications of generational targeting on marketing effectiveness, emphasizing the benefits of improved audience engagement, brand resonance, and higher conversion rates.

1 The Importance of Generational Differences in Social Media Marketing

Generational differences in the social media use are very important for businesses that want to reach their target audience in an effective way. By understanding the social media habits of various generations, businesses can optimize their marketing strategies for better effectiveness. Here are some key takeaways from a literature review:

- Different generations have unique ways of using social media to engage with brands, from initially learning about them to becoming loyal supporters (Sprout Social, 2023).
- Different generations use social media differently, and their platform choice varies according to how that generation interacts with the world (True Anthem, 2023).
- Generational marketing efficiently segments and addresses a target population based on the year of their birth.
- Social media use varies among generations, with some more loyal to brands than others.
- Millennials and Gen Xers are twice as likely to follow firms on social media than Baby Boomers. Gen X follows companies for sales, discounts, and promotions; Millennials follow brands for information and enjoyment; and Baby Boomers look for deals/promotions as well as information (Lesonsky, 2024).

- About 40 per cent of US customers belong to Gen Z, representing the most active group on social media. They are strongly influenced by visual content and their top application is Snapchat (Kamble, 2023).
- The main social media channels used by millennials are YouTube, Facebook, and Instagram. They also rely greatly on online evaluations and word-of-mouth (WOM) recommendations (Kowalewicz, 2020).
- Born into a world of social media and technological innovation, Generation Z uses social media to research products before deciding to buy (Kowalewicz, 2020).

2 Generational Characteristics and Social Media Use

2.1 *Understanding the Unique Characteristics of Each Generation*

Assessing the unique characteristics of each generation is crucial for businesses to create better campaigns for social media marketing. The following are some insights on the ways in which the generations use social media.

2.1.1 Baby Boomers (born 1946–1964)

Below are some characteristics of Baby Boomers that influence their social media use:

- They are active on at least one social media site, and make up the majority of new members on Facebook.
- Their primary reason for using social media is to stay in touch with friends and family.
- Compared to Millennials and Gen Xers, they follow fewer companies on social media.
- A startling 58 per cent of Baby Boomers who first encountered a company or brand on social media will go on to interact with it further on its website.

2.1.2 Generation X (1965–1980)

This is a tech-savvy generation that uses the internet just as much as Millennials. The following summarizes what influences their social media use:

- They are more interested in acquiring information from the internet rather than broadcast or cable news, and choose to get their news and current events from social media and TV at roughly the same rates.
- They account for 1.5 billion daily views on YouTube and spend most of their time on Facebook.
- They have a strong inclination for nostalgia, with 75 per cent watching videos about historical events (Dusek, 2021).

2.1.3 Millennials (1981–1996)

The Millennial generation uses social media to pass the time between work, find interesting information, keep up to date with current affairs, and connect with friends and family. Social media has a big impact on them, especially as they lead busy lives. They frequently use Facebook, Twitter (now X), and YouTube, but are also keen to explore new things — for example, quickly embracing platforms such as Snapchat and Instagram (Kowalewicz, 2020). To summarize:

- Although Millennials have become accustomed to social media's continual presence in their daily lives, they can recall times before it.
- They use social media to pass the time, connect with friends and family, look for interesting material, and remain informed about current events.
- Social media is a major influence, especially given how busy they are.
- They often use Facebook (including Stories), Twitter/X, and YouTube, but are open to experimenting with other social media platforms.

2.1.4 Generation Z (1997–2012)

This generation have grown up in the age of digital technology, so are accustomed to using digital devices. Despite using a variety of social media sites, they are flexible and frequently select their favourites. Instagram, YouTube, and TikTok are ranked highly; however Snapchat is their primary social media platform as they are heavily motivated by visual content (Kowalewicz, 2020).

- As this generation has always used digital technology, it is the most adaptable to change.
- They represent nearly 40 per cent of US customers and are the most active on social media.
- They primarily use Snapchat, and are heavily influenced by visual content.
- They use various social networking sites but usually have a few favourites.
- They establish the patterns that will eventually find widespread acceptance.

2.2 Analysing Differences in Social Media Use

The following outlines some key takeaways in differences in content consumption and engagement behaviours across the different generations.

2.2.1 Generation Z

A report by digital marketing agency Fractl (2015), 'Content engagement by generation', found the following unique characteristics for Generation Z:

- They are more likely to consume content between noon and 3 p.m. than Baby Boomers.
- They use up to 2 or 3 platforms daily, mainly YouTube, Instagram, and TikTok.
- They spend most of their time on social media platforms, particularly those that allow them to create and consume content.

2.2.2 Millennials

A factsheet published by Content Science (2023) summarizes this generation's social media habits as follows:

- They use 5–6 platforms at least weekly, most commonly Facebook, Facebook Stories, Twitter/X, and YouTube.
- They spend an average of 2.25 hours per day on social media.
- They are more likely to these platforms because the content is highly personalized, bite-sized, and 'snackable', and thus more appealing to them.

2.2.3 Generation X

Fractl (2015) notes the following:

- This generation accounts for 1.5 billion daily views on YouTube and spends the majority of their time on Facebook.
- Large numbers of them watch videos about historical events, showing a strong inclination towards nostalgia.

2.2.4 Baby Boomers

- They are less likely to follow businesses on social media than Millennials and Gen Xers (Fractl, 2015).
- They mainly use social media to keep in contact with friends and family (Westcott et al., 2018).
- They use social media at different times from Millennials and Gen Xers, with less consumption between noon and 3 p.m (Fractl, 2015).

3 Behavioural Analysis for Audience Identification

3.1 Motivations and Goals of the Generational Segments

Behavioural analysis helps businesses identify target audiences by examining their behaviour. Below are some steps in the process:

- **Identify priority audience segments**: Segmenting audiences according to their level of engagement with the brand will enable businesses to identify the most valuable audiences and understand how, where, and when best to reach them (Keane, 2017).
- **Collect data**: Marketers can collect behavioural data from websites, mobile apps, call centres, digital help desks, and billing systems (Adobe, 2021).
- **Create personas**: Use first-, second-, and third-party data to create personas that represent the target audience segments (Keane, 2017).
- **Categorize customers**: Categorize customers by the characteristics that are most valuable to the business (for example, demographics, psychographics, geographic segmentation), or by behaviours such as frequent actions and product use, preferred media channels, and online shopping habits (Adobe, 2021).
- **Segment the audience**: Categorize audiences based on the characteristics identified in the previous step (US Department of Energy, n.d.).
- **Understand motives and barriers**: Understand the motives and barriers to participation for each audience segment (US Department of Energy, n.d.).
- **Apply the analysis to a campaign**: Once the company/brand has carried out this level of behavioural analysis, it can apply the findings to better shape campaigns (Keane, 2017).

3.2 Analysing Social Media Data for Generational Insights

Analysing social media data is a valuable way to uncover generational insights. Here are some key takeaways from this study:

- A crucial component in identifying target audiences on social media is demographic data. From awareness to advocacy, people's interactions with businesses are greatly influenced by the subtle differences between generations.
- Generational insights can help marketers gain a deeper sociocultural and psychological understanding of their customers by looking beyond standard data and demographics.
- Understanding who the audience is and what they want is the first step to identifying and leveraging social media trends across generations. Firms need to segment their audience by age, location, interests, preferences, and behaviours. The use of tools such as Google Analytics, Facebook Insights, or Twitter/X Analytics will help gain insights into consumer demographics, psychographics, and social media habits.
- Over the next five years, Gen Z's use of social media will surpass that of previous generations, and usage patterns reflect both a rejection of and a reaction to the norms established by earlier generations. In the meantime, it is important to focus on Millennials because of their numbers and purchasing power.
- Social media is used differently by different generations (as outlined in Section 2).

3.3 Analytic Tools for Audience Profiling

Audience profiling is a valuable way to learn about the characteristics of different generations. Analytic tools can help businesses create detailed audience profiles to help tailor their marketing strategies to reach their target audiences more effectively. Below are some tools that can be used for audience profiling:

- **SparkToro**: This searches through more than 80 million social media accounts and webpages to discover what (and who) an audience follows, reads, listens to, watches, shares, and discusses online. It provides information about any online audience, including demographics, interests, and sources of influence.

- **Audience**: This can help businesses identify valuable insights about their target audience. It uses a comprehensive psychology-based analysis to understand what makes an audience tick, including their core values and purchase behaviour.
- **Similarweb**: This analyses consumer behaviour, building audience segments, and creating targeted strategies to attract more customers. It offers information about audience demographics, geographies, interests, and loyalty.
- **Customer surveys**: Surveys can be used to collect data about audience preferences, behaviours, and attitudes which can be used to create detailed consumer profiles.
- **Social media analytics**: Analytic tools are also available on social networking platforms such as Facebook, Twitter/X and Instagram, and can be used to collect information on user demographics, interests, and behaviours.

3.4 Patterns and Trends in Generational Behaviours

Generational differences can be identified by analysing patterns and trends in consumer behaviour across the age groups.

- It is known there are generational cycles, and harmful patterns and qualities can be passed down through family dynamics and learnt behaviours.
- When it comes to making purchases, every generation has its own unique set of values, objectives, and expectations. Reversing generational differences in consumer behaviour is a key factor driving market development.
- Generational marketing is the process of dividing and focusing on a target population based on their year. Generational marketing methods were established when marketers discovered that different age groups responded to different messages on different platforms.
- It is possible that generational changes will influence behaviour more than socioeconomic disparities. For example, people of all ages and income levels are now greatly influenced by young people in terms of both brand perception and consumption habits.
- Understanding generational behaviour and design trends can set a brand apart as different generations of consumers are attracted by different design trends and styles.

4 Managerial Strategies for Effective Generational Targeting

The various social media usage patterns shown across generations highlight the need for managerial techniques for successful generational targeting. Regarding time spent, platforms, and engagement with content, all generation demonstrate distinct preferences. When it comes to media consumption, Generation Z is more likely to use visual and interactive platforms like YouTube, Instagram, and TikTok, whereas Millennials favour Facebook and Twitter/X. Baby Boomers use social media mostly for business, whereas Generation X values nostalgia and spends a lot of time on YouTube. Businesses must therefore be aware of these generational distinctions in order to properly customize their social media marketing strategy. By doing so, they can maximize engagement and return on investment (ROI) by reaching the right audience with the right material at the right time.

Below are some managerial strategies for effective generational targeting:

- **Focus on goals and set clear expectations**: Each age group has a different work ethic, but all generations can be on an equal footing if there is a clear objective and set of expectations.
- **Avoid overgeneralization**: Generational marketing can help businesses successfully reach out to consumers across different age ranges, but overgeneralization about the groups can cause more harm than good. Marketing teams should therefore avoid launching campaigns that are based on age alone.
- **Use attitudinal segmentation**: Creating diverse plans with attitudinal segmentation and patterns based on generational behaviour will prevent businesses/brands alienating key target audiences.
- **Customize marketing strategies**: Tailoring a marketing strategy to the target client demography is the most efficient way to promote a firm. Given the various preferences and behaviours of different generations, firms should adjust their marketing strategies appropriately.
- **Use multiple channels**: The way that marketing teams create campaigns for the different generations is becoming more sophisticated as social media use varies among generations, with some more brand loyal than others. In order to efficiently reach their target audience, businesses need to employ a variety of channels.
- **Understand communication styles**: Employees who are aware of various communication styles are encouraged to pause and consider their options before acting on impulse or making assumptions. In order to create more productive and cohesive work teams, managers should make use of a variety of experience, skill, and expertise levels.

4.1 Tone, Language, and Visual Elements

The following considerations will help firms choose the best way to communicate with the different generations, adapting strategies where necessary.

- **Adjust tone and language**: The generations may have different expectations and sensitivities when it comes to tone and language. For example, Baby Boomers may expect a respectful and formal tone; Millennials and Generation Z may appreciate a friendly and casual tone; and Generation X may prefer a straightforward and honest tone.
- **Choose appropriate channels**: The generations may have different comfort levels with the various communication channels (whether textual or visual). For example, Baby Boomers may prefer phone calls or face-to-face meetings; Millennials and Generation Z may prefer email or chat; and Generation X may be flexible and adaptable to any channel.
- **Use visual elements**: Visual elements such as emojis and images can be used to communicate with different generations. Emojis are popular with the younger generations, while Baby Boomers may prefer (traditional) images that relate to their age group.
- **Incorporate values and interests**: Each generation has its own set of values and interests. For example, Gen Z is passionate about social justice issues, environmental sustainability, and mental health awareness. By incorporating these topics into a content strategy in a genuine and informative way, businesses can appeal to their values, capture their attention, and build more meaningful relationships with this generation.
- **Create informative and persuasive content**: Gen Xers are the most loyal and active generation on social media. They are open to advertisements and offers, and use social media to investigate, evaluate, and purchase goods and services. Convenience, trust, and value are important to them, so they like content that is compelling, succinct, and straightforward. Businesses should therefore provide actionable, enlightening, and persuasive material to appeal to this cohort.

4.2 Cultural References and Trends

Utilizing relevant cultural references and trends is an effective way to create engaging content for different generations. The following offers some insights on this marketing strategy.

- **Incorporate pop culture**: Popular culture speaks a language most people understand. By embracing it in their content, businesses can build strong relationships with their customers and create a sense of community.

References to pop culture – such as TV shows, movies, music, and fashion trends – in marketing campaigns can help businesses create engaging content that resonates with different generations (Mghames, 2022; Sinekovich, 2023).

- **Target crowd culture**: Subcultures have become more widespread and accessible thanks to social media. Companies can capitalize on this by focusing on emerging ideologies from crowd culture, whereby brands may distinguish themselves in the crowded media landscape (Holt, 2016).
- **Keep up to date with current trends**: Businesses must actively seek and even create pop culture allusions that generate 'buzz' and connect with their target audience if they want to remain culturally relevant. This means keeping abreast of the latest trends and using creativity to work them into advertising efforts (Mghames, 2022).
- **Be authentic**: When using pop culture in marketing campaigns, it is important to ensure that they align with the brand's values and goals. This will help businesses be authentic and build trust with their target audience (Sinekovich, 2023).

4.3 Platform-Specific Approaches for Generational Targeting

As we have learnt, different generations tend to prefer or gravitate toward different devices and social media channels. Therefore, by knowing which platforms the target audience uses can help businesses create single or multi-channel campaigns that will consumers wherever they are spending time. To effectively target different generations on social media businesses can use the following platform-specific approaches:

- **Language and tone**: Each platform has its own unique culture and language. For example, Twitter/X is known for its short and snappy messages, while LinkedIn is more professional and formal. Businesses should therefore adapt their language and tone to fit the platform and the target audience.
- **Content format**: The generations have different preferences for content formats. For example, Gen Z prefers short videos and Baby Boomers prefer longer content, so businesses should adapt their formats to fit the platform and the target audience.
- **Advertising format**: As this is unique to each platform – for example, Facebook offers carousel ads, while Instagram offers sponsored posts – businesses should use appropriate advertising formats to reach their target audience effectively.

- **Hashtags**: Hashtags can be used to reach a wider audience on social media. Again, each platform has its own unique hashtag culture, so businesses should use appropriate hashtags to better reach their target audience.

4.4 Selecting Appropriate Social Media Platforms

Baby Boomers

As we have learnt, Baby Boomers (born between 1946 and 1964) use social media to stay in touch with friends and family. Facebook is therefore a great venue for marketing targeted at this cohort because research shows that 68 per cent of them use this platform. According to other research, 82 per cent of this group who use the internet have at least one social media account, with an average of 4.6 accounts among the top platforms – Facebook and LinkedIn. Many Baby Boomers solely use Facebook (83 per cent of people over 55), making it the most popular social network among this group, according to Dixon (2024).

Generation X

Born between 1965 and 1976, this generation is open to advertisements and offers, and uses social media to explore, compare, and purchase goods and services. Convenience, trust, and value are important to them, and they like content that is compelling, succinct, and straightforward. Facebook, Instagram, Twitter, and LinkedIn are the most popular social media networks with this group, but they also platforms such as Pinterest and YouTube. Compared to previous generations, this cohort is frequently more active on social media and more likely to interact with brands and content.

Millennials

Millennials, those born between 1981 and 1996, interact with peers and the outside world through social media, with Facebook, Instagram, and YouTube the most popular networks. However, they also use TikTok, Snapchat, and Twitter/X, and are likely to interact with companies via Facebook, Instagram, and Twitter/X. Businesses can effectively reach this generation by leveraging influencer marketing (see Chapter 18) and developing a strong review system approach because these users value reviews and word-of-mouth recommendations highly. As almost 90 per cent of Millennials visit Facebook and YouTube at least once a week (and a majority also using Instagram and Snapchat), businesses should think about using those platforms for marketing in order to connect with this generation.

Generation Z

Born after 1995, this generation also connects with peers and spends a lot of time on social media, with Instagram, TikTok, Snapchat, and YouTube the most popular sites, along with others such as Discord and Twitter/X. Businesses should concentrate on producing visually appealing and engaging short-form video content because Generation Z is known for its short attention span and preference for visual material.

4.5 Optimizing Content for Maximum User Engagement

To optimize content for maximum engagement, businesses should consider the preferences and behaviours of their target audience.

- **Blog posts**: Blogs are a popular content format that can be used to inform and engage audiences. They can provide educational content, share opinions, and provide tips and tricks. To optimize blog posts for maximum engagement, businesses should aim for headlines or captions of between 10 and 20 words, use subheadings to break up the content, and include high-quality visuals.
- **Long-form articles**: Longer articles can also be used to inform and engage audiences through in-depth analysis, opinions, and tips and tricks. To optimize long-form articles for maximum engagement, businesses should aim to provide unique data, include high-quality visuals, and evoke emotion.
- **Original research**: This content can be used to provide audiences with unique insights and data. As above, for maximum engagement, businesses should aim to provide unique data, include high-quality visuals, and provide actionable insights.
- **Video**: This is a popular content format that can be used to inform and engage. For maximum engagement, businesses should aim to provide high-quality visuals, keep the video short and to the point, and include a call to action.

- **Infographics**: This format can provide information in a visually appealing way. To optimize engagement with infographics, businesses should again provide unique data, include high-quality visuals, and keep the design simple and easy to understand.
- **Images**: Images can naturally be used to provide information in a visually appealing way, and businesses should aim to provide high-quality visuals, use relevant and eye-catching images, and include a call to action.

5 Case Study and Implications

The case study below of PepsiCo's 'Uncle Drew' campaign showcases a successful campaign aimed at different generational groups, and gives rise to the following questions:

- How did PepsiCo's 'Uncle Drew' campaign leverage the popularity of sports and entertainment to engage with Millennials and Generation Z, and what elements of the campaign contributed to its viral success?

This question encourages analysis of the campaign's strategy and its appeal to specific generational audiences. It also prompts discussion on the use of sport and entertainment as marketing tools.

- In what ways did the 'Uncle Drew' campaign differentiate PepsiCo's marketing approach from traditional advertising methods, and what impact did this have on brand perception and sales?

This focuses on the innovative aspects of the campaign and how it contrasted with conventional advertising, leading to changes in brand perception and a measurable increase in sales.

- What role did cinematic storytelling and humour play in the success of the campaign, and how did these elements contribute to the creation of a full-length movie?

This question explores the importance of storytelling and humour in the campaign's effectiveness, as well as the transition from a series of commercials to a feature film, highlighting the campaign's lasting impact and broader cultural influence.

With reference to the questions above, the following outlines the PepsiCo Campaign.

PepsiCo's 'Uncle Drew' Campaign (2012)

This targeted Millennials and Generation Z through a series of videos on YouTube and other social media featuring the US National Basketball Association (NBA) star Kyrie Irving disguised as an elderly man named 'Uncle Drew' who amazed players on local courts by showcasing his exceptional basketball skills. The initial commercial, shot in New Jersey, showcased Uncle Drew's critique of the younger generation's focus on style over substance, before revealing his true identity as Irving and dominating the game.

The campaign was a huge success, with over 52 million views on YouTube, and resulted in a 23 per cent increase in sales for PepsiCo's 'Mountain Dew' brand. The overwhelming popularity of the inaugural video inspired the production of five cinematic episodes. Each episode showcased Uncle Drew reconnecting with his former team, comprising actual NBA and Women's NBA stars such as Kevin Love, Nate Robinson, and Maya Moore, also cleverly disguised as elderly individuals. Beyond advertising Pepsi Max, the campaign prioritized the production of compelling content that sparked connections with basketball enthusiasts and the general public.

The campaign's unique blend of cinematic storytelling and humour was key to its viral spread. Featuring iconic basketball stars in relatable, amusing storylines, it captivated viewers and generated anticipation for each new episode. The tagline – 'a zero-calorie cola in disguise' – skilfully echoed the campaign's motif of transformation, emphasizing the product's delicious taste despite its zero-calorie content.

The huge success of the character and show sparked the creation of a full-length movie in 2018, *Uncle Drew*, which cost $18 million and earned $46.5 million worldwide. Featuring a cast of famous US athletes such as Shaquille O'Neal, Reggie Miller, and Lisa Leslie, the story followed Uncle Drew as he reunited with his former team to play in a basketball competition, blending humour, fond memories, and thrilling sport.

The 'Uncle Drew' campaign and film were not just about Kyrie Irving's acting skills. They also showed how PepsiCo thinks outside the box when it comes to marketing. By using basketball's popularity and creating a relatable, funny character, the company reached a lot of people and broke away from typical ads. The fact that the campaign was still popular years later and turned into a successful movie shows how well it connected with and influenced people.

Other interesting and successful marketing campaigns include Airbnb's 'Live There', Apple's 'Shot on iPhone', Coca-Cola's 'Share a Coke', and Nike's 'Dream Crazy'.

5.1 *The Impact of Generational Targeting on Marketing Effectiveness*

Marketing efficacy is significantly impacted by generational targeting. Businesses may generate highly focused and relevant content that resonates with their target audience by understanding the distinct traits, values, and preferences of the various generations. Below are some ways generational targeting can impact marketing effectiveness:

- **Better reception and responses to content**: Businesses can customize content to suit the tastes of their target audience by using generational targeting. Better reactions to and reception of the material as a result may boost engagement, conversions, and income.
- **More efficient allocation of resources**: By concentrating on the content, campaign types, and channels that work best for their target demographic, businesses can manage their resources more effectively to maximize ROI and minimize expenses.
- **Improved brand awareness**: Concentrating on the platforms and advertising channels that work best for their target demographic will increase brand identification and awareness, helping companies stand out in a crowded market.
- **More successful campaigns**: By providing each cohort with relevant and meaningful material, generational targeting can result in campaigns that are more successful. This can boost client loyalty and help firms forge closer bonds with their target market.
- **Enhanced creativity**: Generational targeting can enhance the efficacy of marketing creatives by helping businesses resonate with each generation in terms of the images, language, and other elements used in their campaigns. This can help businesses create more compelling and effective marketing campaigns.

5.2 *Challenges and Considerations*

Targeting multiple generations can be challenging for businesses, so the following are some factors to bear in mind.

- **Preferences and behaviours**: Each generation has its own unique preferences and behaviours when it comes to social media and marketing. For example, Baby Boomers may prefer traditional advertising methods, while Generation Z may prefer short-form video content.

- **Communication styles**: Each generation has its own unique communication style, which can make it challenging to create content that resonates with everyone. For example, Baby Boomers may prefer phone calls or face-to-face meetings, while Millennials and Generation Z may prefer email or chat.
- **Values and beliefs**: Each generation has its own unique values and beliefs, which can impact their purchasing decisions and brand loyalty. For example, Baby Boomers may value job security, while Millennials may value work–life balance.
- **Tech-savviness**: Each generation has its own level of tech-savviness, which can impact users' ability to engage with certain types of content or platform. For example, Baby Boomers may be less comfortable with social media than Millennials and Generation Z.
- **Financial circumstances**: Each generation has its own unique financial circumstances, which can impact their purchasing decisions and brand loyalty. For example, Millennials and Generation Z may be burdened with student loan debt, while Baby Boomers may be more financially stable.

Conclusion

This chapter emphasized the importance of understanding and effectively engaging with different generational segments on social media. By using behavioural analysis, providing managerial strategies, and presenting a case study, this chapter equips marketers with practical guidance to optimize their campaign efforts in the diverse landscape of generational preferences. Understanding and capitalizing on generational differences can lead to improved audience targeting, increased engagement, and, ultimately, better marketing outcomes.

References

Adobe.(2021, September 3). *Behavioral analysis*. Retrieved from https://business.adobe.com/blog/basics/behavioral-analysis

Content Science. (2023). Millennial content consumption fact sheet. *Content Science Review*. Retrieved from https://review.content-science.com/millennial-content-consumption-fact-sheet/

Dixon, S. J. (2024). *U.S. social network users 2023, by income*. Statista. Retrieved from https://statista.com/statistics/1337616/us-distribution-leading-social-media-platforms-by-income

Dusek, B. (2021, July 30). *Generational media consumption trends*. Colorado State University. Retrieved from https://social.colostate.edu/trends/generational-media-consumption-trends/

Fractl. (2015). *Content engagement by generation*. Retrieved from https://www.frac.tl/work/marketing-research/content-engagement-by-generation/

Holt, D. (2016, March). Branding in the age of social media. *Harvard Business Review*. Retrieved from https://hbr.org/2016/03/branding-in-the-age-of-social-media

Johnson, B., & Williams, R. (2019). Targeting audiences in the digital age: The role of generational marketing. *International Journal of Market Research, 61*(4), 384–402.

Kamble, S. (2023, July 28). *How different generations use social media*. Feedough. Retrieved from https://www.feedough.com/how-different-generations-use-social-media/

Keane, L. (2017, August 7). *Behavioral analysis*. GlobalWebIndex (GWI). Retrieved from https://blog.gwi.com/marketing/behavioral-analysis/

Kowalewicz, R. (2020, January 9). *What to consider for generation-based social media marketing*. Forbes. Retrieved from https://www.forbes.com/sites/forbesagencycouncil/2020/01/09/what-to-consider-for-generation-based-social-media-marketing/?sh=5521eca14242

Lee, S., & Kim, H. (2021). Understanding generational differences in social media behaviour: A study on engagement and communication preferences. *Social Media Studies, 3*(1), 17–34.

Lesonsky, R. (2024, June 13). *How do different generations act on social media?* SCORE. Retrieved from https://www.score.org/resource/blog-post/how-do-different-generations-act-social-media

Martinez, L., & Gomez, E. (2022). Leveraging social media analytics for effective target audience identification. *Journal of Business Analytics, 5*(3), 112–128.

Mghames, F. (2022). Marketing today: Pop culture, TikTok, and everything in between. *Advertising Week*. Retrieved from https://advertisingweek.com/marketing-today-pop-culture-tiktok-and-everything-in-between/

Rishi, B., & Bandyopadhyay, S. (Eds.). (2018). *Contemporary issues in social media marketing*. London: Routledge.

Sinekovich, E. (2023, June 1). *How brands can thrive adding a pinch of pop culture to their marketing strategy*. Awario. Retrieved from https://awario.com/blog/pop-culture-in-marketing-strategy/

Smith, A. (2020). Generational differences in social media use and their implications for marketing strategies. *Journal of Digital Marketing, 4*(2), 45–59.

Sprout Social. (2023). *Social media use by generation*. Retrieved from https://sproutsocial.com/insights/guides/social-media-use-by-generation/

Thompson, C., & Davis, J. (2018). The impact of generational marketing on consumer behaviour in the digital era. *Consumer Behaviour Research Journal, 2*(2), 75–89.

True Anthem. (2023). *Generational differences on social media*. Retrieved from https://www.trueanthem.com/generational-differences-on-social-media/

US Department of Energy. (n.d.). *Better buildings neighborhood Program: Step 4: Identify target audiences and behavior changes*. Retrieved from https://www.energy.gov/eere/better-buildings-neighborhood-program/step-4-identify-target-audiences-and-behavior-changes

Westcott, K., Loucks, J., Srivastava, S., & Ciampa, D. (2018). *Digital media segments: Looking beyond generations*. Deloitte. Retrieved from https://www2.deloitte.com/us/en/insights/industry/telecommunications/media-consumption-behavior-across-generations.html

Social Media's Role in Customer Experience Creation

14

User-Generated Content Quality vs. Firm-Generated Content Quality

Olli Tyrväinen, Heikki Karjaluoto and Pinja Karjala
University of Jyväskylä, Finland

1 Introduction

Customers experience real-time interactions with their entire social network in online retail stores (Piotrowicz & Cuthbertson, 2014). In recent years, the explosive growth of social media (SM) has changed not only our daily lives but also consumer behavior. Thus, firms are investing in their SM channels and building interactions with their customers on various SM platforms (Rishi & Bandyopadhyay, 2018).

The relationship between SM content quality and customer experience has not been considered extensively in prior research. While existing studies have focused on SM from the perspective of the information source in the decision-making process (Erkan & Evans, 2018) and as a channel for sharing views and ideas in real time (Piotrowicz & Cuthbertson, 2014), research has

DOI: 10.4324/9781003412656-14

not widely addressed the impact of SM content quality on customer experience. This online interaction between a firm and a customer is important because customers share their opinions and thoughts in real time within their networks. Because companies cannot control a customer's individual SM network, negative effects such as harmful comments and fake information may spread rapidly. Therefore, monitoring SM networks and discussions has become essential for marketers (Al-Abdallah et al., 2024).

This chapter aims to clarify the impact of firms' participation in SM discussions, and contributes to previous research by demonstrating the role of firms' and consumers' SM discussions in customer experience. These results will help managers consider the efficiency of their SM activities and estimate the value of their communication with consumers.

Previous research has presented contradictory results concerning the outcomes of SM content quality. Some studies have indicated significant effects on behavioral intentions and loyalty, whereas others have shown no clear impact (Dabbous & Barakat, 2020; Erkan & Evans, 2018; Tyrväinen et al., 2023). However, previous research has mainly focused on the direct outcomes of content quality, and has overlooked the mechanisms behind these effects. To address this gap, the present study addresses the effects of SM content through analysis of the cognitive and emotional components of the customer experience. Investigating the link between SM discussions and customer experience provides valuable information by demonstrating the effects across components of the customer experience, therefore guiding companies' presence on SM.

Consumers who are strongly attached to SM are more active in discussions and more likely to generate content on SM (VanMeter et al., 2015, 2018). In previous studies, SM attachment has been linked with consumers' emotional responses (Wan et al., 2017). However, research has not examined the link between SM attachment, cognitive responses, and behavioral outcomes. This chapter aims to address this gap by exploring the effects of SM attachment on the relationship between emotional and cognitive responses and behavioral outcomes.

To provide a holistic understanding of the customer experience on SM, this study adopted a mixed-methods approach. According to Davies et al. (2011), using multiple methods provides researchers with more comprehensive, complete, and convincing findings on a given topic.

2 Conceptual Framework and Hypothesis Development

2.1 User-Generated and Firm-Generated SM Content

According to Kaplan and Haenlein (2010), *social media* refers to digital platforms that enable individuals to create and exchange content. In recent years, SM has evolved from simple online word-of-mouth platforms to interactive places for content, information, behavior, people, organizations, and institutions (Appel et al., 2020). For consumers, SM works as an information source that also allows them to share their experiences of companies, brands, and products with others. Compared with traditional face-to-face communication, user-generated SM content differs in its non-simultaneous nature, anonymity, social risk, confidentiality, and geographical and spatial freedom. For example, consumers have instant access to information, whenever they want, through their smartphones (Balaji et al., 2016).

SM has created new challenges (as well as opportunities) for companies. Because SM conversations between customers are beyond a firm's control, negative effects such as harmful comments spread rapidly. Companies should therefore develop strategies to minimize the harmful effects of negative word of mouth on their reputation and future business (Balaji et al., 2016).

2.2 Customer Experience

Customer experience refers to consumers' subjective and internal responses to any direct or indirect contact with a firm, such as those that occur during the search, purchase, consumption, or after-sale phases (Verhoef et al., 2009). In this study, we follow the logic of Rose et al. (2012), who stated that cognitive and emotional components are at the core of customer experience. Their customer experience framework was employed because its constructs illustrate the core interest of the present study.

2.3 Loyalty Intentions

Here, we operationalize word of mouth and purchase intention as components of customer loyalty. We use *word of mouth* to refer to a consumer's likelihood to recommend or say positive things about his or her experience to other consumers (Zeithaml et al., 1996); and *purchase intention* to refer to the likelihood of purchasing behavior (Rose et al., 2012).

2.4 SM Attachment

According to Bowlby (1979), attachment theory explains the interpersonal bonds that connect a person with a specific object. Attachment guides the targeting of individuals' emotional, cognitive, and behavioral resources, leading to motivational and behavioral outcomes such as willingness to invest in resources (Whan Park et al., 2010).

2.5 Hypothesis Development

The research model of Study 1 in this chapter posits user-generated SM content quality as an independent variable and firm-generated SM content quality as a moderating variable, and it demonstrates how they are related to cognitive and emotional responses. In Study 2, emotional and cognitive responses to user-generated SM content are independent variables; the firm's response and SM attachment are moderating variables; and negative word of mouth and negative purchase intention are dependent variables. Study 1 considers the positive outcomes of user-generated SM content, whereas Study 2 focuses on its negative impacts. Study 3 addresses the (quantitative) issues identified in Studies 1 and 2, and provides more in-depth insights by using a qualitative research setting. The conceptual framework is presented in Figure 14.1.

Conversations on a firm's page excite, stimulate, and interest customers, leading to continued interaction. For example, an affective state can result from emotions evoked by a stimulus. Positive or negative messages might lead to emotional reactions such as excitement, fear, liking, or joy. Kim and Johnson (2016) showed that user-generated content on SM induces an emotional response in other customers, while Dabbous and Barakat (2020) found similar effects for firm-generated content. We argue that a company's

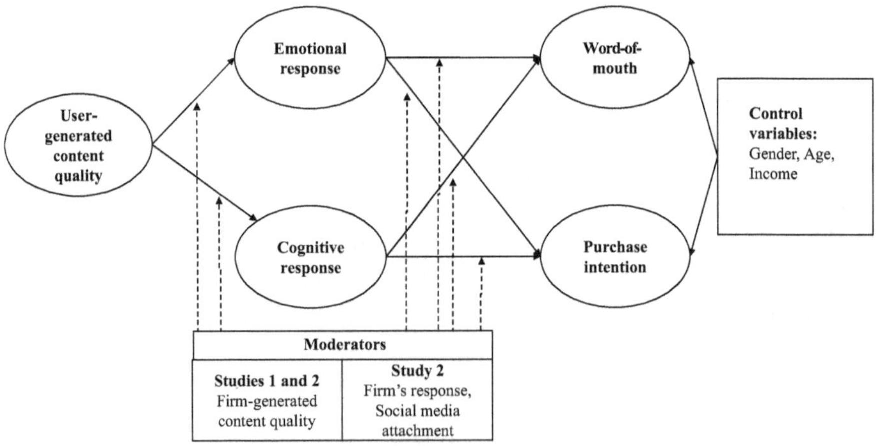

Figure 14.1 The conceptual framework

participation in SM discussions may strengthen the effects of user-generated content, and hypothesize the following:

H1a: Firm-generated SM content quality moderates the effect of user-generated content quality on a customer's emotional response in such a way that the effect is weaker if the customer perceives the firm-generated SM content to be of high quality.

H1b: Firm-generated SM content quality moderates the effect of user-generated content quality on a customer's cognitive response in such a way that the effect is weaker if the customer perceives the firm-generated SM content to be of high quality.

Prior research has presented contradictory results regarding the relationship between SM stimuli and loyalty. For example, Tyrväinen et al. (2023) showed a significant positive effect of information quality on brand loyalty, and Yusuf et al. (2018) found that SM information quality influences purchase intentions. Conversely, Erkan and Evans (2018) found no significant relationship between SM information quality and online purchase intentions. Lee and Hong (2016) studied the effect of the emotional appeal and informativeness of SM posts on behavioral responses (such as likes) and purchase intention, with results indicating that informativeness results in such responses but emotional appeal does not. Firm-generated content has a positive impact on brand loyalty (Ibrahim & Aljarah, 2023). Wu et al. (2020) studied the influence of firms' responses to positive reviews, and found that friendly responses strengthened the effect of the reviews on purchase intention. However, negative reviews and posts can harm a firm's reputation, so developing resilience to negative information has a key role in consumers' purchase intentions. Building on previous studies, we indicate that firms' participation in negative SM discussions may reduce the harmful effects of negative SM content on loyalty outcomes. Therefore, we hypothesized the following:

H2a: A firm's friendly responses weaken the relationship between the customer's emotional response to user-generated content and negative word of mouth.

H2b: A firm's friendly responses weaken the relationship between the customer's emotional response to user-generated content and negative purchase intention.

H3a: A firm's friendly responses weaken the relationship between the customer's cognitive response to user-generated content and negative word of mouth.

H3b: A firm's friendly responses weaken the relationship between the customer's cognitive response to user-generated content and negative purchase intention.

Consumers use SM for various reasons. Individuals who are strongly attached to SM are more likely to share positive word of mouth on platforms and buy products (VanMeter et al., 2015, 2018; Dinh & Lee, 2022). However, this relationship is still unclear with regard to negative SM content (VanMeter et al., 2018). Thus, unlike the original perspective, we are interested in whether SM attachment influences the strength of negative consumer responses, and argue that attachment could play an important role in the effects of negative word of mouth.

H4a: The moderating effect of SM attachment strengthens the relationship between a customer's emotional response and negative word of mouth.
H4b: The moderating effect of SM attachment strengthens the relationship between a customer's emotional response and negative purchase intention.
H5a: The moderating effect of SM attachment strengthens the relationship between a customer's cognitive response and negative word of mouth.
H5b: The moderating effect of SM attachment strengthens the relationship between a customer's cognitive response and negative purchase intention.

3 Empirical Studies

3.1 Study 1: Quality of User-Generated and Firm-Generated Content in Customer Experience Creation

3.1.1 Research Design

The objective of here was to examine the direct effects of user-generated SM content quality on customer experience and the moderating effects of firm-generated content quality on this relationship. The research setting aimed to have respondents reflect on their SM use during a recent purchasing process; therefore, all the key terms were explained at the beginning of the survey form. The target population included retail customers in Finland, and a market research company was employed to recruit participants.

Table 14.1 Study 1: Profile of respondents versus general population of Finland

	Study respondents				**General population**
	2019		**2020**		
	N	%	N	%	%
Gender					
Male	1096	50.8	1283	50.0	49.4
Female	1060	49.2	1285	50.0	50.6
Age (years)					
15–24	207	9.6	312	12.1	11.2
25–34	266	12.3	507	19.7	12.3
35–49	296	13.7	716	27.9	19.0
50–60	416	19.3	524	20.4	13.9
61–80	971	45.0	509	19.8	22.3
Household size					
1	703	32.6	838	32.6	44.0
2	1069	49.6	1057	41.2	32.7
3	182	8.4	289	11.3	10.3
4	136	6.3	246	9.6	8.4
5+	66	3.1	129	5.0	17.2

Note: Data for the general population is derived from Statistics Finland (2020).

Two samples of 2,156 and 2,565 valid responses were collected during December 2019 and October 2020. The demographic profiles of both samples are presented in Table 14.1.

3.1.2 Measurement Scales

All variables were measured on a seven-point Likert scale, and instruments were validated in advance. Items measuring the user-generated content quality were adapted from Kudeshia and Kumar (2017); scales measuring firm-generated SM content quality were adapted from Dwivedi et al. (2019) and Bruhn et al. (2012); and items measuring cognitive and emotional responses were adapted from Brakus et al. (2009).

3.1.3 Measurement Model

The hypotheses were tested using SmartPLS 3 software (Ringle et al., 2015). Composite reliability (CR), average variance extracted (AVE), Cronbach's alpha (C_α), and factor loadings were used to evaluate the model's reliability and validity (Table 14.2). These were acceptable, and we found no evidence of common-method bias using the marker-variable approach.

Table 14.2 Study 1: Average variances extracted, composite reliabilities, Cronbach's alphas, discriminant validity, and descriptive statistics

	AVE	CR	α	1	2	3	4	5	6	7
Firm-generated content quality (1)	0.794 (0.702)	0.951 (0.922)	0.935 (0.894)	**0.936 (0.838)**						
User-generated content quality (2)	0.877 (0.856)	0.966 (0.960)	0.953 (0.944)	0.560 (0.231)	**0.934 (0.925)**					
Cognitive customer experience (3)	0.788 (0.745)	0.931 (0.897)	0.866 (0.828)	0.359 (0.460)	0.300 (0.200)	**0.855 (0.863)**				
Emotional customer experience (4)	0.770 (0.752)	0.931 (0.924)	0.900 (0.890)	0.242 (0.403)	0.175 (0.069)	0.608 (0.641)	**0.868 (0.867)**			
Gender (5)				–0.057 (–0.048)	–0.019 (0.007)	0.028 (0.033)	0.041 (0.045)	**n/a**		
Age (6)				–0.226 (–0.040)	–0.352 (–0.425)	–0.114 (–0.088)	–0.042 (0.019)	–0.017 (–0.026)	**n/a**	
Income (7)				–0.086 (–0.035)	–0.101 (–0.079)	–0.047 (0.017)	–0.032 (0.018)	–0.050 (–0.113)	0.052 (0.191)	**n/a**
Mean				4.371 (4.415)	2.325 (2.409)	4.778 (4.819)	5.498 (5.478)			
s.d.				0.948 (1.002)	1.611 (1.631)	1.303 (1.276)	1.244 (1.198)			

Notes: AVE: average variance extracted; CR: composite reliability; α: Cronbach's alpha; s.d.: standard deviation. Data for Study 1b (2020) is shown in parentheses.

Table 14.3 Results of Study 1

Direct effects	2019		2020	
	β	*p*-value	β	*p*-value
Firm-generated content quality: Cognitive customer experience	0.402	<.001	0.445	<.001
Firm-generated content quality: Emotional customer experience	0.398	<.001	0.415	<.001
User-generated content quality: Cognitive customer experience	0.169	<.001	0.109	<.001
User-generated content quality: Emotional customer experience	0.023	0.307	–0.017	0.394
User-generated content quality × firm-generated content quality: Cognitive customer experience	–0.058	<.001	–0.028	0.087
User-generated content quality × firm-generated content quality: Emotional customer experience	–0.033	0.077	0.024	0.159

3.1.4 Results

The results of Study 1 are presented in Table 14.3. The relationship between user-generated content quality and emotional customer experience was not significant. However, user-generated content quality had a positive direct effect on cognitive customer experience. Firm-generated SM content quality had positive direct effects on both the emotional customer experience and the cognitive customer experience. Firm-generated SM content quality moderated the effect of user-generated content quality on the cognitive customer experience but not on the emotional customer experience (so H1b is supported and H1a is not). Therefore, firm-generated SM content quality slightly reduced the effect of user-generated content quality on the cognitive customer experience but not on the emotional customer experience. After controlling for demographics (gender, income, and age), we found a slight positive effect of gender on cognitive customer experience and emotional customer experience, which indicated that female respondents have slightly stronger customer experiences.

3.2 Study 2: Does Firm-Generated Content Reduce the Harmful Effects of Negative User-Generated Content?

3.2.1 Research Design

Study 2 extends Study 1 by further investigating the moderating effects of a company's participation in a customer's SM conversation by using an experimental research setting. In Study 1, we found that user-generated SM content positively affects the cognitive customer experience, but we found no such effect on the emotional customer experience. The mechanism behind these findings was unclear; therefore, the goal here was to complement these results. Study 2 examined the moderating effect of firm-generated content on the relationship between consumers' responses to negative user-generated content and the components of customer loyalty. It also investigated the moderating effects of SM attachment on this relationship.

3.2.2 Procedure

A total of 674 participants were recruited via an online ground-sourcing marketplace. Some were dropped due to double answers, resulting in the final sample of 659 (65.9 percent men, 34.1 percent women) with a mean age of 33.6 years. Most respondents were from the USA. They were asked to complete a survey consisting of manipulation stimuli and a questionnaire. A 2 × 2 between-subjects design was used. The manipulated independent variables were the type of SM post (emotional vs. cognitive) and the company's action (response vs. no response).

Respondents were randomly assigned to one of four scenarios. In the first scenario, the respondents viewed an emotional SM post on a firm's Facebook page. In the second, the respondents viewed the same post but with the firm's response. In the third scenario, the respondents viewed a cognitive SM post on a firm's Facebook page. Finally, the fourth scenario showed the respondents the same post as in the third scenario but added the firm's response. The respondents then answered the survey about the Facebook post. We used content from actual customer posts and firm answers, which we modified to fit the fictional case.

3.2.3 Measurement Scales

All variables were again measured on a seven-point Likert scale, except for negative word of mouth, which was measured on a ten-point scale.

We adopted Kim and Johnson's (2016) scale to measure perceived information quality as a cognitive response. To measure emotions, we adopted a scale from Rose et al. (2012). The scale measuring negative word of mouth was based on the work of Leppäniemi et al. (2017), and that measuring negative purchase intention was based on the purchase-intention scale of Chen and Barnes (2007). Information on age, gender, and occupation was gathered to form demographic profiles of the respondents.

3.2.4 Measurement Model

As in Study 1, the hypotheses were tested using SmartPLS 3 software, and we used CR, AVE, C_{α}, and factor loadings to evaluate the reliability and validity of our model, which again were acceptable (Table 14.4). We found no evidence of common method bias using the marker-variable approach.

3.2.5 Results

Multigroup analysis was used to test the moderating effects between groups. The analysis found that the firm's friendly response negatively moderated the effect of the cognitive response to a negative purchase intention ($\Delta\beta = 0.280$, $p < 0.1$) and negative word of mouth ($\Delta\beta = 0.173$, $p < 0.1$) (H3a, H3b). Therefore, the firm's friendly response to negative SM posts reduced the harmful effects on purchase intention and word of mouth. The other relationships did not exceed the threshold of significance ($p < 0.1$ or $p > 0.9$).

Structural equation modeling was performed on the complete sample to test the moderating effects of H4a, H4b, H5a, and H5b. We found that SM attachment positively moderates the relationship between emotional response and negative word of mouth (H4a; $\beta = 0.075$, $p < 0.05$) and between emotional response and negative purchase intention (H4b; $\beta = 0.177$, $p < 0.01$). This indicates that the more attached consumers are, the more negative behavioral responses they will generate to emotional posts. H5a and H5b were not supported, indicating that attached SM users generate stronger emotional responses that influence their purchase intentions and word-of-mouth behavior.

After controlling for demographics (gender and age), we found a slight positive effect of age on negative purchase intention ($\beta = 0.070$, $p < 0.05$), which implies that older consumers generate stronger negative purchase intentions than younger consumers.

Table 14.4 Study 2: Average variances extracted, composite reliabilities, Cronbach's alphas, discriminant validity, and descriptive statistics

	AVE	CR	α	1	2	3	4	5	6	7
Cognitive response (1)	0.640	0.842	0.719	**0.800**						
Emotional response (2)	0.704	0.877	0.790	0.379	**0.839**					
Negative word of mouth (3)	0.796	0.887	0.748	0.438	0.697	**0.892**				
Negative purchase intention (4)	0.767	0.868	0.695	0.308	0.638	0.645	**0.876**			
Attachment (5)	0.781	0.915	0.860	0.575	0.335	0.383	0.179	**0.884**		
Gender (6)				0.097	0.045	0.043	0.011	0.114	**n/a**	
Age (7)				–0.108	–0.021	–0.014	0.047	0.106	0.040	**n/a**
Mean				5.266	4.67	6.68	5.039	5.43		
s.d.				0.963	1.27	2.36	1.04	1.14		

Notes: AVE: average variance extracted; CR: composite reliability; α: Cronbach's alpha; s.d.: standard deviation.

3.3 Study 3: How Do Consumers Perceive the Relationship between User-Generated Content and Firm-Generated Content?

3.3.1 Research Design

To address the issues identified in Studies 1 and 2 and deepen our understanding of the obtained findings, we conducted a qualitative interview study to explore how user-generated and firm-generated SM content drives customer experience. Study 3 also aimed to clarify the mechanism behind firm-generated content's moderating effects on user-generated content and its outcomes.

3.3.2 Procedure

In-depth interviews (n = 17) were conducted among consumers in Finland with rich prior experience of SM use in the retail context during October 2020. The purposeful criterion sampling method was used to gather knowledge about the research topic (Patton, 2002, pp. 40–46). The interviewees' demographic information is presented in Table 14.5.

Table 14.5 Demographic profiles of Study 3 respondents

ID	Gender	Age	Occupation
F1	Female	26	School teacher
F2	Female	25	Marketing assistant
F3	Female	23	University student
F4	Female	27	Junior personal banker
F5	Female	51	Practical nurse
F6	Female	24	University student
F7	Female	25	University student
F8	Female	24	University student
F9	Female	31	Senior communication specialist
M1	Male	25	University student
M2	Male	24	University student
M3	Male	18	High school student
M4	Male	27	Electrical engineer
M5	Male	24	University student
M6	Male	68	Pensioner
M7	Male	32	Product owner
M8	Male	55	Sales engineer

The interviewees were asked to reflect on their SM use during the purchasing process regarding one recent customer experience. Semi-structured questions were designed to lead the interview, encourage deeper discussion, and allow the interviewees to express their views (Järvenpää & Lang, 2005). The interviews (each lasting 13 minutes on average) were audio-recorded, transcribed into text files after each session, and translated from Finnish to English. Data analysis followed the three-stage content approach of Miles and Huberman (1994), including data reduction, data display, and drawing conclusions.

3.3.3 Results

Our interview data suggests that the role of user-generated SM content is to offer information to other consumers. Typically, SM is used during the early stages of the decision-making process for both passive inspiration searches and more active product-related information searches. Conversely, consumers create content on SM after their purchase to recommend those goods/services or share negative experiences. These experiences seem to play an important role in the decision-making process.

Negative posts leave a deeper impression than positive posts, and are perceived as more influential if consumers are unfamiliar with their intended purchase. However, consumers tend to filter negative posts because it is important to differentiate between real feedback and online trolls (i.e., people who browse sites with the sole intent of leaving baseless negative comments). The level of information, argumentation, and facts influences the effectiveness of posts. For example, informative content is perceived as more influential for rational decision-making than emotional posts, whereas emotional content is more effective with regard to impulse buying. Credible posts are objective, clear, and transparent.

> If I don't have [a] lot of experience [with a] specific product or company, I find recommendations more important.
>
> (female, 26)

> Reviews on a company's pages do not have [a] great impact because I often see that the people behind the most negative posts are just trolling, so I do not take those posts so seriously. But constructive criticism and, for example, feedback about delivery times would affect my behavior.
>
> (female, 23)

The interviewees expected firm-generated content to offer purchase-related information and inspiration and support their decision-making process. However, firm-generated content was perceived as less important and objective than content created by other consumers. Consumers want to read product reviews, and they appreciate companies that share those reviews on their SM pages. For user-generated content, the effectiveness of informative or emotional content is related to the type of product features available. Rational decision-making requires informative support, whereas emotional content drives impulse-buying behavior.

> Posts from other consumers are most effective. If a retailer picks up and shares consumer reviews (positive and negative reviews), that is effective.
>
> (male, 24)

> In my opinion, companies should provide as comprehensive information about products as possible. For me, informative content is important, mostly technical information.
>
> (male, 55)

According to the interviewees, one important role of a company's SM channels, which is not often used as effectively as consumers would like, is as a channel for feedback. The interviewees highlighted SM's role as a customer service channel, stating that it should offer quick responses and easy interaction between customers and companies.

> Customer service via social media is notably important in some situations. Social media can be a channel where consumers can contact retailers if something is wrong.
>
> (female, 25)

> Facebook chat is often a good channel for me if I want to ask something or make a complaint. So far, I have often gotten an answer.
>
> (male, 32)

To conclude, the importance of informative and emotional content varies according to the type of product. For both user-generated and firm-generated content, cognitive posts are more important in rational and active information searching, whereas emotional content can result in impulsive purchases during passive SM browsing. In addition, our data highlight the importance of effective interaction between companies and consumers. This supports our findings regarding the positive influence of firms' participation in SM discussions. Firms' active SM behavior may reduce the harmful influence of consumers' negative SM posts.

4 Discussion

4.1 Theoretical Contributions

A mixed-method approach allows researchers to draw consistent conclusions from findings. Consequently, this chapter contributes to marketing theory from several viewpoints: it reveals how customers' user-generated content quality affects customer experience and behavioral responses; explores how firm-generated SM content quality influences these relationships; and examines the influence of consumers' SM attachment on consumer responses and behavioral outcomes.

Study 1 found that user-generated content quality has a positive influence on the cognitive response. However, the relationship with the emotional response was insignificant. In Study 2, the firm-generated content was not found to moderate emotional outcomes. Prior studies have lacked a clear explanation of why the moderating effect is significant in cognitive responses but not significant regarding emotional responses; yet some have highlighted SM's role as an informative channel. Providing relevant information reduces the harmful effects of negative posts from other consumers. We suggest that firm-generated SM content stimulates consumers' cognitive processes; therefore, SM's influence on cognitive responses seems to be significant.

As per Swani and Milne (2017), an emotional appeal in SM messages does not influence SM message popularity, which led them to suggest that messages should match offerings – such as using emotional appeals for hedonic products and functional appeals for utilitarian offerings. This is one possible explanation for the insignificant relationship regarding emotional responses.

In addition, our results suggest that the level of a consumer's SM attachment strengthens the relationship between emotional response and loyalty intentions. This indicates that SM content generates stronger responses among heavy SM users. The findings of Study 3 illustrate that the required features of content may depend on the type of product.

4.2 Managerial Implications

The results of this study have several implications for managers. We found that firm-generated SM content quality lessens the importance of user-generated content quality in relation to a customer's cognitive responses. Therefore, we suggest that retailers invest in their SM pages, especially if the cognitive customer experience plays an important role in their customers' purchasing processes. Our results indicate that monitoring and participating in SM conversations related to these customer experiences may reduce the harmful effects of negative posts. Hence, we encourage retailers to actively participate in SM discussions.

SM is more important from a cognitive viewpoint, and we highlight the importance of creating cognitive stimuli for customers' internal processing. Therefore, we encourage retailers to develop their SM pages as an information source for consumers. Our results suggest that retailers should invest in interactions with consumers on SM to increase loyalty among their customers. In view of these findings, we highlight the role of informative content as a key factor behind SM success.

Finally, we found that SM attachment moderates the relationship between emotional customer experience and loyalty intentions. Consequently, if consumers' intention to use SM is high, emotional content is more effective. Therefore, retailers should target emotional SM content to frequent SM users. We assert that providing the right content to the right consumers should be the goal in every retailer's SM marketing strategy.

4.3 Limitations and Further Research

Research generalizability is one notable limitation of this study. While the samples were large (Surveys 1 and 2: $N_{2019} = 2{,}156$, $N_{2020} = 2{,}565$, respectively; experiment: $N = 659$), the data were only collected from US and Finnish retail customers. Therefore, additional research outside these countries is needed in order to generalize the findings. Future research can expand on the present study by gathering longitudinal data, which might better capture the dynamism of customer experience. In addition, Study 1 considered SM on a general level, and Study 2 only considered Facebook. However, the field of SM channels is heterogeneous, so we urge future studies to elaborate on specific channels separately.

Case Example: XXL Sports & Outdoors' Marketing on Instagram

Norwegian sporting goods retailer XXL Sports & Outdoors uses multiple channels to drive traffic to its physical and online stores. One of the key components of the company's digital marketing strategy is investment in SM, which enables it to provide tailored marketing communications, generate content, and actively monitor and participate in online discussions. Consequently, investments in SM result in increased brand visibility, better connections with customers, and enhanced customer experience and loyalty. SM content can be classified as firm-generated or user-generated, depending on the information source. Firm-generated content and user-generated content are interconnected elements of XXL's digital marketing strategy, together contributing to the brand narrative. This case example explores the role of both content types in XXL's SM marketing.

Firm-Generated Content

Firm-generated content is a strategic cornerstone of XXL's digital marketing efforts. The company has invested in its presence on Instagram, where it has separate profiles for each of its primary markets (Norway, Sweden, Finland, and Denmark). This allows XXL to tailor marketing communications to specific regional preferences and demographics, and thus provide more targeted content to its audiences. As a result, XXL's Instagram activities resonate with each market's characteristics, and local audiences can be served in their own language.

On its Instagram profiles, XXL produces firm-generated content to engage with its followers and promote its products. The company employs a mix of paid and unpaid content to optimize its digital marketing efforts. By curating content specific to each market, the company manages to find a balance between global branding and local relevance. More specifically, XXL produces content that includes, for example, product showcases and promotional campaigns aimed at these specific markets. Producing firm-generated content in SM increases XXL's brand visibility, and thus helps the company attract new customers.

Firm-generated content can be divided into paid and unpaid content. Paid content involves sponsored content, which reaches a wider audience. By investing in sponsored posts, the company can target content for specific segments. Consequently, the content is shown to SM users who might be interested in XXL's products (potential customers). Unpaid firm-generated content is aimed at followers of XXL. This content differs from paid posts as its target audience is already familiar with the brand. Unpaid content can be used to foster community interaction by inviting followers to share their experiences.

User-Generated Content

Customers of XXL actively share their experiences on SM. This user-generated content plays a key role from the perspective of XXL's digital marketing strategy. As SM discussions affect consumer's decision-making process, XXL actively monitors these discussions and takes a proactive stance in interacting with its customers. Consumer-to-consumer SM discussions allow people to share their experience in real time, which makes XXL's presence on SM vital. As consumers often use Instagram to seek out information or voice their concerns, XXL responds promptly to questions and addresses customer complaints as a part of its service strategy. Addressing customer queries and concerns in real time demonstrates the company's commitment to its customers. This responsiveness contributes to a positive customer experience, which turns into customer loyalty.

On the other hand, SM discussions often reflect consumer sentiments and preferences. SM provides an open platform where customers can share their feedback with companies. Thus, SM discussions are a rich source of customer data, offering an understanding of market trends. By continuously monitoring these discussions, XXL gains insight into market trends. This real-time data helps the company stay ahead of trends.

Encouraging customers to generate SM content offers numerous benefits for retailers. As user-generated content gives an authentic portrayal of products, it helps build trust among potential customers. When customers share their experiences of XXL, they not only promote its products but also contribute to the brand narrative. Sharing user-generated content on the company's channels deepens customer engagement with the brand. Moreover, responding to user-generated content strengthens customers' relationship with the retailer, which again turns into customer loyalty.

In conclusion, XXL's strategic approach to SM reveals a powerful driver of brand visibility, positive customer experience, and loyalty. The synergistic use of firm-generated content and user-generated content forms a cohesive narrative, reaching diverse audiences with tailored communications. Through active engagement, responsive customer service, and data collection from SM discussions, XXL enhances its understanding of its customers, improves customer experience, and fosters loyalty.

References

Al-Abdallah, G., Barzani, R., Dandis, A., & Eid, M. A. H. (2024). Social media marketing strategy: The impact of firm-generated content on customer-based brand equity in the retail industry. *Journal of Marketing Communications*. 1–30. https://doi.org/10.1080/13527266.2023.2300076

Appel, G., Grewal, L., Hadi, R., & Stephen, A. (2020). The future of SM marketing. *Journal of the Academy of Marketing Science*, *48*, 79–95.

Balaji, M. S., Khong, K. W., & Chong, A. Y. L. (2016). Determinants of negative word-of-mouth communication using social networking sites. *Information and Management*, *53*, 528–540.

Bowlby, J. (1979). The Bowlby–Ainsworth attachment theory. *Behavioral and Brain Sciences*, *2*(4), 637–638.

Brakus, J., Schmitt, B., & Zarantonello, L. (2009). Brand experience: What is it? How is it measured? Does it affect loyalty? *Journal of Marketing*, *73*(3), 52–68.

Bruhn, M., Schoenmueller, V., & Schäfer, D. (2012). Are SM replacing traditional media in terms of brand equity creation? *Management Research Review*, *35*(9), 770–790.

Chen, Y.-H., & Barnes, S. (2007). Initial trust and online buyer behavior. *Industrial Management and Data Systems*, *107*(1), 21–36.

Dabbous, A., & Barakat, K.-A. (2020). Bridging the online offline gap: Assessing the impact of brands' social network content quality on brand awareness and purchase intention. *Journal of Retailing and Consumer Services*, *53*, 101966.

Davies, D., Golicic, S., & Boerstler, C. (2011). Benefits and challenges of conducting multiple methods in marketing. *Journal of Academy of Marketing Science*, *39*, 467–479.

Dinh, T., & Lee, Y. (2022). "I want to be as trendy as influencers": How "fear of missing out" leads to buying intention for products endorsed by SM influencers. *Journal of Research in Interactive Marketing*, *16*(3), 346–364.

Dwivedi, A., Johnson, L., Wilkie, D., & De Araujo-Gil, L. (2019). Consumer emotional brand attachment with SM brands and SM brand equity. *European Journal of Marketing*, *53*(6), 1176–1204.

Erkan, I., & Evans, C. (2018). SM or shopping websites? The influence of eWOM on consumers' online purchase intention. *Journal of Marketing Communications*, *24*(6), 617–632.

Ibrahim, B., & Aljarah, A. (2023). The era of Instagram expansion: Matching SM marketing activities and brand loyalty through customer relationship quality. *Journal of Marketing Communications*, *29*(1), 1–25.

Järvenpää, S. L., & Lang, K. R. (2005). Managing the paradoxes of mobile technology. *Information Systems Management*, *22*(4), 7–23.

Kaplan, A., & Haenlein, M. (2010). Users of the world, unite! The challenges and opportunities of SM. *Business Horizons*, *53*(1), 59–68.

Kim, A., & Johnson, K. (2016). Power of consumers using SM: Examining the influence of brand-related user-generated content on Facebook. *Computers in Human Behavior*, *58*, 98–108.

Kudeshia, C., & Kumar, A. (2017). Social eWOM: Does it affect the brand attitude and purchase intention of brands? *Management Research Review*, *40*(3), 310–330.

Lee, J., & Hong, I. (2016). Predicting positive user responses to SM advertising: The roles of emotional appeal, informativeness, and creativity. *International Journal of Information Management*, *36*(3), 360–373.

Leppäniemi, M., Karjaluoto, H., & Saarijärvi, H. (2017). Customer perceived value, satisfaction, and loyalty: The role of willingness to share information. *International Review of Retail, Distribution and Consumer Research*, *27*(2), 164–188.

Miles, M. B., & Huberman, A. M. (1994). *Qualitative data analysis* (2nd ed.). Thousand Oaks, CA: SAGE Publications.

Patton. M. Q. (2002). *Qualitative research and evaluation methods* (3rd ed.). Thousand Oaks, CA: Sage Publications.

Piotrowicz, W., & Cuthbertson, R. (2014). Introduction to the special issue information technology in retail: Toward omnichannel retailing. *International Journal of Electronic Commerce*, *18*(4), 5–16.

Ringle, C., Wende, S., & Becker, J. M. (2015). *SmartPLS 3*. Bönnignstedt: SmartPLS. Retrieved September 2, 2023, from http://www.smartpls.com

Rishi, B., & Bandyopadhyay, S. (Eds.). (2018). *Contemporary issues in social media marketing*. London: Routledge.

Rose, S., Clark, M., Samouel, P., & Hair, N. (2012). Online customer experience in e-retailing: An empirical model of antecedents and outcomes. *Journal of Retailing*, *88*(2), 308–322.

Statistics Finland. (2020). Retrieved September 2, 2023, from https://www.stat.fi/til/vaerak/.

Swani, K., & Milne, G. (2017). Evaluating Facebook brand content popularity for service versus goods offerings. *Journal of Business Research*, *79*, 123–133.

Tyrväinen, O., Karjaluoto, H., & Ukpabi, D. (2023). Understanding the role of SM content in brand loyalty: A meta-analysis of user-generated versus firm-generated content. *Journal of Interactive Marketing*, *58*(4), 400–413.

VanMeter, R., Grisaffe, D., & Chonko, L. (2015). Of "likes" and "pins": The effects of consumer attachment to SM. *Journal of Interactive Marketing*, *32*, 70–88.

VanMeter, R., Syrdal, H., Powell-Mantel, S., Grisaffe, D., & Nesson, E. (2018). Don't just "like" me, promote me: How attachment and attitude influence brand-related behaviors on SM. *Journal of Interactive Marketing*, *43*, 83–97.

Verhoef, P. C., Lemon, K., Parasuraman, A., Roggeveen, A., Tsiros, M., & Schlesinger, L. (2009). Customer experience creation: Determinants, dynamics and management strategies. *Journal of Retailing*, *85*(1), 31–41.

Wan, J., Lu, Y., & Zhao, L. (2017). How attachment influences users' willingness to donate to content creators in SM: A socio-technical systems perspective. *Information and Management*, *54*, 837–850.

Whan Park, C., MacInnis, D. J., Priester, A. B., Eisingerich, J., & Iacobucci, D. (2010). Brand attachment and brand attitude strength: Conceptual and empirical differentiation of two critical brand equity drivers. *Journal of Marketing*, *74*(6), 1–17.

Wu, J., Wu, T., & Schlegelmilch, B. (2020). Seize the day: How online retailers should respond to positive reviews. *Journal of Interactive Marketing*, *52*, 52–60.

Yusuf, A., Hussin, R., & Busalin, A. (2018). Influence of e-WOM engagement on consumer purchase intention in social commerce. *Journal of Services Marketing*, *32*(4), 493–504.

Zeithaml, V. A., Berry, L. L., & Parasuraman, A. (1996). The behavioral consequences of service quality. *Journal of Marketing*, *60*(2), 31–46.

Augmenting the Analyst 15

Artificial Intelligence in the Age of Social Media Big Data

Faniza Joshi
Chitkara Business School, Chitkara University, Punjab, India

Amandeep Kaur
MCM DAV College for Women, Chandigarh, India

Nidhi Malhotra
Chitkara Business School, Chitkara University, Punjab, India

Introduction

The basis for the evolution of social media began after the dotcom bubble burst in 2001, which is seen as the defining moment for Web 2.0 (O'Reilly, 2007). Yet, the term 'social media' was introduced by Bruce and Susan Abelson when they founded an 'open diary' in 1998. Previously, companies had more control over any information available about them through official statements and advertisements. However, in the current social media age, companies have less impact as clients can freely post remarks and opinions on the web (Kaplan and Haenlein, 2010; Rishi & Bandyopadhyay, 2018). Social media standards allow individuals to distribute data more frequently. Thus, there is a requirement for users to be aware of where to get new and

DOI: 10.4324/9781003412656-15

relevant data and how to consume it (Breslin et al., 2009, pp. 21–44). These platforms generate massive volumes of data every second. Managing this vast amount of information becomes challenging without proper strategies in place. However, social media analytics is being used to address this challenge (Zeng et al., 2010; Leskovec, 2011).

Social media analytics is defined as gathering, analysing, and disseminating information from relevant social media in order to support business activities such as intelligence gathering, opportunity detection, problem identification, sense-making, insight generation, and/or decision-making undertaken in response to sensed business needs (Holsapple et al., 2018, p. 33). Wu et al. (2019) proposed a theory-driven social media analytics framework based on the following contributions: theories of the middle range (Merton, 1949, pp. 39–53); the model of sociocultural evolution (Campbell, 1965); and a three-stage process based on an input–output model (Fan & Gordon, 2014). Rahman and Reza (2022) proposed a 'Sunflower Model for Big Data', which describes big data in ten domains of social data analytics for social media platforms.

By integrating these theories, the present study provides a comprehensive framework for various stages – i.e. formulate, determine, capture, implement, understand, and present. While social media analytics provided valuable insights, the analysis was limited to basic statistical methods, and the scale and complexity of the data made it difficult to derive comprehensive and real-time insight. Artificial intelligence has revolutionized social media analytics, enabling more sophisticated and automated techniques (Finn & Mustafaraj, 2013; Cresswell et al., 2021).

Artificial intelligence can perform tasks that typically require human intelligence, such as visual perception, speech recognition, decision making, and language translation. Artificial intelligence involved the theory and development of simulating and replicating human-like intelligence to accomplish these tasks (Babu & Kanaga, 2022, pp. 2–4).

Artificial Intelligence Techniques

This section deals with various deep learning (DL) and machine learning (ML) techniques. Social media platforms have become important communication channels, but the data they generate is not fully utilized due to its uncertain nature (Chan et al., 2016; Eberendu, 2016; Wang & Zhang, 2024). An effective text-mining method is necessary to extract useful data. Deep learning is one such approach, and can be seen as the AI function that mimics data processing in the human brain (Sarker, 2021).

Deep Learning Techniques

Deep learning is thought to originate from a paper by computer scientist Geoffrey Hinton in the 1980s (Smith, 2018), and was based on the concept of artificial neural networks (ANN) (Sarker, 2021; Wazirali et al., 2023), which can be categorized as 'discriminative' or 'generative'. In the discriminative approach, data is passed from input to output via hidden layers. Thus, it focuses on supervised training problems.

In the generative approach, training can be broadly divided into two categories – supervised and unsupervised. Here the data is labelled under a supervised learning structure which is further used to train the network (Mintz et al., 2009). Under unsupervised training, neural networks prepared models such as restricted Boltzmann machines (RBMs), which could later be adjusted using supervised algorithms (Shrestha & Mahmood, 2019).

Chen and Lin (2014) utilized both labelled and unlabelled data for their study, and discovered the modified neural network – i.e., deep belief network (DBN). Deep neural networks (DNNs) are training algorithms used to address two major challenges: premature convergence and overfitting. Premature convergence happens when the DNN settles into a suboptimal state at a local level, missing the global minima of the entire space. Overfitting occurs when the DNN becomes too specialized for the training data, making it less adaptable to other test data and rigid in its predictions (Shrestha & Mahmood, 2019, p. 53048). DNN structure comprises the following:

- convolutional neural networks (CNNs)
- recurrent neural networks (RNNs)
- long short-term memory networks (LSTMs)
- gated recurrent units (GRUs).

Convolutional Neural Networks

CNNs have revolutionized visual computer tasks, including image generation and classification, object detection, and semantic segmentation. Their ability to automatically learn hierarchical features and patterns has made them highly effective in various applications involving visual data (Li & Yu 2016; Shrestha & Mahmood, 2019; Abid et al., 2020). Social media platforms have vast amounts of visual context, and CNNs excel in tasks such as image classification, object detection, and video analysis (Johnston & Elyan, 2019). For instance, Niklaus et al. (2017) used a CNN to interpolate frames obtained from high frame-trained YouTube data. CNNs can be trained to recognize and flag certain content (such as violence or nudity) by examining the visual elements and examples present in pictures and recordings (Tahir et al., 2019), and much research is being carried out on object recognition, shape coordinating, and pattern recognition.

Recurrent Neural Networks

RNNs are particularly used in sequential and temporal information (Baccouche et al., 2011), and have shown the potential to detect depression using textual data (Zogan et al., 2021). By considering their context and sequence, RNNs can capture dependencies and relationships between words, enabling accurate sentiment classification and understanding of user sentiment on social media (Ain et al., 2017; Nemes & Kiss, 2021).

Long Short-Term Memory

LSTM networks were introduced to address the challenges faced by RNNs when processing sequences of data with long-range dependencies (Hochreiter & Schmidhuber, 1997). They have become popular for various tasks involving sequential data, such as natural language processing, time series analysis, and sentiment analysis (Wang et al., 2018). LSTMs are therefore used to generate text based on the patterns and structures learned from social media data. For example, to detect 'fake news' posted on Twitter (now X), Bangyal et al. (2021) conducted a survey using machine learning and deep learning models (LSTM, CNN, RNN, and GRU); and Miao et al. (2022) employed an LSTM model to explore tweets to track and identify events during the coronavirus crisis in New York City. This model can help in understanding the dynamics of emergency situations and even fake news/misinformation. By analysing the sequential patterns and linguistic cues in news articles or social media posts, LSTMs can detect inconsistencies, misleading information, or suspicious sources, thus helping combat the spread of fake news.

Gated Recurrent Units

This modification of the LSTM network was proposed by Cho et al. (2014) as a simplified LSTM by merging the cell state and hidden state into a single hidden state vector (see also Greff et al., 2017). It achieves this by introducing two gating mechanisms: the update gate and the reset gate. GRUs carry out similar roles to LSTMs, such as sentiment analysis, event detection and trend analysis, behaviour modelling, fake news detection, trend forecasting, and so on.

Machine Learning Techniques

These techniques help AI systems learn and make predictions or decisions without being explicitly programmed (Panda et al., 2021, p. 53). Some common machine learning techniques are supervised, unsupervised, and reinforcement.

Supervised techniques recognize the relationships between input and output, on the basis of which the model can predict values, whereas unsupervised learning data is analysed without predictions (Panda et al., 2021, p.248). Under reinforcement techniques an agent tries to gain proficiency in specific cost functions on conceivable actions that can be performed (Fahle et al., 2020).

Systematic reviews of machine learning algorithms and applications on social media data by Habernal et al. (2013) and van Zoonen and Toni (2016) suggested that supervised methods are mainly used. Algorithms tend to include:

- neural networks
- logistic regression
- decision trees
- support vector machines
- random forests
- k-nearest neighbour
- naïve Bayes classifiers.

Neural Networks

These include deep learning models as DL is considered to be subset of machine learning. It is an area of research that deals with deep artificial neural networks that replicate the human brain (Parekh & Jacobs, 2019).

Logistic Regression

This standard machine learning process depicts the relationship between one binary variable (dependent) and other nominal, ordinal, interval, and ratio level independent variables (Babu & Kanaga, 2022). Kim and Ko (2010) performed a logistic regression using platforms such as Twitter and Facebook to analyse the effect of social media marketing of luxury fashion brands. Oh et al. (2013) studied social driven information based on rumour theory. FakeNewsNet is a data repository constructed by Shu et al. (2020) which uses the logistic regression to facilitate fake news detection and mitigation, and provides promising research directions.

Decision Trees

This methodology illustrates the possible outcomes of decisions through multiple regression tree algorithms, providing paths from root to leaf nodes (Balaji et al., 2021). Decision trees can be used to classify social media posts, comments, or reviews into different sentiment categories by analysing the textual context on social media data.

Support Vector Machines (SVMs)

The objective of SVMs is to find an optimal hyperplane that isolates the information into various classes (Pradhan, 2012, p. 83). The hyperplane is selected in such a way that maximizes the margin, which is the distance between the hyperplane and the nearest data points (support vectors) of each class. This model can be used in financial time-series forecasting (Tay & Cao, 2001). For example, Huang et al. (2004) introduced this technique in an attempt to solve an issue credit rating prediction, and Singh et al. (2018) proposed an approach using SVM in social media data analytics to improve supply chain management in the food industry.

Random Forests

This technique is used for classification as well as regression. It works on accuracy and control over fit by averaging the data set by fitting several decision tree classifiers on various samples. The model has operational value on high-dimensional data (Cui et al., 2018). Zhang et al. (2008) proposed a systematic framework based on a random forest algorithm to develop a network intrusion system.

K-Nearest Neighbour (KNN)

This technique makes predictions based on similarities between new and available data, and puts the new data into the category which is similar to the available data (Babu & Kanaga, 2022, p. 9). It is a non-parametric technique used in statistical estimation and pattern recognition by calculating numeric target of 'k', the nearest neighbour (Arora et al., 2019, pp. 93–94). Balaji et al. (2021) quoted the example of a Google search, explaining the use of a k-means algorithm to cluster webpages based on specific type to make online searches more appropriate.

Naïve Bayes

This is commonly applied to data sets with labelled instances and discrete series. The algorithm learns from labelled data to build a probabilistic model that can arrange new novel instances into proper classes (Zhang & Sakhanenko, 2019). The data sets are conditionally independent of each other given the class label. The value of this assumption will decisively reduce the number of parameters to be estimated. It can be trained on labelled data where sentiments and opinions are expressed in social media posts (Benlahbib & Nfaoui, 2020). Isnain et al. (2021) applied this algorithm to predict the sentiment of unseen social media data, and Gupta and Kaushal (2015) proposed a novel integrated approach to improve the detection of spammers, as for instance, the naïve Bayes and Bayesian network algorithm outperforms others in detecting spam accounts and malicious URLs in social media networks (Yang et al., 2013).

Media Giant: The Case of Netflix

Netflix, founded by Reed Hastings and Marc Randolph on 29 August 1997, is a movie streaming giant that has changed the way people consume content. To start with, Netflix offered online DVDs, using a subscription model where consumers could rent DVDs monthly. This was a major shift from the usual DVD rental systems in place. In 2007, Netflix moved its strategy from renting DVDs to streaming services whereby it allowed its users to watch movies and TV shows on their computers. This became the defining moment in Netflix in providing digital content services.

In another major shift, in 2013 Netflix started producing its own original content, which differentiated it from its competitors and increased its subscriber base worldwide. By 2020, Netflix had over 200 million global subscribers and became one of the leading streaming platforms. Its success led to the entry of competitors such as Amazon Prime Video and Disney+ Hotstar, among others. Facing intense competition, the streaming giant has been leveraging technology to maintain and increase its user base. Netflix has experienced a significant increase due to the era of technological advancement, which has led to the expansion of models based on blended algorithms using machine learning (Tibrewal et al., 2021).

In addition to being the market leader in North America, Netflix is the undisputed leader in terms of audiences in Spanish households (Martínez-Sánchez et al. (2021). Netflix reported over 238.39 million paid subscribers worldwide as of Q2 2023, and produced over 891 original productions, generating $31.61 billion in revenue and $4.49 billion in net income (Shewale, 2023).

It is a continuous and developing endeavour of Netflix to apply artificial intelligence with the objective of enhancing user experience, reducing expenses, and preserving its standing as the industry leader in streaming services. In order to stay ahead of the competition and adjust to shifting viewer preferences, the corporation continually funds research and development (R&D) into artificial intelligence. There are many ways in which Netflix leverages technology, such as for content creation, curation, and optimization, adaptive streaming, and the most widely used recommendation algorithms. Recommendation lists, generated by dedicated engines, are one of the most productive aspects of machine learning in day-to-day contexts (Kotu & Deshpande, 2019, pp. 340–361).

The movie and television industries have made great strides owing to Netflix's machine learning techniques. Netflix and other personalized experiences are made possible by data science. In this age of technology, users have assistance when sifting through thousands of possibilities to choose the ideal products (Codecademy Team, 2023). Recommender systems are a good illustration of how much machine learning and data mining are used in the mainstream industry. Applications ranging from e-commerce to searching, online gaming, music and video, and online dating make use of substantial amounts of data to more effectively and individually meet the needs of users. It is noted that they are also highly effective in increasing core business metrics such as customer satisfaction and revenue (Amatriain & Basilico, 2015).

The first company to include a recommender system was Amazon (Amatriain & Basilico, 2015). Recommendation algorithms offer a kind of mass personalization on the internet that is gaining popularity (Ansari et al., 2000), with most e-commerce sites and applications leveraging some sort of recommendation system to enhance the customer experience. Besides Amazon, businesses that successfully employ such systems for e-commerce include YouTube, MovieLens, and Netflix (FadhelAljunid & Manjaiah, 2017). Netflix was one of the early adopters of big data analytics in 2006, when it came up with a challenge – popularly known as the Netflix Prize – that would award $1 million to anyone who could improve its existing recommendation system, 'Cinematch', by 10 per cent (Maddodi &Krishna Prasad, 2019).

Conceptual Model of Recommendation System

Over the years, Netflix has learned that using recommendations to customize the user experience as much as possible has substantial financial benefits. The literature shows that recommendation systems can be divided into two categories – content filtering and collaborative filtering. They also take into account components such as genre, demographics, customer heterogeneity, content heterogeneity, and so on. The company's recommender system is built on a deep neural network, combined with unsupervised and supervised machine learning algorithms that contribute to creating the complete Netflix experience (Tibrewal et al., 2021).

RecSysOps, a collection of best practices and insights from running extensive recommendation systems, was introduced by Netflix. It consists of four main parts: (1) problem identification; (2) prediction; (3) diagnosis; and (4) resolution techniques, including continuous integration, unit and integration testing, data volume checks, and model metrics checks. The next stage is to observe the system as a whole from the user's point of view. Many teams are frequently involved in large-scale recommendation systems: from the standpoint of an ML team, there are upstream teams (who supply the data) and downstream teams (who use the model). Understanding the interests of stakeholders is the third stage in achieving comprehensive inclusion. This is seen to be the best approach to increase the issue detection section's inclusion.

In order to predict issues, Netflix also uses predictive analytics. Making use of past data, it developed a model that was able to forecast the production model's behavioural statistics on the day that any video was released, which enables the early detection of any problems related to a show's premiere. This is supported by the fact that, on the premiere of *House of Cards*, Netflix spent $100 million on the first two seasons based solely on predictive research.

Netflix's use of issue diagnostics is another important component. This data is logged for a very small percentage of traffic in order to save money. This involves recording the item, the context, the characteristics, and anything else required to reproduce the problem. In this instance, a meticulously planned sampling strategy is used, providing enough coverage of all significant traffic slices. If all the information highlights are accurate, the next step is to go further into the machine learning model and its data to identify the root cause of a problem.

Growing such components for a large-scope proposal framework is a challenging iterative cycle that paves the way for further effort in the future. For example, several kinds of model may be needed to provide identification and expectation. A deeper understanding of ML models and strategy is needed for issue resolution and aim.

Netflix's Strategy

Netflix uses an algorithm for content suggestion or internet video streaming to a home device. Data is used to answer a variety of questions, such as:

- How can we improve the product experience even further?
- Which TV series and films do our members enjoy watching the most?
- Who can we collaborate with to expand access to our service in new markets?

These and other significant issues are handled by specialists who are assisting the organization with research-based numbers in all aspects of the business (Jackman & Reddy, 2020).

Netflix has an edge over strategizing the recommendation system to predict and answer various important business questions, with a major focus on collaborative filtering. It is seen that Netflix has successfully leveraged data analytics in solving major business questions with continuous R&D funding to offer users a seamless experience. The primary motivation behind its decision to implement a recommendation system was to improve user experience and engagement on the network. Various other major companies use these techniques to recommend items to their customers that are similar to those they have searched for or have bought recently. For example, recommendation systems are widely used by travel agencies such as Booking.com and Expedia so that visitors can discover their ultimate holiday destinations based on their search behaviour, historic bookings, or similar users (Postmus, 2018).

Netflix sought to tailor content recommendations for every single user by employing advanced algorithms and machine learning techniques, taking into account their viewing habits and tastes. From time to time, Netflix employs best practices for operating a large-scale recommendation system, such as in-session adapted recommendations, collaborative filtering, and deep learning techniques (Invisibly, 2021). Factors that considerably enhanced this user experience are outlined below.

Personalization

Netflix saw the value of offering its users customized recommendations. As a result of the large content repository, it became crucial to assist users in finding content that aligns with their preferences and interests. To increase the possibility of viewers discovering content they appreciate, Netflix therefore attempted to provide personalized recommendations by examining user data, including viewing history, ratings, and interactions (Molina Fernández, 2018).

User Engagement and Retention

Retaining subscribers and their engagement with the platform are essential to Netflix's business strategy. It therefore sought to enhance user retention and engagement metrics by providing tailored suggestions that would entice viewers to return for more content. This was done to regularly update users about latest related content on the platform.

Competitive Advantage

Gaining an edge in the fiercely competitive streaming market requires offering better customer experiences. Utilizing recommendation algorithms, Netflix aimed to set itself apart from its rivals by providing a more individualized and carefully selected content discovery experience.

Data-Driven Decision Making

Netflix is renowned for using data to inform both platform optimization and content creation. Its recommendation system adheres to this theory by using machine learning and data analytics to inform decision-making. Netflix may gradually increase the precision and potency of its suggestions by examining user behaviour on a regular basis and fine-tuning its algorithms (Amatriain & Basilico, 2015).

Scale and Efficiency

It would be difficult to manually curate content recommendations for every user, given the millions of subscribers the platform has worldwide. Netflix can effectively respond to the varied preferences of its user base by delivering personalized recommendations at scale through the automation of recommendation algorithms.

All things considered, Netflix's choice to employ a recommendation engine is indicative of its dedication to giving its customers a tailored, interesting, and data-driven streaming experience, which has ultimately helped it succeed in the fiercely competitive streaming industry. The abovementioned factors led to the following outcomes for Netflix:

- **Enhanced user engagement**: The platform has successfully improved user engagement by offering customized recommendations based on personal interests. When users find information that interests them, they are more likely to explore it further, which results in longer viewing sessions (binge-watching) and increased levels of pleasure generally.
- **Increased retention**: By keeping subscribers happy with the content options, Netflix's personalized content recommendations have helped retain them for longer. Users are more inclined to stay with the platform and are less likely to cancel their subscriptions when they regularly find material they appreciate.
- **Improved user experience**: Netflix's general user experience has been greatly improved by its recommendation system. It is now easier and more convenient for users to find new movies and episodes of shows because they do not need to spend a lot of time searching for content. Instead, personalized recommendations are displayed on their home screen (Invisibly, 2021).
- **Finding niche content**: Netflix is now able to present obscure and niche content to viewers who may find it interesting thanks to its recommendation engine. As a result, users' content consumption has become more diverse, and smaller productions and genres are now more visible on the site.
- **Data-driven content strategy**: Netflix bases its content generation and acquisition strategy on the information gathered from the recommendation system. It can find trends and insights that inform decisions about what kinds of content to invest in or license by examining user behaviour and viewing preferences.

- **Competitive advantage**: Netflix enjoys a competitive advantage in the streaming market thanks to the efficacy of its recommendation system. Other streaming providers have since implemented their own recommendation algorithms, but Netflix's early adoption and technological advancements have allowed it to remain at the top of the industry.

Overall, it can be seen from Netflix's deployment of the recommendation system that it has been crucial in increasing user engagement and retention rates, and giving users a more fulfilling and customized streaming experience.

Case Study Questions

- Identify the best practices implemented by Netflix to enhance its user overall experience.
- What competitive advantage does Netflix have in terms of resources and enhancing the user experience?

Conclusion

The immense and multifaceted network of requests for online entertainment information requires efficient routes to navigate through it, and human brainpower emerges as the priceless map maker. Deep learning AI tools enable us to interpret customer experiences, track patterns, and even predict future designs. Convolutional neural networks untangle the complexities of visual data, while recurrent neural networks tap into the emotional undercurrents of online expressions. Robust knowledge enables advertisers to contact the right audience with the right message, while at the same time protecting clients from the entanglements of falsehood. Just as Netflix leverages AI to personalize its content and expand its reach, organizations across the spectrum can harness this power to navigate the ever-evolving social media landscape with confidence and precision. The future of social media lies not just in the data we generate but in the intelligence we apply to understand and utilize it.

References

Abid, F., Li, C., & Alam, M. (2020). Multi-source social media data sentiment analysis using bidirectional recurrent convolutional neural networks. *Computer Communications*, *157*, 102–115.

Ain, Q. T., Ali, M., Riaz, A., Noureen, A., Kamran, M., Hayat, B., & Rehman, A. (2017). Sentiment analysis using deep learning techniques: A review. *International Journal of Advanced Computer Science and Applications*, *8*(6), 424–433.

Amatriain, X., & Basilico, J. (2015). Recommender systems in industry: A Netflix case study. In F. Ricci, L. Rokach & B. Shapiro (Eds.), *Recommender systems handbook* (pp. 385–419). Boston, MA: Springer.

Ansari, A., Essegaier, S., & Kohli, R. (2000). Internet recommendation systems. *Journal of Marketing Research*, *37*(3), 363–375.

Arora, A., Bansal, S., Kandpal, C., Aswani, R., & Dwivedi, Y. (2019). Measuring social media influencer index-insights from Facebook, Twitter and Instagram. *Journal of Retailing and Consumer Services*, *49*, 86–101.

Babu, N. V., & Kanaga, E. G. M. (2022). Sentiment analysis in social media data for depression detection using artificial intelligence: A review. *SN Computer Science*, *3*, Art. 74.

Baccouche, M., Mamalet, F., Wolf, C., Garcia, C., & Baskurt, A. (2011). Sequential deep learning for human action recognition. In Salah, A. A. & Lepri, B. (Eds.), *Human behavior understanding: Second international workshop, HBU 2011, Amsterdam, The Netherlands, November 16, 2011. Proceedings* (pp. 29–39). Berlin: Springer.

Balaji, T. K., Annavarapu, C. S. R., & Bablani, A. (2021). Machine learning algorithms for social media analysis: A survey. *Computer Science Review*, *40*(C), 100395.

Bangyal, W. H., Qasim, R., Rehman, N. U., Ahmad, Z., Dar, H., Rukhsar, L., … & Ahmad, J. (2021). Detection of fake news text classification on COVID-19 using deep learning approaches. *Computational and Mathematical Methods in Medicine*, *2021*, 5514220.

Benlahbib, A., & Nfaoui, E. H. (2020). A hybrid approach for generating reputation based on opinions fusion and sentiment analysis. *Journal of Organizational Computing and Electronic Commerce*, *30*(1), 9–27.

Breslin, J. G., Passant, A., & Decker, S. (2009). *The social semantic web*. Berlin: Springer.

Campbell, D. T. (1965). Variation and selective retention in sociocultural evolution. In H. R. Barringer, G. I. Blankstein, & R. W. Mack (Eds.), *Social change in developing areas* (pp. 19–49). Cambridge, MA: Schenkman.

Chan, H. K., Wang, X., Lacka, E., & Zhang, M. (2016). A mixed-method approach to extracting the value of social media data. *Production and Operations Management*, *25*(3), 568–583.

Chen, X.-W., & Lin, X. (2014). Big data deep learning: Challenges and perspectives. *IEEE Access*, *2*, 514–525.

Cho, K., van Merriënboer, B., Gulcehre, C., Bahdanau, D., Bougares, F., Schwenk, H., & Bengio, Y. (2014). Learning phrase representations using RNN encoder–decoder for statistical machine translation. In *Proceedings of the 2014 Conference on Empirical Methods in Natural Language Processing (EMNLP)* (pp. 1724–1734). Doha, Qatar: Association for Computational Linguistics.

Codecademy Team (2023). *Netflix recommendation engine.* Available at: https://www.codecademy.com/article/how-netflix-recommendation-works-data-science

Cresswell, K., Tahir, A., Sheikh, Z., Hussain, Z., Domínguez Hernández, A., Harrison, E., ... & Hussain, A. (2021). Understanding public perceptions of COVID-19 contact tracing apps: Artificial intelligence-enabled social media analysis. *Journal of Medical Internet Research, 23*(5), e26618.

Cui, R., Gallino, S., Moreno, A., & Zhang, D. J. (2018). The operational value of social media information. *Production and Operations Management, 27*(10), 1749–1769.

Eberendu, A. C. (2016). Unstructured data: An overview of the data of big data. *International Journal of Computer Trends and Technology, 38*(1), 46–50.

FadhelAljunid, M., & Manjaiah, D. H. (2017). A survey on recommendation systems for social media using big data analytics. *International Journal of Latest Trends in Engineering and Technology*, Special issue, 48–58.

Fahle, S., Prinz, C., & Kuhlenkötter, B. (2020). Systematic review on machine learning (ML) methods for manufacturing processes: Identifying artificial intelligence (AI) methods for field application. *Procedia CIRP, 93*, 413–418.

Fan, W., & Gordon, M. D. (2014). The power of social media analytics. *Communications of the ACM, 57*(6), 74–81.

Finn, S., & Mustafaraj, E. (2013). Learning to discover political activism in the Twitterverse. *KI – Künstliche Intelligenz, 27*, 17–24.

Greff, K., Srivastava, R. K., Koutník, J., Steunebrink, B. R., & Schmidhuber, J. (2016). LSTM: A search space odyssey. *IEEE Transactions on Neural Networks and Learning Systems, 28*(10), 2222–2232.

Gupta, A., & Kaushal, R. (2015, March). Improving spam detection in online social networks. *In 2015 International conference on cognitive computing and information processing (CCIP)* (pp. 1–6). IEEE.

Habernal, I., Ptáček, T., & Steinberger, J. (2013, June). Sentiment analysis in Czech social media using supervised machine learning. In A. Balahur, E. van der Goot, & A. Montoyo (Eds.), *Proceedings of the 4th workshop on computational approaches to subjectivity, sentiment and social media analysis* (pp. 65–74). Atlanta, GA: Association for Computational Linguistics.

Hochreiter, S., & Schmidhuber, J. (1997). Long short-term memory. *Neural Computation, 9*(8), 1735–1780.

Holsapple, C. W., Hsiao, S. H., & Pakath, R. (2018). Business social media analytics: Characterization and conceptual framework. *Decision Support Systems, 110*, 32–45.

Huang, Z., Chen, H., Hsu, C. J., Chen, W. H., & Wu, S. (2004). Credit rating analysis with support vector machines and neural networks: A market comparative study. *Decision Support Systems, 37*(4), 543–558.

Invisibly. (2021, November 10). *Behind the scenes of the Netflix recommendation algorithm*. Retrieved from https://www.invisibly.com/learn-blog/netflix-recommendation-algorithm/

Isnain, A. R., Marga, N. S., & Alita, D. (2021). Sentiment analysis of government policy on corona case using naive Bayes algorithm. *Indonesian Journal of Computing and Cybernetics Systems, 15*(1), 55–64.

Jackman, M., & Reddy, M. (2020, September 18). *Analytics at Netflix: Who we are and what we do*. Netflix Technology blog. Available at: https://netflixtechblog.com/analytics-at-netflix-who-we-are-and-what-we-do-7d9c08fe6965

Johnston, P., & Elyan, E. (2019). A review of digital video tampering: From simple editing to full synthesis. *Digital Investigation, 29*, 67–81.

Kaplan, A. M., & Haenlein, M. (2010). Users of the world, unite! The challenges and opportunities of social media. *Business Horizons, 53*(1), 59–68.

Kim, A. J., & Ko, E. (2010). Impacts of luxury fashion brand's social media marketing on customer relationship and purchase intention. *Journal of Global Fashion Marketing, 1*(3), 164–171.

Kotu, V., & Deshpande, B. (2019). *Data science: Concepts and practice*. Cambridge, MA: Morgan Kaufmann.

Leskovec, J. (2011, March). Social media analytics: Tracking, modeling and predicting the flow of information through networks. In *Proceedings of the 20th international conference companion on World Wide Web* (pp. 277–278). New York: Association for Computing Machinery.

Li, G., & Yu, Y. (2016). Deep contrast learning for salient object detection. In *Proceedings of the IEEE conference on computer vision and pattern recognition* (pp. 478–487).

Maddodi, S. & Krishna Prasad, K. (2019). Netflix bigdata analytics: The emergence of data driven recommendation. *International Journal of Case Studies in Business, IT, and Education, 3*(2), 41–51.

Martínez-Sánchez, M. E., Nicolas-Sans, R., & Díaz, J. B. (2021). Analysis of the social media strategy of audio-visual OTTs in Spain: The case study of Netflix, HBO and Amazon Prime during the implementation of Disney+. *Technological Forecasting and Social Change, 173*, 121178.

Merton, R. K. (1949). *Social theory and social structure*. New York: Simon & Schuster.

Miao, L., Last, M., & Litvak, M. (2022). Tracking social media during the COVID-19 pandemic: The case study of lockdown in New York State. *Expert Systems with Applications, 187*, 115797.

Mintz, M., Bills, S., Snow, R., & Jurafsky, D. (2009, August). Distant supervision for relation extraction without labeled data. In *Proceedings of the joint conference of the 47th annual meeting of the ACL and the 4th international joint conference on natural language processing of the AFNLP* (pp. 1003–1011).

Molina Fernández, L. E. (2018). *Recommendation system for Netflix*. Master's thesis, Vrije University, Amsterdam.

Nemes, L., & Kiss, A. (2021). Social media sentiment analysis based on COVID-19. *Journal of Information and Telecommunication*, *5*(1), 1–15.

Niklaus, S., Mai, L., & Liu, F. (2017). Video frame interpolation via adaptive separable convolution. In *Proceedings of the IEEE international conference on computer vision* (pp. 261–270).

O'Reilly, T. (2007). What is Web 2.0: Design patterns and business models for the next generation of software. *Communications & Strategies*, *65*(1), 17.

Oh, O., Agrawal, M., & Rao, H. R. (2013). Community intelligence and social media services: A rumor theoretic analysis of tweets during social crises. *MIS Quarterly*, *37*(2), 407–426.

Panda, S. K., Mishra, V., Balamurali, R., & Elngar, A. A. (Eds.). (2021). *Artificial intelligence and machine learning in business management: Concepts, challenges, and case studies*. Abingdon, UK: CRC Press.

Parekh, V. S., & Jacobs, M. A. (2019). Deep learning and radiomics in precision medicine. *Expert Review of Precision Medicine and Drug Development*, *4*(2), 59–72.

Postmus, S. (2018). *Recommender system techniques applied to Netflix movie data. Research Paper Business Analytics*, pp. 1–31.

Pradhan, A. (2012). Support vector machine: A survey. *International Journal of Emerging Technology and Advanced Engineering*, *2*(8), 82–85.

Rahman, M. S., & Reza, H. (2022). A systematic review towards big data analytics in social media. *Big Data Mining and Analytics*, *5*(3), 228–244.

Rishi, B., & Bandyopadhyay, S. (Eds.). (2018). *Contemporary issues in social media marketing*. London: Routledge.

Sarker, I. H. (2021). Deep learning: A comprehensive overview on techniques, taxonomy, applications and research directions. *SN Computer Science*, *2*(6), 420.

Singh, A., Shukla, N., & Mishra, N. (2018). Social media data analytics to improve supply chain management in food industries. *Transportation Research Part E: Logistics and Transportation Review*, *114*, 398–415.

Shewale, R., 2023. *Netflix statistics 2023 (users, revenue & trends)*. Available at: https://www.demandsage.com/netflix-subscribers/

Shrestha, A., & Mahmood, A. (2019). Review of deep learning algorithms and architectures. *IEEE Access*, *7*, 53040–53065.

Shu, K., Mahudeswaran, D., Wang, S., Lee, D., & Liu, H. (2020). FakeNewsNet: A data repository with news content, social context, and spatiotemporal information for studying fake news on social media. *Big Data*, *8*(3), 171–188.

Smith, P. D. (2018). *Hands-on artificial intelligence for beginners: An introduction to AI concepts, algorithms, and their implementation*. Birmingham, UK: Packt Publishing.

Tahir, R., Ahmed, F., Saeed, H., Ali, S., Zaffar, F., & Wilson, C. (2019, August). Bringing the kid back into YouTube kids: Detecting inappropriate content on video streaming platforms. In *Proceedings of the 2019 IEEE/ACM international conference on advances in social networks analysis and mining* (pp. 464–469).

Tay, F. E., & Cao, L. (2001). Application of support vector machines in financial time series forecasting. *Omega, 29*(4), 309–317.

Tibrewal, A., Sehgal, R., & Singh, S. (2021). Antecedents of recommendation framework enabled through artificial intelligence on Netflix platform. *Journal of General Management Research, 8*(1), 34–48.

van Zoonen, W., & Toni, G. L. A. van der Meer (2016). Social media research: The application of supervised machine learning in organizational communication research. *Computers in Human Behavior, 63*, 132–141.

Wang, J. H., Liu, T. W., Luo, X., & Wang, L. (2018, October). An LSTM approach to short text sentiment classification with word embeddings. In *Proceedings of the 30th conference on computational linguistics and speech processing (ROCLING 2018)* (pp. 214–223).

Wang, X., & Zhang, N. (2024). Uncertain spreading model of internet rumors on social media platforms. *Journal of Industrial and Management Optimization, 20*(1), 1–14.

Wazirali, R., Yaghoubi, E., Abujazar, M. S. S., Ahmad, R., & Vakili, A. H. (2023). State-of-the-art review on energy and load forecasting in microgrids using artificial neural networks, machine learning, and deep learning techniques. *Electric Power Systems Research, 225*, 109792.

Wu, G. J., Xu, Z. J., Tajdini, S., Zhang, J., & Song, L. (2019). Unlocking value through an extended social media analytics framework: Insights for new product adoption. *Qualitative Market Research: An International Journal, 22*(2), 161–179.

Yang, C., Harkreader, R., & Gu, G. (2013). Empirical evaluation and new design for fighting evolving Twitter spammers. *IEEE Transactions on Information Forensics and Security, 8*(8), 1280–1293.

Zeng, D., Chen, H., Lusch, R., & Li, S. H. (2010). Social media analytics and intelligence. *IEEE Intelligent Systems, 25*(6), 13–16.

Zhang, Y. C., & Sakhanenko, L. (2019). The naive Bayes classifier for functional data. *Statistics & Probability Letters, 152*, 137–146.

Zhang, J., Zulkernine, M., & Haque, A. (2008). Random-forests-based network intrusion detection systems. *IEEE Transactions on Systems, Man, and Cybernetics, Part C: Applications and Reviews, 38*(5), 649–659.

Zogan, H., Razzak, I., Jameel, S., & Xu, G. (2021). Depressionnet: A novel summarization boosted deep framework for depression detection on social media. *arXiv preprint*, arXiv:2105.10878.

16 Leveraging the Role of Social Media Platform Data in Enhancing the Effect of Cause-Related Marketing

Krishna Teja Perannagari
Indian Institute of Management Tiruchirappalli, Trichy, India

Shaphali Gupta
MICA, Ahmedabad, Gujarat, India

Introduction

In today's rapidly changing marketplace, cause-related marketing (CRM) has emerged as a transformative force for positive societal impact and enhancing brand reputation (Thomas et al., 2020). CRM blends philanthropy with marketing by focusing on marketing strategies that promote a business offering by associating it with a social cause (Bhatti et al., 2022; Varadarajan & Menon, 1988). CRM campaigns primarily involve two approaches: (1) an independent approach involving the company's direct engagement in addressing social issues through programmes such as corporate social responsibility (CSR); and (2) a collaborative approach involving a social alliance between companies and a non-profit organizations (NPOs) to implement the promotional campaign (Liu & Ko, 2011). While multinational corporations (MNCs) often favour the first approach (due to their size,

DOI: 10.4324/9781003412656-16

resources, and global reach), the second approach of using partnerships can benefit companies of various sizes, including small and medium enterprises (SMEs), start-ups, local businesses, and social enterprises.

While pursuing an independent cause-related marketing (I-CRM) campaign allows companies to exert direct control and customization aligned with their business values, objectives, and brand identity, it poses challenges in terms of establishing and maintaining authenticity, requiring substantial resource investments, and necessitating the development of expertise to effectively execute the campaign (Brønn & Vrioni, 2001). Similarly, social alliance-based cause-related marketing (SA-CRM) allows companies to leverage the strengths, resources, and expertise of NPOs. However, it presents challenges in finding the right partner, maintaining coordination, and ensuring long-term commitment (Till & Nowak, 2000). In recent years, SA-CRM campaigns have gained popularity as businesses can maintain credibility while incorporating CRM campaigns into mandatory financial disclosure and leverage the competencies of NPOs in CRM campaigns.

Of the various challenges impacting the success of CRM campaigns, the existing literature emphasizes the cause–brand fit as the most critical factor (Rohit & Panda, 2018). Cause–brand fit reflects how consumers perceive the fit between the social cause and the business offering as rational, compatible and complimentary (Bigné et al., 2012). Extant CRM literature has measured cause–brand fit using various methods, including surveys, interviews, experiments, and netnography (Thomas et al., 2020). In the context of I-CRM, cause–brand fit primarily focuses on the functional fit between the characteristics of the business offerings and the targeted social cause (Guzmán & Davis, 2017). On the other hand, cause-brand fit in SA-CRM emphasizes image fit, which reflects the congruence between the brand image perceptions of the business and the NPO (Kim et al., 2012). Compared to functional fit, measuring image fit is more challenging due to its reliance on subjective consumer perceptions, which are susceptible to variations and influenced by individual beliefs, values, and experiences.

This study investigates a novel text-mining technique to assess the brand image fit between a business entity and an NPO. To determine brand image fit, the authors opted for unstructured textual data as it enables the measurement of consumer perceptions using valuable real-time unfiltered data obtained from a diverse and extensive pool of individuals (Pournarakis et al., 2017). Utilizing consumer text enables a more comprehensive and immediate understanding of consumers' opinions and sentiments. It also enables researchers to identify emerging trends, capture spontaneous reactions, and gather rich contextual information that may not be easily obtained through traditional surveys or interviews (Humphreys & Wang, 2017). While the current research utilizes social media text data to demonstrate the technique, users can employ free-form text emerging from various sources (such as comments, reviews, social media posts, and testimonials) to apply this text analysis method.

Conceptual Background

Organizations around the globe are growing more attentive to the mounting expectations from stakeholders, who are pushing them to operate their businesses with a sense of responsibility and to tackle the social and environmental challenges stemming from their activities (Cillo et al., 2019). Since an organization's viability is significantly linked to its reputation in the eyes of stakeholders, corporate governance regulations have introduced numerous new strategies to foster social responsibility and ethical business conduct among firms (Daromes & Gunawan, 2020). These strategies include: publishing comprehensive sustainability reports; reducing environmental footprints by adopting sustainable practices; committing to ethical supply chains; implementing diversity and inclusion initiatives; following regulatory compliance and staying ahead of emerging legislation; adopting circular economy practices; and seeking certification to showcase commitment (Ewing, 2020).

Further, to effectively demonstrate their commitment to responsible and sustainable practices, companies recognize the need to implement these initiatives and communicate them to the stakeholders (Verk et al., 2021). By promoting their social and sustainability endeavours, businesses can gain credibility among stakeholders and engage employees, investors, and the broader community (Fazli-Salehi et al., 2019). The promotions are done through various means, including sustainability reports and white papers, dedicated sections on corporate websites, social media posts, advertising campaigns, press releases, and philanthropic events (Lafferty et al., 2016). It is also noteworthy that, among the numerous avenues available for communicating corporate responsibility, extant scholarly research highlights the effectiveness of advertising campaigns centred on CRM (Andersen & Johansen, 2016; Bergkvist & Zhou, 2019).

CRM is an effective strategy for promoting corporate responsibility as it connects with individuals emotionally by highlighting a cause to which many customers feel firmly attached (Yucel-Aybat & Hsieh, 2021). Further, companies that engage in CRM often see improved staff morale as employees are more likely to feel proud of their company's values and commitment to a cause, which can enhance productivity and engagement (Woodroof et al., 2019). Despite CRM being empirically proven to improve corporate image, foster long-term favourable consumer attitudes, and increase profitability, it is essential to note that the tactical use of CRM can potentially jeopardize a company's reputation and its alignment with broader community interests if not managed appropriately (Vrontis et al., 2020). Firms must therefore actively pursue CRM campaigns to ensure positive impacts on stakeholders, with proper planning, implementation, and evaluation (Thomas et al., 2020).

The increasing popularity and the expanding utilization of CRM campaigns have led to a rapid proliferation of CRM research since 2000. Early CRM literature focused on investigating the advantages and potential drawbacks of CRM, considering various perspectives, including the viewpoints of businesses, non-profit organizations, and consumers (Brønn & Vrioni, 2001). Furthermore, empirical studies in the initial years primarily focused on examining CRM campaigns' influence on consumer behaviour, including the impact on branding outcomes and profitability (Barone et al., 2000; Chang & Cheng, 2015). Recently, research has shifted toward the strategic marketing and campaign management aspects associated with CRM (Vrontis et al., 2020; Yucel-Aybat & Hsieh, 2021). This focuses on evaluating the impact of CRM initiatives using a resource-based view (Christofi et al., 2020; Singh & Dhir, 2019) and identifying the most effective promotional strategies for CRM campaigns (Kipp & Hawkins, 2019; Xu & Zhou, 2020).

Realizing the potential differences between CRM and conventional marketing campaigns, researchers developed new models and frameworks to study CRM campaigns. Prominent frameworks featured in the CRM literature include the evolutionary process model (Lafferty et al., 2016), the dual-path model of CRM persuasion (Bergkvist & Zhou, 2019), and the iterative model of CRM partnership (Svensson & Wood, 2011). Likewise, prevailing academic works have predominantly employed the attribution model to explore CRM phenomena in conjunction with theories such as the self-construal theory, persuasion theory, associative learning theory, and the theory of reasoned action (Thomas et al., 2020).

In the context of SA-CRM, existing studies have focused on investigating partnership management approaches (Bhatti et al., 2022; Liu & Ko, 2011; Rishi & Bandyopadhyay, 2018), social media campaign management (Deng et al., 2023; Kim et al., 2017), and co-branding strategies (Huertas-García et al., 2017; Natarajan et al., 2016). Similarly, in recent years, social media CRM campaigns have become a primary communication tool for CRM campaigns, providing opportunities for two-way dialogue between consumers and firms while reducing campaign costs (Kim & Kim, 2023). Since social media-driven CRM campaigns leverage viral communication strategies involving priming and framing techniques, companies should exercise caution during their implementation to mitigate unforeseen outcomes (Tanford et al., 2020).

Recent literature on SA-CRM has also stressed the importance of aligning the values of partners engaged in SA-CRM initiatives and the need to develop campaigns that are compatible with the brand image perceptions of all the partners involved (Rego & Hamilton, 2021; Rohit & Panda, 2018;

Yucel-Aybat & Hsieh, 2021). While a thorough examination of consumer preferences is crucial for successful SA-CRM collaborations, research has often favoured primary data methods, which are costly and time-consuming (Thomas et al., 2020). Unfortunately, this dependence on resource-intensive primary data collection restricts the broader adoption and replicability of the research. Using secondary data sources (such as social media text, online reviews, and market research reports) remains an underexplored area in marketing research, necessitating further investigation to bridge this knowledge gap (Bhatti et al., 2022; Xu & Zhou, 2020). The current study proposes an approach that uses the concept of mutual followers, semantic similarity, and Euclidean distance to analyse social media posts and identify suitable partners for SA-CRM initiatives. Next, we detail the method employed.

Method

The proposed text-mining approach is extensive and includes various processes, such as data extraction, filtering, dictionary development, sentiment analysis, and similarity calculation. The authors divided the methodology into four phases to comprehensively demonstrate the proposed approach. In the first phase, they employed the Twitter (X) application programming interface (API) to collect social media data from that platform. The study uses the concept of mutual followers to identify business–NPO pairs that could benefit from a social alliance. It uses generic placeholders for organization names while providing detailed information about the specific domain or field in which these organizations operate to provide context for the research to protect users' privacy and confidentiality. Table 16.1 provides an overview of the NPOs examined in the present study.

In the second phase, the authors developed a construct-specific dictionary using the methodology proposed by Tsao et al. (2019). This dictionary uses social media posts and Aaker's (1997) brand personality framework to analyse consumers' perceptions of the businesses and NPOs identified in the first phase. Aaker's framework was chosen to assess brand–image fit as it provides a structured and standardized approach to capturing brand image perceptions comprising functional, emotional, and psychological dimensions, and enables meaningful brand comparisons. Using the proposed approach, researchers can leverage the power of alternative frameworks – such as the Big Five personality traits model and the DISC (dominance, influence, steadiness, conscientiousness) personality traits model – or tailor their approach by using personality constructs that align with their specific research needs. Table 16.2 summarizes the composition of the brand personality dictionary.

Table 16.1 Overview of phase 1 of the study

NPO Alias	Core Focus Area	Follower Count	Screened NPO–Business Pairs (100+ followers)
Progress Makers	Various socio-developmental issues	1752	17
Empower Future	Child education and women empowerment	3082	31
Comforting Hands	Palliative care	2383	6
Hope Rise	Child education and slum transformation	1484	3
Enable All	Assisting people with disabilities	1414	5
Skill Spectrum	Skill development	1487	15

Table 16.2 Brand personality dictionary snapshot

Dimension	Seed Words	Lemmatized Seed Words	Words Extracted from *Roget's Thesaurus*	Unique Words in the Final Dictionary
Competency	156	148	21945	5503
Excitement	133	128	22982	6785
Ruggedness	152	151	24466	5288
Sincerity	164	158	23299	4823
Sophistication	161	158	20028	4955

The authors collected publicly available tweets from the identified businesses and NPOs in the third phase, and used the construct-specific dictionary developed in the second phase to compute brand personality dimension scores (Tsao et al., 2019). Extracting scores from Twitter posts required extensive data pre-processing, and the final brand personality dimension scores were derived through the transformation of sentiment analysis results using the formula in Equation 16.1:

$$\text{Brand Personality Dimension score} = \Sigma\left(Word\_Count \times Avg\_Sent\right) \div \left(TS\_Count \times DW\_Count\right) \quad (16.1)$$

In the final phase, the authors assessed the similarity between business and NPO pairs using the Euclidean distance formula (Equation 16.2):

$$\text{NPO} - \text{firm similarity} = \sqrt{\Sigma\left(Dimension\ Score_{NPO} - Dimension\ Score_{firm}\right)^2} \quad (16.2)$$

Further, the authors used radar charts to visualize the most compatible business–NPO pairs for social alliances (Figure 16.1). Due to confidentiality concerns and the absence of explicit permission from the brands involved, we have anonymized the brand names while providing detailed descriptions of these entities. Table 16.3 details the compatible NPO–brand pairs identified in the study.

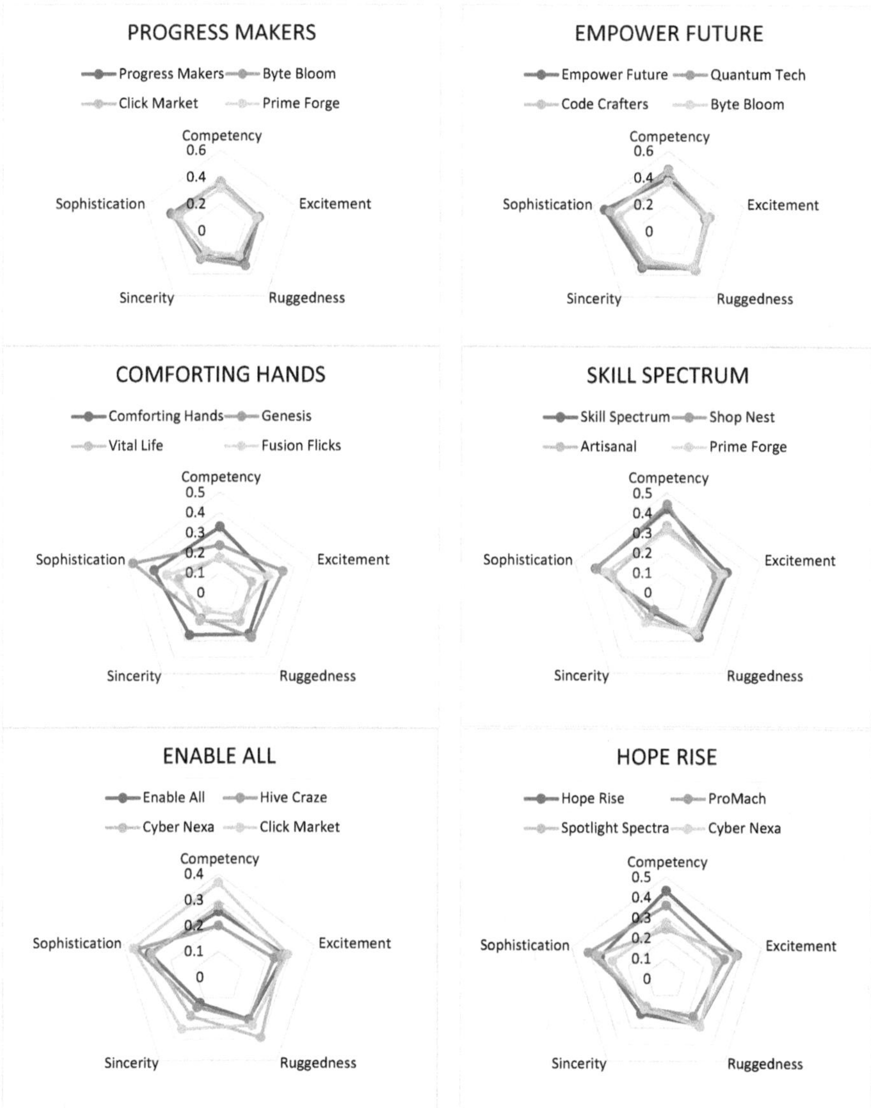

Figure 16.1 Radar charts illustrating brand personality similarities between businesses and NPOs

Table 16.3 Business–NPO pairs with compatible brand personalities

NPO Alias	Business Alias	Business Industry/Sector	Euclidean Distance
Progress Makers	Byte Bloom	IT-Service Company	0.05978125
	Click Market	E-commerce	0.06855297
	Prime Forge	Multinational Conglomerate	0.09938288
Empower Future	Quantum Tech	IT-Service Company	0.090889
	Code Crafters	IT-Service Company	0.095632
	Byte Bloom	IT-Service Company	0.148411
Comforting Hands	Genesis	Automobile Manufacturer	0.194911
	Vital Life	Healthcare Provider	0.250983
	Fusion Flicks	Entertainment Service Provider	0.254776
Skill Spectrum	Shop Nest	E-Commerce	0.069982
	Artisanal	Consumer Electronics Manufacturer	0.130366
	Prime Forge	Multinational Conglomerate	0.142969
Enable All	Hive Craze	Social Media Service Provider	0.089956
	Cyber Nexa	IT-Service Company	0.106886
	Click Market	E-commerce	0.183327
Hope Rise	ProMach	Aerospace Company	0.131967
	Spotlight Spectra	Lifestyle Magazine	0.193403
	Cyber Nexa	IT-Service Company	0.202713

Findings and Discussion

The proposed text-mining approach provides researchers with a powerful tool for studying the relationship between brand personalities, cause marketing, and social alliances. The approach exhibits flexibility in its application across various social media platforms, allowing for the use of different constructs and frameworks that measure brand perceptions. Further, by combining automated and manual text-mining processes, the study benefits from the efficiency, scalability, and objectivity of computerized techniques while leveraging human expertise to provide nuanced, context-aware, and accurate analysis of the text data.

The findings suggest that variations in brand personality dimensions exist between firms and NPOs, reiterating the need to account for these differences when formulating CRM initiatives. This suggestion is also valid in the context of the specific industry/sector and the advocated social/environmental cause. Any misalignment can make or break the campaign, as exemplified by the failure of CRM campaigns involving food manufacturing companies/brands such as Nestlé, Kellogg's, and Skittles. For example, Kellogg's launched a campaign that encouraged individuals to share pictures of their morning meals on social media as a part of its 'No Kid Hungry' initiative.

In return for each post, the company committed to providing breakfast to an underprivileged child through an NPO, Action for Healthy Kids (Kellogg Company, 2012). The campaign faced criticism as people perceived the promotion of sugary and less healthy breakfast options and raised concerns about Kellogg's' alignment with the issue of child nutrition and welfare. Our analysis revealed similar findings wherein the business–NPO pairs involving food manufacturing companies had few common followers. In one case with shared followers, the company exhibited a distinct brand personality compared to the NPO, and so was an incompatible pair for CRM.

The analysis also revealed a strong alignment between information technology (IT) businesses and NPOs dedicated to children's education and the empowerment of women, mirroring the success stories of prominent IT companies such as Google, Intel, IBM, and Oracle. Google launched its visionary 'Made with Code' campaign in collaboration with NPOs such as Girls Who Code and Code.org to motivate girls to embrace coding (Golod, 2016). The success of the 'Made with Code' campaign is evident on multiple fronts, including completing more than 1 million coding projects in just 365 days and the development of numerous coding camps and groups across the world (Google, 2014). Similarly, Oracle partnered with Room to Read, a global education non-profit, to improve children's literacy in India's underserved regions of Rajasthan and Chhattisgarh. Through this CRM alliance, Oracle offered financial grants, provided Room to Read with free access to Oracle's cutting-edge cloud services, and even invested in training NPO employees to ensure they could leverage the technology effectively (Room to Read, 2020). Oracle has achieved significant brand awareness and recognition in even the most geographically isolated and underserved communities through this initiative.

The e-commerce industry has also emerged as a suitable platform for CRM partnerships that support various social causes, including skill development, promoting social progress, and aiding individuals with disabilities. In tune with the findings, e-commerce companies such as Amazon, Patagonia, and Seventh Generation have formed successful CRM partnerships with multiple NPOs supporting various social causes. One of the best-known business–NPO CRM campaigns is Amazon's 'Delivering Smiles', whose main goal is to donate 4G-enabled tablet computers to 18 NGOs partnering with government and aided schools in India (Amazon, 2020).

Amazon also runs a device donation programme in partnership with local NPOs and schools to facilitate the donation of electronic devices and gift cards to children near Amazon fulfilment centres throughout the US (Romano et al., 2020). In another CSR initiative, Amazon donated $1 million to the Red Cross and deployed its 'Disaster Relief Hub' to help coordinate relief efforts after Hurricane Harvey (Weise, 2017). Amazon has leveraged social media and its e-commerce platform to mobilize funding for CRM initiatives, increasing donations, brand awareness, and trust among customers, employees, and the general public.

Another e-commerce company that is known for its CRM initiatives involving environmental sustainability, social justice, ethical business practices, and economic vitality is Seventh Generation, whose notable CRM campaigns include 'Come Clean' (Tugend, 2016) and the 'Greatest Generation' (Williams, 2020). The 'Come Clean' campaign aims to educate consumers about the importance of 'clean' and sustainable cleaning products in collaboration with NPOs such as Earth Echo, Toxic-Free Future, and Informed Green Solutions. The main goal of the 'Greatest Generation' campaign was to raise awareness of climate change, and involved the collaboration of NPOs such as Sierra Club, the Sustainability Academy, and Vermont Public Interest Research Group.

Social media played a significant role in the success of both campaigns, raising awareness among citizens and building a community of socially and environmentally responsible users. It also helped Seventh Generation promote social media channels and drive traffic to its website, where consumers could learn more about the campaigns, purchase its products, and donate to its partner NGOs.

Other recent successful campaigns and case studies also demonstrate that a data-driven social media strategy is crucial for improving the effectiveness of cause-related marketing initiatives (Bhatti et al., 2022; Schamp et al., 2023). Leveraging social media data allows for a nuanced understanding of demographic segments and individual interests, fostering a sense of relatability and authenticity in the campaign elements (Chang & Cheng, 2015). For example, Patagonia, the renowned outdoor apparel corporation, has garnered acclaim for its CRM campaigns, reflecting its steadfast dedication to environmental activism (Shourkaei et al., 2023; Zint & Frederick, 2001). In alignment with its commitment to environmental activism, and in tune with its CRM and CSR initiatives, Patagonia has introduced its 'Action Works' and 'Worn Wear' campaigns.

'Worn Wear' allows customers trade in their old Patagonia clothes for store credit, sell them to give them a second life, or buy lightly-used Patagonia gear at lower prices. The company even mends damaged gear to make it last longer and reduce waste. The initiative is considered a game-changer in outdoor gear (Patagonia, 2024b).

'Patagonia Action Works', meanwhile, goes beyond the conventional 'click here to donate' campaign, serving as a digital hub linking passionate individuals with local grassroots organizations dedicated to preserving the planet they cherish. This initiative aims to empower people by equipping them with the tools and resources to translate environmental concerns into real-world impact (Patagonia, 2024a). To further reflect the company's commitment to the planet, Patagonia has also created numerous CRM campaigns in collaboration with the Holdfast Collective, a non-profit dedicated to fighting the environmental crisis and defending nature (Agafonow & Perez, 2024; Firebelly, 2022).

Social media data and insights are pivotal in shaping Patagonia's CRM campaigns, blending seamlessly with its core initiatives: 'Patagonia Action Works', the Holdfast Collective Collaboration, and 'Worn Wear'. 'Patagonia Action Works' stands as a prime example of leveraging social media data. Through comprehensive data analysis, the company harnesses social media insights to identify emerging environmental concerns, gauge public sentiment, and pinpoint areas of passionate engagement among its audience (Dawson & Brunner, 2020; Zhao et al., 2022). This data-driven approach assists the matching process, facilitating connections between environmentally conscious individuals and local grassroots organizations via the 'Action Works' platform.

The Holdfast Collective Collaboration builds upon these insights, utilizing social media data to identify potential partners aligned with Patagonia's mission and values. Through strategic alliances with like-minded entities identified from social media insights, Patagonia extends its reach and impact within the environmental advocacy sphere (Agafonow & Perez, 2024). Social media analytics aid in evaluating partner compatibility, gauging audience overlap, and optimizing collaborative efforts to amplify shared messages and initiatives. Moreover, the 'Worn Wear' programme integrates social media data to promote sustainable consumer behaviour.

Insights into consumer preferences and behaviours inform the design of promotional campaigns and engagement strategies. By highlighting the environmental benefits of recycling and repurposing clothing, Patagonia leverages CRM to foster a culture of conscious consumption (Shourkaei et al., 2023). Its CRM initiatives are not one-time expeditions but rather continual ascent, with Patagonia consistently refining its campaigns as the environmental landscape evolves (Rivera, 2021). This refinement is facilitated by social media feedback loops, enabling continuous fine-tuning of marketing approaches and delivering personalized experiences that resonate with environmentally conscious consumers (Dawson & Brunner, 2020).

Initiatives similar to 'Patagonia Action Works' can adopt our proposed approach to enhance partner matching through user-generated social media content and by precisely aligning customers with local organizations based on shared values and objectives. Moreover, organizations like Patagonia can use social media platforms to broaden their outreach efforts to identify business–NPO pairs exhibiting genuine interest in socially responsible goals (Bulmer et al., 2024). The proposed approach would also assist the organization's endeavours by identifying influencers, activists, and environmentally conscious individuals/businesses, amplifying the reach of its CRM campaigns and driving grassroots advocacy efforts. With continuous monitoring of user-generated content through the proposed approach, organizations like Patagonia can adapt their campaign tactics, optimize resource allocation, and maximize the effectiveness of their CRM initiatives, ensuring a solid commitment to sustainability and impactful engagement within the online community.

In addition to proposing a novel approach to determining ideal CRM campaign partners, this study extends Opoku et al.'s (2006) brand personality dictionary to create a dictionary that classifies text based on Aaker's five brand personality dimensions. While the existing CRM campaign literature focused on advertising strategies to improve brand image and reputation, the present study contributes to the partnership management literature by introducing a text-mining technique to identify sustainable NPO–firm partners. Resource-constrained NPOs can significantly benefit from the proposed approach as it allows them to target only compatible businesses for CSR grants, thereby saving time and money. Next, we provide some underlined implications of this study.

Implications

The results of the proposed approach can serve as statistical evidence for NPOs seeking corporate funding, enabling them to demonstrate to companies the potential benefits of partnering with them. Likewise, firms can use the approach's statistics to determine the scope and budget of their CRM initiatives and design promotional messages. Moreover, the developed brand personality dictionary can be used in other studies to effectively measure brand personality dimensions from textual data, offering a valuable tool for researchers in the field. By leveraging the abundant and freely available organic social media content, the techniques reduce the need for extensive financial resources typically required for partner identification, enabling cost-effective and efficient collaborations.

Researchers can incorporate other construct-specific dictionaries within the text-mining approach, enabling the evaluation of strategic fit between organizations based on the chosen construct. This adaptability enables researchers to explore various dimensions and construct frameworks, enhancing their understanding of strategic alignment and facilitating comprehensive assessments of organizational compatibility. The proposed framework also offers versatility in assessing brand image fit across various contexts and industries. Finally, the proposed technique allows the integration of more advanced techniques involving deep learning and artificial intelligence algorithms to measure the similarity between organizations engaged in social alliances.

Future Research Directions

The findings of this study reveal several fruitful avenues for future research. First, it is essential to explore the applicability of the proposed approach by analysing the social media posts of organizations engaged in successful and unsuccessful CRM campaigns. This investigation should assess whether there is a correlation between the similarity scores of the entities involved in CRM campaigns derived using the proposed methodology and their outcomes. Research should also concentrate on implementing advanced AI techniques to automate the manual process employed in the current approach and facilitate the use of big data. Finally, researchers should extend the proposed approach by using alternative frameworks to assess brand image fit and explore its applicability in identifying the strategic fit among organizations engaged in joint ventures.

References

Aaker, J. L. (1997). Dimensions of brand personality. *Journal of Marketing Research, 34*(3), 347–356. https://doi.org/10.1177/002224379703400304

Agafonow, A., & Perez, M. (2024). In search of a non-anthropocentric middle-range theory of the firm: On how the Patagonia Purpose Trust granted a controlling stake to nature. *Ecological Economics, 217*, 108076. https://doi.org/10.1016/j.ecolecon.2023.108076

Amazon. (2020, October 28). *Amazon India launches 'Delivering Smiles' program to support online education of students from low income communities*. https://www.aboutamazon.in/news/community/amazon-india-launches-delivering-smiles-program-to-support-online-education-of-students-from-low-income-communities

Andersen, S. E., & Johansen, T. S. (2016). Cause-related marketing 2.0: Connection, collaboration and commitment. *Journal of Marketing Communications, 22*(5), 524–543.

Barone, M. J., Miyazaki, A. D., & Taylor, K. A. (2000). The influence of cause-related marketing on consumer choice: Does one good turn deserve another? *Journal of the Academy of Marketing Science, 28*(2), 248–262.

Bergkvist, L., & Zhou, K. Q. (2019). Cause-related marketing persuasion research: An integrated framework and directions for further research. *International Journal of Advertising, 38*(1), 5–25.

Bhatti, H. Y., Galan-Ladero, M. M., & Galera-Casquet, C. (2022). Cause-related marketing: A systematic review of the literature. *International Review on Public and Nonprofit Marketing, 20*, 25–64.

Bigné, E., Currás-Pérez, R., & Aldás-Manzano, J. (2012). Dual nature of cause-brand fit: Influence on corporate social responsibility consumer perception. *European Journal of Marketing, 46*(4), 575–594.

Brønn, P. S., & Vrioni, A. B. (2001). Corporate social responsibility and cause-related marketing: An overview. *International Journal of Advertising, 20*(2), 207–222.

Bulmer, S., Palakshappa, N., Dodds, S., & Harper, S. (2024). Sustainability, brand authenticity and Instagram messaging. *Journal of Business Research, 175*, 114547. https://doi.org/10.1016/j.jbusres.2024.114547

Chang, C. T., & Cheng, Z. H. (2015). Tugging on heartstrings: Shopping orientation, mindset, and consumer responses to cause-related marketing. *Journal of Business Ethics, 127*, 337–350.

Christofi, M., Vrontis, D., Leonidou, E., & Thrassou, A. (2020). Customer engagement through choice in cause-related marketing: A potential for global competitiveness. *International Marketing Review, 37*(4), 621–650.

Cillo, V., Petruzzelli, A. M., Ardito, L., & Del Giudice, M. (2019). Understanding sustainable innovation: A systematic literature review. *Corporate Social Responsibility and Environmental Management, 26*(5), 1012–1025.

Daromes, F. E., & Gunawan, S. R. (2020). Joint impact of philanthropy and corporate reputation on firm value. *Jurnal Dinamika Akuntansi, 12*(1), 1–13.

Dawson, V. R., & Brunner, E. (2020). Corporate social responsibility on wild public networks: Communicating to disparate and multivocal stakeholders. *Management Communication Quarterly, 34*(1), 58–84.

Deng, N., Jiang, X., & Fan, X. (2023). How social media's cause-related marketing activity enhances consumer citizenship behavior: The mediating role of community identification. *Journal of Research in Interactive Marketing, 17*(1), 38–60.

Ewing, A. P. (2020). Corporate responsibility. In J. Doorley & H. F. Gracia (Eds.), *Reputation management* (pp. 360–387). Routledge. https://doi.org/10.4324/9781351235020

Fazli-Salehi, R., Torres, I. M., & Angel Zúñiga, M. (2019). Customer, corporation, and cause: A comprehensive model of cause selection in cause-related marketing. *Journal of Relationship Marketing, 18*(3), 173–195.

Firebelly. (2022, September 26). *Recently donated Patagonia spearheads cause marketing.* https://www.firebellymarketing.com/blog/recently-donated-patagonia-spearheads-cause-marketing

Golod, A. (2016). *Google: Girls can achieve great things through coding.* U.S. News. https://www.usnews.com/news/stem-solutions/articles/2016-10-18/google-girls-can-achieve-great-things-through-coding

Google. (2014). *Coding resources: Made With Code projects.* https://sites.google.com/smusd.org/hourofcode/code-resources/made-with-code-projects

Guzmán, F., & Davis, D. (2017). The impact of corporate social responsibility on brand equity: Consumer responses to two types of fit. *Journal of Product & Brand Management, 26*(5), 435–446.

Huertas-García, R., Lengler, J., & Consolación-Segura, C. (2017). Co-branding strategy in cause-related advertising: The fit between brand and cause. *Journal of Product & Brand Management, 26*(2), 135–150.

Humphreys, A., & Wang, R. J. H. (2017). Automated text analysis for consumer research. *Journal of Consumer Research, 44*(6), 1274–1306.

Kellogg Company. (2012). *Kellogg's® rallies Americans to share the power of their breakfast.* P.R. Newswire. https://www.prnewswire.com/news-releases/kelloggs-rallies-americans-to-share-the-power-of-their-breakfast-141408843.html

Kim, J., & Kim, M. (2023). Using personalization for cause-related marketing beyond compassion fade on social media. *Journal of Research in Interactive Marketing, 17*(2), 299–316.

Kim, J., Lee, J., & Kim, S. (2017). The efficacy of cause-related marketing within a social network: The effects of congruency, corporate credibility, familiarity of cause brands, and perceived altruistic motive. *Journal of Marketing Communications, 23*(5), 429–455.

Kim, N., Sung, Y., & Lee, M. (2012). Consumer evaluations of social alliances: The effects of perceived fit between companies and non-profit organizations. *Journal of Business Ethics, 109*, 163–174.

Kipp, A., & Hawkins, R. (2019). The responsibilization of 'development consumers' through cause-related marketing campaigns. *Consumption Markets & Culture, 22*(1), 1–16.

Lafferty, B. A., Lueth, A. K., & McCafferty, R. (2016). An evolutionary process model of cause-related marketing and systematic review of the empirical literature. *Psychology & Marketing, 33*(11), 951–970.

Liu, G., & Ko, W. W. (2011). An analysis of cause-related marketing implementation strategies through social alliance: Partnership conditions and strategic objectives. *Journal of Business Ethics, 100*, 253–281.

Natarajan, T., Balasubramaniam, S. A., & Jublee, D. I. (2016). A journey of cause related marketing from 1988 to 2016. *International Journal of Business and Management, 11*(11), 247–263.

Opoku, R. Abratt, R., & Pitt, L. (2006). Communicating brand personality: Are the websites doing the talking for the top South African business schools? *Journal of Brand Management*, *14*(1), 20–39.

Patagonia. (2024a). *About: Patagonia Action Works*. https://www.patagonia.com/actionworks/about/

Patagonia. (2024b). *Worn Wear: Patagonia*. https://wornwear.patagonia.com/

Pournarakis, D. E., Sotiropoulos, D. N., & Giaglis, G. M. (2017). A computational model for mining consumer perceptions in social media. *Decision Support Systems*, *93*, 98–110.

Rego, M. M., & Hamilton, M. A. (2021). The importance of fit: A predictive model of cause marketing effects. *Journal of Marketing Theory and Practice*, *30*(4), 1–19.

Rishi, B., & Bandyopadhyay, S. (Eds.). (2018). *Contemporary issues in social media marketing*. London: Routledge.

Rivera, R. G. (2021). Green cause-related marketing for social innovation: Helping people to reimagine plastic recycling and sustainability. In M. M. Galan-Ladero, C. Galera-Casquet, & H. M. Alves (Eds.), *Cause-related marketing: Classroom companion: business*. Springer. https://doi.org/10.1007/978-3-030-65455-9_2

Rohit, D., & Panda, R. (2018). Cause-brand association: A review. *Journal of Management Research*, *18*(1), 13–26.

Romano, B., Bazzaz, D., Clarridge, C., & Cornwell, P. (2020, April 6). Amazon will donate 8,200 laptops to help Seattle public schools students learn online during coronavirus closures. *Seattle Times*. https://www.seattletimes.com/seattle-news/education/amazon-will-donate-8200-laptops-to-seattle-public-schools-to-help-families-with-coronavirus-closures/

Room to Read. (2020). *Celebrating change: Annual report – special edition*. Room to Read India. https://www.roomtoreadindia.org/media/1ffnmoca/india-2020-annual-report.pdf

Schamp, C., Heitmann, M., Bijmolt, T. H., & Katzenstein, R. (2023). The effectiveness of cause-related marketing: A meta-analysis on consumer responses. *Journal of Marketing Research*, *60*(1), 189–215.

Shourkaei, M. M., Taylor, K. M., & Dyck, B. (2023). Examining sustainable supply chain management via a social-symbolic work lens: Lessons from Patagonia. *Business Strategy and the Environment*, *33*(2), 1477–1496.

Singh, S., & Dhir, S. (2019). Structured review using TCCM and bibliometric analysis of international cause-related marketing, social marketing, and innovation of the firm. *International Review on Public and Nonprofit Marketing*, *16*(2), 335–347.

Svensson, G., & Wood, G. (2011). A model of cause-related marketing for 'profit-driven' and 'non-profit' organizations. *European Business Review*, *23*(2), 203–214. https://doi.org/10.1108/09555341111111219

Tanford, S., Kim, M., & Kim, E. J. (2020). Priming social media and framing cause-related marketing to promote sustainable hotel choice. *Journal of Sustainable Tourism*, *28*(11), 1762–1781.

Thomas, S., Kureshi, S., & Vatavwala, S. (2020). Cause-related marketing research (1988–2016): An academic review and classification. *Journal of Nonprofit & Public Sector Marketing, 32*(5), 488–516.

Till, B. D., & Nowak, L. I. (2000). Toward effective use of cause-related marketing alliances. *Journal of Product & Brand Management, 9*(7), 472–484.

Tsao, H. Y. J., Campbell, C. L., Sands, S., Ferraro, C., Mavrommatis, A., & Lu, S. Q. (2019). A machine-learning based approach to measuring constructs through text analysis. *European Journal of Marketing, 54*(3), 511–524.

Tugend, A. (2016, April 18). Seventh Generation taps Maya Rudolph for its biggest campaign yet. *New York Times*. https://www.nytimes.com/2016/04/18/business/media/seventh-generation-taps-maya-rudolph-for-its-biggest-campaign-yet.html

Varadarajan, P. R., & Menon, A. (1988). Cause-related marketing: A coalignment of marketing strategy and corporate philanthropy. *Journal of Marketing, 52*(3), 58–74.

Verk, N., Golob, U., & Podnar, K. (2021). A dynamic review of the emergence of corporate social responsibility communication. *Journal of Business Ethics, 168*, 491–515.

Vrontis, D., Christofi, M., & Katsikeas, C. S. (2020). An assessment of the literature on cause-related marketing: Implications for international competitiveness and marketing research. *International Marketing Review, 37*(5), 977–1012.

Weise, E. (2017, 29 August). Hurricane Harvey Amazon wish list shows the toll taken on children. *USA Today*. https://www.usatoday.com/story/tech/talkingtech/2017/08/29/hurricane-harvey-amazon-wish-list-shows-toll-taken-children/614581001/

Williams, R. (2020). *Seventh generation brings climate change stance to new campaign. Marketing Dive.* https://www.marketingdive.com/news/seventh-generation-brings-climate-change-stance-to-new-campaign/571973/

Woodroof, P. J., Deitz, G. D., Howie, K. M., & Evans, R. D. (2019). The effect of cause-related marketing on firm value: A look at Fortune's most admired all-stars. *Journal of the Academy of Marketing Science, 47*, 899–918.

Xu, S., & Zhou, A. (2020). Hashtag homophily in Twitter network: Examining a controversial cause-related marketing campaign. *Computers in Human Behavior, 102*, 87–96.

Yucel-Aybat, O., & Hsieh, M. H. (2021). Consumer mindsets matter: Benefit framing and firm–cause fit in the persuasiveness of cause-related marketing campaigns. *Journal of Business Research, 129*, 418–427.

Zhao, L., Lee, S. H., Li, M., & Sun, P. (2022). The use of social media to promote sustainable fashion and benefit communications: A data-mining approach. *Sustainability, 14*(3), 1178.

Zint, M., & Frederick, R. (2001). Marketing and advertising a 'deep green' company: The case of Patagonia, Inc. *Journal of Corporate Citizenship, 1*, 93–113.

Social Media Renaissance with Audio Content 17

Bolstering a Personalized Approach

Ruchi Jain and Uday Thareja
Amity School of Business, Amity University Uttar Pradesh, India

1 Introduction

Content marketers create experiences to connect with target audiences for amplified brand preference and mitigated mental barriers. Digital content marketing has been pivotal for increasing awareness, engagement, conversion and loyalty (Hollebeek & Macky, 2019), and is described as a management process responsible for effective identification, anticipation and customer satisfaction. Content marketing on digital platforms aims to increase customers' brand satisfaction via means such as newsletters, e-books, podcasts, blogs and so on (Järvinen & Taiminen, 2016). Thus, the intention of content strategy is to reinforce brand messaging. However, it is observed by marketers that overabundant sources and page after page of content are becoming an imposition for brands, as content clutter is making it hard to reach potential customers in view of their enhanced exposure to marketing posts (Opreana & Vinerean, 2015).

As people spend more time on social media, there is a realization that brands today are looking for ways to appear more human with content that is visually appealing. Brands do not want to be perceived as serious all the

DOI: 10.4324/9781003412656-17

time; rather, they want to be seen as real people who are responsible for every post, ad campaign, and slogan (Ciccarelli, 2021a). Marketers are therefore innovating to create the most efficient way to fix their message in the minds of customers (Batra & Keller, 2016; Keller, 2016) and generate electronic word of mouth (e-WOM) as an essential peg for driving engagement (Thareja et al., 2021) thus, extending inbound marketing channels.

In the effort to introduce 'human-ness' into brands, we are seeing a massive increase in the use of audio in an otherwise visual world as there is nothing more authentic than a human voice. Audio content is providing much-needed space for creators, experts, thought leaders, students, educationists, and all those who are not stereotypical marketers. Along the same lines, written content repurposed in audio format is also a differentiating tangent in content strategy that is mainly preferred by brands targeting digital natives.

The present study discusses the emerging significance of audio content for digital marketers and the personalization of content through audio formats to advance established digital marketing strategies. It also considers audio content as the futuristic approach for customer engagement in the business-to-business (B2B) market. A case study methodology is used to examine why and how companies use audio content as a marketing tool, and to assess how it can operate in combination with other digital marketing strategies for personalization. For this purpose, a mixed methodology is used, including personal interviews with the founders of the company under study, surveying its clients and assessing the impact of audio content with the help of social media analytics.

2 Literature Review

2.1 Digital Content Marketing

Content marketing is aimed at producing and sharing meaningful content that the consumer wants and is an active recipient of (Lögdberg & Wahlqvist, 2020). Previous studies have shown that content has a large impact on consumer purchase decision (Minsky & Quesenberry, 2016). Digital content marketing is uses social media, web pages and other digital content to build brand trust (Lögdberg & Wahlqvist, 2020). It is becoming an extremely important part of brand marketing as it attempts to add value to consumer lifestyles by educating them about brands and driving positive business outcomes. In other words, the aim of content marketing is to bolster brand perception and appreciation, eventually leading to increased sales.

In practice, the different forms of content include podcasts, articles, live broadcasts, online events, informative literature, white papers and virtual conferences (Hollebeek & Macky, 2019). Digital content marketing shifts the focus from sales to advocacy, which encourages using new marketing skills and methods compared to traditional approaches to marketing (Holliman & Rowley, 2014). Digital content marketing is seen to enable a 'pull' technique, and Jefferson and Tanton (2015) suggested three mainstream trends for changing consumer purchase behaviour: (1) the advent of the World Wide Web; (2) the emergence of social media: and (3) the increasing mistrust of sales-led advertising content that shifts the focus of marketers to the distribution of relevant content rather than 'push' techniques.

The end goal of all marketing led activities is incremental sales, and digital content marketing is no exception. However, this uses an indirect approach of building trust, higher levels of engagement and strong relationships, looking at long-term sales impact (Lögdberg & Wahlqvist, 2020) and to hit the sweet spot where the consumer is receptive to messaging and discovery (Thareja & Jain, 2019). As digital content marketing's main objective is to influence rather than sell, audio content can play a large role in enabling the shift.

2.2 Audio Content

Audio-first experiences are playing an integral role in the digital age and impacting the landscape of both social media and marketing. Audio has expanded exponentially over the last few years to become a staple of our everyday lives, with podcasts growing in popularity across almost all communities (Douglass, 2021). This trend seems to be continuing, with more than 2.4 million podcasts distributed globally in 2021 to more than 116 million listeners, and numbers are still growing (Berry, 2022). In the Indian perspective, audio content is especially relevant as the country has a history of storytelling.

India's linguistic diversity – with more than 22 official languages and 834 or more further languages/dialects spoken by at least 10,000 people – adds to the opportunity for audio content. India had more than 57.6 million podcast listeners in October 2020, making it the third largest consumer of audio content after China and the USA (PwC, 2020). This is set to more than treble given that this has only scratched the surface, with only 14 per cent of India's population listening to podcasts. Podcasts therefore present a significant opportunity for revenue monetization; they can complement conventional radio- and video-based platforms; and can to be accessed safely and comfortably because of relatively small bandwidth requirements.

Digital audio is defined by the Interactive Advertising Bureau (IAB, 2016) as audio programming available for consumers over the internet, while podcasts are audio programmes that are available on portable devices. Even though the content of each podcast is created with different goals in mind, the content must attract the consumer (Lögdberg & Wahlqvist, 2020). As there is a large amount of information clutter to break through to reach desired audiences (Jefferson & Tanton, 2015, understanding target customers and then developing relevant content is of utmost importance. Furthermore, the IAB suggests that podcasts are a medium where the user 'leans in' – i.e. leading to strong responsiveness and thus impacting purchase behaviour.

Digital audio content breaks the barrier of being dependent on screen viewership for consumption by telling stories via immersive audio content. While traditionally audio was consumed through radio broadcasts, delivered to many users at the same time, digital audio content is being consumed as an on-demand service: users are building individual playlists, and content is delivered to each listener as a personalized experience. The IAB suggests that audio content is a growing medium that has no screen dependency, high measurability and reach, and that attracts strong engagement.

With content consumption shifting to mobile devices, screens are getting smaller and more consumption is taking place during other activities (such as driving, walking or jogging), which is giving audio content an edge as there is no requirement for a screen while listening. There are many other documented benefits of audio content (Russell, 2022), including:

- audience targeting basis demographics, geographic and interest
- multi-channel impact to add to the optimal number of brand touch points for conversion
- data and consumption tracking on key metrics such as completion rates and listen through rates
- improved brand recall and relevance to listeners' interests.

Audio content is much more economical and less time-consuming to create than video ads, which have a much longer gestation cycle. Audio content has various other advantages, ranging from providing personalized messaging, public relations (PR) and brand advocacy to building credibility.

3 Personalization Practices Using Audio Content

There are increasing numbers of digital devices owned by households; with the world moving towards connected cars and smart homes, consumers are always digitally connected. Now, more than ever, audio devices are multiplying, with audio consumption now easier and always available. This makes it extremely important for brands to offer effective and personalized messaging to consumers. Audio is the medium of the moment, so making the content as relevant as possible and focusing on individuals are keys to engagement at a deeper level (Martin, 2020). This is evident in the change in the way today's consumers are interacting with brands, both socially and financially, wanting to get to know them in more personal ways (Ciccarelli, 2021b).

Besides using social media, brands showcase their expertise and own their niche through a steady supply of high-quality content. They can collaborate with partners whose expertise complements theirs and engage in conversations to share knowledge. Visual advertising is mostly fleeting or flipping – i.e. viewers are often either moving away from the message or moving ahead to reach something more interesting. However, when listening to audio content, they have the same content with them even when walking or doing other things. Therefore, the same advertising strategy that brands use in mass media cannot be used for their audio content strategy and podcasts. Audio consumption patterns are an added incentive for marketers due to their passive and flexible nature: audio is easier to consume than other formats as users can just plug in a headset or play it on speaker and engage with it while doing other tasks such as household chores, commuting and other activities.

Hence, brands venturing into the world of audio are paying more attention to the context in which their content appears, the speed required to attract their audience, and tailoring their creative ouput to audio (Douglass, 2021). Audio content is being distributed and used by organizations in various ways. One of the most prevalent is recorded ad spots (or native spots), which means they are commercials for the brand; they are inserted in the content stream to create impact or can be permanently integrated into the audio content as part of the story (IAB, 2016). Brands are also leveraging audio content in different ways to increase reach and personalized engagement with their target audience, as in the following examples:

- **Audio content marketing** – Complete storytelling of the brand, distributed across various channels to drive awareness.
- **Podcasts** – Brands are creating company podcast or sponsoring existing ones to increase their reach to target groups.
- **Audio identity** – Creating short jingles that are sound mnemonics, with string audio signatures.
- **Audio branding and ads** – Advertising on various audio and over-the-top platforms (OTTs) to reach out to listeners.

While there are other brand-led activities that are used – such as voice activation ads that integrate audio engagement with users or branded customized playlists – one of the most upcoming engagement tools is creating audio content or podcasts for brands. As shown in Table 17.1, many firms are

Table 17.1 Audio content use by brands/firms and their objectives

Brand/firm	Country	Audience	Digital platform	Duration (mins)	Objectives and other details
HDFC Bank	India	B2C	Official website	15	User awareness initiative for investment: a financial expert talks about wealth creation, complaints and markets
Economic Times	India	B2C	Official website	2	Short podcast about the stock market; general roundup
Manipal Hospitals	India	B2C	Official website, Apple, Spotify	30	Biweekly roundup taking a deep dive into trends and insights
The Hindu	India	B2C	Official website	25	Deep dive into important news items from India beyond
Barclays Bank	UK	B2C	Official website, Apple	20	Multiple weekly podcasts to help ordinary investors make sense of latest financial news and events
Schneider Electric	France	B2C	Official website/blog	5–25	Blog has mix of articles and podcasts, specifically on energy conservation and sustainability
Exxon Mobile	USA	B2B	Official website	20	Leading maritime experts evaluate the far-reaching impacts of emission reforms

now using podcasts as a part of their content marketing strategy to increase brand awareness and engagement, building on thought leadership (Berry, 2022) using integrated and organic conversations, which is in complete contrast to the archaic template of pre- , mid- and end-roll ads.

As the digital audio landscape continues to expand, a wealth of information is emerging about listenership and engagement trends (Nielsen, 2022). Thus, audio clearly cuts though the literacy barrier for brands compared to other media by telling stories while 'humanizing' brands. Moreover, they are available in any language, of any length, and in personalized ways by users plugging into their headphones. Podcasts can create extremely loyal audiences who share content with their friends, thus cultivating communities via meaningful dialogue. Many podcasts are very niche, and therefore target specific groups and individuals. Adding to personalization and delivering higher consumer engagement is the fact that audio content is largely unavoidable in comparison to text and video messaging because the consumer is only listening to one broadcast at any point in time.

4 Case Study: Earshot – Audio Evangelist

Earshot Digimedia Private Limited is an Indian company dedicated solely to audio content, and is widely recognized and integrated with its audiences across channels – social, digital, podcasts services, audio OTTs and so on – in flexible in distinct ways. The three founders of Earshot – Abhijit Majumder, Rohit Upadhyay and Gaurav Choudhury – are stalwarts from across the media and entertainment industry, combining their rich experience to create the magic.

Abhijit Majumder is a renowned journalist with 25 years of experience with media outlets such as *Mid-Day* and the *Hindustan Times*. He has a strong presence on social media, with more than 500k X (formerly Twitter) followers and 130k followers on Facebook. Rohit Upadhyay is an audio evangelist and managing director of iBroad7 – India's first and largest full-service radio agency with in-house recording facilities. Rohit is also a media veteran with a stellar career spanning over 23 years, and has leadership roles with *The Indian Express*, *The Times of India* and the private station Radio City. Gaurav Choudhury, an economist from the Delhi School of Economics, is also a professional journalist with more than 24 years of experience in leading media companies such as Network 18, Moneycontrol and *Hindustan Times*.

The trio founded Earshot in 2019 after an immense amount of brainstorming to understand the gaps that existed in the Indian media and content space. It was clear that there was a massive, hence the decision to become audio evangelists and create India's first multilingual destination for audio originals. Earshot has a comprehensive library of audio content in a range of languages. Its journalistic mission is to use the audio medium to create mainstream content and maintain its reputation as credible, well-researched, and editorially independent.

Earshot works with a wide range of companies, from small businesses seeking to increase customer retention to multinationals wanting to make a large impact. They create content to start conversations/interviews with leaders and business owners while handling their post-production, coaching hosts (and even guests) and consciously looking for their stories. Earshot believes that audio content in India is no longer just an 'experimental format' and that it can be used at any stage of a purchase cycle – whether for creating awareness and interest, generating demand, answering queries and assisting with purchases, or for employee engagement or even managing cause-related marketing (see Chapter 16).

5 Leveraging Audio Content: Inducing Personalization

Earshot is leveraging audio content not only in the business-to-customer (B2C) context, but also aims at business-to-business (B2B) marketing opportunities and business-to-business-to-customers (B2B2C) prospects (see Table 17.2 and Table 17.3).

Business to business (B2B) refers to any marketing strategy or content that is geared towards a business or organization – i.e. companies that sell products or services to other businesses or organizations typically use B2B marketing strategies (Zenn, 2021). In the case of audio content, B2B refers to 'white label' productions, which includes creating content for businesses and brands. These are commissioned podcasts, and are generally distributed by the brands on their websites and social media platforms, or are specifically for internal employee communication.

In B2B marketing, podcasts are a great way to provide valuable information in a format that audiences can dip in and out when they have time to spare (whether a few minutes or an hour). B2B businesses celebrate storytelling and highlight their struggles in their podcasts for their audience to connect with them at a deeper level. Not only do podcasts create a human touch with consumers for B2B business, they also contribute to search engine optimization (SEO) ratings of the brand and help boost page ranking.

Business to customer (B2C) describes businesses whose customers are individuals rather than professional (trade) buyers. Therefore, all these

Table 17.2 Sample cases of Earshot audio content for B2B

Industry	Brand/firm	Platform	Objective	Details
Financial services	HDFC Bank	Internal	Newsfeed about the organization	Weekly update for white-collar employees on latest company news; forwarded via WhatsApp and email
Financial services	HDFC	Internal team	Employee newsfeed for business (customer facing)	Daily financial update: like first page of *Economics Times*, giving roundup of important news of the day to keep business team abreast and better able to serve clients; aimed at brand uplift
NGO	Better India	Own website only	Consumer education	White label: specific educational content produced solely for Better India on various issues (e.g., cleft lips/palates)
NGO	Room2Read	Own website only	Consumer education	White label: specific content for NGO website (e.g. on awareness of girls' education)
NGO	PFI	Own website only	Consumer education	White label: multipart series on comprehensive sex education

Table 17.3 Sample cases of Earshot audio content for B2B2C

Industry	Brand/firm	Objective	Details
Real estate	Signature Realty	Thought leadership	Weekly update on latest events in city of Gurugram (podcast and YouTube video)
Medicine	Indraprastha Hospital	Awareness campaign to showcase their doctors as the country's best	Monthly medical update: 25-min podcasts featuring specialist doctors sharing medical knowledge and explaining issues (e.g. can men get breast cancer, one of the most heard)
Technology	Mediatek	Thought leadership in mobile technology	Weekly update on new technology and trends with Mediatek leaders discussing tech
Financial services	Equitas Bank	Key opinion leader (KOL) voice	10-part series of insights from the bank's CEO
Real estate	Housing.com	Thought leadership	Complete roundup of real estate sector every two weeks, with deep dives into important industry topics

Note: The platforms used are Earshot, social media and podcast channels such as Apple, Google, Gaana, Spotify and Saavn.

businesses' marketing is dedicated to the needs, interests and challenges of people in their everyday lives (Zenn, 2021). In case of audio content, all the podcasts would be based on the topics of interest of consumers and would range from hobbies to entertainment. B2C podcasts provide real value because they are not just branding tools; listeners can also feel connected, have a sense of belonging, learn more about their interests and be part of the podcast community while engaging in discussion.

The distribution pathway of *business to business to customers* (B2B2C) is a combination of B2B and B2C. In the audio context, this refers to podcasting partnerships between the brand and Earshot, aimed at creating podcaster intellectual property (IP). Earshot works on creating the end-to-end solution, bearing in mind, however, that the brand's goals are spreading information and generating interest among consumers rather than direct advertising. Earshot's work ranges from deciding the episode structure to scripting, anchoring/guests, production and post-production, and even publishing and sharing material on partner websites, social platforms and audio OTT players.

6 Data Analysis: Sectoral Penetration of Audio Content

The authenticity of the human voice is established in an otherwise visual world. Audio content is creating much-needed space for creators. Likewise, written content is being repurposed into audio format by brands and companies to add a different slant to content strategy. The intensive study of Earshot demonstrates how the company has penetrated various sectors with equal ease, as outlined below:

- **Financial services**: Given the high percentage of money-minded listeners, financial services providers have an already-educated audience to engage with. Case in point: a notable banking institution, HDFC, was struggling to keep its staff up to date with latest events in the ever-changing financial world in order to create confidence among customers and showcase its extensive knowledge of the finance sector. As the requirement was real time with daily updates and to a wide range of internal customers, audio content was ideal due to its quick production and easy dissemination via messaging apps, and has come as a welcome solution to the challenging situation. As another example, HDFC, has thousands of employees and operations throughout India, and thus a need for a 'self-portrait' of employee branding and information. An audio content solution therefore provided a roundup of newsworthy happenings in the organisation, which employees can tune into to keep abreast of latest events.
- **Real estate**: Property is (and always will be) one of the most important decisions in a person's life as well as a desirable investment strategy (whether in India or elsewhere). Housing.com is an app that gives customer the power of transparent and easy purchase of a home/real estate, and wanted the position of thought leader in the sector. An audio content solution that consolidated all the major sectoral highlights, hot topics and events into interesting newsfeeds was therefore created and distributed across many platforms, creating a pioneering podcast in the real estate sector. Because investing in real estate is a somewhat advanced skill, it can take a lot of effort to learn it well. For that very reason, the Signature team creates educational content to help advance knowledge and give tips on the real estate space. The content was largely centred on the Delhi National Capital Region. Besides the primary goals of increasing demand and brand awareness, audio content also adds to the top-funnel content requirement and aids SEO rankings.
- **Non-profit organizations**: The strategist at Room2Read wanted to highlight the ability of podcasts to play a role in an important CSR initiative regarding the education of girls in India. A multipart series was therefore created that highlighted the pain points associated with the subject,

along with the opportunities to overcome them and make Indian society more equitable. In an earnest attempt to address and clarify misconceptions about cleft lips and palates, Better India and Smile Train used audio content to create a series of podcasts led by experts. They highlighted cleft care, and featured parents of patients and individuals living with these conditions to raise awareness of them, break misconceptions, and 'normalize' people living with clefts.

- **Medical services**: The core focus of this audio content series was to enable listeners to be proactive about health and provide holistic information about current topics. The episodes featured everything from new medical breakthroughs to smart daily health habits, with doctors, researchers and experts (from Apollo Hospitals and others) sharing their discoveries about medicine and well-being. The benefit goes far beyond a branding and informational exercise to being more visible among the medical fraternity.
- **Information technology services**: Mediatek powers most of the everyday tech gadgets in India, from smartphones to routers and laptops. The company therefore wants to tell its stories and offer insights on the emerging technology shaping the future, from transformative digitization to innovative solutions. Audio content worked extremely well due to its flexibility of recording in remote locations, along with shorter lead time needed to put together the content as the interviewees were senior leaders powering these innovations in the rapidly evolving technology environment. This assists brands in ascertaining thought leadership while driving traffic on their platforms to enhance their reputations.

7 Conclusion

This study aimed to contribute to and enrich the limited literature on branded audio content. It tried to build a deeper understanding of sample cases in the B2B and B2B2C contexts, and provided an overview to benefit brands interested in opting for audio content. While reasons for using audio content in the marketing mix could differ from company to company according to their key performance indicators (KPIs), the benefits to organisations will have many commonalities. The benefits could range from cost/time efficiency to active listening and human voice nurturing relationships, and even branding and employee relationships. Hence greater opportunities await brands as audio content can be created quickly at considerably lower cost, and can be spread to engaged and loyal audiences that regularly listen to the content. In terms of content, brands tend to focus on providing meaningful, valuable and personalized content aimed at sharing knowledge or for entertainment. It has been noticed that creating content internally might result in compromised quality both in terms of sound and activity flow. Therefore, hiring professional audio companies to create content for both B2B B2B2C will lead to good sound quality as well as optimal flow of conversation, hence assisting in better reach and engagement.

The chapter shows how audio content is currently seen as a supplement to the marketing arsenal, with brands sceptical of its use, and thus not many are seen to be making significant investment in the medium. Some of the strategies that brands can adopt to increase engagement with their target customers are shared in this study, and marketers who work with content development and inbound marketing can benefit from these options. Due to the nature of audio as a medium, there are infinite opportunities to adapt the topics – ranging from language and communication to planning – which can lead to its successful implementation. In today's ecosystem there is a need to be present across numerous environments (i.e. omnichannel distribution) in both B2B and B2B2C options.

The present study identifies opportunities for different kinds of research in this field. Podcasting is still an evolving concept, and organizations are still gearing up to it. Hence, there is little research into discovering and reviewing audio media, so in-depth research with respect to the strategic implications of audio content could be looked at. It would also be fruitful for further studies to look at the unique motivations of listeners and how they interact with brand-led audio content. The personalization induced by audio content has immense potential to fortify the digital marketing strategy of brands.

References

Batra, R., & Keller, K. L. (2016). Integrating marketing communications: New findings, new lessons, and new ideas. *Journal of Marketing*, *80*(6), 122–145.

Berry, Z. (2022, March 2). *Branded podcasts*. ZMC Podcasts. Retrieved from https://zmcpodcasts.com/2022/03/branded-podcasts-the-research-behind-why-theyre-taking-off/

Ciccarelli, D. (2021a, October 28). *How audio-first experiences are changing the social and marketing landscape in a visual-focused world*. LinkedIn. Retrieved from https://www.linkedin.com/pulse/how-audio-first-experiences-changing-social-marketing-ciccarelli/?trackingId=781vsM2FR1iq4gCF%2BNvzuA%3D%3D

Ciccareli, D. (2021b, December 21). *Why audio needs to be part of your marketing strategy in 2022*. LinkedIn. Retrieved from https://www.linkedin.com/pulse/why-audio-needs-part-your-marketing-strategy-2022-david-ciccarelli

Douglass, L. (2021, Jaunary 4). *Audio is the medium of the moment: So how can brands use it to connect?* Retrieved from https://www.clickz.com/audio-is-the-medium-of-the-moment-so-how-can-brands-use-it-to-connect/264605/

Hollebeek, L. D., & Macky (2019). Digital content marketing's role in fostering consumer engagement, trust, and value: Framework, fundamental propositions, and implications. *Journal of Interactive Marketing, 45*, 27–41.

Holliman, G., & Rowley, J. (2014). Business to business digital content marketing: Marketers' perceptions of best practice. *Journal of Research in Interactive Marketing, 8*(4), 269–293.

IAB. (2016). *Digital audio buyer's guide 2.0*. New York: Interactive Advertising Bureau.

Järvinen, J., & Taiminen, H. (2016). Harnessing marketing automation for B2B content marketing. *Industrial Marketing Management, 54*, 164–175.

Jefferson, S., & Tanton, S. (2015). *Valuable content marketing: How to make quality content your key*. London: Kogan Page.

Keller, K. L. (2016). Unlocking the power of integrated marketing communications: How integrated is your IMC program? *Journal of Advertising, 5*(3), 286–301.

Lögdberg, A., & Wahlqvist, O. (2020). *Podcasting as a digital content marketing tool within B2B*. Master's thesis, Linköping University, Sweden.

Martin, E. (2020, May 8). *How to give your personalized marketing strategy the human touch*. Retrieved from https://www.ceros.com/inspire/originals/personable-content-marketing-human-touch/

Minsky, L., & Quesenberry, K. A. (2016, November 8). How B2B sales can benefit from social selling. *Harvard Business Review*.

Nielsen. (2022, May). *Podcasting today: Insights for podcast advertisers*. Retrieved from https://www.nielsen.com/insights/2022/podcasting-today/

Opreana, A., & Vinerean, S. (2015). A new development in online marketing: Introducing digital inbound marketing. *Expert Journal of Marketing, 3*(1), 29–34.

PwC. (2020). *Global entertainment & media outlook: 2020–2024*. https://images.assettype.com/afaqs/2020-10/5418760e-4a65-4054-94fd-da3deb6c67dc/afaqs.pdf

Russell, A. (2022, August 23). *Why audio advertising is the next big trend in marketing*. Grapeseed Media. Retrieved from https://grapeseedmedia.com/blog/why-audio-advertising-is-the-next-big-trend-in-marketing-and-how-to-get-started/

Thareja, U., & Jain, R. (2019). Artificial intelligence enabled in-video advertising : Infiltrating the fashion Industry. *International Journal of Innovative Technology and Exploring Engineering, 9*(1), 3826–3832.

Thareja, U., Jain, R., Gupta, N., & Batra, B. (2021). Fortifying social media content with behavioural engagement for purchase intention of fast fashion brands. *Turkish Online Journal of Qualitative Enquiry, 12*(10), 388–402.

Zenn, J. (2021, December 2). *We break down B2B vs. B2C marketing*. HubSpot. Retrieved from https://blog.hubspot.com/agency/differences-b2c-b2b-marketing

Influencer Marketing and Customer Engagement through Social Media 18

A Promising Avenue in a New Normal

Bhavna Sharma and Nupur Taneja
BPS Women University, Khanpur Kalan, Sonipat, Haryana, India

1 Introduction

Social media platforms have modified our lives and choices in the era of technical transformation as there is an increasing trend for people to post items and share their opinions on social platforms such as YouTube and Instagram, which has affected preferences and decision-making (Sharma &Vasuja, 2022; Rishi & Bandyopadhyay, 2018). Social media's impact on the marketing field can also be observed as it is used by both consumers and marketers. Marketers use social media to spread awareness (Yogesh & Yesha, 2014), while consumers watch review videos and posts by influencers that highlight details of products. This has made it necessary for sellers to create positive relationships with their customers using social media as it is the requirement of the day.

The entertainment content in the social media posts by influencers has a major impact on consumers which encourages them to form positive attitudes toward products (Arli, 2017). Customers are attracted to things that connect them to the lives of social media influencers. They remember and

DOI: 10.4324/9781003412656-18

prefer reviews posted by influencers about the products rather than advertisements as they connect to them (Nandagiri & Philip, 2018). This engagement of consumers using the internet saves companies a lot of money that they used to spend on traditional advertising as online advertising is noted as an effective option on social platforms for promoting brand (Pütter, 2017; Balakrishnan et al., 2014).

The COVID-19 pandemic transformed the way people interacted; it was a time when social media became a major platform where information and experiences were shared. Social media became a great tool for interaction; but, at the same time, it enhanced panic buying by consumers. People started stockpiling items at home as they watched videos on social media about shortages of stock in shops and markets. For example, World Health Organization advice about using hand sanitizers caused a sudden spike in demand for sanitizers (Naeem, 2021). It is shown that social media enhances impulsive buying of products by consumers; when people come across products they like while scrolling, the chance is that they will order them without a second thought (Abdelsalam et al., 2020). Although social media might trigger excessive buying, it has also been seen as a great tool to address various issues. For example, it can be used to encourage positive attitudes toward green products (Pop et al., 2020).

The social media sphere is constantly changing and will continue to do so because of changes to and the increasing role of mobile phones in people's lives (Kohli et al., 2015). The present study aims to uncover the nuanced strategies employed by influencers for audience engagement, scrutinize the role of influencer marketing in product and service promotion, and assess the nature of audience-generated comments. The chapter follows a logical progression, commencing with a clear conceptual framework and delineation of research objectives. A comprehensive literature review in Section 2 lays the groundwork, while Section 3 elucidates the chosen research methodology. Section 4 then presents and analyzes the results; implications drawn from the study are discussed in Section 5; and Section 6 critically addresses limitations while proposing future research directions. This structured approach ensures a thorough exploration of the multifaceted aspects surrounding influencer dynamics, providing valuable insights for both academia and the industry.

2 Literature Review

2.1 Influencer Marketing and Purchase Intentions

Influencer marketing is the process of collaborating with parties who have an engaged audience that can be targeted to enhance sales of a particular brand as it is easier to influence consumers through blogs than with traditional written advertisements (Sudha & Sheena, 2017). The behavior of consumers regarding a brand and their purchasing decisions can be modified by an influencer (Pop et al., 2022), who is generally believed to have a positive impact on consumer attitudes toward brands (Nafees et al., 2021). There are many factors that impact social media influencing, such as cultural background and interaction. It is seen that what consumers have encountered in the past and what they learn anew in the present affects how they behave and what they purchase online (Kizgin et al., 2018). Brand awareness is found to influence buying decisions, but only a little bit; the major impact comes from social media content (Ansari et al., 2019). When consumers are acquainted with a brand, it may lead them to the brand's social media pages; but what matters most is the quality of information on those pages to attract consumers (McClure & Seock, 2020). On the other hand, it is also believed that those who are highly knowledgeable about a brand are not influenced much by other people's opinions (Cheung et al., 2014).

There are several ways to influence consumers. For example, brands may interact directly with an audience in a friendly way on social media, which helps them inculcate a strong effect on the audience that increases purchase intentions (Barcelos et al., 2018). Social influencers also play an indirect yet crucial role in engaging consumers as, when they post reviews, their audience relates them to the brand image, which somehow encourages purchase (Hermanda et al., 2019).

To attract consumers of this generation, it is found to be crucial to interact with them; when interaction through social media is done properly, there are more chances for them to purchase (Alalwan, 2018). It has been observed that, due to influencer marketing, the intention to mimic the influencers is positively related to purchase intentions (Ki & Kim, 2019). A brand may gain huge benefits using influencer marketing, but it should be used with due care because it might not always influence consumers positively (Zak & Hasprova, 2020). Some consumers like uniqueness, and it is found that those who prefer to purchase differently from others are less likely to be influenced by their peers (Wang et al., 2012).

2.2 The Role of Trust in Consumer Engagement through Social Media

Social media influencers are people who post content on social platforms such as YouTube, Instagram, and Facebook, and the content they provide significantly affects the audience. Social media creates awareness among consumers; but, for initiating any purchase decision, they trust someone with whom they are personally acquainted (Cooley & Parks-Yancy, 2019). Some believe that consumers are more easily influenced if they trust the influencer in the videos posted on social media (Al Kurdi et al., 2022), while others say that shopping websites are considered more trustworthy as they contain reviews by actual people who have used them (Erkan, 2016).

Influencer marketing therefore aims to build loyal followers through social media by cultivating trust in them (Sudha & Sheena, 2017). It is found that consumers even buy high-value products promoted on social media (Forbes, 2013), so it is advantageous for companies to gain consumers' trust by encouraging reviews and engaging with customers. It is suggested that good communication must be developed with consumers so that they post content in favor of the brand because user reviews can play a more influential role in attracting customers (Schivinski & Dabrowski, 2016), so regular posts related to the brand by influencers are advised to gain the confidence of consumers (Hanaysha, 2022). Still, it is a challenge for consumers as, with the growing number of influencers, it is difficult to identify who to trust as some post reviews for commercial purposes (Schwemmer & Ziewiecki, 2018).

The present study reviewed literature from 2005 to 2024 that contained research on influencer marketing and how brands create image and develop trust in consumers. Some studies explored the strategies of influencers to engage consumers and promote products and services. However a gap was found as there were limited studies that targeted specific social media platforms and examined influencer content to determine their strategies. Studies on audience comments were also limited, so a need was felt to conduct a study that viewed the content of influencers on YouTube and Instagram. This study bridges the gap by examining the content of the top three influencers in different categories and analyzing their strategies by reviewing their videos, posts, and comments.

Case Study: Starbucks

Starbucks is well known for its coffee, and is the world's largest coffeehouse chain. It is one of the brands with a strong presence on social media, using various tactics to remain in people's minds. It has been observed that Starbucks not only promotes its products on social media but also attracts audiences by being on trending lists by showcasing opinions on various issues prevailing in society, sharing content on a regular basis, reposting content to loyal customers, and responding quickly to customer queries and comments because prompt replies make the audience feel valuable (Sadhu, 2024). For example, as mentioned in the study by Sam and Cai (2015, p. 213), when Starbucks in Singapore posted about the "hazel nut macchiato", a user shared the experience by commenting that it "was nice but too sweet". In response, Starbucks suggested that the customer could ask for a less sweet version, as available for all drinks. This showcases the importance of positive as well as negative comments on social media, which plays a crucial role in the success of a company as it creates a strong bond with customers by making them feel valued.

Starbucks has used many more strategies to attract large audiences through social platforms such as Twitter (now X), Instagram, and Facebook. These include using social media to update customers on announcements, promotions, and tips related to Starbucks products. Hashtags have often been used to draw the audience's attention to the pro-tips offered by Starbucks, which helps boost the customer experience, with content likely to be used that strikes the emotions of the audience with a blend of humor and storytelling. Similarly, Starbucks creates action-oriented content to directly encourage customers to purchase its products by offering limited-time discounts (Taecharungroj, 2017).

Starbucks has built its customer base not only through promotion on social media but also by increasing the quality of its products and services on a regular basis by conducting surveys and feedback drives to gather data from customers about their views and experiences; and the issues faced have been addressed properly. To enhance its reach, the company has collaborated with various influencers and content creators who promote brand and their experience of it (New Waves Technology, 2023).

Starbucks is one of the reputed brands that collaborate with influencers who have a strong audience base, attractive lifestyle content, and a good reputation on social media. According to Anderson (2020), for the launch of "Starbucks Sunrise Blend", the company partnered with Will Taylor – a style blogger and social media influencer with a large base of dedicated followers who described the product through captions in his social media posts as "bright and smooth" to steer followers towards the new product. Starbucks then analyzed the effect of the influencer's post on the sale of coffee through the conversion rate of links clicked from the post. Starbucks' motive behind the collaboration with Will Taylor was to enhance the reach and increase sales of its newly launched Sunrise Blend.

It is evident that different tactics used by Starbucks on social media helped the company gain a higher position in the global market. But sometimes in the competitive world a small decision can have a large impact, as in the case where Starbucks launched an advertisement with #whatsyourname to support the transgender community by depicting a person struggling with his identity when misnamed "Jemma" by people, which caused stressed and disturbed his mental health. The ad ended by showed him entering a Starbucks outlet, where he was asked his name and said "It's James." With this, the barista wrote on the cup his correct name, "James", and the ad ended with the line "Every name's a story" to support transgender people. The aim of this advertisement was to prompt social change and, through it, a positive impact on the goodwill of the brand. However the outcome was very different. Employees of the company took to social media to reveal Starbucks and the transphobia residing in the company. Many of them tweeted about their experience with Starbucks for the denial of surgery for gender reassignment, and some shared how the company had forced them to change their name on its login. This was a major controversy for the brand that diluted all its efforts to create a particular social image by targeting transgender people (Bredava, 2023).

3 Research Methodology

As influencer marketing is appearing as a promising avenue, the present authors decided to explore its recent status through a detailed analysis of the content of selected social media influencers. Literature data was meticulously curated from reputable databases such as Scopus, encompassing previous research conducted from 2005 to 2024.

The sampling frame targeted top-tier social media influencers on YouTube and Instagram, specifically focusing on the lifestyle, health and fitness, and educational categories. Within each category, the top three influencers in India were then selected, namely: Sejal Kumar, Kritika Khurana, and Kusha Kapila for lifestyle; Fit Tuber (Vivek Mittal), Gaurav Taneja, and Rujuta Diwekar for health and fitness; and Abhi and Niyu, Ranveer Allahbadia, and Ankur Warikoo for education. Each category underwent an in-depth qualitative analysis through the observation of five videos from each of the selected influencers.

The choice of these limited yet popular influencers is strategically aligned with this study's focus on the qualitative exploration of influencer strategies, particularly in the context of product promotion. Recognizing industry trends, the inclusion of well-known influencers adds significance as brands often seek partnerships with such influencers for effective product promotion, making the study highly relevant to current marketing practices.

Table 18.1 Influencer study overview

Aspect	Details
Literature Data Collection	Data was collected from reputable databases such as Scopus from 2005 to 2024
Sampling Frame	Top influencers in the lifestyle, health and fitness, and education categories
Selected Influencers	Lifestyle: Sejal Kumar, Kritika Khurana, Kusha Kapila Health and fitness: Vivek Fit Tuber, Gaurav Taneja, Rujuta Diwekar Education: Abhi and Niyu, Ranveer Allahbadia, Ankur Warikoo
Number of Videos Studied	45 in total (five from each influencer)
Qualitative Nature	In-depth qualitative analysis through observation of influencers in different categories
Rationale for Selection	The inclusion of limited yet popular influencers aligns with industry trends, with brands preferring well-known influencers for effective product promotion. Recognizing India's dominance in the digital landscape, the study strategically selected influencers from YouTube and Instagram, the platforms with the highest number of users in the country (Asrani, 2024)
Survey Insights	According to Statista, 30% of responses concern lifestyle and fashion, highlighting the significance of this area in the influencer landscape in India

Source: The Authors.

Table 18.1 provides a concise summary of the key details in relation to the research methodology, influencer selection, and relevant insights.

According to reports by Statista: India is the leading market for YouTube globally, with approximately 462 million users, followed by the United States (Ceci, 2024); most of the country's social media users are active on Instagram and YouTube (Basuroy, 2024); and 30 percent of posts/comments relate to lifestyle and fashion (Basuroy, 2023).

In the aftermath of the coronavirus, people have become more guarded and aware of their health and fitness. Consumers now monitor their well-being through a broader and more sophisticated lens. To improve their levels of awareness, they prefer more suggestions for healthier lifestyles from various platforms. One of these is influencers who provide them with dietary plans promoting products that have a significant impact on consumers. Fit Tuber is India's most popular influencer in the category of health and fitness, with 6.94 million subscribers (AJ Marketing, n.d.).

Social media is now widely used by students to enhance their knowledge to compete in their field, and educational practitioners are also adopting social media to provide access to their knowledge-based content through online courses (Roblyer et al., 2010). Social media is therefore now a significant bridge for students to be motivated and become involved in the distributed learning environment (Baird & Fisher, 2005), so it is important to study the effect of social media influencers in the field of education.

As mentioned earlier, the present study explored five videos from each of the content creators, which resulted in the analysis of 45 videos from nine influencers (Table 18.2).

Analysis of the YouTube videos focused on: identifying the strategies the influencers used to attract audiences, assessing how they promote products and services and the response of their audiences. To learn about the type of strategies used by influencers and their effectiveness (or otherwise) we examined whether they used live chats, question/answer (Q&A) sessions, humor, polls, and asking followers to like, share, and subscribe. The videos were assessed on the criteria used to attract consumers to products and services – such as whether products were shown on screen through pictures or used personally by influencers themselves, or whether consumers were offered discount codes and links to purchase. Finally, the types of audience comment (praise, criticism, questions asked) relating to the videos were evaluated to assess the overall impact of influencers on audiences.

4 Results and Analysis

To achieve the research objectives data was collected from the videos uploaded to YouTube and Instagram by influencers while viewing the videos. The focus was to analyze how the influencers presented the content/information, how they engaged the audience, and how the audience responded. The first objective was to examine the strategies used by influencers in their videos to engage the audience, which was achieved by analyzing the content in the videos. The influencers engaged the audience through various tactics, such as connecting through personal stories and the use of humor to entertain viewers. This trend was found in all the influencers who shared lifestyle content: they often engaged their audience by incorporating Q&As in their content; and educative content was created on topics of concern, answering questions to actively engage the audience. To engage audiences in the healthcare and fitness category, influencers also often included topics of concern, Q&As, and polls, thus showing that they care about their audience.

Table 18.2 Description of videos

Category	Name/Username of Influencer	Followers/ Subscribers	Platform	Video Title/Description
Lifestyle	Sejal Kumar (YouTube: Sejal Kumar Instagram: sejalkumar1195)	842K followers on Instagram 1.42 million subscribers	YouTube	Q&A with my brother
			YouTube	Life as a content creator (weekly vlog)
			YouTube	Gua Sha, retinol and more: Skincare Q/A with my Mom@maitriwomanhealth
			YouTube	How to style? Styling outfits according to different days of the week (Vogue inspired)
			Instagram	[Post on personal life update, asking what content audience wants and real discussion]
	Kritika Khurana (YouTube: Kritika Khurana Instagram: thatbohogirl)	1.8M followers on Instagram, 807K subscribers on YouTube	Instagram	[Poll to determine what type of content the audience prefers]
			YouTube	Life update! Career, fitness, creativity block, skincare and more!
			YouTube	Kritika Khurana opens up about her divorce, Aditya & rumors. What happened between them?
			Instagram	[GRWM for #kerastase party Outfit @themeshstore.co Bag: Singapore Earrings & heels: @hm]
	Kusha Kapila (YouTube: Kusha Kapila Instagram: kushakapila)	3.4M followers on Instagram, 1.02M subscribers on YouTube	Instagram	In my TT best
			Instagram	@badboyshah What a bangerrrr and @theshilpashetty is such a vision in this
			YouTube	When you are poor at comebacks
			Instagram	Hostel ki roti>>>> discus throw
			Instagram	[Q&A about local brands]

Health & Fitness	Vivek Mittal (YouTube: FitTuber Instagram: fittuber)	295K followers on Instagram, 7.39M subscribers on YouTube	Instagram	The miracles of 100% cold-pressed castor oil
			Instagram	[Directions for washing hands properly after COVID-19]
			Instagram	[Q&A on healthy food]
			Instagram	It's the beginning!
			YouTube (extract from Sandeep Maheshwari)	Meet Vivek Mittal (Fit Tuber, episode 5)
	Gaurav Taneja (YouTube: Flying Beast Instagram: taneja.gaurav)	4M followers on Instagram, 8.62M subscribers on YouTube	YouTube	Q&A with Mummi Papa
			YouTube	Reason behind suspension from my pilot job
			Instagram	[Discussion about bodybuilding and protein shakes]
			Instagram	[Promotional video with a brand]
			YouTube	Reason behind suspension from my pilot job
	Rujuta Diwekar (YouTube: Rujutadiwekarofficial Instagram: rujuta.diwekar)	1.5M followers on Instagram, 1.02M subscribers on YouTube	Instagram	Three easy things you can do if you suffer from arthritis or RMD
			Instagram	[Story of how their team works]
			YouTube	How to prevent cravings
			Instagram	[Guidance for following a healthy diet]
			Instagram	[Top three mistakes people make when dieting]
Education	Abhiraj & Niyati (YouTube: Abhi and Niyu Instagram:abhiandniyu)	2.7M followers on Instagram, 5.08M subscribers on YouTube	YouTube	Abhi and Niyu exposed!!! (2 million special Q&A)
			YouTube	Why does India flood so easily?
			Instagram	Level of aliens
			Instagram	If you have a complicated relationship with your parents
			Instagram	[A promotional video about the tribal hair oil]

(*Continued*)

Table 18.2 (Continued) Description of videos

Category	Name/Username of Influencer	Followers/ Subscribers	Platform	Video Title/Description
	Ranveer Allahbadia (YouTube: Ranveer Allahbadia Instagram:ranveerallahbadia)	2.9M followers on Instagram, 6.48M subscribers on YouTube	YouTube	Pyaar Aur breakup (special Q&A, livestream)
			YouTube	Watch this before it's too late: Insurance and its importance (in Hindi)
			Instagram	[Discussion about Janmashtami with Jaya Kishori]
			Instagram	[Video with an officer about a Delhi murder case]
			Instagram	[Personal development: how to interact with the opposite sex]
	Ankur Warikoo (YouTube:warikoo Instagram:ankurwarikoo)	2.7M followers on Instagram, 3.24M subscribers on YouTube	Instagram	[Informative video on helping nature]
			YouTube	Buying jewellery is not the only way! Gold investing in 2023 (Hindi)
			YouTube	These financial methods will not help you become a Crorepati! (Hindi)
			YouTube	10 questions to ask before buying health insurance
			Instagram	[Guide about the dilemma of making the right decision]

Source: Compiled by the Authors.

Table 18.3 Elements used by influencers to attract viewers

Category	Influencer	Humor	Polls	Q/A	Shoutout	Call to Action	Storytelling	Concern
Lifestyle	Sejal Kumar	✗	✗	✓	✗	✗	✓	✓
	Kritika Khurana	✗	✓	✓	✗	✗	✓	✗
	Kusha Kapila	✓	✓	✓	✗	✗	✓	✗
Health & Fitness	Fit Tuber	✗	✗	✓	✗	✗	✓	✓
	Gaurav Taneja	✗	✗	✓	✗	✓	✓	✓
	Rujuta Diwekar	✗	✗	✓	✗	✗	✓	✓
Education	Abhi & Niyu	✗	✗	✓	✗	✗	✗	✓
	Ranveer Allahbadia	✗	✗	✓	✗	✓	✗	✓
	Ankur Warikoo	✗	✗	✓	✗	✗	✗	✓

Source: The Authors.

Table 18.3 shows that elements such as polls, Q&A sessions, shoutouts to fans, calls to action (including asking viewers to like, share, and subscribe), and storytelling were used to attract audiences.

To achieve the second objective – to assess how influencer marketing has been used to promote products and services – the study examined whether the influencers used brand names, demonstrated the products, provided links in descriptions, and offered discount coupons. It was enjoyable watching the influencers as they promoted the products by way of personal demonstration, which ultimately encourages viewers to purchase them.

Table 18.4 shows that lifestyle and health and fitness influencers mostly promoted products through live demonstrations and mentioned the brand name, while a few provided links and discounts. However the content for educational videos lacked product promotion, demonstrations, or any kind of link to purchase.

The final objective of the study was to evaluate audience responses, which was accomplished through the classification of the comments left below the videos as positive (praise), questions asked, and negative. This was the most entertaining part of the study as the ways in which viewers expressed their opinions of the influencers showed whether or not they were satisfied and influenced by them.

As indicated in Table 18.5 (and in line with Karamustafic et al., 2020), most comments in all three categories (lifestyle, health and fitness, and education) were positive or asked questions, and few negative comments were found in the analysis.

Table 18.4 Techniques used to promote products

Category	Influencer	Brand Name	Product Demo	Links Provided	Discount
Lifestyle	Sejal Kumar	✓	✓	✓	✓
	Kritika Khurana	✓	✓	✓	✗
	Kusha Kapila	✗	✗	✗	✗
Health & Fitness	Fit Tuber	✓	✓	✓	✓
	Gaurav Taneja	✓	✓	✓	✓
	Rujuta Diwekar	✓	✓	✓	✓
Education	Abhi & Niyu	✗	✗	✗	✗
	Ranveer Allahbadia	✗	✗	✗	✗
	Ankur Warikoo	✗	✗	✗	✗

Source: The Authors.

Table 18.5 Comments generated by audiences

Category	Influencer	Positive	Questions Asked	Negative
Lifestyle	Sejal Kumar	✓	✓	✓
	Kritika Khurana	✓	✓	✗
	Kusha Kapila	✓	✓	✗
Health & Fitness	Fit Tuber	✓	✓	✗
	Gaurav Taneja	✓	✓	✓
	Rujuta Diwekar	✓	✓	✗
Education	Abhi &Niyu	✓	✓	✓
	Ranveer Allahbadia	✓	✓	✗
	Ankur Warikoo	✓	✓	✗

Source: The Authors.

5 Implications

The present study has several implications for stakeholders regarding influencer marketing and consumer engagement. The results show that influencers use various strategies, such as humor, Q&As, storytelling, polls, and emotional support, among others. In the lifestyle category, Q&As and storytelling are the most effective strategies, whereas in health and fitness, along with these two strategies, concern is also proven to be effective. Educational influencers also mostly use Q&As and show concern to influence social media users. On this basis, influencers can focus on these strategies and enhance their skills to attract increasing numbers of followers.

The study found that influencer use is the new normal and an effective option to attract customers and engage them through social media. Brands are therefore advised to collaborate with influencers to promote their products. They should also showcase their presence to audiences on social media by actively posting content on their websites and replying to customer queries (Barcelos et al., 2018). Businesses are also advised to invest time and effort to analyze customer data and strategize to create content that combines information with humor to help them engage a large audience.

Finally, the study showed that social media users mostly left positive responses to the videos in the comment section. This can therefore motivate influencers not just to maintain their skills but to try to improve them in future to increase their number of followers and subscribers.

6 Limitations and Future Directions

The study collected the data by observing videos posted by nine famous Indian social media influencers on YouTube and Instagram, which may not be an ideal representation for a wider area. Other influencers who are rapidly gaining followers and who may become popular in the near future could be selected for further research. Moreover, other categories could be explored that might have significant influence in the near future due to changes in the social environment. The present study was based entirely on observation, whereas future studies could be conducted through personal interviews with influencers and/or from the perspective of social media users influenced by them. The role of artificial intelligence and algorithms in influencer marketing is also a fruitful area to explore, and future research could also involve experimental studies between different persuasive actors using different social media theories.

References

Abdelsalam, S., Salim, N., Alias, R. A., & Husain, O. (2020). Understanding online impulse buying behavior in social commerce: A systematic literature review. *IEEE Access*, *8*, 89041–89058. https://doi.org/10.1109/ACCESS.2020.2993671

AJ Marketing. (n.d.). *10 best health & fitness influencers in India*. Retrieved September 29, 2023, from https://www.ajmarketing.io/post/10-best-health-fitness-influencers-in-india

Al Kurdi, B., Alshurideh, M., Akour, I., Tariq, E., Alhamad, A., & Alzoubi, H. M. (2022). The effect of social media influencers' characteristics on consumer intention and attitude toward Keto products purchase intention. *International Journal of Data and Network Science*, *6*(4), 1135–1146. https://doi.org/10.5267/j.ijdns.2022.7.006

Alalwan, A. A. (2018). Investigating the impact of social media advertising features on customer purchase intention. *International Journal of Information Management, 42*, 65–77. https://doi.org/10.1016/j.ijinfomgt.2018.06.001

Anderson, K. (2020, June 11). *Starbucks partners with Instagram influencer Will Taylor*. Medium. https://medium.com/@knowltonanderson/starbucks-partners-with-instagram-influencer-will-taylor-bcaf01bd14a7

Ansari, S., Ansari, G., Ghori, M. U., & Kazi, A. G. (2019). Impact of brand awareness and social media content marketing on consumer purchase decision. *Journal of Public Value and Administrative Insight, 2*(2), 5–10. https://doi.org10.31580/jpvai.v2i2.896

Arli, D. (2017). does social media matter? Investigating the effect of social media features on consumer attitudes. *Journal of Promotion Management, 23*(4), 521–539. https://doi.org/10.1080/10496491.2017.1297974

Asrani, R. (2024, August 1). *Top 10 upcoming education influencers in India. Confluencer.* https://confluencr.com/top-10-education-influencers-in-india/#:~:text=Top%2010%20Education%20influencers%20in%20India%201.201.,5.%20Raj%20Shamani%20%E2%80%93%201.2m%20followers%20More%20items

Baird, D. E., & Fisher, M. (2005). Neomillennial user experience design strategies: Utilizing social networking media to support "always on" learning styles. *Educational Technology Systems, 34*(1), 5–32. https://doi.org/10.2190/6WMW-47L0-M81Q-12G1

Balakrishnan, B. K. P. D., Dahnil, M. I., & Yi, W. J. (2014). The impact of social media marketing medium toward purchase intention and brand loyalty among Generation Y. *Procedia: Social and Behavioral Sciences, 148*, 177–185. https://doi.org/10.1016/j.sbspro.2014.07.032

Barcelos, R. H., Dantas, D. C., & Sénécal, S. (2018). Watch your tone: How a brand's tone of voice on social media influences consumer responses. *Journal of Interactive Marketing, 41*, 60–80. https://doi.org/10.1016/j.intmar.2017.10.001

Basuroy, T. (2023, December 14). *Most followed influencer content categories in India as of 2022*. Statista. https://www.statista.com/statistics/1295939/india-most-followed-influencer-categories/

Basuroy, T. (2024, April 8). *Leading social media platforms for influencer marketing across India in 2023*. Statista. https://www.statista.com/statistics/1241426/india-social-media-influencer-market-by-most-active-platform/

Bredava, A. (2023, April 6). *Starbucks: 10 best and worst marketing campaigns*. Awario. https://awario.com/blog/starbucks-best-and-worst-marketing-campaigns/#anchor2

Ceci, L. (2024, May 31). *Leading countries based on YouTube audience size as of April 2024*. Statista. https://www.statista.com/statistics/280685/number-of-monthly-unique-youtube-users/

Cheung, C. M. K., Xiao, B. S., & Liu, I. L. B. (2014). Do actions speak louder than voices? The signaling role of social information cues in influencing consumer purchase decisions. *Decision Support Systems*, *65*(C), 50–58. https://doi.org/10.1016/j.dss.2014.05.002

Cooley, D., & Parks-Yancy, R. (2019). The effect of social media on perceived information credibility and decision making. *Journal of Internet Commerce*, *18*(3), 249–269. https://doi.org/10.1080/15332861.2019.1595362

Erkan, I. (2016). *The influence of electronic word of mouth in social media on consumers' purchase intentions*. PhD thesis, Brunel University, London. https://bura.brunel.ac.uk/bitstream/2438/12972/1/FulltextThesis.pdf

Forbes, L. P. (2013). Does social media influence consumer buying behavior? An investigation of recommendations and purchases. *Journal of Business & Economics Research* *11*(2), 107–112. https://doi.org/10.19030/jber.v11i2.7623

Hanaysha, J. R. (2022). Impact of social media marketing features on consumer's purchase decision in the fast-food industry: Brand trust as a mediator. *International Journal of Information Management Data Insights*, *2*(2), 100102. https://doi.org/10.1016/j.jjimei.2022.100102

Hermanda, A., Sumarwan, U., & Tinaprilla, D. N. (2019). The effect of social media influencer on brand image, self-concept, and purchase intention. *Journal of Consumer Sciences*, *4*(2), 76–89. https://doi.org/10.29244/jcs.4.2.76-89

Karamustafic, S., Stockmaster, T., Palladina, S., Harris, A., & Perloff, R. M. (2020). Social media influencers: Who they are and how they influence. *Student Scholarship*, *1*. https://engagedscholarship.csuohio.edu/stu_pub

Ki, C. W., & Kim, Y. K. (2019). The mechanism by which social media influencers persuade consumers: The role of consumers' desire to mimic. *Psychology and Marketing*, 36(10), 905–922. https://doi.org/10.1002/mar.21244

Kizgin, H., Jamal, A., Dey, B. L., & Rana, N. P. (2018). The impact of social media on consumers' acculturation and purchase intentions. *Information Systems Frontiers*, *20*(3), 503–514. https://doi.org/10.1007/s10796-017-9817-4

Kohli, C., Suri, R., & Kapoor, A. (2015). Will social media kill branding? *Business Horizons*, *58*(1), 35–44. https://doi.org/10.1016/j.bushor.2014.08.004

McClure, C., & Seock, Y. K. (2020). The role of involvement: Investigating the effect of brand's social media pages on consumer purchase intention. *Journal of Retailing and Consumer Services*, *53*, 101975. https://doi.org/10.1016/j.jretconser.2019.101975

Naeem, M. (2021). Do social media platforms develop consumer panic buying during the fear of Covid-19 pandemic. *Journal of Retailing and Consumer Services*, *58*, 102226. https://doi.org/10.1016/j.jretconser.2020.102226

Nafees, L., Cook, C. M., Nikolov, A. N., & Stoddard, J. E. (2021). Can social media influencer (SMI) power influence consumer brand attitudes? The mediating role of perceived SMI credibility. *Digital Business*, *1*(2), 100008. https://doi.org/10.1016/j.digbus.2021.100008

Nandagiri, V. & Philip, L. (2018). Impact of influencers from Instagram and YouTube on their followers. *International Journal of Multidisciplinary Research and Modern Education*, 4(1), 61–65.

New Waves Technology. (2023, May 29). *Brewing a buzz: A Starbucks social media marketing case study*. LinkedIn. https://www.linkedin.com/pulse/brewing-buzz-starbucks-social-media-marketing-case#:~:text=The%20company%20also%20uses%20social,communication%20channel%20with%20its%20customers

Pop, R.-A., Săplăcan, Z., & Alt, M. A. (2020). Social media goes green: The impact of social media on green cosmetics purchase motivation and intention. *Information, 11*(9), 447. https://doi.org/10.3390/INFO11090447

Pop, R.-A., Săplăcan, Z., Dabija, D. C., & Alt, M. A. (2022). The impact of social media influencers on travel decisions: The role of trust in consumer decision journey. *Current Issues in Tourism, 25*(5), 823–843. https://doi.org/10.1080/13683500.2021.1895729

Pütter, M. (2017). The impact of social media on consumer buying intention. *Journal of international business research and marketing*, 3(1), 7–13. https://doi.org/10.18775/jibrm.1849-8558.2015.31.3001

Rishi, B., & Bandyopadhyay, S. (Eds.). (2018). *Contemporary issues in social media marketing*. London: Routledge.

Roblyer, M. D., McDaniel, M., Webb, M., Herman, J., & Witty, J. V. (2010). Findings on Facebook in higher education: A comparison of college faculty and student uses and perceptions of social networking sites. *Internet and Higher Education, 13*(3), 134–140. https://doi.org/10.1016/j.iheduc.2010.03.002

Sadhu, S. (2024, Jan 20). *Top 3 stellar social media case studies to inspire you*. SocialPilot. https://www.socialpilot.co/blog/social-media-case-study#:~:text=Starbucks%20mastered%20the%20advertising%20transition,in%20content%20across%20multiple%20platforms

Sam, C.-Y., & Cai, Y. (2015). A study on the use of social media to understand consumer preference: The case of Starbucks. *International Journal Management Business Research, 5*(3), 207–214.

Schivinski, B., & Dabrowski, D. (2016). The effect of social media communication on consumer perceptions of brands. *Journal of Marketing Communications, 22*(2), 189–214. https://doi.org/10.1080/13527266.2013.871323

Schwemmer, C., & Ziewiecki, S. (2018). Social media sellout: the increasing role of product promotion on YouTube. *Social Media and Society*, 4(3). https://doi.org/10.1177/2056305118786720

Sharma, B., & Vasuja, K. (2022). Investigating social media induced polarization on national education policy 2020. In I. Qureshi, B. Bhatt, S. Gupta, and A. Tiwari (Eds.), *Causes and symptoms of socio-cultural polarization* (pp. 177–209). Singapore: Springer. https://doi.org/10.1007/978-981-16-5268-4_8

Sudha, M. & Sheena, K. (2017). Impact of influencers in consumer decision process: The fashion industry. *SCMS Journal of Indian Management, 14*(3), 14–30.

Taecharungroj, V. (2017). Starbucks' marketing communications strategy on Twitter. *Journal of Marketing Communications, 23*(6), 552–571.

Wang, X., Yu, C., & Wei, Y. (2012). Social media peer communication and impacts on purchase intentions: A consumer socialization framework. *Journal of Interactive Marketing, 26*(4), 198–208. https://doi.org/10.1016/j.intmar.2011.11.004

Yogesh, F. & Yesha, M. (2014). Effect of social media on purchase decision. *Pacific Business Review International, 6*(11), 45–51.

Zak, S., & Hasprova, M. (2020). The role of influencers in the consumer decision-making process. *SHS Web of Conferences, 74*, 03014. https://doi.org/10.1051/shsconf/20207403014

19

Perceived Source Credibility of Social Media Influencers and Consumer Attitudes toward Brands

An Exploration of Differences between India and the United States

Lubna Nafees, Christy Cook
Appalachian State University, USA

Atanas Nik Nikolov
Kennesaw State University, USA

James Stoddard
Appalachian State University, USA

Introduction

Social networking is one of the most popular online activities, and the number of active users continues to increase. In 2023, 4.9 billion people were actively using social media worldwide, and projections are for 5.85 billion by

DOI: 10.4324/9781003412656-19

2027 (Wong, 2023). The COVID-19 pandemic has contributed significantly to an increased interest in social networking as lockdowns left people at home and looking for alternate ways to socialize. The most popular social networks worldwide as of October 2023 were Facebook with 3.03 billion monthly active users, followed by YouTube, WhatsApp, Instagram, and WeChat. TikTok saw an exceptional increase in monthly active users worldwide, with 1.5 billion in 2023. This short-form video sharing application was downloaded over 3 billion times and generated an estimated 9.4 billion US dollars in revenue in 2022 (Iqbal, 2023).

Because of the tremendous growth in social media, the global influencer marketing is also on the rise, having more than tripled from 2019 to 2023, from 6.5 billion to 21.1 billion US dollars (Dencheva, 2023). Influencer Marketing Hub defines an influencer as someone who has "the power to affect the purchasing decisions of others because of his or her authority, knowledge, position, or relationship with his or her audience accompanied with a following in a distinct niche, with whom he or she actively engages" (Geyser, 2024). King (2024) states that the size of an influencer's audience depends on both reach and niche (e.g., business vs. beauty).

Social media influencers (SMIs) can be found virtually across all industries, from electronic gaming (Jiang et al., 2020) to cosmetics. Instagram alone accounts for over 500,000 active influencers. The majority are nano-influencers, with fewer than 10,000 followers; 27.73% of Instagram influencers have between 10,000 and 50,000 followers; 6.38% have 50,000 to 500,000; 0.28% have between 500,000 and 1 million; and only 0.23% have more than 1 million followers (West, 2023).

The impressive growth in overall social media usage, as well as that of SMIs, calls for more academic and practitioner research to understand the role of SMIs in building consumer brand attitudes as well as the processes to explain these outcomes. The current situation with influencer marketing is one of the rare cases where academic interest and industry needs/developments merge to make the need for additional research urgent. Gen Z (born around 1997–2012) and millennials (mid-1990s to early 2000s) are more likely to buy products based on influencer recommendations (Droesch, 2020). Consequently, studying the drivers of SMI influence on consumers' brand attitudes is of paramount importance for both practice and academia.

The purpose of the present study is to explore the relationship between perceived SMI source credibility and consumer attitudes toward brands. Specifically, it aims to answer the following research questions:

RQ1: Does a particular dimension of source credibility assume more significance in one culture as opposed to another?

RQ2: Will the dimensions of source credibility found in the United States also emerge for India?

The next section reviews the literature on perceived source credibility and its relationship with consumer brand attitudes.

Perceived Influencer Credibility and Consumer Attitudes to Brands

Perceived source credibility has been demonstrated to affect consumer attitudes long before social media was in existence (e.g., Whitehead, 1968). Perceived source credibility has been defined as "judgements made by a perceiver … concerning the believability of a communicator" (O'Keefe, 2002, p. 181). Ohanian (1990) defined source credibility as "a communicator's positive characteristics that affect the receiver's acceptance of a message" (p. 41). A highly credible source is commonly found to be more persuasive than a less credible source (Lirtzman & Shuv-Ami, 1986). Gotlieb et al. (1987) found that a more credible source gathered more customers/followers than one with lower credibility. Source credibility has also been found to influence confidence versus doubt in individuals as well as their intention to consume/purchase (Briñol et al., 2004; Bannister, 1986; Suzuki, 1978). The trustworthiness, goodwill, and expertise dimensions of source credibility might also have varying degrees of importance in affecting attitude formation and change.

Various conceptualizations of source credibility have been proposed in the literature. For example, Lou and Yuan (2019) suggested that expertise, trustworthiness, and attractiveness comprised the three dimensions of source credibility, with attractiveness regarded as physical attractiveness or likeability. In addition, Munnukka et al. (2016) proposed a four-dimensional construct of source credibility including trustworthiness, expertise, similarity, and attractiveness. In that study, "similarity" refers to attachment to an SMI on demographic or ideological grounds. However, in this chapter we follow the more traditional conceptualization of source credibility as consisting of expertise, goodwill, and trustworthiness. The following sections will elaborate on these three dimensions.

Perceived SMI Expertise

This refers to the extent to which an SMI is considered capable of making correct assertions (Hovland & Weiss, 1951). Homer and Kahle (1990) found that in high-involvement consumer decisions, a high-expertise source was more influential than a low-expertise source, but in a low-involvement situation a high-expertise source was less influential than a low-expertise source. DeBono and Klein (1993) found that consumers are influenced equally by powerful and weak arguments when the source is perceived to have high expertise. Different individuals are influenced differently based on source credibility (Nafees et al., 2021). For instance, a consumer's ability to direct and balance their actions will determine their reactions to an expert versus a non-expert source (DeBono & Klein, 1993; DeBono & Harnish, 1988).

Perceived SMI Goodwill

This refers to the SMIs' intention toward the consumer (Hovland et al., 1954). Previous research has identified goodwill as the SMIs' attitude toward the well-being of the consumer (McCroskey & Young, 1981). Goodwill is of unique intrinsic value, described as caring and empathy (McCroskey, 1992), and McCroskey and Teven (1999) introduced perceived caring, also termed goodwill, composed of three elements – understanding, empathy, and responsiveness. Understanding is knowing another individual's ideas, needs, and feelings; empathy is the ability of an individual to identify with another individual's feelings; and responsiveness is one individual's attentiveness to another's communication.

Perceived SMI Trustworthiness

Perceived trustworthiness has been defined as the degree of confidence the consumer has that the SMI will communicate the arguments they consider most legitimate. Perceived SMI credibility has been proposed as positively related to SMI trustworthiness (Hovland et al., 1954). In addition, trustworthiness has been found to be more impactful on decision making than expertise (McGinnies & Ward, 1980). However, other studies have shown that trustworthiness alone may not be enough to explain perceived source credibility or may be less important than expertise (Hovland & Weiss, 1951; Kelman & Hovland, 1953).

Based on the aforementioned three-dimensional model of perceived SMI source credibility (i.e., expertise, goodwill and trustworthiness) and their relationship with consumer attitudes towards brands, the conceptual model is advanced and shown in Figure 19.1. The next section discusses the research method used to explore the relationships in the model.

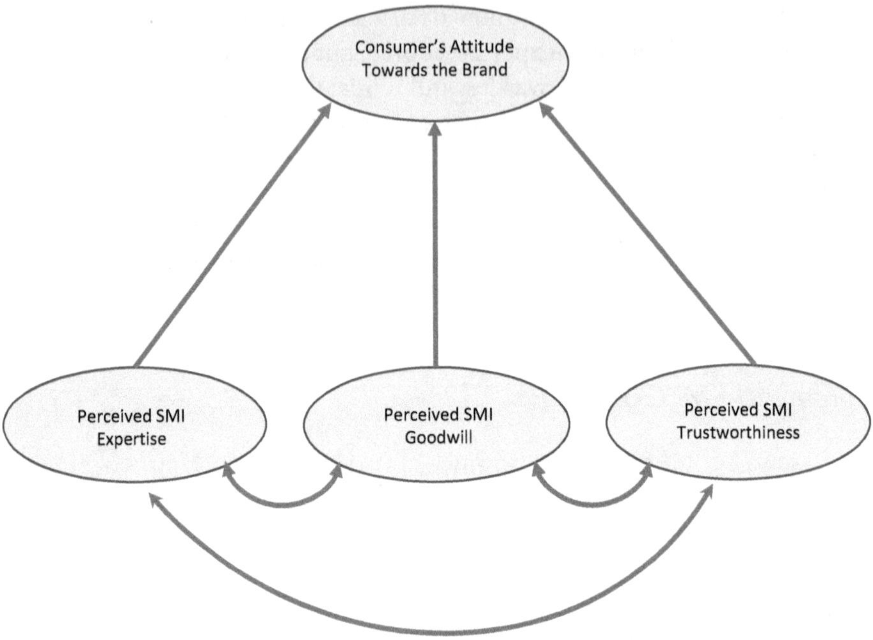

Figure 19.1 Proposed relationships between perceived SMI expertise, goodwill and trustworthiness and consumer attitudes to brands

Research Method

This section describes the survey instrument used and the data collection method.

Survey Instrument

To test the relationships in the proposed model a survey was developed that asked respondents to think about an Instagram social media influencer they follow. They were then questioned about why they followed that particular SMI. The scales were adapted from McCroskey and Teven (1999) with items measured using a six-item scale ranging from "Strongly Agree" (5) to "Strongly Disagree" (1). For perceived SMI expertise the items included "intelligent," "trained," "expert," "informed," "competent," and "qualified." Items for perceived SMI goodwill included "they care about me," "they have my interest at heart," "they are not self-centered," "they are concerned with me," "they are sensitive," and "they are understanding." Perceived SMI trustworthiness included "honest," "trustworthy," "honorable," "moral," "ethical," and "genuine."

Consumer attitude toward brands was measured by asking respondents to think about a brand that their Instagram influencer discussed. Then they were asked to respond to statements using the same scale as above. They included "makes the brand appealing to me," "makes the brand look good to me," "makes the brand seem pleasant to me," "makes the brand seem favorable to me," and "makes the brand likeable to me" (Spears & Singh, 2004).

Data Collection

The data was collected using a Qualtrics panel from India and the United States, resulting in 176 completed surveys from India and 231 from the US.

- *US statistics*. Ages varied from 16 to 78 (mean = 38, standard deviation = 16). Most respondents were female (male = 16%, female = 84%). Educational attainment included 41.1% high school, 22.1% two-year degree or technical education, 24.2% Bachelor's degree, 11.8% Master's degree, and 0.9% Doctoral degree.
- *India statistics*. Ages varied from 19 to 74 (mean = 37, standard deviation = 15). Most respondents were female (male = 44%, female = 64%). Educational attainment included 7% high school, 4% two-year degree or technical education, 33.5% Bachelor's degree, 54% Master's degree, and 1% Doctoral degree.

Analysis and Results

Confirmatory Factor Analysis

The survey measures were analyzed via confirmatory factor analysis (CFA) to determine their psychometric properties. All data was used for the CFA (i.e., for India and the US combined). Based on the analysis, one item (G3) was excluded from the goodwill construct. The standardized results are shown in Figure 19.2.

The final CFA model suggests an adequate model fit: $\chi^2/df = 3.096$; normed fit index (NFI) = 0.902; comparative fit index (CFI) = 0.931; and root mean square error of approximation (RMSEA) = 0.072). Discriminant validity was evidenced using the Fornell and Larcker (1981) criterion (see Table 19.1). Convergent validity was demonstrated as all model items loaded significantly on their latent variables ($p < 0.001$). In addition, the composite reliabilities were acceptable (see Table 19.2).

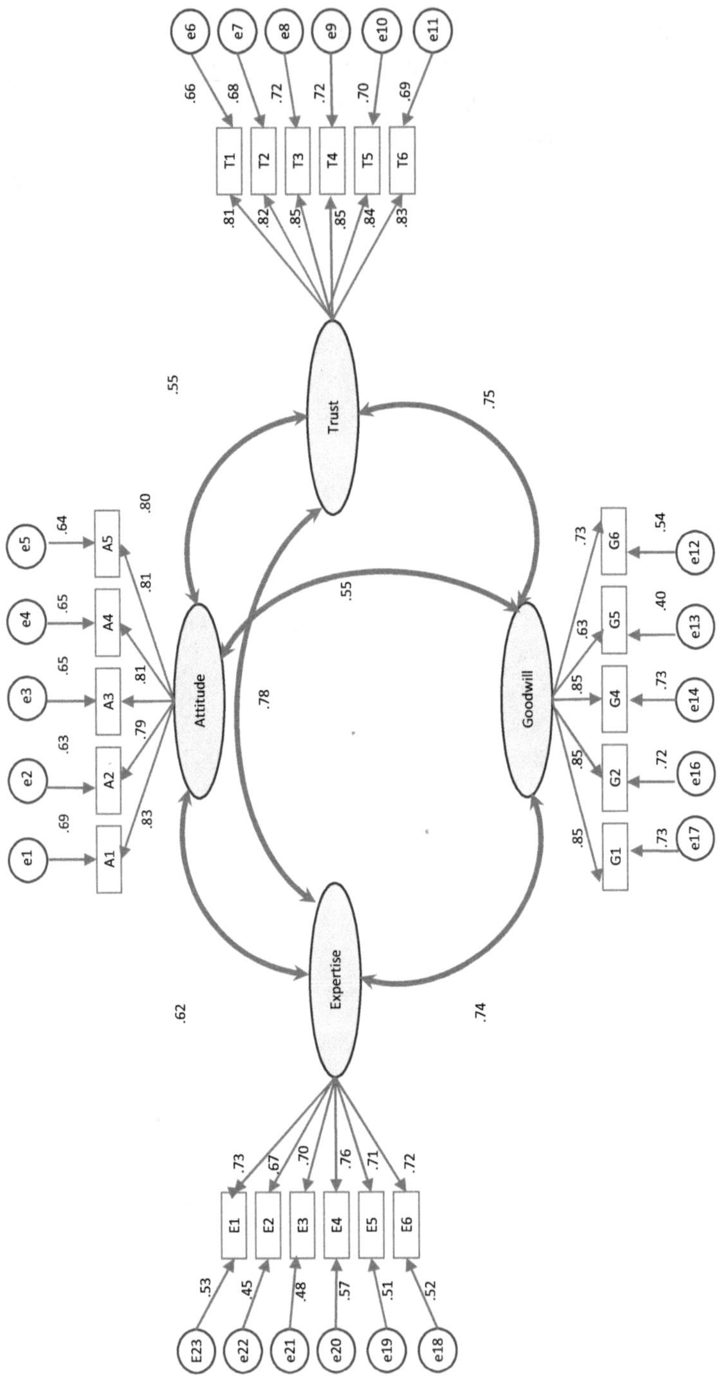

Figure 19.2 Standardized CFA results

Table 19.1 Evidence of discriminant validity between latent factors in the model

Brand Attitude (A)				Expertise (E)			
Factor/Item	**Factor Loading**	**Loading Squared**	**Error Variance**	**Factor/Item**	**Factor Loading**	**Loading Squared**	**Error Variance**
A1	0.831	0.690561	0.178	E1	0.721	0.519841	0.225
A2	0.795	0.632025	0.199	E2	0.711	0.505521	0.239
A3	0.807	0.651249	0.202	E3	0.756	0.571536	0.231
A4	0.809	0.654481	0.196	E4	0.695	0.483025	0.264
A5	0.797	0.635209	0.206	E5	0.668	0.446224	0.391
				E6	0.73	0.5329	0.293
Sum		3.263525	0.981	Sum		3.059047	1.643
Average Variance Extracted	0.769			Average Variance Extracted	0.651		
Fornell/ & Larcker Comparisons				Fornell & Larcker Comparisons			
	Correlations Squared				Correlations Squared		
Brand Attitude & Trust	0.302			Brand Attitude & Trust	0.384		
Brand Attitude & Goodwill	0.302			Brand Attitude & Goodwill	0.608		
Brand Attitude & Expertise	0.384			Brand Attitude & Expertise	0.547		
Average Variance Extracted by Brand Attitude Factor > all squared correlations with other factors in the model, Discriminant Validity				Average Variance Extracted by Brand Attitude Factor > all squared correlations with other factors in the model, Discriminant Validity			

(*Continued*)

Table 19.1 (Continued)

Goodwill (G)				Trustworthiness (T)			
Factor/Item	**Factor Loading**	**Loading Squared**	**Error Variance**	**Factor/Item**	**Factor Loading**	**Loading Squared**	**Error Variance**
G1	0.732	0.535824	0.294	T1	0.811	0.657721	0.232
G2	0.631	0.398161	0.544	T2	0.823	0.677329	0.227
G3	Excluded			T3	0.849	0.720801	0.167
G4	0.853	0.727609	0.356	T4	0.847	0.717409	0.185
G5	0.849	0.720801	0.625	T5	0.836	0.698896	0.219
G6	0.854	0.729316	0.321	T6	0.828	0.685584	0.204
Sum		3.1111711	2.14	Sum		4.15774	1.234
Average Variance Extracted	0.593			Average Variance Extracted	0.769		
Fornell & Larcker Comparisons				Fornell & Larcker Comparisons			
	Correlations Squared				Correlations Squared		
Brand Attitude & Trust	0.302			Brand Attitude & Trust	0.302		
Brand Attitude & Goodwill	0.563			Brand Attitude & Goodwill	0.563		
Brand Attitude & Expertise	0.547			Brand Attitude & Expertise	0.608		
Average Variance Extracted by Brand Attitude Factor > all squared correlations with other factors in the model, Discriminant Validity				Average Variance Extracted by Brand Attitude Factor > all squared correlations with other factors in the model, Discriminant Validity			

Table 19.2 Composite reliabilities for factors in the model

Construct/Item	Standardized Regression Coefficient	Composite Reliability
Brand Attitude		
B1	0.831	
B2	0.794	
B3	0.807	
B4	0.809	
B5	0.798	
All relationships significant at p<0.001		0.851
Trust		
T1	0.811	
T2	0.823	
T3	0.849	
T4	0.846	
T5	0.835	
T6	0.829	
All relationships significant at p<0.001		0.933
Goodwill		
G1	0.732	
G2	0.631	
G3	Excluded	
G4	0.853	
G5	0.849	
G6	0.854	
All relationships significant at p<0.001		0.819
Expertise		
E1	0.721	
E2	0.711	
E3	0.756	
E4	0.696	
E5	0.668	
E6	0.729	
All relationships significant at p<0.001		0.916

Since the psychometric properties of the model were acceptable (i.e., model fit, composite reliability, convergent validity, and discriminant validity), it was retrofitted into a structural model to see whether perceived SMI expertise, goodwill, and trustworthiness were related to consumer attitude towards the brand. The standardized structural model results are shown in Figure 19.3 for the whole sample.

All the observed items loaded significantly on their respective latent variables, and all covariances and correlations between the exogenous variables

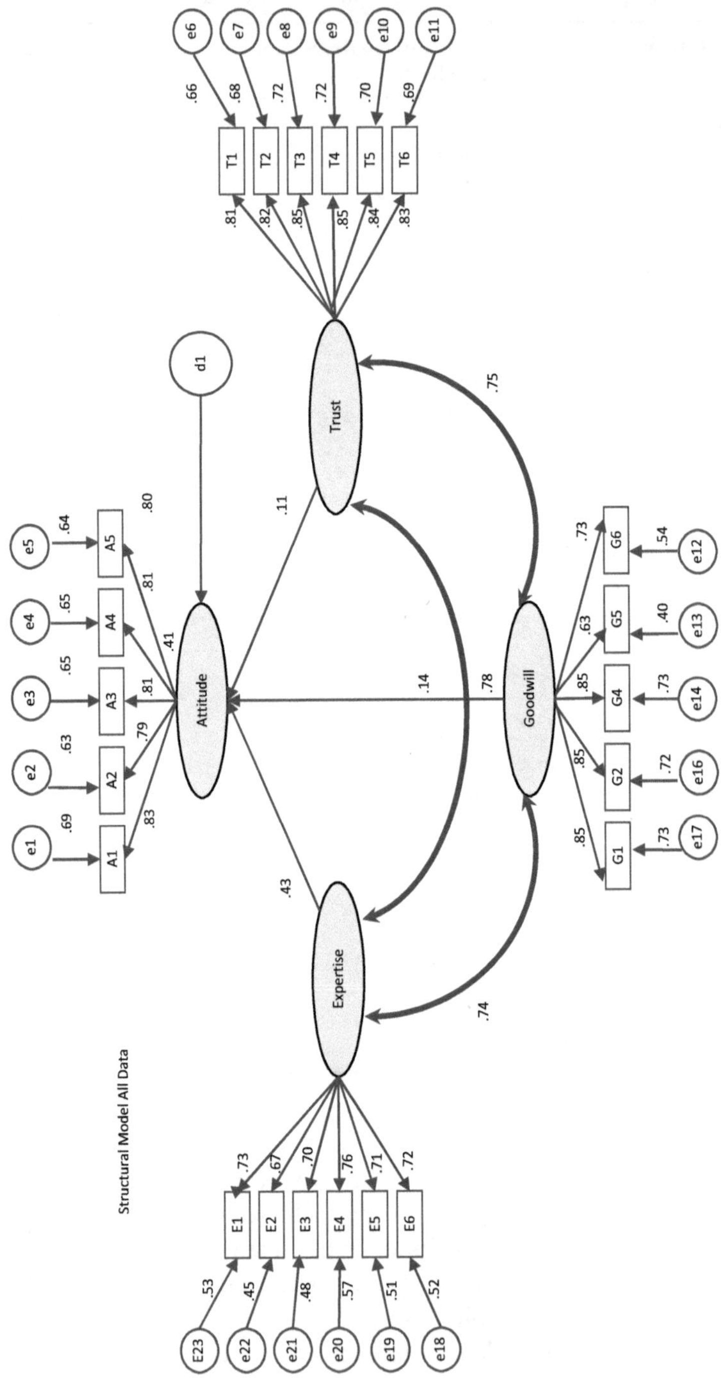

Figure 19.3 Standardized structural model results

are significant. The model fit is acceptable (χ^2/df = 3.096, NFI = 0.902, IFI = 0.932, CFI = 0.931, RMSEA = 0.072). Perceived SMI expertise was found to be significantly positively related to consumer attitude towards the brand (CR = 4.528, $p < 0.001$). The relationship between perceived SMI goodwill and consumer attitude towards the brand was found to be marginally positive (CR 1.745, $p = 0.081$); and no relationship between perceived SMI trustworthiness and consumer attitude towards the brand was found (CR = 1.269, $p = 0.204$).

Sampling for India and the United States

Since the main purpose of this study was to explore whether the relationship between perceived SMI source credibility and consumer attitude towards brands was viewed the same way by consumers in India and the US, further analyses were conducted on split samples for India (n = 176) and the US (n = 231). The structural model was then run with each sample. The standardized results from the Indian sample are shown in Figure 19.4.

The fit of the model to the India data was not acceptable ($\chi^2/df = 2.356$, NFI = 0.815, IFI = 0.884, CFI = 0.883, RMSEA = 0.0888), suggesting that the model might be modified. However, all items loaded significantly on their respective factors, and all covariances and correlations between the exogenous variables were significant ($p = 0.001$). Neither perceived SMI expertise ($p = 0.126$) nor perceived trust ($p = 0.211$) was related to consumer attitude towards the brand, but perceived goodwill was found to be related to consumer attitude towards the brand ($p = 0.009$). As a result, a modified structural model was analyzed with perceived SMI goodwill as the sole exogenous variable. That final model exhibited acceptable fit (χ^2/df = 1.613, NFI = 0.940, IFI = 0.976, CFI = 0.976, RMSEA = 0.059).

The same structural model was used to analyze the US data, with the standardized results shown in Figure 19.5.

The model fit here was tenuous ($\chi^2 = 2.775$, NFI = 0.860, IFI = 0.906, CFI = 0.905, RMSEA = 0.088). All items significantly loaded on their respective factors, and the covariances and correlations between the exogenous variables were significant ($p < 0.001$). Perceived SMI expertise was found to be related to consumer attitude towards the brand ($p < 0.001$); perceived goodwill was not related to consumer attitude towards the brand ($p = 0.777$); and perceived trustworthiness was found to be marginally related to consumer attitude towards the brand ($p = 0.054$). In an attempt to improve fit, the model was modified to eliminate perceived SMI goodwill and re-analyzed. Some fit indices improved (NFI = 0.884, IFI = 0.918, CFI = 0.918), while

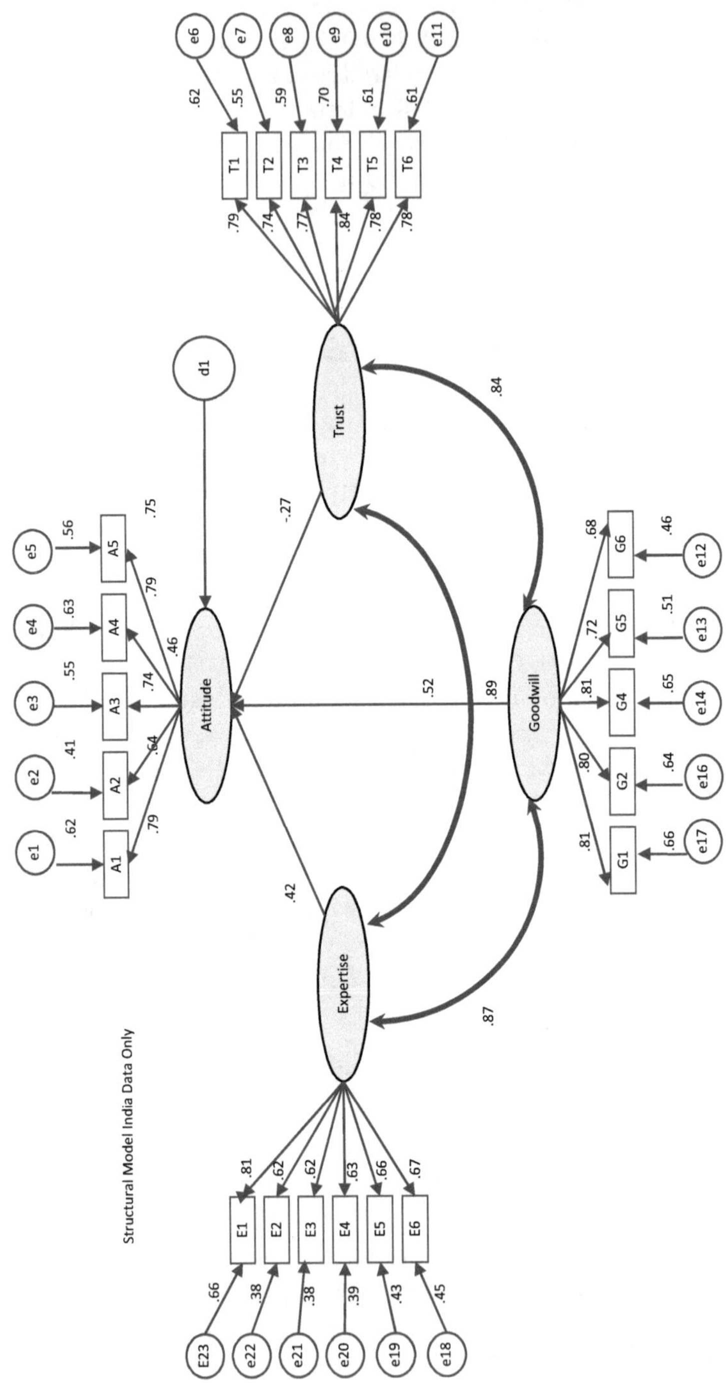

Figure 19.4 Standardized structural model results for India

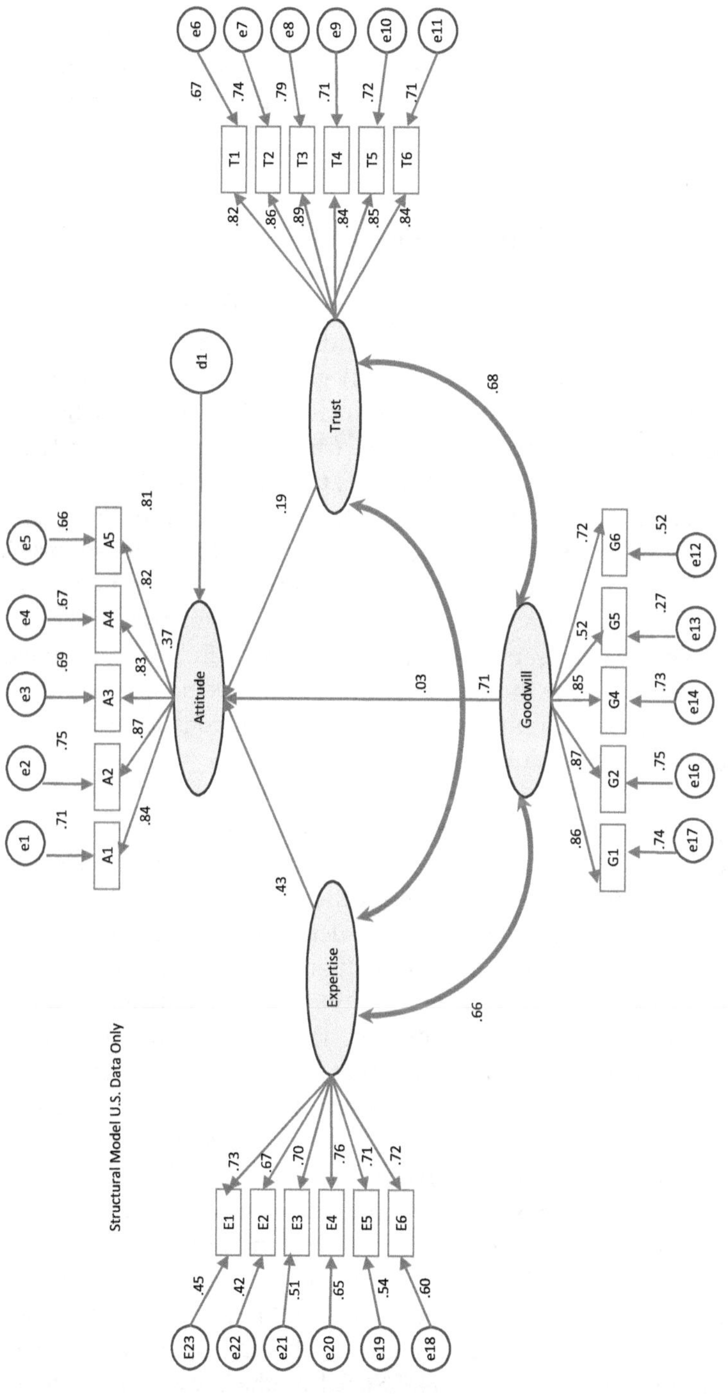

Figure 19.5 Standardized structural model results for the US

others worsened ($\chi^2/df = 3.071$, RMSEA = 0.095). Perceived SMI expertise and trustworthiness were found to be significantly related to consumer attitude towards the brand ($p < 0.001$ and $p = 0.025$ respectively). The next section presents conclusions, limitations, and suggestions for further research.

Conclusions, Limitations, and Future Research

This chapter explored the relationship between perceived SMI source credibility and consumer attitude toward brands in India and the United States. Results indicate that only perceived SMI goodwill is positively related to consumer attitudes toward the brand in the Indian sample, whereas perceived SMI expertise and trustworthiness (marginally) are positively related to consumer attitudes toward the brand in the US sample. This is consistent with the findings of Yoon et al. (1998) – who studied the three dimensions of source credibility in a non-social media context (expertise, trustworthiness, and attractiveness) and how they are applicable to a US versus a Korean sample – and with Kapoor et al. (2003), who found that American and Indian people have different communication styles and interpret messages differently. For example, Indians have a more positive perception of silence than Americans. Okabe (1983) suggested that what constitutes source credibility might differ from culture to culture.

Hofstede's cultural theory suggests a possible explanation for the differential impact of SMIs on brand attitudes across the two cultures: "Culture is the collective programming of the mind that distinguishes the members of one group or category of people from others" (2011, p. 3). One dimension of his model (power-distance) is of particular importance in the present study. *Power-distance* refers to the notion that not all individuals are equal, as well as to people's attitudes toward existing social inequalities. Here India scores high on power-distance, indicating that it has a social hierarchy and a top-down structure. This implies that (1) members of Indian society are dependent on the power holder for direction; (2) society accepts unequal rights between those with power and those who hold less power; and (3) a high degree of paternalistic leadership, where leaders take an interest in the personal lives of those they supervise and look out for individual well-being.

In the United States the concept of "liberty and justice for all" and equal rights for all members of society is a guiding philosophy. This could possibly explain why perceived SMI goodwill is the more prominent dimension of source credibility in the Indian culture, whereas expertise and trustworthiness dominate in the US sample. Social media users in India follow an influencer when they perceive them to be more understanding, empathetic, and responsive, whereas the US audience connects with influencers based on their expertise and the legitimacy of their communication. The Indian audience also accepts hierarchies and allows the emergence of leaders, who are then idolized, while the US audience evaluates based on expertise and builds trust.

In summary, this study demonstrates that the mechanics of influencer marketing may vary across cultures/countries – in this case, India and the United States. This has significant implications for both practitioners and academics, especially as more marketing firms are exploring influencer marketing to reach bigger audiences in a highly networked world. This research explored relationships in the context of the social networking site Instagram, which has emerged as the leading platform for influencer marketing. This is also one of the first works to explore these relationships on Instagram and study the differences in influencer marketing across different cultures. In addition, this research was not restricted to a specific product or service category, further broadening its implications beyond a few narrow product categories.

This study makes the following theoretical contributions. First, it is the first effort to extend the literature on the dimensions of source credibility to the domain of social media in general, and influencer marketing in particular. In doing so, it enriches the literature on the role of social media influencers in shaping consumer brand attitudes by proposing that the dominant dimension of source credibility can vary across cultures. This research further explains the difference in the emergence of a dominant dimension based on Hofstede's culture theory.

This study used the source credibility scale developed by McCroskey and Teven (1999), but, as previously noted, there are other conceptualizations. For example, Lou and Yuan (2019) proposed that source credibility consists of three dimensions – expertise, trustworthiness, and attractiveness; and Munnukka et al. (2016) suggested a four-dimensional construct composed of trustworthiness, expertise, similarity, and attractiveness. Future research could therefore study alternative conceptualizations of perceived source credibility to understand the dimensionality of the construct.

For practice, this study suggests that marketers closely examine and monitor an SMI's perceived credibility when engaging influencers to promote their brands. It has shown that, in the Indian sample, only perceived SMI goodwill was positively related to consumer attitude towards the brand, whereas in the US sample, perceived SMI expertise and trustworthiness were positively related to consumer attitude towards the brand. This has implications for brands working in multiple markets. This research tried to explain the difference using Hofstede's cultural theory, which classifies India as more accepting of power-distance than the US. The implication here is that society's strong perceived SMI goodwill is perhaps sufficient for them influencers in India to have substantial followings. For example, some popular influencers in India (not discussed here) are renowned movie stars (such as Amitabh Bachchan, Salman Khan, and Shahrukh Khan) and cricket players (such as Virat Kohli), and respondents cited "liking" or "loving" these celebrities as reasons to follow them. On the other hand, influencers in the US belong to different fields and are followed for their expertise and trustworthiness. For example, Black History, It's All Chic To Me, Les Do Makeup, vegginintheci ty, Bexa Boss Lady (among others) are influencers of choice because they have expertise in a specialized topic (history, makeup, cookery, business, etc.) that is informational and useful to followers.

In today's digitally driven world, traditional advertising methods have evolved into new marketing techniques that are more personalized and customer-centric, such as influencer marketing (IM). IM leverages the popularity and credibility of social media influencers (SMIs) with large followings on social media platforms to promote products, services, or brands to their audience.

IM is not a new phenomenon, and can be traced back to celebrity endorsements. However, with the advent of social media, particularly platforms such as Instagram, IM has evolved significantly. Its success can be attributed to the trust and authenticity that SMIs have built with their followers. IM feels more organic and relatable than traditional advertising, which can be judged as intrusive or insincere. Followers connect with SMIs as peers or friends they can trust, thus making them more receptive to product and brand reviews and recommendations.

Influencer marketing, while sharing similarities across regions/countries, can also vary significantly due to differences in culture, customer behavior, legal and regulatory environment, and digital landscape. For example, the present study specifically looked at cultural differences. India and the US have distinct cultural norms, values, and customer preferences, so IM strategies need to be customized to resonate with the cultural sensibilities of each country's audience. For instance, humor, family-centric content, and traditional values may be more effective in India, while individualism, diversity, and innovation may have more emphasis in the US. These cultural differences are highlighted here by followers in India connecting with SMIs based on perceived goodwill and those in the US connecting more on perceived expertise and trustworthiness. This can be illustrated with two case studies of popular Instagram influencers – one from India and one from the US.

Case Study: Popular Influencers in India and the US

Virat Kohli – renowned cricketer and former captain of the Indian team – is the most popular and influential figure on Instagram in India (Forbes India, 2023). With 263 million followers and strong engagement, his presence on Instagram makes him a household name not just in sports but also in the realm of social media influencing.

Kohli's Instagram account (@virat.kohli) serves as a window into his life, offering followers an intimate look at his career, personal milestones, and off-the-field endeavors. Despite his celebrity status, he comes across as approachable and down to earth through his content, connecting with followers on a personal level, which generates a lot of goodwill. Whether sharing glimpses of training sessions, match highlights, or moments with his family, Kohli's posts resonate deeply with his audience. His posts are perceived as authentic and relatable, and often convey messages of perseverance, teamwork, and self-belief, inspiring followers to chase their dreams and overcome challenges.

Kohli also actively uses Instagram to champion social causes and initiatives close to his heart, such as the environment, children, and education. His influence extends beyond the realm of sport as he collaborates with brands across various sectors, including fashion, fitness, and lifestyle. His endorsements and partnerships on Instagram highlight the commercial power of his influence. In conclusion, Virat Kohli's position as the most popular Instagram influencer in India is a testament to his ability to connect with followers, both on and off the field, based on perceived goodwill.

Moving to the US, "Les Do Makeup" is well known for her expertise in beauty and makeup (Marshall, 2024). Les Do Makeup (@lesdomakeup) – the online persona of Leslie Quezada (known as Les) – is one of the most popular Instagram accounts in the beauty and makeup niche. This account has garnered a significant following and engagement due to Les's captivating makeup tutorials, product reviews, and beauty tips, and is a popular destination for enthusiasts seeking inspiration, education, and entertainment. With her expertise, authenticity, and commitment to inclusivity, Les has a significant impact on the beauty industry and her followers. Her position as one of the top Instagram influencers in the United States is based purely on her expertise built up over the years. Les collaborates with leading beauty brands, and frequently features sponsored content and product recommendations on Instagram. Her honest reviews and endorsements contribute to her credibility and influence within the beauty community as followers trust her recommendations when making purchase decisions. Les also uses Instagram to advocate for diversity, equity, and inclusion within the beauty industry, often showcasing makeup looks on individuals of different ethnicity and gender, and with different skin tones. By championing representation and celebrating beauty in all its forms, she fosters a supportive and inclusive audience of beauty lovers on Instagram.

Questions

1. How do cultural values and norms in India and the US shape the effectiveness of influencer marketing strategies, and what specific elements should brands emphasize in each market to maximize impact?
2. In what ways can brands leverage the unique strengths of influencers like Virat Kohli in India and Les Do Makeup in the US to enhance their marketing efforts, and what lessons can be learned from their differing approaches to connecting with their audiences?

References

Bannister, B. D. (1986). Performance outcome feedback and attributional feedback: Interactive effects on recipient responses. *Journal of Applied Psychology, 71*(2), 203–210. https://doi.org/10.1037//0021-9010.71.2.203

Briñol, P., Petty, R. E., & Tormala, Z. L. (2004). Self-validation of cognitive responses to advertisements. *Journal of Consumer Research, 30*(4), 559–573. https://doi.org/10.1086/380289

DeBono, K. G., & Harnish, R. J. (1988). Source expertise, source attractiveness, and the processing of persuasive information: A functional approach. *Journal of Personality and Social Psychology, 55*(4), 541–546. https://doi.org/10.1037//0022-3514.55.4.541

DeBono, K. G., & Klein, C. (1993). Source expertise and persuasion: The moderating role of recipient dogmatism. *Personality and Social Psychology Bulletin, 19*(2), 167–173. https://doi.org/10.1177/0146167293192005

Dencheva, V. (2023, September 27). *Global influencer market size 2023*. Statista. https://www.statista.com/statistics/1092819/global-influencer-market-size/ (Accessed on November 6, 2023).

Droesch, B. (2020, February 13). *Influencers more likely to inspire Gen Zer and millennial purchases*. Insider Intelligence. https://www.insiderintelligence.com/content/influencers-more-likely-to-inspire-gen-zer-and-millennial-purchases

Forbes India. (2023, November 13). *Top 10 Indians with highest followers on Instagram in 2023*. Forbes India. https://www.forbesindia.com/article/explainers/indians-highest-followers-instagram/85725/1

Fornell, C., & Larcker, D. F. (1981). Evaluating structural equation models with unobservable variables and measurement error. *Journal of Marketing Research, 18*(1), 39–50. https://doi.org/10.2307/3151312

Geyser, W. (2024, January 30). *What is an influencer? Social media influencers defined.* Influencer Marketing Hub. https://influencermarketinghub.com/what-is-an-influencer/ (Accessed on November 6, 2023).

Gotlieb, J., Gwinner, R., Schlacter, J., & St. Louis, R. (1987). Explaining consumers' reactions to price changes in service industries: The effects of the location of the service provider, the credibility of the information source and the importance of the service to the consumer. *Services Marketing Quarterly, 3*(1), 19–33. https://doi.org/10.1080/15332969.1987.9984864

Hofstede, G. (2011). Dimensionalizing cultures: The Hofstede model in context. *Online Readings in Psychology and Culture, 2*(1). https://doi.org/10.9707/2307-0919.1014

Homer, P. M., & Kahle, L. R. (1990). Source expertise, time of source identification, and involvement in persuasion: An elaborative processing perspective. *Journal of Advertising, 19*(1), 30–39. https://doi.org/10.1080/00913367.1990.10673178

Hovland, C. I., & Weiss, W. (1951). The influence of source credibility on communication effectiveness. *Public Opinion Quarterly, 15*(4), 635. https://doi.org/10.1086/266350

Hovland, C. I., Janis, I. L., & Kelley, H. H. (1954). Communication and persuasion: Psychological studies of opinion change. *American Sociological Review, 19*(3), 355. https://doi.org/10.2307/2087772

Jiang, S., Hua, X., & Parviainen, R. (2020). How do popular online streamers influence viewers' purchase intention? Evidence from a mobile game campaign on YouTube. *Journal of Digital & Social Media Marketing, 7*(4), 332–343. https://hstalks.com/article/5558/how-do-popular-online-streamers-influence-viewers-/

Kapoor, S., Hughes, P. C., Baldwin, J. R., & Blue, J. (2003). The relationship of individualism–collectivism and self-construals to communication styles in India and the United States. *International Journal of Intercultural Relations, 27*(6), 683–700. https://doi.org/10.1016/j.ijintrel.2003.08.002

Kelman, H. C., & Hovland, C. I. (1953). "Reinstatement" of the communicator in delayed measurement of opinion change. *Journal of Abnormal and Social Psychology, 48*(3), 327–335. https://doi.org/10.1037/h0061861

Iqbal, M. (2023, October 31). *TikTok revenue and usage statistics (2024).* Business of Apps. https://www.businessofapps.com/data/tik-tok-statistics/ (Accessed on November 6, 2023).

King, J. (2024, August 5). *Guide to influencer marketing: Trends, tactics, creators and KPIs.* EMarketer. https://www.emarketer.com/insights/influencer-marketing-report/.

Lirtzman, S. I., & Shuv-Ami, A. (1986). Credibility of sources of communication on products' safety hazards. *Psychological Reports, 58*(3), 707–718. https://doi.org/10.2466/pr0.1986.58.3.707

Lou, C., & Yuan, S. (2019). Influencer marketing: How message value and credibility affect consumer trust of branded content on social media. *Journal of Interactive Advertising, 19*(1), 58–73. https://doi.org/10.1080/15252019.2018.1533501

Marshall, T. (2024, January 23). Behind the beauty: The rise of Les Do Makeup and her million-dollar net worth 2024. *Asia Media Journal (AMJ)*. https://www.asiamediajournal.com/les-do-makeup-net-worth/

McCroskey, J. C. (1992). *An introduction to communication in the classroom*. Edina, MN: Burgess International Group.

McCroskey, J. C., & Teven, J. J. (1999). Goodwill: A reexamination of the construct and its measurement. *Communication Monographs, 66*(1), 90–103. https://doi.org/10.1080/03637759909376464

McCroskey, J. C., & Young, T. J. (1981). Ethos and credibility: The construct and its measurement after three decades. *Central States Speech Journal, 32*(1), 24–34. https://doi.org/10.1080/10510978109368075

McGinnies, E., & Ward, C. D. (1980). Better liked than right. *Personality and Social Psychology Bulletin, 6*(3), 467–472. https://doi.org/10.1177/014616728063023

Munnukka, J., Uusitalo, O., & Toivonen, H. (2016). Credibility of a peer endorser and advertising effectiveness. *Journal of Consumer Marketing, 33*(3), 182–192. https://doi.org/10.1108/jcm-11-2014-1221

Nafees, L., Cook, C. M., Nikolov, A. N., & Stoddard, J. E. (2021). Can social media influencer (SMI) power influence consumer brand attitudes? The mediating role of perceived SMI credibility. *Digital Business, 1*(2), 100008. https://doi.org/10.1016/j.digbus.2021.100008

O'Keefe, D. J. (2002). *Persuasion: Theory and research* (2nd ed.). Thousand Oaks, CA: SAGE Publications.

Ohanian, R. (1990). Construction and validation of a scale to measure celebrity endorsers' perceived expertise, trustworthiness, and attractiveness. *Journal of Advertising, 19*(3), 39–52. https://doi.org/10.1080/00913367.1990.10673191

Okabe, R. (1983). Cultural assumptions of East and West: Japan and the United States. In W. B. Gudykunst (Ed.), *Intercultural communication theory: Current perspectives* (pp. 21–44). Beverly Hills, CA: SAGE Publications.

Spears, N., & Singh, S. N. (2004). Measuring attitude toward the brand and purchase intentions. *Journal of Current Issues & Research in Advertising, 26*(2), 53–66. https://doi.org/10.1080/10641734.2004.10505164

Suzuki, K. (1978). Acceptance and rejection of a suggestion. *Japanese Psychological Research, 20*(2), 60–70. https://doi.org/10.4992/psycholres1954.20.60

West, C. (2023, October 26). 22 influencer marketing statistics to guide your brand's strategy in 2023. *Sprout Social*. https://sproutsocial.com/insights/influencer-marketing-statistics/ (Accessed on November 6, 2023).

Whitehead, J. L. (1968). Factors of source credibility. *Quarterly Journal of Speech, 54*(1), 59–63. https://doi.org/10.1080/00335636809382870

Wong, B. (2023, May 18). Top social media statistics and trends of 2023. *Forbes Advisor*. https://www.forbes.com/advisor/business/social-media-statistics/

Yoon, K., Kim, C. H., & Kim, M.-S. (1998). A cross-cultural comparison of the effects of source credibility on attitudes and behavioral intentions. *Mass Communication and Society*, *1*(3–4), 153–173. https://doi.org/10.1080/15205436.1998.9677854

Index

Pages in *italics* refer to figures and pages in **bold** refer to tables.

Kolibri 360 GmbH
Ferdinand-Jühlke-Straße 7
99095 Erfurt, Deutschland
produktsicherheit@kolibri360.de